ACCOUNTING FOR PUBLIC POLICY

DAVID ROSENBERG

Accounting for public policy

*Power, professionals and politics
in local government*

Manchester University Press
Manchester and New York

distributed exclusively in the USA and Canada by St Martin's Press

Published by Manchester University Press
Oxford Road, Manchester M13 9PL, UK
and Room 400, 175 Fifth Avenue,
New York, NY 10010, USA

Distributed exclusively in the USA and Canada
by St Martin's Press, Inc.,
175 Fifth Avenue, New York, NY 10010, USA

British Library cataloguing in publication data
Rosenberg, David
    Accounting for public policy: power, professionals and politics in local government.
    1. Great Britain. Local government. Financial management
    I. Title
    352.1'0941

Library of Congress cataloging in publication data
Rosenberg, David
    Accounting for public policy.
    Bibliography: p.
    Includes index.
    1. Central-local government relations – Great Britain. 2. Local government – Great Britain. 3. Local officials and employees – Great Britain. 4. Local finance – Great Britain. 5. Intergovernmental fiscal relations – Great Britain. I. Title.
    JS3137.R67 1989 352.041 88-32610

    ISBN 0 7190 2565 6 *hardback*

Printed in Great Britain
by Courier International, Tiptree

CONTENTS

FOREWORD *Aaron Wildavsky*

The perpetual outsider inside the inner sanctum; a memoir of David Rosenberg*

David Rosenberg forcibly called himself to my attention: At a conference in Sweden, he took vigorous exception to the lecture I gave. This did not prevent him at subsequent meetings from plying me with readings (a) opposed to and (b) supportive of my position. From remote places there came even more obscure books that turned out to be important. Where will I find his like again, this in-house critic who looked out for me (and for others he adopted) better than I could for myself?

It has been a long time since I allowed other people to choose my enemies for me. This attitude turned out to be especially fortuitous in regard to David Rosenberg, who had developed getting off on the wrong foot into a high art. Nowadays, when 'the character' is universally beloved (a lack of discrimination masquerading as broadmindedness), It takes a David to slay the Goliath of false tolerance. 'Characters' are people who, understanding the mores, choose to disregard a single, hopefully unessential, one. Not our David. Nothing retail about him. He violated social norms, like he bought his books, wholesale. It was not that he didn't care, only that he didn't know how many or how often or how much he discomforted people on whose good opinion he depended.

Among the most delicate subjects I discussed with David, aside from how I should reorganize my life, was why he had difficulty obtaining a permanent position in academia. I mean, why don't these earth people like us Androjens? The answer was at once self-evident and discomforting. For every possible rationale – he was too odd, too radical, too truthful, too noisy, too open, too insistent – David had rehearsed, as well as any philosopher, his exceptions. The only person he had not got was someone who fit not one but all these categories. After all, who else would sell copies of the *Socialist Worker* nearby his civil servant colleagues, only to express surprise that they took umbrage.

No sense speaking Eskimo to the Hottentots. I told David that, despite all, his work would eventually lead to recognition in the form of *a position*. Even now, I am confident that as his work gets published its drawing power will grow.

Among the minor fascinations of this man, so unlike others, was the devotion of his

*This is an expanded version, written after reading the essays that follow, of a note about David that appeared in *Accounting, Organizations and Society*, Vol. 10, No. 3 (1985), pp. 353–7.

scholarly life to a seemingly staid and rule-bound group – local budget officials. The contrast could hardly be greater. And that, surely, was the point. Evidently lacking socialization into the ways of this world, David set out to discover the customs of the earthlings. Through a detailed reconstruction of their roles – who expected what of them and how these conventional types responded – David hoped to understand how the social world works. His gift was the outerside of his misadventures, for David was so distant from the conventions that he had to treat his treasury men as if they were strangers from another civilisation. His ability to see them as if they were born anew is the secret of his ability, similar in some ways to Jane Austen, to recreate before our eyes a whole moral universe.

There was more to it. For I have yet to take a stab at explaining why he identified so strongly with these local government treasurers who, in other eyes and perhaps earlier in David's life, might have seemed, not to put too fine a point on it, not the hard done-by but the doers-in, 'the ruling class'. A short detour may help.

Among the topics I discussed with David, but with no one else, was the Marxist theory of the state under capitalism. This subterranean interest could not be discussed with my fellow political scientists because they never heard of it. It was impossible to discuss it with Marxists I met because they were so serious, whereas, on this subject, I couldn't be. Imagine treating the American state-cum-bureaucracy, straight from its latest triumph in Panama, portentiously, as *The State*. David Rosenberg was so instinctively schooled at mocking everyone's pretensions, including his own, including pretensions over other people's pretensions, that we were able to trade stories about the absurdities of our favorite systems. Here was the United States of America, the cause of other countries' consequences, shipping its raw materials to Japan and receiving back manufactured goods, the very position alleged to be assumed by those under the sway of imperialist powers. David liked that. But he did not like it so well when the protagonists in his standard political dramas refused to play their assigned parts. And herein may lie our clue.

The Tories may always have been awful but David could bear them if they were predictably awful. Incompetent they were, parasitic, no doubt, but classy too. Their fuddy-duddyism had a certain protective quality about it helpful to the odd-man-out. Their incapacities extended to toleration of dissent, even if they did think it beneath their notice. Alas, under Mrs Thatcher, this was to be no more. By attempting to centralize local finance, this prime minister was not only violating long and dearly held conservative doctrine, she was also to do worse by playing into the Labour Party's centralizing tendencies. David suspected the worst; so he supported his local establishment against theirs (or, to be precise, hers).

'System blame', unless one means all possible modes of organizing social life, was not David's thing, not for long; he felt too acutely the pain of the participants to do that. But he was able, as those who read his papers can attest, to ascertain the hidden ambiguities beneath the supposedly solid surface.

Disqualified from acting like others – do what I do, not what I say – David

Rosenberg over-identified with the norms of scholarship. Constant criticism (never mind when or of whom) clarifies. So he did. Scholarship ought to be a co-operative enterprise. And he did co-operate, not always waiting to discover whether others wanted to be co-operated with. Abandon views when refuted. Quick to discard what new evidence showed to be faulty, David wondered – often out loud – why others present did not. The principle was widely approved but its instant applicant was deemed unfortunate. The air of discomfort David carried, clinging to him like a well-worn slipper, was due, I believe, to his insistence on raising questions of theory and practice most of us would rather forget.

It should be clear by now (if not, consult his essays) that David was a born subversive. He was loyal to people in his way but he could not, for long, be loyal to ideas. This held true for his own ideas. Because he was so acutely sensitive to social pressure, David was an admirer of Gramsci on hegemony. I would offer American counter-examples – egalitarian Catholic bishops, the leftward influence of universities, the utter weakness of hierarchical organizations from trade unions to big churches to political parties. In turn, David was adept at counter-counter-examples, from infant mortality rates to computer surveillance to the ordinariness of policy ideas. David might challenge my data but he never lost respect for the possibility that something unexpected just might be true. Wouldn't that be something! He saved himself from believing too much in what he said last year, I think, by an understanding, deeper than his other understandings, that whatever the promise of a new society, nonconformists, even if it was only to nonconformity, would still be in trouble. And that meant him.

David's analytic power rested on the understanding, so hard won, that as man was a social creature, social life was both indispensable and unsatisfactory. Even those most determined to obey its rules could not succeed in doing so without grave damage to themselves and to others. And that, for him at least, would never change.

The unsocialized also need friends. David did have his way, though not one likely to produce results very often. He attacked on scholarly grounds, I suspect, in order to apologize in personal terms. This may not be everyone's road to instant intimacy but, for want of more soothing ways, as I can testify, it occasionally worked for David.

One day, I imagined, as his talent overwhelmed all obstacles, his defects retrospectively rationalized into virtues, at a distance, a safe distance, David would have had *his position*. Others would tell him what he was by reading his title. Why, to add to his endless promotion of the young and, as yet, undiscovered and under-appreciated scholars, he might even have had a bit of patronage to distribute.

What, then, would have become of our David in power? Alas, alas, I shall never be able to enjoy this perpetual outsider inside the inner sanctum. The world has a way of getting even but only, I think, with people who know what that means. And my friend David would never get even because that would mean he no longer cared about scholarship. Acceptance meant a great deal to him (as it must to those who do without for so long) but, in the end, he could never be like us if only because he cared more about our profession than we do.

EDITORS' PREFACE AND ACKNOWLEDGEMENTS

David Rosenberg died of heart failure at the age of 42 on 22 November 1984. He studied sociology at Leicester University, and wrote a post-graduate dissertation at Bristol University on the Probation Service before teaching and researching at Oxford Polytechnic and the Universities of Dar es Salaam and Nairobi. Returning to England in 1978, he worked for three years in the School of Management at the University of Bath on an SSRC project directed by Cyril Tomkins investigating local government budgetary processes under stress. He continued this work in the Department of Accounting and Finance at Manchester University. He was thus one of the first sociologists to be employed in a university department of accounting, with a brief to carry out fieldwork on the behaviour of accounting professionals. At the time of his death he was about to take up a post at the New University of Ulster, and to begin a new ESRC research project with Allan Cochrane on local authority bugetary processes.

A listing of David's publications, including many book reviews mainly for the *Sociological Revew*, is provided as an appendix to this book. The papers in this collection were intended to form the core of a PhD thesis to be submitted to Bath University. They were left at various stages of preparation. Some were published, or accepted for publication, some were in typescript, others (including the 'semi-autobiographical appendix' which we have used as a conclusion) were longhand drafts. In these papers, David Rosenberg contributes to key policy and academic debates in two vital ways. He breaks new ground in the development of social research methods for the exploration of decision-making by elite professionals. But he also contributes directly to debates about the operation of accounting professionals in local government and, more generally, those concerning professional politics within the state. David rejects any simple technical or organisational explanations and instead sets out to uncover the developing relations which underly the operation of professional politics, in all their richness. It has in the past been easy to acknowledge the importance of this in principle – David takes a crucial step forward by exploring it in practice in the context of severe fiscal stress.

Our task as editors has been to order these papers, where possible to remove repetition and to check some of the references. Mike Cowen has written an introductory essay and Diana Rosenberg prepared the bibliography.

Editors' preface and acknowledgements

We are grateful to the wide circle of David's friends who have encouraged us to complete this project and bring David's work to the attention of a wider audience. We owe a particular debt to Trevor Hopper, of the Department of Accounting and Finance, University of Manchester, who not only supported the project throughout, but facilitated a loan from the Management Control Workshop to cover some of our costs, and introduced us to our Publisher. David himself acknowledged the value of comments by Ian Colville, Rod Rhodes and Cyril Tomkins on the drafts of Chapters 4 and 8. We are grateful to Joanne Robertson, formerly of Birkbeck College for help with typing, and to Francis Brooke and Helen Graham of Manchester University Press for seeing the book through to publication.

The following journals have given permission to reproduce copyright material:

Chapter 2, Budgets and Human Agency: Do the men have to be dragged back in?, from *Sociological Review*, 1985, 33(2), 193-220. Chapter 7, The languages of role: Treasurers in UK local governments, from *Policy and Politics*, 1985, 13(2), 155-774. Chapter 8, The politics of role in local government: perspectives on the role set of Treasurers in their relationships to Chief Executives, from *Local Government Studies*, 1984, 10(1), 47-62. Chapter 9, The assumptive world of managers of personal and social services in UK local government, from *Local Government Studies*, 1985, 11(4), 63-90.

Allan Cochrane, Faculty of Social Sciences, The Open University.

Andrew Coulson, Institute of Local Government Studies, University of Birmingham.

Mike Cowen, Department of Economics, City of London Polytechnic.

Diana Rosenberg, Faculty of Information Science, Moi University, Eldoret, Kenya.

INTRODUCTORY ESSAY *Mike Cowen*

One statement sums up the thesis behind this book: 'To be a good treasurer is to sometimes be a bad accountant but an effective street politician'.[1] In the course of evaluating the position of local government officials who are concerned with the externally imposed task of executing expenditure cuts, David Rosenberg draws on theory, inspired much by Adorno, Foucault and to a lesser extent, Hollis, to confront the most developed empirical work, of for instance Wildavsky, Dunleavy and the INLOGOV school, on British administrative practices. The theoretical is not, and deliberately not, set out separately from the object of the empirical material. The task of showing that the position of a state official is as much grounded in political strategy as in technical rationality, demands that theory should be embedded in the empirical construction of what power and occupational culture entails. This becomes more obvious when it is appreciated that the question 'Do the men have to be dragged back in?' can only be tentatively posed by drawing out the bases of 'why men think what they do when they do'. The knowledge of the bases of action is not separate from action itself.

Rosenberg was subjectively averse to both nominalism and rationalism. He was verbally fulsome in denouncing the kind of conventional academic practice which proceeds through formally stated general sets of abstract concepts and then reducing them to specific and individual phenomena.[2] His aversion was most damning when he encountered formalism within currents of the political left and this aversion was carried over into the forms of his own writing and expression. He did not write academic monographs, texts nor journal articles until he reported on the results of the research which is contained in the chapters of this book. Encounters with theory were expressed through the medium of extended book reviews which were not conventional review articles. A typical review, usually in the *Sociological Review*, would be of about ten pages on a single significant book and contain about thirty references. It represented, as in the case of Poulantzas, the first attempt to theoretically criticise a figure whose work would later become influential. Because this kind of expression is apparently so unconventional it was unnoticed. In this sense Rosenberg made himself abnormal and he stood apart from, for instance, debates on the state in Britain. Likewise, and as this book amply shows, Rosenberg could not be tied down to any area of academic demarcation. Distinctions between theory and the empirical, history and structure, positive and normative had no meaning for David who perpetually ranged over time between therapeutic and accounting practices and social and political theory. No system of concepts to categorise 'real' action is to be found in this book; the author eschews formal definition, demarcation and explicit statement which derive from any one academic or other discourse.

David uses the concepts of *internal* and *external discourse*, and *assumptive world* throughout much of this book and it may be useful for the reader to get an impression of how these concepts have come to be developed and used more generally within certain forms of social theory. In Chapter 2, he says that 'a selective eclecticism will reign over this project'.[3] The eclecticism arises from the way that he draws on discourse and power from Foucault and assumptive world from transactional research, as collated by Young. These two strands by no means exhaust the extent of his reading and the continuities of his previous work which, on the police, production workers and shop stewards, predated and informed the approach to this project. Moreover, through his reading, writing and talking over two decades, there is a strong concern for the historical determinants of the power of the nation state, a concern which is remarkably absent from this book. The nation state appears in this book as the given exogenous determinant of the object which official subjects face and of which they are a part. But, it is the nation state, as both subject of policy and object of analysis, which is the incomplete part of David's sociological life.

CONTINUITIES AND CHANGES FROM EARLIER WORK

During 1971 David circulated an unpublished paper, entitled 'The sociology of the police and institutional liberalism (draft polemic)'. For liberals, David argued, the policeman is assigned the script of Hamlet as 'a tragic dilemma':[4] Laws impose constraint on the police but the policeman must violate these laws to impose others which are designed to enforce order. This dilemma is false because it is inherent in and insoluable for a formally democratic society. Analysis which mediates between Hamlet's dilemma and individual personality cannot provide an explanation of the police because it abstracts from the functions of the state in relation to civil society. Law enforcement should relate to class domination and the police are to be regarded as agents of dominant elites in society. The paper, referred to as 'a sharp statement', merited a footnote in Westergaard and Resler's *Class in Capitalist Society*.[5] Maureen Cain, in *Society and the Policeman's Role*, also refers to the polemical piece: 'the picture is overdrawn, but there is some truth in it' – law and enforcement in the widest social and political context has been largely ignored.[6]

For the purpose of this book a number of points stand out. Firstly, David states that in Britain, most studies on diverse groups such as doctors, magistrates, politicians and lawyers are not done in a social vacuum but are informed by the terms of a functionalist

Durkheimian model which acts to unify social values. Implicity, the studies are criticised because they rest upon Durkheim's premise that individuals embody the collective consciousness of a predetermined *society*. A social structure is independent of individual action so that, for example, when the police act, they do so through the common values or beliefs of 'society'.[7] Instead, social based studies on occupational values should incorporate a historical perspective which includes class conflict and the models for this work should be Weber and Marx. Secondly, Gouldner is correct when he suggests that transactional analysis (particularly of Goffman) fails to incorporate analysis of the agency of control within the institution as a secondary level of power to the primary macrosociological determinants of power. For sociologies based on the institution, it is reductionist to suppose that 'insights gained in an intra-unit enquiry are expected to illuminate exhaustively also extra-unit problems'.[8] Here, David suggests that the analysis of inter-subjective action within the government department or capitalist firm cannot be expected to provide the means for understanding social action or the relations between different institutions, whether or not the institution possesses a corporate subjectivity and acts as if it were an individual agent. Thus, for example, the way in which a police constable may be subordinate to a chief constable within a single constabulary cannot in itself provide the criteria for evaluating any general character of social subordination. The first point, that social values are fragmentary rather than unitary and that history acts on process within the institution and determines the character of organisation as institution, is emphasised throughout this book. However, it is the second point, about the secondary conception of intra-institutional power, which begins to be turned around as David's primary concern, during the course of his academic work.

This was amply acknowledged by David himself when he reviewed Brogden's study of the police, twelve years after the police polemic was written. Brogden stated: 'Rosenberg paid only lip service to the duality of consent and coercion – giving more emphasis to the latter and failing to recognise the cruciality of consent'.[9] David writes that he was surprised by coming across this accusation, particularly in that he was more than aware about the problem of simply tying the police into the service of a dominant master class. Rosenberg of 1983, no matter what the impression of 1971, is no unproblematic radical struggling against the Durkheimians. Brogden does just what David suggests somebody should do when analysing state servants, including the police. The implication is that in 1983 Rosenberg would have drafted his polemic on the police quite differently from what he wrote during 1971. He shows how the relationship between the police and the central and local state changes in terms of 'different fractions of the dominant power bloc at central and local level'. Few studies 'attempt to situate the mechanisms by which the autonomy, whole or partial, of the state agents is reproduced'.[10] The partial autonomy of the state agents is derived from the balances between class forces inside the state. But the autonomy cannot be ascribed, functionalist-wise, to the structure of state power, on the lines that the state *needs* partially autonomous agents. Rather, the police acquire legitimation as autonomous agents by virtue of their legal 'guardship' ideology. As guardians of the nation's safety the police politically intervene to challenge 'even their nominal political masters inside the state itself'. The guardianship is different from that of other state agents but in this book, the same principle is at work – treasurers in local government acquire legitimacy from accounting guardianship and the history of this legitimation permits political intervention of local government servants, for or against elected councillors.

Having looked at the police, David turned his attention to probation officers. A MSc thesis, '*To Advise, Assist and Befriend*' – *English Probation Work as a Form of Social Work*, was submitted to Bristol University during 1972. The thesis, of about 100 pages, lists sixty-five books and ninety articles as references and incorporates the results of observing and talking to probation officers over six months in their Bristol central office. He set out to unravel the 'ideological determinants of the work situation of probation officers'.[11] Liberal sociology sees deviancy as a social problem to be treated through administrative policy rather than as a political issue of the political arena. Deviants are therefore handled by experts rather than by the public who are supposed to be menaced by deviancy. Therefore, 'the main theoretical concern is to understand how the issues of control and rehabilitation are mediated by the work situation of a sample of probation officers'.[12] The theoretical concern for control, vested in and over professionals generally, and rehabilitation as practised specifically by social and probation workers, predates the appearance of the core of Foucault's work. Yet, Rosenberg was grappling with the same issue as was to emerge on the broad canvas of Foucault and it is not surprising, therefore, to find David drawing heavily from Foucault when he comes to formulate the terms of discourse and power in this book.

Punishment, as applied through the practice of probation, is designed to cope with the offender rather than the offence. David argues that the focus of modern utilitarianism on the personality and irrationality of the offender may be more coercive than nineteenth-century utilitarianism with its relative unconcern for the offender but sensitivity to the social plight which produced the deviant child. In modern practice, the deviant as object of reform is seen as 'an intractable defender' of the values of another working class culture, which fails to meet the values of the subject of reform, the middle class probation worker. Yet, there is a striking difference from the argument in the police polemic. The self-image of the probation officer is that of a 'child saver' and images of Florence Nightingale and Octavia Hill are ingrained in the professional culture of 'child care officers'. Moreover, the 'public lay image [of officers] legitimates the licence and mandate of such helping professions and is thus difficult to reject or even to hold at a distance'.[13] This idea of the historical construction of self-image comes later, as we shall see, to be formulated as internal discourse, a part of which is expressed by the conception of the assumptive world of professionals. External discourse is also prefigured in the thesis: If social workers see themselves as helping professionals, their clients see the carers as 'gatekeepers' who control access to private advantage and freedom. 'Guards', 'guardian' and 'gatekeeper' perpetually emerge throughout the body of David's work on state officials, and external discourse is about guarding the guardians, as he puts it. Internal discourse is seen, in the thesis at any rate, as the 'myths, licences, mandates and charters [which] are enhancers and codifiers of beliefs for groups that they protect and enforce existing mores as well as creating new claims'.[14] It is about the ritualisation of professional technique and the pride which the command over technique bestows upon the professional in her image as a practitioner of technique. External discourse is about power. Social workers see themselves 'as trapped by bureaucracies' who are not part of the professional ritual. The social worker becomes an agent of social control to uphold the values of 'society'.

Now, it is revealing that Hamlet reappears in the thesis, not as a tragic figure to be dismissed but as one to be upheld: 'The structural ambivalence probation offers are supposed to feel in their role as social work/social control agents almost postulates a Hamlet-like prototype probation officer'.[15] Insofar as the client resists the control which is imposed on the offender, as part of the rehabilitative ideal, the social worker pursues two 'apparently contradictory strategies' towards the client. The social worker acts as a client coloniser by forcing the client to uphold the rehabilitative ideal; the social worker acts as a client bargainer where the officer as subject uses the bargain, as an adviser to the client, to obtain consent for rehabilitation. Social workers who pursue consent to the exclusion of coercion, who do not ride the centaur into which both consent and coercion is enfolded, are regarded as deviant. Thus, the social worker as subject towards the client is also the object of control by supervisors who are formally responsible to the bureaucracy of lay boards and state authority. The terms of supervision over the officer, through reviewing case records, discussing the client as a case problem and the officer's subjective rapport with the client, are replicated within the terms of the encounter between officer and client. Modern utilitarianism, with its concern for the client as deviant from *the* rational norm or ideal, rests on therapeutic practice, the dynamic enfolding of coercion and consent. But equally, therapeutic practice is the means by which the gatekeepers are supervised and guarded: '[Therapeutic practice] allows the supervisor to exercise considerable surveillance and control over the subordinate in a manner relatively consistent with his professional self-image'.[16] The senior social worker uses the technique of case work to discipline subordinates; junior and deviant officers are not fired but are cooled out within the service.

Within this outline of 'the occupational culture' of social workers (and probation work is seen as a form of social work in this thesis), David develops the argument that the relatively weak professional organisation of the helping professionals makes officers more openly exposed to external control. Unlike the professionals, particularly of accountancy whom we meet in this book, officers in social work readily become the victims of state sponsored reforms and the interpretations of normal society which are conveyed to them by lay boards. Radical social workers may resist the terms of external control but their organisational capacity to do so is limited because they are at the margins of a marginally organised profession. As 'good people doing dirty work' (culled from E. C. Hughes), David concludes thus: 'We can see liberal or neo-liberal ruling groups awarding punitive and social control tasks to marginal occupations and groups yet keeping them at a distance from the reality of power and awarding them the contradictory status and stigma that attaches to people doing such work'.[17] Social workers are ideologically linked to 'master institutions of society'. Casework, as advice through consent, is not possible in an authoritarian society. State sponsored reforms are supposed to reconcile the ambiguity of practice, and are characterised as 'control as help for law and order and help as control for permissiveness'. But reforms lead only to more contradictory reforms and the further dehumanisation of practice.

This conclusion in 1972 is little different from the police polemic of 1971. We have pointed to a significant difference from the polemic in the way that the social work is actively posed for its practitioners, through self-image, ritual and that which will make up internal discourse in this book and the way that elements of internal and external discourse are prefigured for the later work. However, there are substantial differences between the formulation of categories which are used in the MSc thesis and the categorisation which emerges out of the arena of local government. To anticipate, the *bargain* is used as an instrument of the subject in the thesis; in this book, bargain refers to the relation, as a process, between subjects. David refers to 'the *reality of power*' in 1972 but power has no such real existence in the later work and if it does it is specified as a fragmentary as much as unitary conception of control. Likewise, the *bureaucracy* appears earlier as a unitary external subject exercising external control over the practices of work. But here the bureaucracy is broken open as a field within which action takes place. *Strategy* is also given a different implied meaning from the way the term is used for social workers, as expressing their encounter with clients and, as such, as technique rather than an expression of power. Before we turn to establish these terms more precisely for this book, we should look at one striking source of continuity and change – that of method.

In his semi-autobiographical appendix, at the end of this book, David traces out his movement as a sociologist through Leicester, Bristol, Oxford Polytechnic, Dar es Salaam and Nairobi. In 1978, after a brief stay in Durham, he was recruited as a research fellow at Bath University in the Accounting and Finance section of the School of Management, to work for three years on the effect of financial stress on local government. Initially, David did fieldwork in Somerset County Council where he interviewed intensively and was able to sit in, and even contribute to, meetings of management teams. Later, and between 1981 and 1983, his work spread out, through less intensive interviewing in Avon, Bradford, Sheffield, Manchester and London. In the appendix he expresses his 'genuine sympathy and even respect for the elite professionals in their struggle to control their work situation and their public services in the structural clash between central and local governments which specially became the pattern from 1979'.[18] To some extent, he writes, he became the advocate of specific spending departments and the advocate of the partial autonomy of local government.

At the end of the MSc thesis, David appendaged 'Notes on the research process'. The notes reflect on his experience and encounter with probation officers in their central office. The contrast with the later experience, as recounted in the semi-autobiographical appendix, could not be more striking. He was averse towards the probation office and its personnel, except for the deviant or junior workers who were marginalised within the office. 'I was sharply aware of my failure to blend into the background'.[19] He expressed distaste of the location of the office in a new building occupied by police headquarters. A senior probation officer bumped into Rosenberg while he was selling *Socialist Worker* one Saturday morning in the town centre. David writes of his surprise at the reaction of the officer when they renewed their encounter in the office: The officer did not threaten or remove Rosenberg from the office – he cooled him. The subjective experience of fieldwork becomes part of the evaluation of objective material.

The researcher, David insists, cannot suspend his private values for the purpose of participant observation. The method of participant observation is presented as anthropological method but unlike the experience of fieldworkers in Africa, David's natives possess power. The natives as lower-middle-class officers were similar to the class of the researcher but, unlike 'the researcher, possessed power over working-class clients and the socialist researcher, privately identifies with the clients. 'In this period of my research the attempt to present a semi-critical face to my "natives" which they would accept rather than my hostile secret self, enabled me to understand why the best participant obervers are either romantics and/or liberals'.[20] However, in the local government studies, David reflects that his middle-class 'potential' was no hindrance towards studying the natives and no block towards accommodating himself to the object material on which the natives, as accountants and administrators, worked. Despite his understanding that Rosenberg's 'psychological and cultural patterns' were different from those of individual officers, his own middle-class 'potential' and professionalisation permitted reciprocity to be realised in fieldwork practice. He feels proud that he is the only researcher in Britain to be given access to the confidential meetings of the top strata of corporate managers in local government. The real influence of the researcher is upwardly incongruent with his relatively low status; in the probation study the incongruence was the other way around. Above all, and unlike the earlier experience, David finds that the local government project meets both his private political identity and sociological interests. As he puts it, his outsider interests met his job as a hired hand.

There is an obvious paradox here. A committed socialist finds antipathy towards the work of helping professions and empathy towards that of regulatory and managerial professions. We should try to unravel the paradox because it helps to explain what this book is about. It could be suggested that there is no paradox, that David's infinitely capricious capacity for irony has actually found a limit which has got the better of his commitment and, indeed, his socialism. However, his love for the ironical and the big joke is matched, in the scope of this book and the self-reflection that he casts upon it, by an equal seriousness of purpose which extends far beyond the personality of whim. Two other, more serious avenues could be explored. In the semi-autobiographical appendix,

David declares his sociological interest to be the study of elite power on and over decision making. He expresses his sympathy for Weber because when the sociologist arrived in America, he inclined towards an understanding of shoe owners rather than the ethnic origins of shoe shiners. Furthermore, he acknowledges his admiration for Beynon, who when addressing car workers as the object of his factory study, returns the full value of the workers' labour power back to them. Beynon writes for car workers rather than his sociologist and other academic peers. It is not clear whether the fruits of the work which the managers put into reflecting on their culture will be returned to them, but David feels that he has engaged rather than observed and that the work has been grounded rather than abstracted as an object which is alien to the subjects of the study.

At the end of the MSc thesis, David points out that 'a sociological researcher is not born into the research situation with no past nor memories'. He took the memory of probation officers into the research which is contained in this book. For eighteen months between 1976 and 1978, David carried out fieldwork at the Bata shoe factory in Limuru, Kenya. The material from this study, directed at shop stewards and supervisory staff within the factory, was not written up in any form and only fragments of the research notes (interview and archival notes) survive. It was as if David felt a profound amnesia towards this particular project, that the object of the study could not be transcended into subjects and remained as abstract natives, the sources of participant observation for the romantic or liberal anthropologist. Rosenberg had slipped into the pitfalls of an anthropology which cannot engage with its object and the experience of the African fieldwork could only be carried into the English local government research as negative memory. In his own terms, David's failure to transcend anthropology in the shoe factory illuminates the success of his sociological craft in the town halls.

The second way of explaining the paradox of empathy could be to suggest that the character of Rosenberg changed over the decade of the 1970s. The deterministic Marxist of the student revolt of 1968 became the professionally lapsed student a decade or more later, a researcher, grasping with agency and the social expression of individual action. There is a moot point behind this suggestion and we will show precisely how it arises in connection with the eclectic aspects of social theory which David took on board to produce this book. However, we have already indicated the extent to which the outlines of the scope connecting individual intention to rules and social action were laid out in the MSc thesis of the early seventies. Aspects of social theory confirmed the intuitive feel for the significance of agency and interaction which David had always possessed. To invert the supposed break of Marx, there was no discontinuity between the early hard, rationalist and objective focused Rosenberg and the later warmer, interpretive and subjective minded David. If there was a substantial change in the forms of David Rosenberg's attention, it was in his conception and characterisation of the state. We doubt whether David would have considered the autonomy of local government to be a worthwhile subject for engagement at the time that he wrote the police polemic. The change in the treatment of the state was registered by his attachment to Poulantzas, the *partial* switch from regarding the state as that of subject to that of arena for action. This, as we spell out below, did much to inform the congenial regard for embattled state officials but it is by no means the whole story.

The empathy which David feels towards a managerial elite, the antipathy which he expressed towards the work of helpers and the apathy which he suffered as a result of studying factory workers and staff in East Africa are all the result of his profound attachment to politics. David was full of politics – personal politics, politics of academic careers and research and above all, the politics of organisation. However much he was personally detached from his own pursuit of career and involvement in organisation his identity, as he puts it in the appendix, swivelled around 'accountability in a formally democratic political system'. Rosenberg, particularly in his oral utterances, was thoroughly depressed by the lack of history and political analysis in the various marxist writings on the state. He constantly urged that empirical work should focus on how and why decisions are taken politically. The invective in his complaints on this score put him at a tangent to much of marxism.

Rosenberg became apathetic in East Africa because the terms of existence of an expatriate academic researcher could not meet the terms of his political identity. When David reviewed Beynon's book on car workers in Ford's Halewood factory, he berated the author for too much naturalism in his method. But he notes that Beynon is concerned with understanding the ambiguity of the position of shop stewards:

> [Beynon] seems to argue that the role of socialist theory and culture is a crucial determinant in understanding why one steward becomes a supervisor for management and another consciously decides to remain on the shop floor. The stewards themselves seem to be aware of the crucial weakness in not being able openly to articulate a political culture in their role as stewards.[21]

Likewise, when reviewing Van Onselen's renowned book on African mine workers in the then Southern Rhodesia, David asks the following question: Sections of the African petit bourgoisie have been recruited from a migrant working class which 'dream about transforming themselves into shopkeepers, petty traders etc. At what period did they internalise their destinies as members of an increasingly stable working class with little hope of social industry?' The ambiguities and complexity of cultural expression was a source of worry for David. Van Onselen takes a one-sided view of working-class consciousness and treats a love for team and other dancing, for instance, as a safety value which diverted workers' minds from serious issues of exploitation. But David uses anthropological material to show that team dancing, with each team based on a particular ethnic group and naming their leaders after British colonial officials, served no one functional purpose:

> Imagine a miner attired in European dress obscenely posturing and gesturing to an audience of his own people, and all the while addressed and referred to by the symbols of British administrative and military authority. Such dancing obviously does not portray respect or awe for those symbols of Colonial rule. The white man's burden has been reduced to the gyrations of an African miner.[22]

David takes it that 'fragmentation and different traditions among the miners', like that of car workers, give rise to ideological and political expression which cannot be reduced to some prior analytical index of working class consciousness. He found it difficult, and with much diffidence, to capture the expression of factory workers in Kenya.

In England, Rosenberg expressed antipathy towards the work of helpers and social workers because the work was defined in therapeutic rather than political terms. But he feels empathy towards the local government managers because they define themselves and act as much according to political suppositions as to the contours of their professional cultures. The local government managers of this book are virtually all directors of Social Services. As such, he chose to concentrate on the area which he had previously covered in the MSc thesis. We will indicate how David deals with self-definition and professional culture against the background of some contemporary strands of social theory which move tangentically across Marx's statement on the significance of the political.

If there was any sense in which David was not a marxist it is this quote from Marx:

> The political mind is a political mind precisely because it thinks within the framework of politics. The keener and more lively it is, the more incapable it is of understanding social ills ... The principle of politics is the will. The more *one-sided* and, therefore, the more perfected the political mind is, the more does it believe in the omnipotence of the will, the more it is blind to the natural and spiritual limits of the will, and the more incapable is it therefore of discovering the source of social ills.[23]

Marx wrote on the limits of administrative action on the following grounds. Since the state is based on the contradiction between public and private life, between the general and private interests, state administration 'has confine itself to a formal and negative activity, for where civil life and its labour begin, there the power of the administration ends'. He claims that in confronting the 'unsocial nature' of private ownership, trade, industry, and in 'this mutual plundering of the various circles of citizens ... impotence is the law of nature of the administration'.[24] If the state wanted to make administration effective, it would have to abolish private life and to end private life, it would have to abolish itself, the state as embodying the contradiction between the private and general interest. So the twist in the argument is that the state cannot recognise the impotence of administration. Rather, 'every state seeks the cause [of social ills] in accidental or deliberate short-comings of the administration, and therefore it seeks the remedy for its ills in measures of the administration'.[25] In short, the state tries to remedy social ills with administrative practices and procedures.

Now, the message of the MSc thesis was firmly rooted in the ground of Marx's argument. However, during the 1970s, David was drawn towards Poultantzas and the structural analysis which rejects the state as a categorical subject acting, as in the above, to do x rather than y. Later on, he suspended the attachment to this variant of structuralism and moved across towards variants of *critical theory*, from Adorno to

10

Habermas, and Foucault. In different ways, both critical theory and Foucault are attempting, in important parts of their arguments, to extend, limit and transcend and determine whether it is possible to do all this, the basis of Marx's argument. David splices non-marxist theory with that developed within the broadest possible interpretation of any marxist tradition to deal with administration in the arena of local government. This book, unlike the thesis, is not therefore grounded in Marx's original idea on administration. He confines himself to the limits of administration and does not, in any extensive way, range over the formal conception of the relation of administration to the state.

SOCIAL THEORY

This book is rooted in social theory because David sees his task to explain the tension between the subject of agency and the objective structure which shape social action. In this book, the outlines of structure are given by what he refers to as the primacy of the accumulation process of capitalism and 'the totality of corporatist institutions'. His attention is overwhelmingly directed towards agency and how and why individuals are constituted as subjects who act as state officials within the given set of institutions. A field or arena of power expresses the way in which collective action, of officials, is arrived at and is limited or opened by the structure which he takes as given. The terms of *assumptive world* and *bringing the men back in*[26] are taken from the work of Young and Hollis who, in general, reject distinctions between the normative and positive and who search for the roots of autonomous rather than conditioned individual action within a socially constructed world. *Discourse* and *power* are derived from Foucault. David distinguishes between *internal discourse*, as materially specific and different forms of rationality, and *external discourse*, as the power which limits or expands the action of individual practitioners or officials who incorporate the practice of accountancy as one particular form of rationality.

Assumptive World

To anticipate any misunderstanding, the emphasis on the subject, as an active human agent rather than behaving being, does not entail any sympathy towards theories of subjectivism and recourse to subjectivity. The author explains this simply, in another context when he refers to the reaction against technological determinism in sociology. When reviewing Beynon's book, David stated: 'I believe that [the] new sociological humanism perhaps can better be understood as a liberal response to a theoretical political crisis inside the sector of industrial sociology, which takes the form of a return to a metaphysical tradition that places the human subject at the centre of his history'.[27] David draws on Adorno to reject any prior duality between subject and object and follows Adorno's critique of Hegel's transcendental subjectivism. Rather than the idea of the mind as action which culminates in the dissolution, through history, of the separation between subject and object, Adorno sees no means by which thinking, of the subject, can construct the abstract categorisation of the world as objective thought. Thinking is always constrained by history and the object and subject cannot be reduced to each other. For Adorno, the social domination of the objective world over the individual becomes possible because the subject as an active human agent engages in self reflection. The idea of individual free will makes the objective world dominate the particular subject: 'An object can be conceived only by a subject but always remains something other than the subject, whereas a subject by its very nature is from the outset an object as well.... To be an object also is part of the meaning of subjectivity; but is it not equally part of the meaning of objectivity to be a subject'.[28]

This statement encapsulates David's reference to Adorno, that the 'illusory power of the subject' cannot be denied and that any proposition about objective thought demands the individual subject as part of the confrontation with, and explanation, for social domination. The particular individual cannot be subsumed under any general social order but the social world cannot be reduced to subjective agency.

A decade earlier in 1975, David reviewed Gouldner's *For Sociology*. Gouldner engaged in a criticism of ethnomethodology and interactivism as the source of a new subjectivism which subserves institutional sociology by a concentration on the self-reflection of individual agency.[29] Thus, the bureaucracy is no part of an external world, external to the individual, but it is through interpretation of actors that the idea and social meaning of a bureaucratic order is established. In the review, David supports Goulder against the subjectivists but opposes Gouldner for his programme for transcendental sociology. Gouldner puts his bets on Lenin, rather than Marx, for the renewal of an institutional sociology. David retorted:

> Precisely, but a Lenin would have analysed the internal conflict between a Worsley and a Gouldner against a Roy Turner and a Garfinkel[30] as being a class struggle between the ideologists of a classical objectivist bourgeoisie and members of the subjectivist petit bourgeoisie. In the concrete social relations between these two social classes the petit bourgeoisie dances to the tune of big capital. In the world of sociology, unlike the world of history and economics, the petit bourgeoisie can organise to seize the theoretical means of production.[30]

Marxism, unlike sociology, is the objective science of the working class. But Adorno's negative dialectics as a version of critical theory is a far and critical cry from objective science. Over the 1970s, David took on critical theory and ended his flirtation with objectivism and rationalism.

Adorno, against Lukacs's Heglian marxism for instance, cannot accept that the universal or human totality is centred on the proletariat. The universal 'could only be grasped within the particular. Concrete individual phenomena expressed the universal within their very structure ... discrete and disparate phenomena could be grasped only through the recovery of the "ideas" – the symbolic representations – they embody. Crudely put, "ideas" can be represented by concepts of particular configurations of concrete elements'. It is the symbolic representation of action, through particular phenomena, that David brings to this book. Time and time again, he refers to the symbols of action as expressing the trust or bargaining relationship between officials and that between officials and councillors. Officials express themselves effectively on political grounds to the extent that they embody the symbols of politics. The symbols, as language of the actor, equally made the individuals captive of the structure of the state and society, all that is of the historical object which is off stage in this book.

Symbolic representation is the basis of the critique of Wildavsky and Dunleavy. In the case of Wildavsky, for instance, Whitehall officials build coalitions and bargain on the basis of trust and the determinants of trust, as for instance class and education, make .ationality bounded.[32] For Dunleavy, the autonomous capacity of officials to bargain and interact to produce policy is a myth. Officials, like architects who designed high rise housing under the influence of the construction industry or local government treasurers who act through the City of London money markets for council borrowing and investment, are structurally conditioned. They do not act as agents of capital but they are interlocked with firms and markets to achieve their output or financial targets.[33] David intervenes between Wildavsky's model of bounded rationality and Dunleavy's modified structuralism. He intervenes, as we shall see, because of his own earlier attachment to structuralism and his later desire to transcend the duality between agency and structure. Wildavsky's model of bounded rationality rests on a utilitarian conception of the instrumental human agent. The model allows for conflict, and counter conflicting alliances of officials, but the premise of pure rationality, however bounded, cannot explain the administrative process because the language which expresses the boundaries of action are not incorporated, as symbols, into administration as political action.

Symbol representation of concrete, disparate phenomena draws on symbol interactionism but is not reduced to it. Interactionism, as developed by G. H. Mead, rests upon the possibilities of self reflection and interpretation by the individual subject within the objective constraint of the social world.[34] It is quite possible, even necessary, to reject ethnomethodology while advancing the claims for symbolic interactionism as a counterpoint to models of bounded and unbounded subjective rationality. Following Hollis, David rejects Goffman's version of interactionism. Hollis shows that in Goffman's world, individuals enter into social relations so well endowed with human attributes that the roles which they play are social accidents. Actors treat their roles as a public means to private ends and the official positions which they occupy as roles gives rise to 'a stock of reasons' to explain their action.[35] However, this version of individual inter-action through pure rationality, which David takes to inform Heclo and Wildavsky's analysis of Whitehall as the *Private Govemmment of Public Money*, cannot explain how the unity of the individual self is arrived at, how the subject is constituted through creative self expression. The gist of this book is that the individual subject, as official, is socially constructed through the symbols of action. Symbols are not merely derived from social constraints but explain why the constraints come to dominate individual action. For instance, *value for money* studies are imposed upon public sector accountants by the Thatcher government to symbolically fulfil the ideological prerogative of eliminating 'waste' in state expenditure. But when officials engage in these studies, they may incorporate value for money as criteria for their accounting practices and equally be sceptical about the accounting worth of value for money. The assumptive world of officials is the set of symbols which are drawn into the explanation of official action.

There is a further sense in which David owes much to Adorno. Rational identity, between concepts and objects, is denounced by Adorno as the analytical curse of the divorce between subject and object. The definition of concepts is nothing other than rational identification and to refuse to define is to liberate oneself from the curse of rationalism. Conceptual definitions, as normative criteria, grasp more than what is adequate to understand a given, particular object; empirical definitions, as existential conditions, tell less than what is necessary to take in the object under study. There is no separation betweeen objects of reality and the method which is used to confront them; method cannot be independent of the object of analysis and confrontation. To avoid definitions of rationalism, as identities between concepts as subjects of their objects, Adorno 'constructed constellations of concepts in order to "indicate", to "gesture" the particularity of the object'.[36] In this book, David refuses to define his concepts and shows how his material is constructed out of fieldwork which is part of the interaction between officials. Ideas of the constructed self, according to the concepts of assumptive world and discourse, are brought together to give a feel of officials acting politically in their administration of local government services.

The idea of *assumptive world* was developed out of the failure of experimental method, in psychosociological research, to maintain a distinction between normative values and existential beliefs. Weber had realised that belief in any social reality is created by both the observed actor and the observer and, to suspend belief, the ideal type of reality which the observer as sociologist constructed could only be obtained by removing the observer from the procedures of the action of the observed. The failure to resolve the question of how belief could be suspended independently of the procedures or rules of the game of the actors' world let to the different reactions of phenomenology, ethnomethodology and the new subjectivism. The failure of experimental method, and participant observation where the observer is value–neutral, led to the view that perceptual and evaluative components of belief are interdependent for both the individual actor and the observer. Individual decisions emerge as conflicting value positions are negotiated within an environment and becomes 'a socially constructed objectivity'. The assumptive world is the sum total of values which integrates intentions and beliefs to include existential judgements about the social reality. The assumptive world of the individual subject contains, in Young's words, a portfolio of plans which correspond to different possibilities of an uncertain social world. Plans are inhered in images of the world and it is through the image that knowledge of self-reflection and interpretation of the world is accumulated. Given uncertainty of the social world, the choice of particular plans involves constant negotiation, as drama, through a set of changing images of the world. The changing images are the symbols of representation and are worked through the idea of discourse, as we will show. Young states the following, which David reproduces in Chapter 7: 'The assumptive world provides political actors not just with their audience, backcloth and other props but also the stage directors, lines and cues'.[37] Young emphasises cueing as the most important property provided by the assumptive world and suggests that it is best handled by semiology as the theory of signs. David follows the emphasis but does not take up the suggestion. He treats cueing as the means by which officials absorb externally imposed change through their values which change not merely the end of resource allocation decisions, but also the rules of the game by which decisions are taken. Cueing is about politics.

In the case of Dunleavy, 'national corporate structures' override values of the majority local government party and the values of local government officials; officials do not occupy local political space. David criticises Dunleavy by taking up Weber's distinction between living for politics and living off politics. Officials live off politics since local political forces determine whether a successful accountant is successful as a political actor. Cuts, imposed by the Thatcher government after 1979, set off imposed change but managers of local government services do not further the values of accountancy to decide on how the provision of services are to be reduced. David takes on the INLOGOV school of contingency theory to reinforce the intervention between rationality and structure.[38] Contingency theorists argued that the most probable reaction of local governments and their officials to the cuts would be that councils would adopt a more rational view of budgeting and would move away from the irrationality of incremental budgeting. Since the contingency theorists were aware that this general tendency would work through in different ways for different departments of different councils, they were led to argue that the politics of the organisation would determine the degree to which rational budgeting is arrived at. But David does not confine politics to interaction within the organisation according to the premise of a given rationality. He insists that managers of council services act politically to create a counter-rationality. One officer says: 'You have got to master the feel of the situation rather than the logic of the situation'. Political skill, in reading the local balance of political forces and reorganising the claims of other managers in the changed situation, is the cue derived from the assumptive world and which furthers the rationale of management in a political rather than accounting direction. The political is the basis of the counter rationality and politics is the expression of the way in which accounting as internal discourse meets power as external discourse.

Discourse

To recapitulate, David sees tension between two perspectives of agency and structure. The *internal discourse* gives the agent freedom to decide on action but the *external discourse* determines whether the freedom is real or illusory. Accounting as a set of procedures, to balance revenue against expenditure or vice versa, consists of a series of functions which agents perform through a specific technical language. Discourse is the practice of language and internal discourse is concerned with the means by which the language is used to insulate the set of procedures from the balance which is arrived at by agents who perform the accounting functions. The language which is employed to construct a budget is insulated from the budget as resultant financial balance to maintain the authority, the autonomy, the freedom of accountants to act according to their own procedures. Without insulation, the budget would be constructed in a manner which would be determined by the political and social effects of the resulting balance. Individuals constructing a budget would not be constituted as accountants and their action as subjects would not be privileged but determined. Accounting, as David puts it, provides an ideological charter for a particular organisation and gives finance professionals at the apex of their power in the organisation the status of a secularised priesthood. It is through ideology that procedures are insulated from the result of budgeting; the set of procedures for performing technical functions are invested with symbolic meaning or ritual to provide a model of action. Accounting appears to be a rational means of allocating resources because the procedures are invested with the symbols of technical expertise and become, through the assumptive worlds of agents, an internal discourse of rationality.

External discourse is about the expression of power which counteracts the ideological force whereby accountancy is insulated as internal discourse. The symbolism which protects accounting as rational budgeting for resource allocation is also the symbolic discourse of 'the rulers to the ruled who are themselves outside the arena of where the action is'.[39] Budgeting, as external discourse, is the means of legitimating political rule through the state. The Thatcher government legitimates cuts in public sector provision through superimposing a model of rational resource allocation upon the internal discourse of accountancy. When cuts are explained as a means of achieving 'value for money', the procedures of 'accounting for money' are no longer insulated from an externally imposed budget. In making 'accounting' conform to 'value', the ritual of internal discourse is encapsulated through the external expression of power. But, and this is the nub of the problem, the internal discourse of budgeting for the value of money is carried out by an elite who are insulated, through national corporate structures of the state, from the politics of representative democracy. To acquire legitimation, the internal discourse must be incorporated, as rational administration, into the external expression of power. Local government officials resist incorporation through the construction of a counter rationality, through creating alliances with councillors on the basis of the political values of the assumptive world. Also, through extending the insulating force of accountancy into the national arena, ties between central government, professionals and professional authority are strengthened; through acting within local political space, external discourse involves professionals accepting the ritual that local politicians symbolically maintain the reality of their control over decisions. Professionals acknowledge the limits of their procedures locally but extend the boundaries of the internal discourse nationally. Local councils, dominated by the

Labour Party, are encouraged to make political decisions on cuts while professionals in and around the Department of the Environment are encouraged to further the rational accounting for money, as the source of internal discourse, to pre-empt local effects of cuts. Thus, to maintain insulation for their procedures, professionals act politically and political skills determine the extent to which the limits of internal discourse can be compressed and expanded. But here, the capacity to exercise political skill is not itself determined but is contingent. David takes up Foucault to insist that 'agency is constructed by discourses that are contingent in their eruption'.[40] The capacity to resist the external expression of power is not predetermined but is marked by discontinuity and uncertainty.

Foucault is concerned with the failure of the intention behind programmes of social intervention, like reforming the English probation service or the provision of local government services, to correspond to the historical effects of the programmes. Given that programmes express state power over individuals, resistance to external power is the limit of power but the limit cannot be formulated. Limits, as taboo, can be transgressed but not destroyed by investigation: 'An expose of the repressive effects of liberal prison reforms will serve equally the managers as the critics of such a system'.[41] But non-correspondence between historical effects of programmes and intention cannot be explained through structure, as the set of capitalist and state institutions, but through practices in which power and knowledge are dispersed and diffused. If practices 'are the means of historical action' then, as the objects of research, they cannot be reduced to the intention of any individual or to subjectivism in general.[42] It is through history, as a series of conflicts, events and struggles which express particular strategies of power, that agency is constituted. The intentions of individuals which inform programmes for action through administrative action of the state cannot be laid out in advance and separately from administrative practice. Practice involves 'the application of knowledge for a political purpose' and, moreover, the application of knowledge always contains power and thus its limit, resistance.[43]

Knowledge arises out of discourse and is expressed through discourses which necessarily do not correspond to each other. Any presupposed unitary subject is dissolved by knowledge. Foucault makes knowledge take two meanings: formal knowledge of a discipline with a set of definitions, rules, skills and techniques is referred to as *connaissance*. Accountancy is such a discipline with its codified set of rules and corpus of propositions which are standardised and homogenised in textbooks and regulated through examinations. David takes accountancy to be of the internal discourse through which the budgetary game is played. The second meaning of knowledge 'refers to knowledge in general, knowledge dispersed concretely throughout a specific historical social formation'. Knowledge in general, associated with the strategies of power in society, is referred to as *savoir*.[44] Savoir, in implying knowledge as active general practice, turns the discipline into disciplining and regulations into regulating. Thus, the second meaning of knowledge as savoir becomes the external discourse for David in this book.

The production of discourse is regulated through the authority of the internal discourse itself. Sheridan interprets Foucault's accounts of knowledge to show why and how knowledge 'ceaselessly multiplies risks' and creates uncertainty.[45] The discipline, such as accountancy, 'the society of discourse', like the Chartered Institute of Public Finance and Accountancy (CIPFA), the production of commentaries on accounting practice all serve to regulate discourse. Qualification and certification for practice confines particular individuals to the knowledge of practice and excludes others from the profession of practising through the discourse. Ritual invests practitioners with 'the gestures, behaviour, circumstances and the whole set of signs that must accompany the discourse'.[46] But procedures for regulating discourse, which exclude individuals and classify knowledge and confine practice to the ritual of the discourse, are operated through the 'rarefaction of speaking subjects'. Individuals who set examinations or rule on professional practice possess the pure, refined qualities of the profession as the archtypical expression of personality. Rarefaction of the subject, the person as total accountant, proposes an ideal truth or what Foucault refers to as the ideal of the will to truth. The ideal truth is in a constant state of flux in so far as contending individuals of the discourse dispute elements of the practice. Accountants, for instance, argue over how effects of inflation should be included in calculations of profit and thus conflict reigns between proponents of historic and current cost accounting. However, individuals dispute as accountants and the ideal truth is that of accountancy. The ideal truth becomes the law of the discourse and exponents who propose the ideal truth give the discourse the status of an immanent rationality.

By confining knowledge to the single rationality of an ideal truth, knowledge is made more uncertain but 'the specific reality of the discourse is denied'. The reality of the discourse, such as accounting, is carried through institutions, like the capitalist firm or local authority education department, where the discourse of accounting meets other discourses, such as that of the teaching profession. Since the other discourse is regulated through its own ideal truth, discourses necessarily cannot correspond to each other. It is through the non-correspondence of excluding, juxtaposing and intersecting discourses that programmes of administrative action are constructed. Axiomatically, the intention framed by the rarefied subject of the ideal truth of any one discourse will not correspond to the effects of the intention behind any proposed and administered social programme for state action and intervention. Discourses interact to create practice which is discontinuous and it is because of discontinuity and uncertainty that discourse becomes fragmented around segmented, specific practices which are regulated by rarefied subjects: 'A discontinuous series of events shatter the moment into a series of different time scales and disperse the subject into a plurality of possible positions and functions.'[47] But it is practice, as the intersection of discourses, which creates agency. Hollis's autonomous man or the individual's assumptive world are created through multiple rationalities and not the single rationality of *the* internal discourse. And it is through external power of the external discourse, that the subject comes to acquire the autonomy, the capacity to exist in a world of many rationalities.

Knowledge, without the exercising of power, would be amorphous and undefined. For Foucault, power is not a single instrument or the unitary capacity of a subject to secure an outcome. Power is multiple, omnipresent, existing in a network of 'micro-powers, power relations that permeate every aspect of social life'.[48] More specifically, power is a strategic relation of society to establish connections between different elements of the society. Strategies become the basis of the power relation because of the distinction which Foucault makes between events of the rational, rarefied discourse and those of the non-discursive practices of institutions. This is precisely the distinction between the internal and external discourse of this book. Knowledge is codified as ideal truth through the power relation because the capacities to insulate procedures from their supposed outcomes or to produce the internal discourse are determined through events of practice – through conflict and struggle. Likewise, knowledge multiplies risks because the imposition of one discourse upon another creates uncertain events whose outcome cannot be predicted in advance. The external discourse represents the attempt to confront one discourse against another, the means by which power of knowledge is created: 'the ideal of the will to truth, hence, is a norm by which power seeks to protect itself by mystifying its control over knowledge'.[49] Foucault, like Adorno, may go against Hegel's search for universal truth and unitary subject but, in his idea of the dialectic between knowledge and power, he is accompanying Hegel's attempt to join philosophy with history. Unlike Hegel, the two come together through politics, the symbols of power. Strategies apply knowledge for *political purposes* and it is the attraction of the emphasis on the political which draws David towards Foucault.

This is the background against which David uses the concepts of internal and external discourse to show the rules of the budgetary game change and to ask who guards the guardians of money? The exogenous state of expenditure cuts which central government has imposed upon local government sets off a chain of events. Existing rules of the game, through which the internal discourse of accountants becomes the external discourse, are renegotiated. The politically central accounting techniques of the treasurer, the internal discourse, allows the treasurer to steer the allocation of resources away from an open clash, over a diminishing cake, between spending departments. The political position of a treasurer becomes stronger than that of the chief executive, whose assumptive world involves the administrative task of arbitrating between departments. Before the cuts, in a period of rising local government expenditure, departmental allocations of the increasing cake were settled through virement, the power to transfer parts of expenditure from one account to another, and jointed incrementalism: present concessions by one department to another are made in the certain knowledge that the department will be compensated by the other through concessions in the future. Now, after the cuts, knowledge is uncertain and departments create political alliances to bargain over the cake. David's repeated example is that of the Social Services director who creates an alliance with the Housing Department against the director of Education. The bulk of social services and education expenditure consists of recurrent expenditure outlays to meet salaries of social workers and teachers; housing department expenditure is on the capital account and so there is no conflict between social services and housing if the distinction between recurrent and capital is made on the basis of accounting criteria.[50] Since negotiation over allocation is carried out in the discourse of accounting, the treasurer becomes the guardian of spending departments. The treasurer becomes the broker of local government, the representative of chief officers to councillors and of councillors to officers.

As we have emphasised, politics articulates different discourses. The effective treasurer, who has the individual capacity to influence council policy, acts politically at the limit of the internal discourse; the treasurer who cannot transgress the limit remains little more than a book-keeper. An effective treasurer said: 'The subtlety of my position is I have to maintain my right to professional opinions without taking too much advantage of it'.[51] Brokership is possible because the accounting role is seen to be politically neutral. When the treasurer acts politically, through the discourse of councillors whose power is legitimated through representative democracy, the treasurer cannot transgress the limit of the political discourse. David points out that the treasurer plays the broker role reluctantly and the effective treasurer maintains respect for the rituals and nuances of respect and deference towards the symbols of representative democracy: 'The strength of any competent and politically skilled treasurer is that his institutional role allows him to effect policy construction without an automatic challenge by councillors that he is talking politics'.[52] As the guardian of spending departments, the treasurer acts politically by supporting councillors, if necessary, against chief officers. The treasurer, unlike other officers, is insulated from the charge of political intervention because the internal discourse of accounting, unlike other discourses, consists of technical procedures for guarding the use of money. Money is the most abstract source of commensurability between different programmes. It is the treasurer who guards money and by acting at the limit of the discourse, sets out the rules of the budgetary game. But the treasurer is part of the balance which governs the expectations all agents have of the budgetary game. The guard of the guardian is the balance between different discourses and the treasurer can occupy the pivotal position, the balance between bad accounting and effective politiking.

Professionalisation, as Foucault shows, makes it impossible for discourses to correspond to each other.[53] The internal discourse of technique must be a part of the external discourse of power. Negotiation over bargains to achieve balance is continuous but practice is discontinuous. An exogenous shock of state-imposed cuts increases uncertainly within the arena of local government. The power of officials, contained in the ability to withhold or extend the offer of information to each other and to councillors, is increased when they create political alliances to temper uncertainty. All this supposes that local government managers act endogenously within the boundaries of the local arena. They defend localism to resist exogenous change. However, as David points out, officials are not confined to a local arena where they are bureaucrats of a council. Chief officers control the local administration of services as the junior arm of the central state. Within a national arena, the internal discourse is regulated through national institutions and the external discourse expresses a different order of power through a different source of force. At one point in the text, David hints at this problem but he does not extend the analysis to break open the assumed exogeneity of action within a national arena. He suggests, for instance, that treasurers feel alienated from the Whitehall nexus because central government lacks accounting expertise.[54] Thus, in the national arena, treasurers rely on CIPFA, the regulatory institution of the internal discourse, to mediate between central and local government. The problem is that the Thatcher government is averse to mediation. Likewise, he proposes that the power of politicians, local councillors for instance, is evaluated through their specific capacities to restrain central government demands for expenditure cuts. Restraint in effective cutting would reduce the degree of exogenous uncertainty faced by local councillors and so increase the power of councillors in the local arena with respect to that of officials. But in the Shire County of Somerset, for instance, the local Tory notables have become marginalised within the balance of political forces which make up the national Conservative Party. Local politicans cannot temper the external environment and officials act politically to increase their power. These points are no more than hints and this book is locked into a local arena of power. It is off the stage of the book that we can find David's focus on the nation state.

STATE

If an analysis of the given character of the British state is absent from this book, then its absence is remarkable given the overwhelming attention which David showed towards the state in his previous and other concurrent writing. His stance towards the state changed during the 1970s. The 1971 police polemic presents the Hegelian view of the state as a unitary subject acting out the coercive power of the dominant class of capital over labour. By the late 1970s, David has drawn himself towards Poulantzas and he entered into the version of structuralism which separated state power as a concept from the state apparatus as a set of institutions. State power was not a subject but an arena, an area of political space through which the balance of class forces in society was condensed. At the time that he was writing this book, it was apparent that he was arriving at a synthesis, between the Hegelian totality of subject and fragmented system of arenas, to charactise the form of the nation state. The synthesis was inflected, as we have shown, through his later encounter with critical theory and Foucault.

We emphasise that this attempt to arrive at a synthesis is suggestive and tentative but pointers towards it are stuck down in this book. He states that the marxist tradition rests on the prior assumption of the concentration and inequality of power. The 'negotiated order' theory of institutional analysis is premised on the model of relatively fragmented power. 'The fragmentation and concentration can and do exist in a unity'.[55] And again: 'The state is a broker state as well as a Hegelian totality which refuses to recognise that internal structures have internal political systems'.[56] The emphasis on fragmentation, between state departments and between local and central government, is given to this book as the one-sided focus of division in unity: Central-local relations 'are contests, conflicts, negotiations and pseudo negotiations between two unequal power blocs which can themselves be both united and also internally divided'.[57] The unity is taken as given; the internal division is to be explored because it is ignored by state theorists of the academy and of the marxist tradition. In a review of an academic collection of papers which were selected from a conference in Austria, David protests, in 1984, that the collection ignores Australian specificity: 'In this world of universal academic communities bound and bonded together by conferences, internal reference groups and free tickets to each other's bases, the materiality of nation societies and states and their investigation can too often become marginal in the search for universals'.[58] However there is more to the exploration of internal division and fragmentation than this riposte. The professional managers of local government are the subject of provisioning state services and, as an elite, are the focus of David's sociological attention. But within the corporate sphere of the universal or total expression of state power, the professionals are subordinate as the unifying object of corporate control. To make the local managers visible is to unravel 'a dialectic [which] allows subordinate groups some power to negotiate and bargain the terms of formal subordination'.[59] Negotiation, he repeats time and time again, at the 'so-called margins of social life can be of some considerable symbolic significance'.[60] David bent the stick towards fragmentation and the particular because he had long dwelled on the universal and structural. And most significantly, he saw the significance of the margins while he was engaged in work on the general form of the capitalist state.

Extended reviews on Poulantzas's *Fascism and Dictatorship* and *Classes in Contemporary Capitalism* appeared between 1976 and 1978 and were regarded, apparently, by Poulantzas himself as the most useful reviews of his work.[61] Poulantzas argues that fascism is an ideological movement with ties to big property rather than a movement stemming from the rural petit bourgeoisie. In both Italy and Germany, the petit bourgeoisie were deeply divided over support for fascism though in Italy more emphatically, the rich peasantry of the North and Centre gave active support to the movement. The strength of the argument, David suggests, is that Poulantzas uses ideology to analyse 'the much abused concept of the petit bourgeoisie': 'The underlying emphasis he gives in all his work to ideology, politics and economics as structural determinants of class comes out, for example, clearly in his understanding of the importance of ideology in the actual class constitution of the petit bourgeoisie'.[62] *Classes in Contemporary Capitalism* is an analysis of intermediate strata, the new petit bourgeoisie in France. The analysis is carried through the medium, as in the book on fascism, of how modes of production co-exist, through articulation with each other. The question is whether the petit bourgeoisie are likely to stand with a fraction of French non-monopoly capital against the internationalisation of monopoly capital. But here, David berates Poulantzas for failing to grasp ideological determinants of class as real and material rather than as 'a belief system in the minds of different class agents ... It is ironic that Poulantzas, who has consistently argued against all instrumentalist theories of state and class domination which contain certain subjectivist elements can yet bring these elements in by the "back door".[63]

Poulantzas cannot transcend his own critique of the state as subject because of the formalism of his analysis of modes of production. The formalism is a complex rather than simple functional reductionism but it produces a contradiction between the claim that the state and politics are relatively autonomous of class forces and the simplistic conception of a social formation, the social area in which modes of production are articulated. It is through the social formation that class forces are conceptualised as the expression of social relations of production but the nation state cannot be other than the state of the social formation. Poulantzas fails to produce an adequate theory to show how partial 'similarities' of the class location of the petit bourgeoisie at the 'cultural-ideological level' can be arrived at out of totally different 'material bases in production relations'. Poulantzas claimed the following: 'Mental labour is, in fact, encased in a whole series of rituals, know-how and cultural elements that distinguish it from the working class ... If these ideological symbols have little in common with any real differentiation in the order of elements of science, they nevertheless legitimise this distinction as if it had such a basis'.[64] David takes this statement to represent the reduction of a specific technical culture of intermediate strata, the external discourse, to a 'crude sociological manipulation' where agents use their possession of technical knowledge to manipulate the working class. Poulantzas ends up as a moralising conspiracy theorist because he is a sociological formalist.[65]

After he was engaged in the reviews on Poulantzas, David set about writing a PhD thesis on underdevelopment theory. He wrote two chapters, entitled 'The Origins and Function of Sociological and Historical Theories of Underdevelopment', and 'The Development of the Marxist Theory of Imperialism', and then abandoned the thesis. As a theoretical prelude to his factory fieldwork in Kenya, he also wrote a paper, 'Some Myths on the African Working Class'.[66] The aborted thesis centres on a critique of the then rising influence of dependency theories which, in turn, were a reaction against the previous prevailing orthodoxy of modernisation theory: 'The backwardness of modernisation theory of the dominant American kind or the debates over the hypotheses of the English historians Robinson and Gallagher should not blind Marxists to the theoretical ambiguities and mistakes of the founding fathers of Marxism – Marx and Engels'.[67] The failure to engage directly with Marx has led to the theoretical subordination of specifying Marxist theories of imperialism by radicals of the Hobsonite tradition. He takes up Tom Kemp as the then most developed proponent of a Marxist theory of imperialism and comments that the focus on the British state, in an explanation for British imperialism, 'remains at the level of sociology of the personnel of the metropolitan state and the different fractions of the ruling class block':

> Instead of displacing the epistemological terrain of sociology by a theory of the space in
> which the relative autonomy of state power is a part of the overall hegemony of the ruling

class block, an instrumental model of 'interests' emerges (landlord as opposed to industrial 'interests') which is conceptually similar to the work of Hobson. At best it remains a descriptive account rather than a theory of the state as a condensation of a particular balance of social classes.[68]

David is arguing for a purely Poulantzasian theory of the state; the gibe, about the sociology of state personnel, highlights the extent to which he reversed his order of priority when he came to write the second thesis as the contents of this book.

The state, and the question of imperialism, could only be handled through theory which is ingrained in the 'specificity of the mediations of capitalist development'. In typical Rosenberg fashion, David runs through a breathtaking body of historical writing on Russia, the United States, India and Spanish overseas expansion in America to confront Marx's interpretations of these cases of would-be capitalist development.[69] No over-reaching conclusion is drawn and series of tentative statements are made. However, in two earlier reviews, David took the argument further and accused Dunn, as a theorist of revolution, of being incapable of understanding the connections between modern revolution and the classes which are created through capitalist industrialisation. Industrialisers may be semi-feudal ruling groups, including large landowners, military officers or petit bourgeoisies and state functionaries:

> These industrialisers may themselves become industrial bourgeoises or may be displaced by the social classes they have created, or they may fuse with them. It is a characteristic of the post-war period that throughout the underdeveloped world the social forces compelling industrialisation have developed with great and massive rapidity and in most cases clearly in advance of the development of a stable bourgeoisie. This partly explains the importance of the state in most underdeveloped countries where it often assumes the role of a bourgeois ruling class prior to the substantial development of that class.[70]

When reviewing a collection of papers on a critique of underdevelopment, he welcomed the direction and gist of Gunder Frank's work but regarded it as inadequate because Frank does not 'explore conceretely the "forms"' in which backward countries are integrated into a world market through imperialism.[71] Authors in the collection who use Marx to criticise under-development theory suffer from the influence of 'common sense sociology' in their work: 'The occasional quotation from Marx's work does not negate the absence of any concrete direct discussion of the law of value as elaborated in Marx's *Capital* . . . Any radical sociology of development which ignores the law of value of not being central to the examination of underdevelopment and uses the category of 'nation' to explain exploitation is superficial'.[72]

Geoffrey Kay's critique of theories of unequal exchange between nations is presented as the standard which makes value theory essential for the explanation of underdevelopment. Nevertheless, while David popularised Kay verbally, the focus of his writing remained, as ever, on the state.

In the paper on the myth of characterising the African working class as a labour aristocracy, a definite theoretical proposal is advanced.[73] He compares the cases of

South Africa and Northern Rhodesia, where racial prohibitions were placed against the advancement of unskilled migrant African labour towards skilled and semi-skilled jobs, with that of the Belgian Congo, where the colonial state supported the upgrading of a permanently employed black wage labour. In South Africa, unlike the Belgian case where the state acted for the Union Minière Company, the state supported white workers against the mining companies who desired upgrading. Therefore, the determination of the status of skilled labour, whether white or black, is bound up with an analysis of class alliances which are expressed by the contours of state power. Analysis should be concerned with the specificity which allows the possibilities for class alliances to be politically established. Elsewhere, in the review of Van Onselen's book, David spells out the point: white populism, of white workers and the petit bourgeoise, challenged the British South Africa Company: 'This European populism allows the class contradiction inside the colonial state to be expressed. The colonial state which expressed a particular class balance both internally to Southern Rhodesia and externally to the world economy, it not analysed [by Van Onselen] other than in its straightforward consistent support for mining capital'.[74] Later, and in by referring to division in Northern Ireland, a similar point was made.

Sometime during 1980 David warmly reviewed an important book on the state in Northern Ireland. Bew, Gibbon and Patterson had challenged those who struggled in Ireland according to ideas of national self-determination and also those who supposed that politics and ideology are simple reflections of a 'basic material relationship': 'In focusing throughout on the state and the key role it played in perpetrating the Protestant block, we are taken beyond those economistic theories which reduce the politics of crises to conflict between different forms of capital'.[75] The fundamental purpose of the state, to maintain conditions for exploitation of the working class, dictates why different parts of a ruling class dominate over others. The Protestant block in Northern Ireland is a changing form of an alliance between a bourgeoisie and working class. Populism provided one means for cementing the alliance but an anti-populist changing current always threatened to undercut the alliance. In the 1960s, when the alliance broke-up, the Unionist state lost its autonomy from Westminster. These proposals for the focus on politics and ideology were brought to bear on the analysis of English local government. Some experience from reflecting on the post-colonial state in Africa was also incorporated in David's attempt to understand the status of Thatcherism in Britain after 1979.

We have shown how the thesis of this book is set off by the imposition of cuts which since 1979 (and in effect 1976 following IMF conditionality on loans advanced to the Callaghan Labour government). David started his fieldwork a few months after Thatcher came to power. The thesis, as we have mentioned, is that professionals become more aware of liberal democracy at the level of local government and acted to defend localism. However, to manage the impact of the cuts locally, professionals became more incorporated into the corporate structure of central government and thus came 'to provide inputs into national state policy'.[76] David states that when the 'known political environment' at both central and local levels becomes more uncertain, unknowable and unpredictable, professionals act politically and corporate management is politicised: 'The transformation to a Hobbesian politics of a ruthless war of all against all may become the new form of collective cultural understanding in the 1980s in local government'.[77] Bureaucratic structures, as he puts it, can be shaken by earthquakes and the rules of the budgetary game, a form of legitimation of rational administration which attempts to depoliticise cuts as a technical exercise, are subject to an eruption. The question is whether the advent of Thatcherism represents irrevocable change in the structure of the state, whether central or local, or whether it is cyclical reaction to a past period of growth in state expenditure and as such as predictable by reference to post-cyclical variations in, this case, central-local government relations. David poses this question, in its strongest form, through the medium of his book reviewing between 1982 and 1984.

The review of the Brogden book on the police raises the legitimation crisis of the state as the lacuna of the book. The idea of legitimation crisis is inherited from Habermas whose argument is that administrative intervention into welfare makes the state 'more visible and intelligible that "the invisible hand" of liberal capitalism'.[78] Administrative intervention makes control and choice over the provision of welfare services more political and increases the demand for the provision through the state. When increased demands cannot be fulfilled or if they are partially fulfilled at the expense of capital accumulation and economic crisis, then the penalty of 'governmental crisis management' is the withdrawal of legitimation as 'mass loyalty' to the state. David takes the effects of Thatcher cuts to be a legitimation crisis. He follows Brogden's point that legitimation fixes the limits of the partial autonomy of state agents from dominant classes and from capital. But, structural analysis, like that of Poulantzas, is neo-functionalist if it supposes that capitalism needs state officials to act relatively autonomously. A distinction should be made, David insists, between the partial autonomy of state agents 'in a society where a dominant hegemonic class or block of classes rules through representatives ties to party and state' and autonomy when 'a formerly dominant class experience a major crisis of legitimation'.[79] It is this second case which is what Thatcherism represents.

Habermas presumes that the underlying cause of the legitimation crisis is a change in class structure which makes it difficult for the loyalty of one class to be secured through state while state policy is systematically directed towards the advantage of another class. In a review of Dunleavy's work on corporatism, which rests on a study of post-war mass housing in Britain, David makes his strongest statement on Thatcherism: 'While English state corporatism has been weakened, if not broken by the impact of Jacobin right-wing populism and the partial collapse of a hegemonic bourgeois class at the political level, this does not mean a necessary gain for the working class'.[80] The political gain, by implication, is that of the petit bourgeoisie but David is too wary to further this contentious argument. Rather, he looks at the change in the position of state officials that follows from Thatcher's command over state power:

In such a conjunctural crisis of legitimation chief police officers now intervene in public as loyal 'servants' and guardians of the nation's safety and, being placed above mere politics, can often pressure and challenge even their nominal political masters inside the state itself. The English ethical state was built by a liberal elite which highly prized professionalism and saw it as a cultural civiliser of vulgar interest politics. A radical police chief of Devon and Cornwall or a narrow reactionary police chief of Manchester are merely the inheritors of such a classical liberal tradition.[81]

What he writes of the managerial police here is generalised elsewhere, for instance, in the review of the Australian Conference collection on the state. Only one paper, by Ferraresi on the Italian state, is recommended as having any value. To signify his break with Poulantzas, David welcomes this critique of structuralist models of the state. He repeats the gist of the one-sided Hegelian view in commenting that the Italian state has ceased 'to be a unitary subject, capable of planning and enforcing major strategies'. But the decline of parliament does not reinforce the cohesion of the central state. Basic structures and practices of the state apparatus are left intact and this has all meant that 'arbitrary powers of state agents are even enhanced'.[82] More generally for Britain, the same conclusion is reached. Change in the political, public profile of state officers emerges from the continuous structure of the state.

Thatcherism, David claims in the review of Dunleavy, as a form of 'anti-corporatist symbolic politics' has only modified the politics of administrative practice within the state apparatus and has not shifted the historic balance inside the corporatist politics of state power. To repeat, he does not explicitly emplify on the historic balance of state power and the presumption can only be that the political gains of the petit bourgeoisie can be reversed and are by no means irrevocable. But there is no mistaking, throughout the whole of this book, the emphasis which he gives to modification of practices within the state apparatus. Whereas structuralism, of Dunleavy's variety, can only explain continuity in state form and practice, corporatism or any other state form cannot be reproduced continuously. State practices are reproduced through continuous 'negotiations and struggle'. It is the change in the profile of state officers, the transgression of the external discourse of power, which signals discontinuity in state practice while the agents, in and beyond themselves, keep the structure of state power intact. David offers this final homily: 'The absence of an advanced analysis of governmental politics by both conventional political scientists and Marxists which examines the breaks and the continuities in the English variants of corporatism … creates mythologies which trap the political left'.[83]

NOTES AND REFERENCES

1 Ch. 7, 176.
2 A useful account of nominalism and rationalism can be found in Johnson, T.*et al., The Structure of Social Theory,* 1984, chs. 1-5; also, see Hindess, B. *Philosophy and methodology in the Social Sciences,* 1977.
3 Ch. 2, 46.

4 Rosenberg, D. The sociology of the police and institutional liberalism (draft polemic) *unpublished paper*, 1971, 4.

5 Westergaard, J. and Resler, H. *Class in a capitalist society*, 1975, 186.

6 Caine, M. *Society and the policeman's role*, 1973, 21.

7 Johnson, T. *et al., op. cit.*, 158-9.

8 Rosenberg, D. *op. cit.*, 1971, 2.

9 Rosenberg, D. Review of 'The Police: Autonomy and Consent by M. Brogden', *Sociological Review*, 1983, 31(4), 801.

10 Rosenberg, D. *op. cit.*, 1983, 800.

11 Rosenberg, D. '*To advise, assist and befriend*' – *English probation work as a form of social work*, MSc thesis, Univeristy of Bristol, 1972, 18.

12 Rosenberg, D. *op. cit.*, 1972, 19.

13 Rosenberg, D. *ibid.*, 1972, 18.

14 Rosenberg, D. *ibid.*, 1972, 17.

15 Rosenberg, D. *ibid.*, 1972, 119.

16 Rosenberg, D. *ibid.*, 1972, 67.

17 Rosenberg, D. *ibid.*, 1972, 121; see Hughes, E. C. *Men and their work*, 1958.

18 Appendix, 244.

19 Rosenberg, D. *op. cit.*, 1972, 125.

20 Rosenberg, D. *op. cit.*, 1972, 126.

21 Rosenberg, D. Extended review of 'Working for Ford by Huw Beynon, Allen Lane and Penguin, 1973', *Sociological Review*, 1974, 22(4) 634.

22 Rosenberg, D. Review article of 'C. Van Onselen, Chibaro: African Mine Labour in Southern Rhodesia 1900-1933, 1976', *African Review* 1977, 7(2), 113.

23 Marx, K. Critical notes on the article, The King of Prussia and Social Reform, in *The Collected Works of Marx and Engels*, International Publishers, 1975 (quoted in Connolly, W. (ed.) *Legitimacy and the State*, 1984, 27).

24 Marx, K. *op. cit.*, 27.

25 Marx, K. *ibid.*, 26.

26 For *assumptive world*, see Chapters 2 and 9; for *bringing the men back in*, Chapter 2.

27 Rosenberg, D. *op. cit.*, 1974a, 631.

28 Adorno, T. W. *Negative Dialectics*, 1973, 183 (quoted in Held, D. *Introduction to Critical Theory*, 1980, 213).

29 Johnson, T. *et al., op. cit.*, 100-112.

30 The reference to Peter Worsley arises because Worsley ('The state of theory and the status of theory' *Sociology* 8(1) 1974, 1-17) attacked the growth of subjectivism within sociology during the early 1970s; Garfinkel is represented as a leading light of ethnomethodology; Turner is the editor of a basic text on ethnomethodology and has researched, for instance, on 'the formal properties of therapy talk', an account of communication between analyst and client. See Turner, R. (ed.), *Ethnomethodology*, 1974; Sudnow, D. (ed.), *Studies in Social interaction*, 1972; Rogers, M. F. *Sociology, ethnomethodology and experience*, 1983. Also see Filmer, D. *et al., New Directions in Sociological theory*, 1972; Cicourel, A. *Cognitive Sociology*, 1972.

31 Rosenberg, D. Extended review of 'For sociology by Alvin W. Gouldner, 1973', *Sociological Review*, 1975, 23(4), 969.

32 See Heclo, H. H. and Wildavsky, A. *The private government of public money*, 1974.

33 See Dunleavy, P. *The politics of mass housing in Britain, 1945-75*, 1981.

34 Johnson, T. *et al., op. cit.*, 100.

35 Hollis, M. *Models of man*, 1977, 102-3.

36 Held, D. *op. cit.*, 218.

37 Young, K. Values in the policy process, *Policy and Politics*, 1977 5(3), 5.

38 INLOGOV refers to the Institute of Local Government studies at the University of Birmingham. See for instance Greenwood, R. *et al.*, *The organisation of local authorities in England and Wales*, 1967-75, 1975; Greenwood, R. *et al.*, The organisational consequences of financial restraint in local government in Wright, M. (ed.), *Public spending decisions*, 1980.

39 Ch. 2, 56.

40 Ch. 2, 59.

41 Lemart, C. C. and Gillian, G. *Michel Foucault*, 1982, 134.

42 See Smart, B. Foucault, sociology and the problem of human agency, *Theory and Society*, 1982, 11(2).

43 Lemert, C. C. and Gillan, G. *op. cit.*, 136.

44 Lemert, C. C. and Gillan, G. *op. cit.*, 133.

45 Sheridan, A. *Michel Foucault*, 1980, 119.

46 Sheridan, A. *ibid.*, 127.

47 Sheridan, A. *ibid.*, 129.

48 Sheridan, A. *ibid.*, 139.

49 Lemert, C. C. and Gillan, G., *op. cit.*, 138.

50 Apparently, the example was drawn from the singular experience of Bradford but was not so neat and logical for other cases, such as Sheffield.

51 Ch. 7, 170.

52 Ch. 6, 155.

53 See Foucault, M. *The archaeology of knowledge*, 1972.

54 Ch. 6, 154.

55 Ch. 1, 33.

56 Ch. 3, 91.

57 Ch. 3, 76.

58 Rosenberg, D. Review of 'State, Class and Recession by S. Clegg *et al.* (eds.), 1983', *Sociological Review* 32(1) 1984, 153.

59 Ch. 3, 92.

60 Ch. 3, 92.

61 Rosenberg, D. Extended review of 'Fascism and Dictatorship by N. Poulantzas, 1974', *Sociological Review* 24(3) 1976; extended review of 'Clauses in Contemporary capitalism by N. Poulantzas, 1975', *Sociological Review* 26(3) 1978.

62 Rosenberg, D. *op. cit.*, 1976, 670.

63 Rosenberg, D. *op. cit.*, 1978, 691.

64 Poulantzas, N. Classes in Contemporary Capitalism, 1975, 258 (quoted by Rosenberg, D. *op. cit.*, 1978, 691).

65 Rosenberg, D. *op. cit.*, 1978, 692.

66 Rosenberg, D. Some myths on the African working class, IDS, University of Nairobi (WP 294), 1978.

67 Rosenberg, D. The origins and functions of sociological and historial theories of underdevelopment, *unpublished paper*, 1977, 31.

68 Rosenberg, D. *ibid.*, 5.

69 Rosenberg, D. The development of the Marxist theory of imperialism, *unpublished paper*, 1977.

70 Rosenberg, D. Review article of 'John Dunn, Modern revolutions, 1972', *The African Review*, 1974 4(3), 485-86.

71 Rosenberg, D. Review article of 'Beyond the Sociology of Development' by Ivor Oxaal, Tony Barnett and David Booth (eds.), 1976, *Sociology*, 10(2), 1976, 362.

72 Rosenberg, D. *ibid.*, 368.

73 Rosenberg, D. *op. cit.*, 1978.

74 Rosenberg, D. *op. cit.*, 1977, 115.

75 Rosenberg, D. Review article of 'The State in Northern Ireland, 1921-72: Political forces and social classes', by Paul Bew, Peter Gibbon and Henry Patterson, 1979, unpublished review article.

76 Rosenberg, D. *op. cit.*, 1983 (Review of Brogden), 801.

77 Rosenberg, D. *op. cit.*, 1984 (Review of Dunleavy), 128.

78 See Held, D. *op cit.*, 291.

79 Rosenberg, D. *op cit.*, 1983a, 801.

80 Rosenberg, D. Review article of 'The politics of mass housing in Britain 1945-1975, by Patrick Dunleavy, 1982', *Sociological Review*, 31(1), 1983c, 128.

81 Rosenberg, D. *op. cit.*, 1983a, 802.

82 Rosenberg, D. *op. cit.*, 1984, 153.

83 Rosenberg, D. *op. cit.*, 1983c, 127.

CHAPTER ONE

The existing literature, methodology and the research process

The sociological literature on the professions is both extensive and impressive. E. C. Hughes's writings have been influential in the formation of this literature and some extent it has accepted empirical research as a natural practice of fieldwork.[1] The literature on budgeting in organizations is rather more controversial and organizational theorists, political scientists and accountants have mainly concentrated on the end results while paying homage to the idea, voiced mainly by Wildavsky, that budgeting is a form of politics.[2] The process whereby a budget becomes a budget has rarely, if ever, been satisfactorily discussed. The human, sometimes all too human, actors in their individuality and authenticity have no substantial presence in this literature. Yet it is fair to admit that the literature on budgeting has a certain strength. Research has focussed on such factors as conditions when prices have been stable. It has also dealt with hypotheses about what happens when currency loses its power to predict the value of things to be purchased. Questions have been posed about the continuous primacy of the budget in policy making and what changes occur in the behaviour of the actors.

It is ironical and amusing that Caiden and Wildavsky's study of budgeting in poor countries[3] offers also some indication on how state budgeting operates in more 'developed societies'. A survey of different poor countries shows a possible overlap in the practices of governmental budgets with relatively 'advanced' and wealthy western societies. To that extent there has been a breakdown from the classical pattern of a balanced budget which nineteenth-century political economy advocated. A tendency exists and is now recognised that the annual character of budgeting surrenders to repetitive budgeting, as the central budget office and spending departments struggle constantly to divert the flow of ill-defined and slippery resources. Actors invent tricks and counter tricks to protect their share of the budget pie. Sometimes, though not always, the central collection and publication of data suffers. Spending departments attempt to satify debtors and contractors with vouchers that may wait for months before

---

*This chapter was in the process of being written at the time of David Rosenberg's death. The section on the literature of budgets and human agency had only just been started and was torn off the author's writing pad.

they are honoured by the Treasury. Spending departments also do what they can to establish autonomous accounts free from Treasury control. The Treasury for its part, can hide information in order not to disclose how much it actually can allocate to hungry departments. There is a difference between the official published budget and the 'real budget' that is paid to be in the notebooks or minds of a inner budgetary elite.[5] Under conditions of high inflation the true rate of inflation, as well as the true allocation of resources, may be hidden in a system of poor data and purposeful efforts to mislead. Local government finance in Israel, argues Sharkansky, has all these characteristics. As one official explained to him 'we offer Jerusalem the opportunity of aiding us before we cause a crisis of unpaid bills and unmet service needs, or after we cause that crisis'.[4]

In studies of UK local governments it is accurate to recognise that the patterns of interactions, structures of bargaining and negotiation between both professional and political actors have been noted. The customs, 'rules of the game', which form the background to decision-making have also been recognised. Noted and recognised but not adequately studied.

However, certain types of organizational analysis did allow for the possibility of bargaining between and inside a diverse range of organizations. Indeed one school of analysis is commonly known as 'negotiated order' – perhaps a more dignified title than is warranted for its meaning: bargains and offers which cannot be refused. The most well known exponents, Strauss and his associates, derive their models from highly specific studies of the dominance of professionals in bureaucratic organizations. A text by Strauss alone to build a universalistic model of negotiations was less useful and successful.[5] In organizational studies, the interactionists played another card. Man the negotiator joined man the exchanger and man the player of games and presenter of diverse identities. The new supposedly master card looked at times similar, if not identical, to previous cards in the sociological game which emphasised the active and conscious element in reality construction.

Two associates of Strauss, Bucher and Stelling, utilize the model as a key to understanding the dominance of professionals over supposed Weberian organizations in which they formally are mere subordinates, though influential ones. They note a continually unfolding internal differentiation within the organization which they liken to a political process involving negotiations, bargaining and the formation and dissolution of alliances.[6] Bucher and Stelling argue a common interactionist position: that the power to determine policy is not clearly located in specific positions. It is more diffuse and the focus and balance of power can shift in response to different issues. Not only in this model is power fragmented but it is articulated through interpersonal influence and represents them.

The implicit critique of different models of power by negotiated order theorists draws attention to the dangers of a reductionism whereby the question of authority relations between agents is a mere zero sum game. However, rather more is claimed. Thus Mangham, pushing his argument to a polemical extreme, has argued that, in every situation, power is relative rather than absolute.[7] Inside even such total institutions as prisons the jailor is forced to negotiate over the terms of his authority with the jailed. Such a humanist perspective (to use Berger's category) tells a part of the story only.[8] Even in fascist concentration camps bargaining went on between the SS guards and inmates. It existed but while it may be significant for negotiated order theory it may be less significant to the life chances of guards and inmates. One category survived, the other largely did not.

This use of 'negotiated order' is linked to an *a priori* pluralism which argues that resources exist in every social setting which can at times be tapped as an individual power base for strategic actors. The weakness rather than the apparent strength of the existing authorities structure is underlined. Bucher and Stelling state that in many professional work contexts there is no pre-existing role structure, 'rather the new member builds his own place in the organization, and creates the role he plays there'. Further 'role creation is a direct consequence of being accorded professional status. The professional is the person who has the right to say what should be done and what is necessary to get it done'.[9] Negotiated order theory stresses bargaining between relative equals and also acknowledges that the distribution of power in organizations is unequal. The emphasis is against the possibility that power is so concentrated that negotiations are merely imposed arbitrarily.

Early 'negotiated order' studies had their origins in hospital studies in which high status medical professionals dominated and subverted their bureaucratic organization. It was later suggested that the model might equally be applied to a range of quite different organizations. The only common variable supposedly was that organizational power was seen as being highly situational and contingent. Day and Day dryly point out that the manner in which negotiations are presented 'suggests a co-operative and unusually smooth process involving temporary disruptions in normal routines ... with little actual domination or oppression emanating from different bases of power within and without the organization'.[10]

If elite theory and marxism start from an *a priori* assumption of inequality of access to power and its concentration, the negotiated order theorists blandly prefer to accept a model of relative fragmentation and ignore those conjunctures and contexts which would weaken its explanatory power. Yet fragmentation and concentration can do co-exist in a unity.

Danziger's study of budget-making in UK local government[11] is one of the few attempts to recognise the actual negotiations inside the budget and the limits to such negotiations. Danziger found, after comparing budget-making in both the USA and the UK, that budget construction in the UK was significantly more fluid than in the USA. Procedures seemed to be dominated by covert and often continual negotiations between budget agents. Elected politicians did not make a comprehensive review of the allocation bids at any specified time. Danziger notes that under such circumstances formal decisions often have a ritualistic character. In two out of four budgetary 'cultures', budget construction was anchored in the application by a limited number of technical specialists of somewhat mechanical procedures.

In these systems, the budget solution, states Danziger, '... is the consequence of the organization's problem solving routines and the impact of individual behaviour is secondary'. In the other two budget cultures Danziger found 'a fluid bargaining process with a series of discrete episodes involving interactions between pruning actors and particular spending advocates. While these episodes are institutionalised and routinised, budgetary decisions are somewhat contingent upon the personal styles of, and the interplay between, specific individuals'.[12] It is suggested that budget processes were dominated by continual negotiations between the Treasurer and the spending departments.

Danziger's research is of obvious importance. The relative concentration on finance professionals in budget making and the willingness to interview and quote from such officers who are normally 'invisible', makes his study a valuable addition to a sparse literature which is too often prescriptive. Nevertheless, it should be emphasised that, while Danziger makes a qualified plea for a qualitative research method, 'configurative approaches at the individual level remain attractive because they provide a rich descriptive data from which to generate stories as explanations and because they capture more of the texture of politics',[13] his own text fails to follow such a method. Heavy reliance on comparative statistical data, a positivistic method which is unwilling to examine the diverse political and organizational cultures in the local governments in the sample, etc., all tend to weaken the potential contribution of the text to a field of knowledge and literature which is amazingly underdeveloped. In addition the study, though published in 1978, was largely carried out before the important 1974 organization of local government which greatly reinforced certain roles and changed others. The Danziger study of expenditure politics also is marked by the political fact that the era was one of a steady rise of expenditure for key spending departments and this was supported by political parties of different values in power at Westminster. As Stewart[14] and others have remarked the present era of fiscal standstill or even contraction has the potential to alter radically and shake up the expectations around growth which in the past have been written into the 'traditions' and procedures.

What follows is, therefore, a tentative attempt to fill a certain lacuna in the literature relating to resource allocation and policy formation in UK local governments. It concentrates on the roles and relationships of officers and their own evaluation of the politics of role playing. In addition, it is an attempt to ask further questions relating to the secular mystery of money and the budget process generally. If, as Rhodes suggests, professionals – one of the major actors in the decision making process – are noticeable primarily for their absence from studies of local politics,[15] this is a partial attempt to redress the situation. Hughes states, in his research on occupations and professions, that his aim 'was to discover patterns of interactions and mechanisms of control, the sanctions which they have or would like to have at their disposal, and the bargains which were made consciously or less consciously – among a group of workers and between them and other kinds of people in the drama of their work'.[16] Any studies of local government professionals and their occupational cultures should do at least this and certainly no less than this. Any study of the professional elites who play significant parts in the drama of policy formation and resource allocation should use Hughes' ideas as a base line from which the research process should be, at least in part, built.

BUDGETS AND HUMAN AGENCY

Social theorists are usually conscious, sometimes even over-conscious of implicit 'models of man', structure and agency. Accountants and budget technicians normally do not feel that such a question occupies significant space in their professional discourses. A typical formulation by Arnold and Hope notes that the field of budgeting theory presents 'behavioural problems ... and the present state of knowledge ... is such that even very broad generalisations can be dangerous'.[17] What follows is a critical survey of some of the more interesting literature on budgeting together with a desire to live somewhat dangerously.

It has been remarked by Adorno that any theory which needs to deny completely the illusory power of the subject would tend to reinstate that illusion even more than one which overestimated the power of the subject. As Adorno acknowledges, the objectivity of truth really demands the subject. Once cut off from the subject it becomes the victim of sheer subjectivity.[18] The contradiction at the heart of a project to retrieve human agency from the grip of structure is that, in the very attempt to make out a case for human agency, structure is invoked to account for the constitution or emergence of the subject/agent.[19]

The category of the human agent, the 'subject', has become the object of a great deal of theorising from the structuralists to the post-structuralists. One consistent and main theme in this diverse group of writers is the challenge to the supposed 'metaphysics associated with the concept of the human subject'. Challenged is the notion of the human agent as a given entity, the author of its acts and centred in a unitary reflexive and directive consciousness. As Hirst and Wooley remark, the reaction of humanist philosophy, psychology and sociology is, and was, to utilize the reserve army of personalist and extentialist ideas which had become established as a main defence against the presupposition of behaviourism. The new challenge appears to threaten a universal determinism rendering human conduct a mere 'effect'. However, as Hirst and Wooley note, 'what is challenged is not the status of person, free agent ... but rather the claimed ontological foundations of that status. The notion that men are "free agents", directed by a sovereign and integral consciousness is metaphysical "fiction"'.[20] While, in principle, the call to abandon the dualism of human agent and society is persuasive,in practice it is almost impossible to accomplish. As Abrams drying noted 'the weight of two and half millennia as the obvious basis for effective thought is remarkably oppressive'.[21] Dualism, the understanding of social reality as a dichotomy of subject and object, meaning and structure, self and society is, and has been, the dominant motif of philosophical and social theory and is unchallenged in humanist social psychology.

[Text is unfinished]

METHODOLOGY

The research, on which the following chapters are based, was part of a research project funded by the Economic Social Research Council between 1978 and 1982. It was directed by Professor C. Tomkins of Bath University and utilized a case study perspective on a non-metropolitan county to examine the process by which accounting systems are linked to resource allocation decision making.

The research design was a very limited form of participant observation augmented by relatively unstructured interviewing and some documentary analysis. The combination of methods was mainly determined by commitment to a form of interpretative sociology which would allow the assumptive worlds of both finance professionals, namely accountants, and service department professionals to be understood 'from the inside'. This perspective was shared by the fellow researcher, Mr I. Colville, and formed much of the base on which the ESRC project was formulated. The case study of processes in one local government was supplemented by somewhat more limited fieldwork in a number of other local governments at different levels, i.e. metropolitan and non-metropolitan counties, districts, etc. It may be noted that questionnaires or interview sample surveys were rejected as inadequate because they could not realistically be expected to reveal the nature and extent of professional involvement in decision making, and also because of too great a possible dependence on respondents' replies. A method was required which situated a specific group of professionals' perceptions and attitudes in an organizational context and allowed for a limited independent observation of decisions, actions and outcomes over time.

The relationship between theory and method is normally problematic, but in the case of this research it is particularly so because there are two macro constrasting perspectives. On the one hand the 'urban managerialist' perspective on local government practices stresses that resources may be controlled by important groups of 'gatekeepers' or urban managers who 'mediate' between Whitehall, national and local politicians and the economy. The questions this literature poses basically revolve around issues of power and decision making and of professional or bureaucratic ideologies. On the other hand, the structuralist literature argues that organizational explanations where the research focus is on the behaviour and ideology of organizational actors is mistaken. The structuralist literature implies that studies of so-called urban managers and their decisions are studies of lower order phenomena of minor significance because their decisions are over-determined either by the totality of corporatist institutions or by the primacy of the accumulation process, the management of collective consumption, and the reproduction of labour. There is a tension, therefore, between the two perspectives.

It is perhaps too optimistically contended that structuralist macro explanations do not prohibit an organizational focus and an interpretative sociology. It is hoped that it is possible to combine data from actors' accounts, interviews, observations, etc., and relate such case study data to macro concepts. The task at its most abstract level is to understand and explain something of what Lukes has termed 'the dialectic of power and structure'.[22]

In quantitative research it is common to see a series of well-planned steps which must be engaged in, from the inception of a project to a final report. Some sociologists such as Denzin, in their attempts to make a qualitative research method more rigorous and thus more respectable, have seen such steps as likewise necessary.[23] Yet it may be objected that the principle of 'messiness', long rejected with some embarrassment, should not be denied in a truthful discussion of the research process itself. Wildavsky in a discussion of how he helped to produce the *Private Government of Public Money* argues 'books may be written in curvilinear fashion, much like fitting together the parts of a puzzle, except that all the pieces are not available at the beginning ... the final shape is made up by the pieces instead of being fitted into a pre-determined form'.[24] Neatness has its own logic whereby a finished product denies its origins and history.

It is common in a qualitative research project to note that in many of its stages the supposed logical sequences become blurred and can even flow together. Attempts to tidy up and impose order can damage the richness of data collection, for the unfolding of the research process, which can be both puzzle and adventure, may carry researchers along rewarding paths as well as wasting time in a utilitarian sense. A fundholder and director of a project, if cut off from this grass roots 'feel' for data, by his institutional position is only too well aware that the final report must be in on time. He or she must hope that the final report should supposedly capture the 'essence' of the data seized and transformed at the bureaucratic end. But the final report has to lock out legitimate data in its packaging and fieldworkers revert to the roles of mere hired hands when this happens. In a phenomenological sense, research if not eternal is timeless. Yet researchers are all too mortal and funding organizations welcome the death of time and a project's end.

The problems of research are limited by such factors as time, context and culture. The survey method was rejected as unsatisfactory to case-study research and unstructured research interviewing was favoured. However, in data collection this method emphasised certain role problem areas. This paradox has been noted by Stebbins. 'Objectivity should be maintained at as high a level as possible while rapport must not be allowed to flag. Rapport is essentially a subjective condition which if successfully established, threatens objectivity'.[25] Stebbins argues that an unstructured interview is also an interpersonal relationship.

The researcher, once access is negotiated, is given a partial licence and mandate to accost others. Not a complete mandate but granted privileges not generally available. Goffman ignores researchers but suggests that priests and nuns are sacred occupations which legitimate accosting.[26] The researcher's licence and mandate is more circumscribed and is open not merely to scrutiny, but challenge. The researcher seeks information from supposed secrets. It is generally assumed in the normative literature on research methods that resistance to the researcher can take place, but a possible empathy and negotiation can overcome such resistance. The humanism in interpretative sociology ignores the human factor as well as recognising it. At least once when interviewing accounting professionals inside the Treasury during the present research, a section head openly expressed resentment and warned another accountant against granting an interview. Such hostility may be linked to many factors and it in turn made the researcher even more conscious of his ambiguity towards the 'hard' values of the occupational culture of the accountants.

A frequent problem for researchers is a belief that the researched manage 'fronts' with researchers. An explosion whereby one accountant openly disrupts the 'front' of a team performance, while being psychologically disturbing allows further awareness of the apparent areas of safety and danger to the researched. Douglas has commented 'epistemologically, any investigator has to believe that the end result of his investigations will be the discovery of truth. To postulate that behind every front lies another front gets one nowhere. But to hold that immutable truth will reveal itself once a front is breached is an equally futile approach. One's interest has to lie in judging the validity of the data one collects regardless of the method used to generate that data'.[27]

Deutscher is aware of the significance of 'fronts' to the researcher and underlined the problem by declaring 'acting out a relationship is not necessarily the same as talking about a relationship'.[28] How to identify the conditions which cause people to behave as they talk and the conditions in which people say one thing and behave in exactly the opposite has still not been resolved. Participant observation is one method of avoiding this particular problem yet it is sometimes extremely difficult if not impossible for a researcher to move into such a research role. Such a difficulty can be partly avoided by seeking out informants who can provide interpretations and information over a period. This presents both problems and advantages.

The present research concentrated, inside the mental division of labour in the ESRC project, on unstructured interviews, direct observation of routine work, and discussions inside the various layers of middle and senior managements in both the Treasury and the Personal Social Services. Direct observation of numerous meetings inside County Hall, including highly confidential ones, enabled the researcher to be both 'fly on the wall' and to spread the information net wide. Fairly regular attendance of several days in a week over a period of two years plus 'informal' conversations allowed informants to be collected – and the researcher in turn was also collected. Observations taken in both formal and informal settings, e.g., the staff restaurant, allowed professionals to give informal as well as formal interpretations. Thus the Director of [Personal] Social Services, at lunch with his senior staff, would provide information and interpretations which he may have been reluctant to place on tape when formally interviewed. Data and interpretations gained in this way were invaluable and they also provided the researcher with a much needed support. The lack of such an informant in the Treasury at an 'informal' level, and the potential antagonism supposedly between professionals in a control department and professionals in a spending department suggests that the informant was drawing the researcher into the milieu and values in his work space. It should also be pointed out that the researcher was probably spotted early on as being sympathetic to the Personal Social Services at the private level.

The research project, in which the data was gathered, was an attempt to investigate the use of accounting information in budget-making in local governments. The researcher, a senior research officer, was a 'hired hand', but after some ambiguous feelings decided to shape the official project and to collect further data. To some extent, while this was not written into a formal contract between the project director and the representatives of the council it did not strain the contract. Indeed, one influential chief officer in a preliminary meeting suggested to the project director that the organizational and political dimensions of resource allocation were of extreme importance and the project director had himself conceded such a point. Both the researcher and his junior colleague were committed to shaping the project and also to aligning it with their own professional ideas about research. This meant a policy of negotiation not only with the council which was covert but also with the research director who was himself not often in the field. The control over data and interpretations forced a conjunctural alliance between the research officers who divided up the research areas. It is interesting that the older and more senior officer believed that the strain of attempting empathy and fieldwork on the culture and organizational structure of a management strata of a police force could better be handled by his colleague. He foresaw tensions in data gathering which may not be present in the other areas of research on a social services department. To that extent, his own values and his desire for self preservation gave him a softer option. It is at times an unreal belief in humanist qualitative research that a researcher can always sympathetically understand, if not identify with, an alien culture. To the extent that the researcher could research and, in part identify, with the soft values of a social services department and its Director, he took the softer option in the division of mental labour in the project.

When research access is granted or negotiated a researcher is faced with a satisfactory presentation of the research self. Role distancing can take place, but a researcher has to present him or herself both convincing and non-threatening to the people he or she proposes to know. Only when this is accomplished can the researcher proceed. Any disruption in this fabric of learning can create not merely tensions but chaos. Thus, while the researcher was able to interview nearly all accountants in the sample with few problems, he found on one occasion that a section head openly intervened and warned a junior accountant not to pass information to the researcher, an outsider and a possible 'spy' who was too close to the values of a spending department. The researcher's neutral and professional role was thus challenged. Until then the accountants in the Treasurer's office had not merely been co-operative but largely took for granted that the researcher, a sociologist working on an accounting project, was largely in sympathy with their culture and goals. Such an encounter repelled the researcher and forced him into closer interaction with staff in the social services who were more welcoming. To that extent the researcher had initial sympathies with a spending department and its goals and was further 'bent' in its direction in the course of the research. A social researcher, if rejected by an alien occupational culture or a particular aspect, has to guard him or herself against the dangers of too close an identification. Awareness of this is useful but hardly sufficient.

Research, in common with all social interaction, involves the control and interpretation of impressions. Indeed, a social researcher should be skilled at what Goffman has called impression management. Yet this can create doubts of bad faith and inauthenticity in the researcher which he or she can only contain by imposing an ethos of professionalism which may itself be built on sand. Attempts to convey a desired impression of one's research self and to interpret accurately the behaviour and attitudes of others, i.e. the impression management of significant others, is of crucial importance in the ability to gather data. The researcher element which may threaten its internal common sense. If it cannot absorb, it rejects or neutralises. It rewards and punishes. Fears of bad faith can run parallel with pragmatic fears of bad data or no data.

Goffman has argued that in impression management 'we find a team of performers who co-operate to present to an audience a given definition of the situation'.[29] Disruptions in the performances can signal to a researcher that if he or she is defined as a threat or a spy rather than a sympathetic audience, that may in turn provide clues to the back region where the public performance is prepared. Normally, access to the back regions where a team performance is prepared is tightly controlled. The researcher found that the Director of Social Services and his staff in practice 'turned him' by a selective introduction to the mystery of the back regions where their managerial professionals prepared for audience presentation to the politicians and fellow officers. Berreman has argued that the researched are normally evaluated by their peers on the basis of the degree to which they protect the secrets of their team.[30] Such a locking out of a researcher may alienate if he or she is aware of the disjunction between preparation and presentation. Selective telling of secrets, especially if they are half guessed, has 'turned' more researchers than admit to it.

The researcher feels and often is vulnerable. While formally he or she has been granted access at a senior level this can guarantee a great deal or nothing. The researcher asks for time and attention and the impressions given will determine the kinds and validity of data to which he or she will gain access. Both researchers and researched are performers and audiences to each other as significant others.

The initial distaste for too close an interaction with the police organization and culture and the open resistance and antagonism of one accountant had consequences. So did the inability to comprehend the technical task of accountants and the uneasiness felt towards their rationalities and their probable lack of sympathy for a 'soft' social researcher. In contrast, the help and partial empathy given by the social services management also had consequences. After one episode, in which the researcher turned up at an early committee meeting after making a long journey and then was reprimanded for openly dozing off, a carrot was also given. The Director invited him to accompany him to highly confidential meetings of the Chief Officers' Group where, with the permission of the collective of Chief Officers, he could observe the interplay as a 'fly on the wall'. This was seen by him, his colleague and research director, as a turning point in the process of data collection. It also significantly raised his research status among the professional staff and, that, in turn, increased both the access to further data and the self confidence of the researcher.

The strategy of artless naivety often advocated as a device in qualitative research is always partly a device and never entirely real. Further, in many settings, it is not an acceptable mode of presentation of self. The actors in the local government worlds being researched, were willing to help a fellow professional researcher as well as a human being, often in some distress. They would perhaps have been less willing to help a researcher who was not able to claim a professional identity. Artless naivety would have resulted in eventual rejection.

Yet there are problems in both unstructured interviewing and using oneself as the main instrument of data collection and analysis. Qualitative research aims to preserve the 'naturalness' of the situations and actions observed, yet there is always the problem of observing and monitoring one's behaviour in order to appear 'natural' and the possible consequences on others of the researcher. The last consequence was of significant importance in the research.

NOTES AND REFERENCES

1 Hughes, E. C. *The sociological eye*, 1971.
2 Wildavsky, A. *Budgeting*, 1975.
3 Caiden, N. & Wildavsky, A. *Planning and budgeting in poor countries*, 1974.
4 Sharkansky, I. Budgeting amidst triple digit inflation. *British Journal of Political Science*, 1984, 14, 86.
5 Strauss, A. L. *Mirrors and masks*, 1977.
6 Bucher, R. & Stelling, J. Characteristics of professional organisations. *Journal of Health and Social Behaviour*, 1969, 10(1), 3-15.
7 Mangham, I. *Interactions and Interventions in Organizations*, 1978.
8 Berger, P. L. & Luckman, T. *The Social Construction of Reality*, 1971.
9 *Ibid.*, 6. But Goldie argues against Bucher and Stelling, who claim that power cannot be identified and located, that medical professionals are still in a position of structural dominance in UK mental hospitals. See Goldie, N. The division of labour among mental hospital professionals. In Stacey, M. (ed.). *Health and the division of labour*, Croom Helm, 1977.
10 Day, R. & Day, J. V. A review of the current state of negotiated order theory. *Sociological Quarterly*, 1977, 18(1), 131.
11 Danziger, J. N. *Making budgets*, 1978.
12 *Ibid.*, 169.
13 *Ibid.*, 205.
14 Stewart, J. From growth to standstill. In Wright, M. (ed.). *Public spending decisions*, 1980, 9-24.
15 Rhodes, R. A. W. The lost world of British local politics? *Local Government Studies*, 1975, 1(3), 43.
16 Hughes, E. C. The humble and the proud. *Sociological Quarterly*, 1970, 11 (2), 150.
17 Arnold, J. & Hope, A. *Accounting for management decisions*, 1983, 278.
18 Adorno, T. W. *Against epistemology*, 1982.
19 Smart, B. Foucault, sociology and the problem of human agency. *Theory & Society*, 1982, 11(2), 121-41.
20 Hirst, P. & Wooley, P. *Social relations and human attributes*, 1982, 131.

21 Abrams, P. *Historical sociology*, 1982.
22 Lukes, S. Power and structure . In his *Essays in social theory*, 1977, 3-29.
23 Denzin, N. K. *The research act in sociology*, 1970.
24 Wildavsky, A. Rationality in writing. *Journal of Public Policy*, 1981, 1(1), 126.
25 Stebbins, R. A. The unstructured research interview as incipient interpersonal relationship. *Sociology and Social Research*, 1972, 56(2), 164.
26 Goffman, E. *Behaviour in public places*, 1963, 129.
27 Douglas, D. J. Managing fronts in observing deviance. In Douglas J. D. (ed.). *Research and deviance*, 1972, 94.
28 Deutscher, I. Words and deeds. *Social Problems*, 1966, 13(3), 235-54.
29 Goffman, E. *The presentation of self in everyday life*, 1971.
30 Berreman, G. D. *Behind many masks*, 1962.

CHAPTER TWO

Budgets and human agency: do the men have to be dragged back in?

In social theory it is still customary to draw a dichotomy between two camps. One, represented perhaps above all by Weber, is that in which social structures are seen as the results of (or as constituted by) intentional or meaningful human behaviour. The other, represented perhaps more commonly by Durkheim, is that in which 'social facts' are seen as possessing a life of their own, external to and coercing human agents. With some bending and stretching, the various schools of social theory, such as phenomenology, existentialism, functionalism, structuralism, etc. can then be seen as instances of one or more of these positions.

Berger and his associates[1] have attempted to synthesize and reconcile these two dichotomized positions. According to this reconciliation 'social structure is not characterizable as a thing able to stand on its own, apart from the human activity that produced it'. But equally, once created, 'it is encountered by the individual (both) as an alien facticity (and) ... as a coercive instrumantality'. 'It is there, impervious to his wishes other than (and resistant to) himself'. This schema seems to be able to do justice both to the subjective and intentional elements of social 'life' and also the externality and coercive power of 'social facts'. Thus, it supposedly avoids any voluntaristic implications associated with the Weberian tradition and any reification associated with the Durkheimian one. A distinction is drawn between natural and social acts, in that the latter, but not the former, depends essentially upon human activity. Thus, the elements of social organization in any society are seen as a process of human objectivization, that under certain conditions, take on an alienated form. According to Berger and his associates, objectivization is the process whereby human subjectivity embodies itself in products that are available to oneself and alienation is the process whereby the unity of the producer and his product is broken. Thus, languages, cultural and ethical norms, etc. are ultimately all embodiments of human subjectivity. The model then understands society as an objectivization or externalization of the human agent. And the human agent is an internalization or reappropriation in consciousness of society. This model of structure and agency draws upon the tradition of Hegel which the Hungarian Marxist G. Lukacs also related to in his classical text *History and Class Consciousness*.

Bhaskar has argued that Berger and his associates encourage a voluntaristic idealism in understanding social structures and mechanistic determinism with respect to human agency. In seeking to avoid the errors of both stereotypes they merely, he argues, succeed in combining them. Human agency and society are not related 'dialectically'. 'Rather they refer to radically different kinds of things ... the properties possessed by social forms may be very different from those possessed by the individuals upon whose activity they depend. Thus one can allow, without paradox or strain, that purposefulness, intentionality and sometimes self-consciousness characterize human actions but not transformations in the social structure'.[2] Bhaskar distinguishes between the genesis of human actions, lying in the reasons, intentions and plans of human agents, on the one hand, and the structures governing the reproduction and transformation of social activities, on the other. Bhaskar attempts to preserve the status of human agency, whilst eliminating the myth of creation which depends upon the possibility of an individualist reduction. 'Speech is governed by the rules of grammar, without supposing either that these rules exist independently of usage or that they determine what we say. The rules of grammar, like natural structures, impose limits on the speech acts we can perform but they do not determine our performances'.[3] Keat and Urry state that Berger especially 'sometimes appears to argue that any explanation of human action in terms of the causal operation of social factors constitutes a reification ... one can in fact distinguish between reified and non-reified causal explanations of human action'.[4] They argue that 'the form that social relations take is unintended by any single individual, but results from the interdependent activities of the past and present members of that and related societies. These social relations are not material things but they are real. They have ontological status, but not that of a person. Such social relations are causally effective but they do not fully determine the course of individual behaviour. Also crucial are the subjective means through which individuals assess, interpret, and actively construct their patterns of action within the given structures. Such meanings are not simply individual. Their content is logically dependent upon the shared meanings, rules and conventions and their structured interrelationships, within the language at the societal level'.[5]

Hollis, in warning that 'traditional' conceptions of the human agent were perhaps buried rather than dead, argues 'they are buried in the roots of the very theories which purport to reject them ... there is no dispensing with a model of man ... even empiricists are again flirting with notions of essence'.[6] He declares his support for a 'strong case of bringing men back in' as 'men need social relations but social relations depend on the psychology of men'.[7] In opposition to 'passive' conceptualizations of human agency he supports a Goffmanite variant of role theory which celebrates man as an autonomous actor. While opposed to the philosophical 'realism' of Bhaskar and Keat and Urry, Hollis also accepts a partial agreement about causality which emphasizes human agency inside the fabric of human history.

The category of the human agent, the 'subject', has become the object of a great deal of theorizing in recent years, in work associated with Althusser, Barthes, Derrida, Foucault and Lacan. One consistent theme, in this otherwise highly disparate corpus of work, is the challenge to the supposed 'metaphysics' associated with the concept of the 'person', the 'human subject'. Challenged is the notion of the human agent as a given entity, the author of its acts and centred in a unitary, reflexive and directive consciousness. It is curious that Hollis does not risk a direct engagement with this important literature in his general polemic on social action. The reaction of humanist philosophy, pyschology and sociology is, and was, to utilize the reserve army of personalist and existentialist ideas which had become established as a main defence against the methodological presuppositions of behaviourism. The new challenge appeared to threaten a universal determinism rendering human conduct a mere 'effect'.

Althusser[8] argues that 'ideology' is an inevitable component of any social totality, because the human agents 'lived' relation to their social relationship can never be an adequate account of the conditions on which those relationships depend. Althusser has tried to produce a category of human agent which does not explain its actions as originating in some pre-given 'subject', in free-will, or as being determined by external causes. Althusser seeks to conceive of a socially constituted agent who is at the same time capable of being a 'bearer' of social relations, and who is not a mere effect or cipher. The thesis that agents are self-conscious subjects and that 'society' is nothing but the results of their inter-subjective relations is rejected as inadequate. Althusser argues, on the contrary, that far from assenting in a constitutive act of will, human agents live in an 'imaginary' relation to it. The agent's 'imaginary' relation is a form of presentation of the agent's existence in such a manner that a definite pattern of behaviour is implied. For Althusser, the 'imaginary' relationship to the totality of the agent's social relations is both constitutive of the subject and the basis for its actions 'as if' it were a free, self-determining consciousness. Thus, the imaginary makes the metaphysical 'fiction' appear to be a reality and, Althusser says, to the extent human agents act 'as if' it were, then it is.

This social construction of reality model explains the interrelation between a particular form of the human agent and a pattern of conduct. It accepts the necessity of constituting agents, that the agent is not given in the individual, and at the same time that the result is an agent, whose conduct – although patterned – is not determined.

Phenomenology and symbolic interactionism have attempted to resolve the dualism in the agent-society dichotomy in a variety of ways, all of which emphasize the self-consciousness of the human subject as an agent. However, it is curious that the banal, but useful, observation that individuality like society is, and can only be, constructed historically, is silenced in these texts. As Anselm Strauss argued, 'identities imply not merely personal histories but also social histories … individuals hold memberships in groups that are themselves products of the past. If you wish to understand persons – their development and their relation with significant others – you must be prepared to view them as embedded in historical context'.[9] Like that of the Marxist, Althusser, this formulation suggests that human agents are the carriers of ideologies and forms of social relations which cannot be reduced to the values of individuals.

A tentative, and by no means final, position is that structure and subject-agent have always been interdependent as categories. A wholesale attack on the latter was, in due course, bound to subvert the former. As Adorno states, the objectivity of truth really demands the subject. 'Once cut off from the subject, it becomes the victim of sheer subjectivity'. Adorno also adds in his reflection on the dialectic of the two 'the question of the share of each is not to be settled generally and invariably'.[10] As an heuristic device and with some rashness, models of social action taken from a diversity of theoretical fields will be utilized to draw attention to the possibility of limited advances. A selective eclecticism will reign over this project. Arnold and Hope have noted that the field of budgeting theory presents 'behavioural problems' and 'the present state of knowledge ... is such that even very broad generalizations can be dangerous'.[11] A survey of some of the available literature on budgeting, and a desire to live dangerously by bringing to the surface the implicit models of man (as Hollis calls them) which dwell in the depths of the budgeting-literature waters, are the motifs for the following arguments.

Homans, two decades ago, protected against the dominance in sociology of system theories which invalidated the human actor in all his or her shyness and courage.[13] In these models, the motivations and the values of human actors did not exist other than those which the social system functionally conferred in a process of socialization, which was without disruption, deviation or pain. Indeed, pain evaporated as a problematic which was existentially and biologically grounded. Social death was over-social and socialization a smooth process in which the necessary values were internalized by human actors. Wrong, too, protested against an over-socialized conception of man in which the motivation of human actors was mechanically determined by a tight fit between the needs of the system and the human actors who live and breathe inside such an 'Iron Cage'.[13]

In social theory, political science and sociology today, whilst such models of functionalism are still powerful, they are no longer dominant. Role theory, which had an orientation in the field of organizational studies to a dry and static reductionism, has become less rigid in sociology together with those variants of interactionism which have penetrated the field of social psychology. The tendency in role theory to reify actors, has been met by a critique which is shared by a number of perspectives and which argues that actors bring to any role their previous biographical experiences and this provides them with sets of meanings by which they give their own interpretation of the role. Behaviour within a role always, then, involves a certain reworking and redefinition of the expectations regarding the way in which role incumbents should behave and there is rarely a complete consensus as to the behaviour expected of the incumbents of a given role.

The weakening of the dominant functionalism in role theory is best documented by Goffman's category of role distancing. It could still be argued that the revision of role theory advocated by E. Goffman and others, while not locking the human agent into an 'Iron Cage', is still a category which is reified and legitimates such reification. However, a loose, soft determinism may well serve analytical purposes which an extreme voluntarism would deny, as even Berger would admit. A more interesting critique of all types of role theory suggests that its orientation is basically static, and defines social behaviour as more or less normative and, furthermore, has a tendency to reduce social relations in which the human agent is a bearer to game-like models of interpersonal relations only.[14]

Models of budgeting span a diversity of intellectual fields and collectively they claim to legitimate the possibility of a scientific theory. Primacy in explanation is claimed by all the models and is thus wholly possessed by none. The vigour of rival models attempting to gain hegemony over each other, suggests a crisis in budgeting theory which is increasingly recognized by a few and shrugged off by many. Each model is both a technical intervention in method and measurement and is also a carrier of an implicit conceptualization of human agents. Such an underlying nuance illuminates and constitutes the formal model and the formal model or models can then only be understood by a recognition of the conceptualization of human agents.

This chapter argues, sometimes directly and sometimes through a more contradictory path, that diverse traditions are articulated in different perspectives on budgeting. An alternative model of human agent is advocated with some reservations. Lukes has argued for the alternative explanation of agency as consisting of a 'set of expanding and contrasting abilities, faced with expanding and contracting opportunities'. Together these constitute structured possibilities which specify the powers of agents, variations between agents and, over time, for any given agent. Lukes emphasizes, 'social life can only be properly understood as a dialectic of power and structure, a web of possibilities for agents, whose nature is both active and structured, to make choices and pursue strategies within given limits, which in consequence expand and contract over time. Any standpoint or methodology which reduces that dialectic to a one-sided consideration of agents without internal or external structural limits, or structures without agents, or which does not address the problem of their interrelations, will be unsatisfactory'.[15]

The 'traditional' conceptualization of budgeting as a quantitative plan to co-ordinate and control resources is related to the managerial functions of the procuring and controlling of resources. 'Budgets do not involve direct, personal surveillance by an actor or actors seeking control', claims one study. 'They represent an impersonal quantitative means for achieving control over the activities of sub-units or organizational members'.[16]

Both state budgets and budgets in 'private' organizations can be viewed as part of technically founded discourse which disguises managerial domination as a rational response to technical problems. Habermas has noted how 'the manifest domination of the authoritarian state gives way to the manipulative compulsions of technical-operational administration'.[17] Budgetary studies are normally articulated through both strong and weak varieties of positivism and the claim to value neutrality not only measures the degree of control but legitimates it as a device of manipulative rationality.

Other dimensions of budgeting have become mainly silenced in the mainstream discourse on budgeting. From the margins, it has been suggested that these other dimensions of budgeting exist; thus, we find those who can analyse it as an 'ammunition machine'[18] or, as a forum for an internal political system of bargaining.[19] It has also been claimed that accounting systems provide a means of legitimizing the activities of agents and interests of sub-units in ambiguous situations: that they provide a convenient 'dramatization' of efficiency in contexts where efficiency is elusive because of the loose linkages between agents' activities and outcomes.[20] And yet other perspectives can exist and flourish on the margins of accounting and organization studies.

Budgeting practices and the significance of those agents located in such practices differ between societies. Wildavsky argues that the origins of gross differences in budgeting across national states is a function of wealth, predictability, size, elite values and political institutions. In his model, wealth and predictability are the most important causal variables in predicting the basic character of the budgetary process itself.

In the construction of governmental budgets, both technocrats and politicians can claim different 'ideological charters'. The problem arises as to how far particular studies of budgets can determine who has real power to formulate fiscal policy? Since budgeting practices provide the outside observer with built-in quantitative indicators, positivism claims that power in budgetary matters can be measured by the capacity to transform spending allocations to increase or cut back the amount granted to one group of ministerial agents. According to this perhaps rather simple notion, the answer is merely to follow a projected budget from the earliest stages of its formulation to its final ratification, paying careful attention to the magnitude of alternatives in each spending request. The stage at which the largest number of decisions are made concerning the largest amount of money is, *ipso facto*, the most important locus of decision making. Conversely, those stages of the budgetary process in which spending proposals are rarely or never transformed, may be regarded as perfunctory and unimportant.

Purely quantitative indicators of power in budgetary matters, however, are deceptively simple, and may lead to serious misinterpretations. Not all modifications in budget estimates constitute decisions about priorities, and not all agents and roles who alter these figures should be regarded as 'powerful'.

Many expenditure decisions are unambiguously determined by legislation previously enacted: budgeters, in these contexts, have little choice but to allocate resources in strict accord with that legislation. In the UK, central government legislation on local government services has had a significant statutory power over the agents of the resource allocation process. Many apparent decisions, too, even when budget agents appear to have a significant amount of discretion and power, are non-decisions in so far as the specific political culture in which the budget system operates is able to impose a normative 'common sense' which withdraws alternatives from the agenda. Thus, the 'rules of the game' in the last years of Franco meant that the budget could only be altered in so far as the whole or parts lay wholly or partly outside the Franquist elite's 'zone of indifference'. Gunther states 'when decisions involved policies on the margins of that "zone of indifference" move, overtly political constraints had to be taken into consideration. In setting the annual budget policy, this meant that certain policy options, whose effects on the economy were fully explored during the preparatory stage of this decision-making process could not be selected'.[21]

A third major qualification which must be imposed on quantitative indicators of 'power' in budgetary decision-making is the awareness that not all monetary changes represent real alterations in spending priorities. Some changes must be made from one budget year to the next, to enable activities of services to continue at previously established levels. These relatively automatic adjustments, over such factors as inflation, entail significant changes in the shape of a budget. Yet, it is the existing 'rules of the game' which rules that these changes are unchallenged.

To identify agents who possess power in the budgetary process, therefore, it is necessary to go beyond quantitative indicators of that concept. Ritual is both a cloak over the naked face of power and broadening of the projects of the agents who can and do wield power. It is important to recognise that the self is in part a ceremonial thing, a sacred object which should be treated in budgeting with proper ritual and with care.[22] And the external discourse of a budget is a power discourse. Olsen insists that the 'expressive' aspects of local government budgeting are strategic elements in a societal 'democratic' discourse between power holders in Norway and the citizens. It is a discourse which allows the elite agents both power to manoeuvre and sharply circumscribes their power.

The lack of a theoretical bridge between such a perspective, which utilizes categories of ritual, power, discourse, and an interactionist perspective, based in methodological individualism which examines actions and activities of agents, is an obvious lacuna in the alternatives to the normative models of budgeting theory. Perhaps only Goffman, rather than any other sociologist in the tradition of G. H. Mead, consciously relates to a Durkheimian sociology of ritual. Goffman's method utilizes ritual, not as a tight-fitting corset which does not allow the occupant to breathe, but as nuanced interpretations of interactions which on the surface only are highly voluntarist. The mainstream of symbolic interactionism exhibits a curious theoretical dislike of structuralist, holist and Durkheimian forms of macro-sociology.

A dramaturgical perspective on budget-making will indicate that the process is both solemn and supposedly systematic. Even if chaos reigns inside the construction of activities, the discourse of a budget is public rather than private and must claim order, justice and rationality as the guiding principles. Ideals of a perfect utopian society, worthy of Sir Thomas More, are superimposed on the surface of budget-making. Backstage, however, the patching up of cracks in the fiscal boat through which water enters, goes on through the activities of the all too human agents who worry, plead, warn and sometimes sweat as they work to reach the shore. The external discourse of rationality and justice drives out not only impure politics but the impure agents who become invisible men – very few women occupy these strategic roles.

The name of the budgetary game then is the legitimization of supposedly rational administration. This relates to an important shift in Western societies away from representative democracies. Habermas has argued that, 'the dependency of the professional on the politician appears to have reversed itself. The latter becomes the mere agent of a scientific intelligentsia, which in concrete circumstances, elaborates the objective and requirements of available techniques and resources as well as an optimal strategy and rules of control'.[23]

The question can then arise: is what Habermas describes as the dominance of a de-politicized technocratic strata merely a strong tendency rather than an iron law, and what are the implications for the critical study of budgeting? The acceptance not merely of reification but of a total alienation in which the administration of things is normal, is explicit in Habermas's pessimistic sociology. Yet, budgets can sometimes collapse and the planning and bureaucratic structures can be shaken by human earth-quakes. Habermas's lack of empirical sociology may also be an element in a vocabulary of motives which starts as a critique of a given dominant technocracy, by noting its hidden kernel of unreason, and ends in a pessimistic half legitimization as unavoidable.

A minor, but still significant, reaction has disrupted a dominant 'common-sense' consensus in budgeting theory which had eliminated or marginalized the organizational context and the social, political, and ideological variables. This minor upheaval has been based largely on a comparatively few case studies which attempted to study budgeting as a process over time rather than assuming perfect knowledge of what a budget is from the outset. A well-known series of studies is by the political scientist, Wildavsky, and his collaborators, and the emphasis on political realism is primary. Wildavsky's study of money politics in UK central government, it should be noted, is both similar and different from his studies of budgeting in American local governments. In both types of study, the emphasis is on budgeting as a political process where human agents represent themselves and organizational sub-units probably have conflicting goals.

It is well known that Wildavsky has argued that the process by which budgetary allocation agreements are initially reached is a political decision-making process, in which conflict is mitigated by following certain 'incremental' procedures. The most important of these is the almost automatic acceptance by budgetary agents of a certain level of minimal expenditure by each spending department. This 'base' figure (usually equal to each department's allocation in the budget of the previous year) is not challenged in the course of negotiations. Instead, bargaining and the application of political pressures of various kinds concern requested 'increments' over and above that base figure. By thus reducing the scope of the issues in dispute, the intensity of inter-departmental conflict is reduced. Nevertheless, since the size of the yearly increment can be very important to spending departments, political pressures brought to bear during negotiations over each requested spending increase may be very extensive. Finally, in most cases, some kind of 'fair shares' principle governs the interdepartmental allocation of the yearly spending increment. This may range from the relatively simple, but highly political, notion that everyone should have a chance to get at least a little extra through these negotiations, to the opposite.

The focus is then on coalition building and bargaining and an assumption is made of 'bounded rationality'. The mode of analysis is very similar to Lasswell's formulation that the important question for political analysis is who gets what, when and how.[24] Wildavsky attempted to formulate a position in these terms. 'If politics is regarded in part as conflicts over whose preference shall prevail in the determination of rational policy, then the budget records the outcomes of this struggle. If one asks, who gets what the government has to give? Then the answers for a moment in time are recorded in the budget. If one looks at politics as a process by which the government mobilises resources to meet problems, then the budget is a focus of these efforts'.[25]

The conceptualization of the budget as a political arena is linked with but also limited by the well-known assertion that the budget process is one of incrementalism in decision-making. A number of writers, apart from Wildavsky, have noted and dissented from the assertion that rational and comprehensive problem-solving approaches assume intellectual capacities, perfect knowledge and available time to a degree real decision-makers do not possess. March and Simon, and Lindbloom, amongst others, developed a critique and an alternative perspective from such a rational process model, centred on an assessment of the characteristics and behaviour of human actors in a complex situation.[26] Complex decisions are, particularly according to Lindbloom's model, made by a continual and marginal series of adjustments from the current situation. Only a few alternatives are considered, and 'feedback' (that reified concept from systems theory), from the total impact of decisions guides yet further adjustments.

The techniques of incremental decision-making are then employed to simplify drastically the options which human actors consider. This effectively limits the amount of information that must be gathered and processed, the permutation of choices that are evaluated and the extent to which overall goals and objectives can be evaluated. This style of decision-making has been particularly attributed to budgets in both political science and accounting research orthodoxy and has thus achieved the status of a conventional wisdom that underpins a broad consensus. Inside this consensus there is some debate concerning the quality of decisions reached but there is comparatively little dissent from the new 'common-sense' that incrementalism describes the behaviour of budget agents in a variety of contexts. The budget process is taken to be incrementalism written large, but neither the reasons for this nor the impact on decisions of the differential behaviour of budget agents are normally specified and, apart from an infinite regress mode of explanation, there is no other explanation of why the present levels of expenditure patterns of allocation exist, other than through reductionist psychological observations based on particular agents.

It is arguable that as a theory, incrementalism is weak as an explanatory model, despite its considerable predictive power in the past. The literature does not seriously explain why incrementalism occurs at all or why some budgeting systems are less incremental than others. Greenwood, Hinings and Ranson dryly note that the literature is tautological. 'If the definition of an incremental change is drawn widely enough then the claims that all budgetary procedures are incremental is easily substantiated'.[27]

Kantor and David charge incrementalist theory as ignoring the importance of changing political and economic forces that act as 'constraints on these patterns of behaviour'.[28] Wildavsky, for example, has shrugged off a budgetary system with a 30 per cent change in budgetary totals and can still write as if incrementalism was, and should be, the normative budget for all seasons.

Wildavsky emphasizes and emphasizes again that budgets are the outcomes of clashes between different agents representing diverse interests. However, the image of man implicit in incrementalism limits the range of choices and so reduces the river of politics to a stream. Budget agents certainly are bureaucratic agents with much of their freedom to choose eliminated by their role-input as representatives of interests. Thus, they cannot take large risks and maybe the divisibility of outputs, the complexities and the need to simplify choices, moves such agents to 'muddle through' and to reduce the risk-taking by socializing these agents to disbelieve in the possible rewards. The lack of choices is apparently over-determined by the tightness of continuity and the actor's *a priori* socialization through past interactions.

Incrementalism, it is commonly agreed, is a particular model of pluralism in which interest groups have their bargains institutionalized in budgets which are rarely overturned. Non-decisions thus reign over significant areas of budget politics. Growth in budget expenditure allows the integration of newer interest groups without a major challenge to the existence of previous institutionalized agreements.

Incrementalism is not the opposite face of pluralist bargaining but is an expression of the political strength of a range of diverse interest groups. The culture of incrementalism is one of consensus construction in which no powerful actor or agent for an interest group is totally invisible. It is thus possible to argue that the model of incrementalism is more than a simple model of causation and action, it is also a mode of legitimization of contemporary budgetary politics. It is rare for the incrementalists to evaluate the who-gets-what aspect of budget analysis because of the 'common-sense' acceptance that the content and process of budgeting is working properly. Wildavsky, especially, has an implicit perspective that views budgeting as an arena of bargaining coalitions in which all major interests in a 'polity' are more or less represented by the budgetary actors. The weak or silent may be recognized in some mode of undemocratic representation in this process but this relationship is unproblematic. Incrementalism tends thus to be a celebration of the strong, while articulating as a variant of the democratic theory of the getting and spending of money.

The emphasis on budgeting as a political struggle means that a 'more adequate theory of budgeting will have to be based', in the words of Greenwood, Hinings and Ranson, 'upon the political features of organizational life, rather than upon the cognitive deficiencies of decision actors'.[29] To that extent, Wildavsky would himself acknowledge the dominance of organizational politics. Implicit in this formulation is a concept of the human agent as a game-playing actor, instrumentalist and perhaps totally utilitarian in goal orientation and values. This model is very similar, not surprisingly, to the Goffmanite model of the human actor as a presenter of self to a diversity of audiences, selecting goals and discarding them when other interests dictate. Only incrementalism denies the voluntarism inherent in some aspects of Goffmanite analysis by emphasizing a model of role as an 'iron cage' which imprisons the actors. The discursive affirmation of a given ideological order is organized through affirmative symbolism or ritual. The waving of a national flag, the Christian Holy Communion or the construction of budget all possess an expressive symbolic quality as well as, in the latter, a pragmatic function. Beattie has argued that though both symbolic and 'practical' modes may be, and often are, combined in the same social practice 'it is necessary to distinguish between them as they imply different attitudes towards experience and call for different kinds of understanding'.[30] Therborn states 'the distinction between a ritual and a material affirmation is an analytical one and not a distinction between intrinsically ritual and non-ritual practices'.[31] Thus, a political election in a western liberal capitalist state is an affirmation of liberal political ideology. To the extent that the outcome is predetermined by limits on who may run and have a chance to campaign effectively, the affirmation is predominantly ritual. But to the extent that the outcome is open, Therborn regards the affirmation as predominantly material.

Olsen, Johnson and others have used the word 'ritual' in their analysis of budgeting as a social process. Unlike the Goffmanite image of man as a free agent not given to altruism, they, too, like Wildavsky, in practice emphasize the patterning of roles, the lack of real freedom in the projects of the actors. If man is born free but everywhere in chains, those chains are both visible and invisible and cast from the world of symbolism. Parts of the totality of budgets have thus been defined as 'ritualistic' in so far as the actors have no power over the script and the script itself has already been written in such a manner that important changes are difficult and indeed impossible to make. Ritual thus becomes an explanatory category in which the past projects of human agents structure and over-determine the responses of contemporary agents. The weight of traditions and the cake of human custom weighs upon the back of human agents and is not consciously always recognized. Like strong models of structural functionalism in the sociology of the 1950s and 1960s, and the more frozen models of roles in social psychology, few radical changes are allowed as possibilities. Yet, it is legitimate and useful to argue that budgets are indeed a form of symbolism. This does not automatically contradict an analysis that budgets are a type of politics. Both recognize that budgets are the attempt to divide 'scarce' resources without too much blood being spilt on the carpets of organizations. Are budgets then to be conceptualized as a type of ritualistic politics or are other perspectives equally valuable?

Political science models of budgeting are not a tightly defined system of explanation as that provided by neo-classical economic theory, yet the attempts to establish linkages in urban political studies, for example, between the vivid tapestries of local political activities and the cold figures in the municipal balance sheets, offer some limited theoretical advances and rewards. Political science today lingers at the boundaries of analyzing budget construction as a political process built on the political

53

theories of both Hobbes and Locke. It articulates a variety of realisms which accept that agents and 'sub-units' may well have conflicting goals and poses questions and answers around the assumption of 'bounded rationalities'. The use of the word 'rational' and its cognates has caused untold confusion in the realm of budgeting theory and social theory in general. Perhaps it should be stressed that Max Weber himself is partly responsible for this as his use of the term is irredeemably opaque and shifting.

A tendency also exists in the usage of the term 'rational' to conceptualize it as a dominant 'rationality', a majestic world spirit of the age in which all alternative discourses lose their meanings and potencies. A variety of sociologies exist which supposedly challenge or reinforce this. Thus, A. Schutz advocated that inside a totality of society, a number of multiple realities exist in social life which are not co-determinate with each other. Unfortunately, Schutz failed to transform his phenomenology into a theoretical or empirical sociology.[32] The perspective known as functionalism also justifies the study of apparent 'non-rational' behaviour by reference back to a not so irrational 'hidden hand' by which all levels of social life work to sustain each other. The explanation in terms of the ends that social pheonomena serve and the explanation of the specific operation of diverse social institutions by reference to their interdependence makes it then unnecessary to pay significant attention to the intentions of human agents, except as a foil to add cogency to latent functions.[33] Still, an analysis of budgeting may well come to a conclusion that a weak model of functionalism which stresses the inter-relation of the different parts of budgetary outcomes could explain many of the events in the political process. That human subjects may well, in constructing a budget as a process, also live and negotiate outcomes from a vantage point of multiple realities has not yet been recognised however.

The utilitarianism of the Wildavsky tradition denies, by not recognizing, that political man is also a human agent who lives in, on, and around political symbolism, which itself is not reducible to the laws of a Benthamite calculation. Edelman and other American political scientists have focussed on the symbolic strategies used by different human agents and groups under specific conjunctural contexts to defend or attain goals. Such symbolism is integral to the importance of ritual.[34]

Olsen's study of budgetary behaviour in Norway argued that data existed which could not be explained by an orthodox decision-making model. Important parts of the budget, argued Olsen, can only be understood as a ritual. The expressive aspects of budgeting with roots deep into political rituals give legitmacy to political agents.[35] While Wildavsky mainly emphasizes the political context of budget construction in his case study of Oakland, he also, at the margins, identifies 'revenue, behaviour, executive dominance, council acquiescence and utopian departmental requests' as important characteristics of local government budgets. The object of the budgetary process in such cases is 'control' rather than 'navigation'. The establishment of 'short-term hedging' against unpredictable events rather than the clear establishment of organizational goals, means that in the event of a fiscal crisis, budgeting tends to become a form of 'maintenance activities'. Agents know where they are, but they cannot go very far. In this argument, Wildavsky seems to suggest the existence of ritual elements but his main emphasis is on describing where the 'action is', which allows an analogy of political systems to become the dominant motif in his writings.[36]

A number of methodological problems exist in the study of ritual in the budgetary process or elsewhere. A major problem is how to establish whether one inter-presentation is more valid than another. The observer simply cannot accept the human agent's interpretations alone; at the same time, he cannot deny the partial legitimacy of such interpretations. The task is to interpret the ritual within the context and this must be empirically established. Often symbolism is not explicit, thus crucial explanatory clues may be generated in comparison with alien contexts as well as more general theoretical categories and ideas. Goffman has suggested that an important perspective in the study of supportive ritual is to try to isolate specialized functions, the assumption being that although all of these rites serve to support social relationships, this can be done at different junctures and in different ways, and these differences provide a means of distinguishing classes of these rituals.[37]

Jönsson, in a valuable study of budgeting in Sweden, has argued that budgets are not the result of a rational process in the manner in which new techniques for planning are defined. Yet, they are not irrational either. 'Rather the budgetary process is characterized by a multitude of rationalities at play'.[38] Thus, the allocation of resources between different and competing programmes is in itself complex and this is compounded in many ways by an absence of acceptable measures of output and an imperfect knowledge of how means are related to ends in the 'common-sense' model of input and output. In a more extensive study of budgeting in Sweden, Jönsson accepts that budgeting in a political environment is a form of ritualistic control in which learning and significant changes do sometimes take place. He argues that the elements in the budget process in Gothenberg Council are 'ritualistic not because it is irrational, but because it has many rationalities ... In spite of the ritual pervading the process, there was learning ... men are smarter than systems, and what is learnt is how to negotiate; not how to make better budgets'.[39] Ritualism, for Jönsson, is not an 'iron cage' but rather a loose fitting suit. He illustrates, through use of the dramaturgical perspective, that in budgeting 'the stage is set by the political circumstances and the financial resources available, but the roles are given in the script. There is always room for interpretation and excellence in performing the role, but it does not take much to make Hamlet into a ridiculous figure'.[40]

This reflection by Jönsson is some distance away from the Wildavsky school, which seeks to create a 'positive' theory of budgeting, a mechanism by which financial resources are translated into human purposes. While Wildavsky, Simons, March, Cyert, Lindbloom in their general critique of the classical model of 'economic man' which assumes 'total rationality', turn to a theory of games and social exchange to various degrees, the organizational context is less loosely coupled to budgeting than a dramaturgical perspective would emphasize. Incrementalism as a theory is not agnostic on such questions. It is true that the assumptions behind a 'muddling through' model implies that budgeting is incremental, fragmented and sequential in time. Decisions are made without clear common goals and reliable information about alternatives and consequences is more often lacking, than otherwise. A 'pure' dramaturgical perspective can accept all of this; the question arises – what are the significant determinants which give the human agents real or apparent freedom? What is the degree of tight or loose coupling between a budgetary process with all the potential human farce of possible banana skins and the organizational requirements of obtaining sufficient financial resources to purchase the future of human agents?

While budgeting theory has a few writers who observe or stress the symbolism and ritual of budgets both in construction and in outputs, the very language of budgeting allocates a discourse which eliminates and makes invisible such a potential rewarding area. Also the anthropological literature is not itself totally clear in the relationship of symbol and ritual to human agents and in fact may merely argue that such symbolism is universal in pre-industrial societies.[41] Yet budgeting theory has failed to theorize adequately that the hustle and bustle of even invisible budgetary elites pivots around ideologies, myths and belief systems which bind the human agents into constructed social structures. It is equally more necessary and important to stress what has been implied earlier, that budgeting is a symbolic discourse by the rulers to the ruled who are themselves outside the arena of where the action is and is thus a major mode of legitimization.

The formalism inside the official governmental culture of the UK political elites document this with some clarity. Thus, prior to the Chancellor of the Exchequer's ritual of budget presentation to the House of Commons, there is speculation in the mass media by ideological gatekeepers and interpreters of the mystery of taxation. The 'rewards' and 'punishments' of changes in forms of taxation are seen as societal discourses to client groups by the governing administration. Raising of taxation through an increase in the price of consumer items like beer and tobacco is not merely a utilitarian act alone but is seen as punishing drinkers and smokers for ills which consumerism creates and sustains. The presentation of a budget in the House of Commons by a Chancellor of the Exchequer is presented in a language, therefore, both of political arithmetic and of morality. The relationship between the two discourses can only be conceptualized by a discovery of the audiences who are democratically captive and bound.

Both Wildavsky and the alternative models of causation possess useful explanatory value and an adequate theory of budgeting would acknowledge such validity and go on to relate one level to the other. Multiple realities exist, with the need for an adequate non-utilitarian sociology that can capture the diversity of means and the apparent coexistence of such diversities. A budget, too, can be both a *rite of passage* with a destination ending in both Stendhal's world of *The Red and the Black* and an entry into the same colours of profit and loss which are unproblematic in the accounting literature.

What is more sacred and secular than the getting and spending of money? Perhaps only motherhood, and even that is now threatened. Budgeting guards the sacredness of money by superimposing a discourse of rational allocation which eliminates any mystery or hides it. Ritual, as Geertz hints, provides both a 'model of' and a 'model for' action.[42] In so far as ritual always entails the enactment of a social relationship, the relationship is shown in such a way that it both portrays and subtly alters the relationship framed in the ritual act. Weber, Sombart and Simmel all attempted to impose a secularization of the mystery of money as a social relation by discussing its commodification and internal rationality as a form of exchange.[43]

It is commonplace that negotiations take place at the margins and the centre of budgets but they rarely, as already has been hinted, are solely over goals which are totally utilitarian even, and especially, when money is concerned. As writers have noted, the budget process is effected by the manner in which ritual penetrates the apparently pragmatic world of resource allocation.

Local governments and budgeting, especially in the UK, are knitted together not merely by the powerful claims of professionalism, but by numerous 'customs' which create traditions of action, roles, scripts, etc.[44] These customs are not located in the background among the other props but fill the stage and give content and meaning to interactions. Freedom perhaps is only the non-recognition of custom. Significant roles inside the local government organization can become, in diverse contexts, ritual specialists and this is especially true of accounting roles. Thus, treasurers may find that they devise new, or adapt old, rituals in order to uphold their definitions of the 'truth' of the budget process. In alliance with other strategic roles they can even rewrite a script to a considerable extent. Such power is differentiated from being a 'master of ceremony', although in practice a role occupant may possess both attributes. Budgeting as a formal structure then, in such a specific organizational context, often dramatically reflects the myths of its institutional environment rather than being simply a response to the demand of the work activities of the organizational context. Agents in any budgetary process not only commit themselves to supporting a specific ceremony which is both more and less than a facade, but also commit themselves to negotiations backstage, which, though often formally inappropriate, keep the apparently technical activities running smoothly. Thus a crisis of legitimization can be avoided and the discourses internal and external to the budgetary processes are not weakened.

Meyer and Rowan argue that modern accounting creates ceremonial production functions and maps them onto economic production functions. Thus, the conventions of modern accounting attempt to assign value to particular components of organisations on the basis of their contributions to the goods and services the organization produces. 'But for many units ... it is utterly unclear what is being produced that has clear or definable value in terms of its contributions to the organizational product'.[45]

Accounting then can provide an 'ideological charter' for a particular organization or a budgetary activity. This gives the finance professionals, at the apex, the power of a secular priesthood as they, more than any other category, can claim to be the central guardians of the system they serve as apparent servants. The anthropological literature notes that in social contexts where meanings and relationships are weakened, specialization in ritual function may not be highly developed and rituals may be generated by those who perform. By contrast, in social contexts which produce conflicts, a division exists between those who devise and those who perform rituals though both are ritualistic in role performance. The creation of ritual activities then can become a conscious effort, an expansion of the legitimacy and power inherent in guardianship roles. If incrementalism as a type of budgetary immobility is linked to a more or less strong ritual pattern, then zero-based budgeting allows greater degrees of volatility in movement and is less paterned. The former is perhaps linked and favoured by those agents and roles less in need of the protection offered and given by ritualism in budgeting. Zero-based budgeting allows and welcomes contests and clashes and encourages a less controlled political input. It changes the 'rules of the game' by adhering to a mimicking of war in budgetary interactions. Negotiations become less smooth and diplomacy less stable.

Rituals of rebellion that mock or question the given order of things are not always alien to budgetary systems, although as Lukes and Gluckman noted they are relatively common in 'civil society'.[46] A mimicry of conflict is part and parcel of the budgetary process as contests between bids by different agents appear and disappear from the agenda. The high degree of institutional formalism, and the 'customs' associated with it, produce the mechanisms that transform the conflict into a resolvable one. The agents are symbolically seen to be representing a diversity of interests and values. To gain organizational legitimacy from peers and subordinates, they must give a more than adequate performance of 'fighting for their corner'. Blood is shed indeed and often, but, as it falls, it fails to permanently damage the tasteful carpets, as frequently it is transformed into a removable tomato sauce by a mysterious alchemy. The agents talk the same language, a language of service values, priorities, and this language unites as well as divides. The budget 'war' is also then understood as a 'game', by these agents, sometimes an unfair game and rough, but a game for all that, though serious consequences can and do follow from playing. Such joint 'play' evokes a team spirit and a team ethos.[47] There are reciprocal bonds which create dependency inside apparent conflicts. What unifies them is a common interest in presenting the 'front' of budgetary construction to external audiences and a collective control of the production of budget drama as 'common-sense'.

Penalties on budgetary agents who allow cracks in the forging of the consensus to be revealed to external audiences, vary between budgetary cultures. Whereas 'teamwork' in many social contexts attempts to present a common definition of the situation as if each agent was autonomous in arriving at the final collective definition; the budget process as democratic drama stresses the collective and just integration of the agents in a final solution, in which the whole is not merely more than the individual parts and interests but an ideal social contract. Budget agents are permitted role distancing but not the illegality of creating a legitimization crisis. Surface cynical deals do not automatically shake the belief in the budget as sacred social drama, and collective control of the audience's milieus provides a protection in some depth from the potentiality of a ritual profanation of the front region.

It has been already implied that accounting systems and budgets do far more than simply record, or reflect a mirror image of aspects of financial performances. To the extent they can constitute a key feature of organizational procedures they determine the dominant discourse as Foucault's work may suggest. He and others argue that the human agent in his humanity is not susceptible to precise and continuous definition by a magisterial and unshakable 'reality'. Rather, human agency is constructed by discourse that are both contingent in their eruption, determining in their effect and yet constrained by significant others who at the same time are constructed by discourse. The discourse is uniquely born out of language and communication between agents.[48]

In the tradition of G. H. Mead, a parallel argument on 'vocabularies of motives' by C. W. Mills points out that human agents 'discern situations with particular vocabularies'. They anticipate the consequences of human action in terms of these same vocabularies. 'In a social situation, implicit in the names for consequences is the social dimension of motives. Through such vocabularies types of societal control operate'.[49]

Accounting systems can structure a dominant discourse with subordinated discourses or (as the Meadian tradition would argue) vocabularies of motives in a variety of ways. Myths, rituals and interests of dominant coalitions and of the apparently neutral technical system form guidelines of behaviour for human agents. Achievement of targets can be its own legitimization. If any agents find difficulty in this, they articulate their 'accounts' in terms of the dominant 'vocabulary of motive' and to that extent strengthen the ritual element. An account is a linguistic device employed, argues Lyman and Scott, whenever an action is subjected to valuative enquiry. 'Moreoever accounts are situated according to the statures of the interactants, and are standardized within cultures so that certain accounts are terminologically stabilized and routinely expected when activity falls outside the domain of expectations'.[50]

The budget as a process is a world taken for granted in contemporary literature perhaps because, as a system of near perfect harmony, it hides the imperfections of the human agents who direct, construct and inhabit it. Human agents are invisible and the discourse of a budget is the ideal representation of the truth of a society, for most of the time.

In liberal democratic capitalist societies governmental budgets are mainly an external discourse and are coupled to its internal strains and conflicts. In contradiction to the apparent breadth of politics, external in these societies, the budget is determined by small elites of agents who carefully insulate themselves from not merely the sea of democracy but even often the respectability of meek pressure groups. Heclo and Wildavsky on the Treasury in UK central government and Danziger's examination of budgets in UK local governments, both document and mechanisms which insulate the elites.[51] Being accountable only to the historical institutions in which these agents are located, attempts to claim bids on the budget are resented and presented as a pollution of the purity of professional authority. In addition, democracy and pressure groups threaten the collective control a team of budget agents has over its collective performance, unless certain agents can neutralize this potential threat by symbolically representing absent but perhaps potent social forces. In budget cultures in which popular democracy could pose such a threat, the external discourse of a budget which emphasizes justice and other attributes of a 'good society' could be damaged by such a populist interpretation.

The charisma of budget actors is partly routinized in the diversity of roles which bind and bond each member. A team's charisma need not suffer in rhetorically calling for a 'good housekeeping'. Indeed, such pieties may strengthen audience control as well as fixing limits on internal negotiations. The Treasury in Whitehall has been defined as an occupational community of reputations. While reputations are like human souls eternal, in a budget culture they can be lost, won and lost again. Reputations represent individual human agents at the level of performances and also imprison the agents in the reputational mask. If reputations are not merely taken but have also to be granted and accepted, the team as a team articulates the ritual of interdependency. And if, as Goffman claims, the world is a wedding, it can also be a separation and a divorce.

Human agents, it has been noted, can commit themselves, even when apparently role-distancing, to public ceremonial facades which are more and less than a facade. Through backstage activities agents commit impure deals and other practices, but keep the sacredness of the budget and ensure its hidden technical agenda. The backstage of a budget has a level of real autonomy from its external discourse into civil society though one level helps to create and reproduce the other. Nevertheless, one level cannot be reduced to the other and indeed, in the discourse external to the budget, agents are forced to deny or avoid the recognition of such impure practices.

Heclo and Wildavsky note the insulation of budget politics from democratic audiences and the openness of budget agents is linked to their invisibility. If the budget agents act, as has been suggested, in the manner of a 'team', then, while individual members may make temporary gains from revealing practices to external audiences and thus robbing them of charisma and legitimacy, the penalties and controls undercut such potential threats. The budget team, in all budget cultures where secrets are to be kept, attempts with great success to convert all agents into insiders. Outsiders or quasi-outsiders quickly learn the dangers of spoiling collective performances with the resulting damage to those 'trust' relationships which are vital elements in the 'common sense' culture. Such apparently secular ideologies as professional bonds and the ethos of professional loyalties can and do co-exist with rituals which guard the purity of the essence of a budget from pullution.[52] Against the authority of the budget 'team', the external audiences and publics can only weakly protest, resist and then comply.

Backstage activities and negotiations are both pragmatic and ritualistic. It would not be wisdom to deny that even the supposed underlife of a budget process is not totally free. The film, *The Godfather*, showed the Don, at the wedding of his daughter, granting favours in the informal audiences awarded by him as the patron. Indeed the supposed backstage in such a context can be even more important than the performance in a front region. The relationship of each to each shifts according to the balances in the context. In the backstage of a budget, the agents while positioning themselves in a team also make offers to each other which they 'can't refuse'. Thus, the internal hierarchy of a team and the authority of each agent is demonstrated. Social death and reputational decline may result from a refusal by one agent an offer by another. Yet, budget cultures emphasize dependencies, reciprocities and norms of 'fairness'. In Danziger's words the budget process can no longer be viewed as a 'single temporal event: rather the decision is seen as a scenario, as a series of episodes in which various participants have made variously important contributions'.[53]

It has been emphasized that budgets define not merely 'what is' but also 'what ought to be'. Some sociologists following Merton use the term ritualist for agents who perform external gestures without inner commitment to the ideas and values being expressed.[54] If ritual is defined as a routinized act it can be, in a subtle manner, a despised form of communication. Other symbolic acts will then accurately convey information about the intentions and commitments of the human agent. Anthropologists are in the habit of using ritual to mean action and beliefs in the symbolic order without reference to the commitment or non-commitment of the human agents.[55] In their studies of small-scale and face-to-face social settings, a gulf does not often exist between personal and public meanings. Rituals are not fixed and discrepancies between the situation being enacted and the forms of expression are immediately reduced by changes in the latter.

Inner withdrawal from the meanings built into the ceremonial facade of a budget by team agents can and does happen and the budget symbolism can then become more threadbare. Everything becomes mere politics but a politics defined as a form of utilitarian interest. Ritual can and does allow non-decisions to preside over whole areas of a budget, but, if an element of it is seen by agents as mere manipulation, it loses its power to hold the half-captive agents.

NOTES AND REFERENCES

1 Berg, P. L. & Pullberg, S. Reification and the sociological critique of consciousness. *New Left Review*, 1966, 35, 56-61. Berger, P. L. & Luckmann, T. *The social construction of reality*, 1971.
2 Bhaskar, R. *The possibility of naturalism*, 1979, 44-56.
3 *Ibid.*, 45.
4 Keat, R. & Urry, J. *Social theory as science*, 1975, 186.
5 *Ibid.*, 193.
6 Hollis, M. *Models of man*, 1977, 3.
7 *Ibid.*, 27.
8 Althusser, L. *Lenin and philosophy*, and other essays, 1971.
9 Strauss, A. L. *Mirrors and masks*, 1977.
10 Adorno, T. W. *Against epistemology*, 1982, 72 and 156.
11 Arnold, J. & Hope, A. *Accounting for management decisions*, 1983, 278.
12 Homans, G. C. Bringing men back in. *American Sociological Review*, 1964, 29(6), 809-18.
13 Wrong, D. H. The oversocialised conception of man in modern sociology. In his *Skeptical sociology*, 1977, ch. 2, 31-54.

14 Urry, J. Role analysis and the sociological enterprise. *Sociological Review*, 1970, 18, 351-63. Goffman, E. Role distance. In his *Encounters*, 1961 83-152.

15 Lukes, S. *Essays in social theory*, 1977, 29.

16 Covaleski, M. A. & Dirsmith, M. W. Budgeting as a means for control and loose coupling. *Accounting, Organizations and Society*, 1983, 8(4), 330.

17 Habermas, J. *Towards a rational society*, 1971, 107.

18 Burchell, S. C. Clubb, A. Hopwood, J. Hughes & J. Nahapiet. The roles of accounting in organizations and society. *Accounting, Organizations and Society*, 1980, 5 (1), 5-27.

19 Wildavsky, A. *The politics of the budgetary process*, 1964.

20 Cooper, D. J., Hayes, D. & Wolf, F. Accounting in organized anarchies. *Accounting, Organizations and Society*, 1981, 6(3), 175-91.

21 Gunther, R. *Public Policy in a no-party state*, 1980, 93.

22 Goffman, E. *Interaction ritual*, 1972.

23 Habermas, *op. cit.*, 66.

24 Quoted in Pfeffer, *Power in Organizations*, 1981, 2.

25 Wildavsky, *op. cit.*, 4.

26 March, J. G. & Simon, H. A. *Organizations*, 1958. Lindbloom, C. E. The science of 'muddling through'. *Public Administration Review*, 1959, 19(2), 79-88. Both represent 'classical' statements.

27 Greenwood, R., Hinings, C. R. & Ranson, S. The politics of the budgetary process in English local government. *Political Studies*, 1977, 25(1), 26.

28 Kantor, P. & S. David. The political economy of change in urban budgetary politics. *British Journal of Political Science*, 1983, 13(3), 251-74.

29 Greenwood (*et al.*), *op. cit.*, 26.

30 Beattie, J. H. M. On understanding ritual. In Wilson, B. R. (ed.), *Rationality*, 1971, 240.

31 Therborn, G. *The ideology of power and the power of ideology*, 1980, 82.

32 Hindess, B. The 'phenomenological' sociology of Alfred Schutz. *Economy and Society*, 1972, 1 (1), 1-27.

33 Wilson, B. R. (ed.) *Rationality*, 1971. This is an important collection of articles centred around this problem.

34 Edelman, J. M. *The symbolic uses of politics*, 1964. Also Cohen, A. *Two-dimensional man*, 1974. The latter book is an anthropological study.

35 Olsen, J. Local budgeting: decision-making or a ritual act. *Scandinavian Political Studies*, 1970, 5, 85-115. It should not be assumed that merely because agents have goals that symbolism is in itself a form of rational action. As Hollis dryly remarks 'instrumental accounts of rationality are not silent about the rationality of goals ... By relying, for instance, on some vacuous universal desire to attain happiness or maximize utility, they can credit the agent with a rational goal without actually saying so. The presumption is thus created that mere desire for an end counts as a reason for pursuing the end'. Hollis. *Op. cit.*, 99.

36 Wildavsky, A. *Budgeting: a comparative theory of budgetary processess*, 1975.

37 Goffman, E. *Relations in public*, 1972, 93.

38 Jönsson, S. Budgeting behaviour in local government. *Accounting, Organizations and Society*, 1982, 7(3), 287.

39 Jönsson, S. *A city administration facing stagnation*, 1982, 82.

40 *Ibid.*, 83. Discussions of the dramaturgical perspective can be found in Harre, R. & Secord, P. F. *The explanation of social behaviour*, 1972 and Ditton, J. (ed.). *The view from Goffman*, 1980.

41 Bocock, R. *Ritual in industrial society*, 1974. His argument is that ritual is universal in industrialized societies and that no secularization has occurred.

42 Geertz, C. *Interpretations of Culture*, 1973.

43 *Ibid.*

44 Stewart, J. *Local government: the conditions of local choice*, 1983, 87. He states that the council,

'above all, a setting for rituals ... the game is important to participants, yet remains a game played as a ritual by relatively unchanging rules'.

45 Meyer, J. W. & Rowan, B. Institutional organizations. *American Journal of Sociology*, 1977, 83 (2), 350.

46 Lukes, S., *op. cit.*, 552-73. Gluckman, M. *Custom and conflict in Africa*, 1973. He argues for a conflict functionalism in which conflicts whether directly or by inversion or in other symbolic forms, emphasize the social cohesion within which the conflict exists. Also Coser, L. *The functions of social conflict*, 1956. He adopts from Simmel the same formulation.

47 Goffman, E. *The presentation of self in everyday life*, 1971, provides a brilliant discussion of the 'team' as a category.

48 James, F. *The prison house of language*, 1972.

49 Mills, C. W. Situated actions and vocabularies of motive. In Horowitz, I. L. (ed.), *Power, politics and people*, 1967, 439-452.

50 Scott, M. B. & Lyman, S. M. Accounts. *American Sociological Review*, 1968, 33 (1), 46.

51 Heclo, H. H. & Wildavsky, A. *The private government of public money*, 1974. See also Danziger, J. N. *Making budgets*, 1978.

52 Douglas, M. *Purity and danger*, 1966, 156. 'Each culture must have its own notions of dirt and defilement which must not be negated'.

53 Danziger, *op. cit.*, 16.

54 Merton, R. K. *Social theory and social structure*, Enl. ed., 1968, 203-7.

55 Douglas, M. *Natural symbols*, 1973.

CHAPTER THREE

Power and professionalism and control in central-local government relations

Recently a political scientist, Rhodes, complained in his survey of central-local government relations literature that it had 'demonstrated a marked aversion to theory'. Later he comments that 'barefooted empiricism' is the usual paradigm of analysis and that the theoretical field is 'too often the preserve of public administration, the subject needs to break out of these confines'. An advance cannot, he argues, 'be achieved by the traditional methods of legal-institutional case studies'.[1] Dearlove claims

> there is a body of traditional wisdom about local government, a well-established discourse ... this conditions and limits the conventional debate. The tradition is made up of simple statements that purport to describe and explain how local government works; to diagnose the faults; and to suggest reforms which will lead to a better system characterized by democracy, efficiency, effectiveness, and co-ordinated rationality. These statements may be termed orthodoxies.

Dearlove argues that even where the statements purport to offer a description and explanation they are not based on any solid empirical research into the practice and behaviour of local governments.[2]

It may be of use to employ Michel Foucault's notion of a discourse to identify this field of 'common-sense' literature on central-local government relations. Texts and supposed descriptions purporting to contain knowledge about something actual are not easily dismissed. Expertise is attributed to the literature by the mere fact of its existence, and the authority of academics, politicians and institutions that can accrue to it, surrounding it with still greater prestige. Most importantly, such a body of literature can create not only knowledge but attempt to create the very reality they appear merely to describe. In time such knowledge produces a tradition, what Foucault calls a discourse, whose presence or weight, not the originality of a given academic, is really responsible for the texts and paradigms produced out of it.[3]

The local government 'system' may well too be a discourse carried by its 'believers' and its priests (including academics) into the very civil society that maintains it. Many believe with pragmatic passion that local government is uniquely democratic. The discourse combines elements of technocracy with a political language of democracy which is equated most strongly with local community. Fittingly one study of local governmental politics had the title *Democracy and Community*.[4] In the literature the value of local 'democracy' is an unquestioned 'common-sense' and detailed evidence to support this is rarely thought necessary. Hill, for example, simply states: 'Democracy is what councillors and officers do in their day to day work. The definition of democratic local government is their definition'.[5]

Dunleavy has dryly noted the formalism of the dominant public administration paradigm inside this discourse is the

> refrain that power lies where it is supposed to be, formally and legally. Some authors are content to maintain the legal fiction that power is exercised by the local council as a whole, and the dictum that council members take policy decisions while officers merely carry them out ... more informed and realistic studies within this tradition at least admit of a pervasive political process dominated by power ... but they put forward a resolutely positional view in which power exertion is seen as confined to individuals in controlling positions in formally responsible locations in the local council or bureaucracy ... nor is much attention given to the ... detailed way in which decisions are made, or to the analysis of policy outcomes.

Dunleavy further notes 'it is not coincidental that this view is essentially similar to the mores inculcated in council members and to the values assigned importance in the professional training of local government officers'.[6]

It is also striking how the field of organizational theory which services local government studies has ignored the implications of 'reforms' of local government. The organizational theory literature, while somewhat different from the public administration literature, has also, with a few honorary exceptions, eliminated power as a problematic in its attempts to demonstrate how decision-making should be 'rational'. In pratice this literature favours entrusing public policy to the professionalism of non-elected officials and the allegedly technical and neutral process of policy construction. Interestingly Dunleavy has noted that the early papers published by the directors of the two most prestigious Centres of Local Government in the field of local politics can evaluate such politics only as a necessary evil, a useful legitimizing device for policy decisions but also a potentially distorting and disruptive influence on policy development.[7]

The rise, since the 1974 reorganization of local governments, of models of corporate management is explained by Dearlove as, at least in part, an attempt to increase the collective authority of the professionals at the expense of the elected politicians. Organizational theorists, while not inventing the system of corporate management, have been foremost in supporting it as a mechanism for containing the volatility of power produced in the local government system which has the potential of escaping the control of the elites of chief officers and selected councillors. Thus, Programme Planning and Budgeting Systems (PPBS), programme budgeting, Zero Base Budgeting (ZBB), and other managerial fads were all legitimated as scientific and prescriptive models on how decisions should be made and became part of a language of politics. Wolin has defined, correctly, contemporary organizational theory as a mode of the sublimination of politics.[8] A critique produced by Benington – an outsider who became a Chief Officer – described corporate management as helping to advance certain interests and values at the expense of others and at the same time making it harder for those biases to be observed and challenged.[9] Cockburn in her study of Lambeth has remarked that one of the important effects of corporate management was to depoliticize issues in local government.[10] This minority but useful tradition of analysis sees corporate management attempts to plan rationally local services as being integral to a process of corporatism, where professionals are given actual power over policy construction, while still being in formal subordinate positions in the bland organizational models. As Clapham recently argued, corporate planning can be constructed as a direct attack on the political process by a technocracy.[11]

It would be a mistake to believe that organizational theorists in high educational institutions were solely or mainly responsible for the initial introduction of corporate management models. In the late 1960's and early 1970's, for example, some important city councils called in firms of management consultants to revise their decision-making machinery and to propose changes. Thus, Hull and Liverpool called in McKinsey and Stockport called in Booze, Allen and Hamilton.

Di Maggio and Powell have argued that in the initial stages of 'their life cycle, organizational fields display considerable diversity in approach and form. Once a field becomes well established, however, there is often an inexorable push towards homogenization'.[12] Meyer and Rowan point out that as early adoptions of organizational innovations spread, a threshold can be reached beyond which adoption provides legitimacy rather than improves performance.[13] Much homogeneity in organizational structures stems from the fact that despite considerable search for diversity, there may be relatively little variation.

Central government departments, networks of influential members of what Dunleavy has usefully called the 'national' local government system, and other elites seem to be important in spreading the message of corporate management as a system of rational salvation. In practice, the fact that corporate management created hybrid systems in which new structures were merely superimposed on older ones was largely ignored and under-researched. Corporate management, as an organizational style, was seen as value-free and unchallenged.

Organizational theory in local government was and is structured by a relative absence of empirical research and observation based on fieldwork. In a manner similar to classical organizational theory, sociological variables of informal organization and power tend not to be problematic.[14] Thus, the body of contemporary 'theory' so often utilized can be seen both as a general legitimization of normative current practices, as well as a specific organizational weapon of particular fractions of management in their attempt to control labour and the organization as a whole. This, too, in part explains, though does not excuse, the acceptance of models that largely ignore power and process as a key to explaining decision-making, which is not recognised to be a form of politics.

Dearlove and others have commented sharply on the limitations of the dominant public administration literature in its discourse on local governments. Dearlove's own 1970 study of the London Borough of Kensington and Chelsea focussed entirely on the roles of council members alone. The rationale he gave was that 'many of the officers were interviewed, but it proved impossible to break through the culture cliche that they were simply servants advising the all-powerful policy-making councillors whose decisions they readily implemented'. He goes on to stress, 'ideally, one would have observed instances of interaction between councillors and officers'.[15] Rhodes has also remarked that the formalism of the institutionalist literature, which sees key professional managerial elites as mere 'servants of the council', has also meant 'that one of the major actors in the decision-making process is noticeable primarily for a major absence from studies of local politics'.[16]

Many other criticisms could be levelled at the public administration literature in its discourses. Power is seen, *a priori*, in pluralist terms and, even those who are critical of pluralist perspectives at a theoretical level, in practice seem to accept it by default. Saunders' valuable and unique study of Croydon is perhaps the only exception to this.[17] It should again perhaps be emphasized that, with the exception of the work of Kogan on Education Directors,[18] there are no useful studies of chief officers' backgrounds, values and ideology. Such elites are invisible or merely 'obedient servants'. Another gap in the literature in this research field was pointed out by Dunleavy who states that 'the significance of professionalism as an intra-departmental influence on policy has never really been analysed', and refers to 'our complete ignorance of the intra-departmental policy process in local government'.[19] Many other examples can be given of the silences on power in the consensus literature. It may not be surprising that two influential writers, at the Institute of Local Government Studies itself, have argued that the study of public administration and research into local government 'should be comparative within the field of organisational theory rather than of political sciences'.[20] Political science, as a field has a stronger awareness of power, even if variants of functionalism inside the field have a similar tendency to conceive it as non-problematic. Studies of power and decision-making in local governments have suffered partly because of the methodology of enquiry and partly, as previously stated, because of the ideological 'common sense' model of local government as a relatively unproblematic form of democratic representation. Theoretical alternatives do exist and could be utilized however.

Radical, non-marxists, like Lukes,[21] who are critics of the predominantly empiricist behavioural and 'pluralist' orthodoxy in the normative political science conceptualization of power, have centred their critique upon the identification of what is seen as a significant aspect of power relations. This is excluded from empirical analysis by the epistemological and methodological assumptions of the dominant tradition. The aspect of power relations to which they draw attention, is the complex processes whereby consent, often active consent by the subordinate groups, to specific exercises of power over them is secured. If it is an exercise of power when A secures the compliance of B to A's wishes, even against the wishes of B, then surely it is also an exercise of power when A secures the complicance of B by modifying B's very wishes in accordance with his, A's, objectives.

In this very simple model, the relationship could be assimilated to one of manipulation, and such manipulative techniques are accessible to empiricist and behaviourist analysis, in so far as they are constituted by detectable actions and decisions of assignable individual actors. However, Lukes and other radical critics claim that, if it is possible for certain actors or groups of actors, by virtue of their social position, to sustain or modify social forms and practices of dominance in such a way that the resulting pattern of wants in subject actors favours the non-conflictual realization of their own wants and aspirations, then this is a situation investigable as a power relation even inside the dominant research tradition.[22] The empiricism of the latter requires the observability of exercises of power, in the form of decisions and actions of specifiable actors which settle conflicts of preference or wants between contending actors or groups of actors. The type of power Lukes is interested in analyzing is exercised to ensure that conflicts never arise. The identification of specific acts of assignable actors as casually responsible for the formation of this or that want would be methodologically out of the question. If powerful actors and groups of actors can affect and/or control the subordinated actors or groups of actors in such a way so that wants are generally satisfiable within the existing framework, then research which is conceptually and methodologically restricted to the analysis of conflicts over the satisfaction or articulated wants within that institutional framework will even contribute to the legitimization of such a situation. Such research will fail to register unarticulated wants, possible preferences, which might have been formed were it not for the hegemony of social practices and relationships which shape wants. Research which takes as 'given' the wants and preferences which are articulated will tend to render 'invisible' the process of how those 'given' wants are socially constructed.

The discourse of power in the field of organizational behaviour can be found expounded in a recent textbook by Pfeffer.[23] Whilst frankly accepting the 'fact' of power, Pfeffer adopts the unproblematic and empiricist model of power which was earlier under attack by Lukes and others in US political science. Pfeffer, quoting Lasswell, defines politics and power as 'the study of who get what, when and how', but no attempt is made to go beyond this criticism.[24] Pfeffer's text, without any recognition of the conceptual epistemology at stake, attempts to measure the dimensions of power in organizations. An earlier study by M. Crozier was more analytical; he has argued that power is a very different problem with which to deal in the theory of organizations. It refers to a kind of relationship that is neither unidimensional nor predictable.[25] He argues that micro power politics cannot be read off from a macro level and vice versa.

Contingency theory is utilized by writers based at the prestigious Institute of Local Government Studies. The heavy emphasis in these writings on structural adaptations and the lack of concern with processes has been linked to a relative distancing from an acknowledgement that organizations are political systems and cultures. Power is seen as being co-determined with and by institutional roles. Contingency theorists do abstractly acknowledge the importance of studying the 'political features of organisational life, rather than the cognitive deficiencies of decision actors'.[26] This has not, however, been their empirical research practice, though at certain times power and politics are formalistically added to the shopping list of organizational determinations in decision-making. The thrust of this perspective is to underline the external 'environment' of the UK local governments as a source of contraints upon action. Pugh and Hickson,[27] who inspired Hinings and others, emphasized the effects of size, dependence and technology on the organizational structure. Similarly, Lawrence and Lorsch,[28] though not writing on local government as a form of organization, have argued that the structure of the organization is shaped and determined by the constraints in the organizational environment. The emphasis on constraints is a legitimate theoretical recognition of a macro-process but the attempt by organizations to control as well as adapt to the external environment is under-researched and not theorized, other than in neo-functionalist terms.

It is theoretically possible to distinguish between power as resources, power as rules governing interactions, and power as the 'mobilization of bias'. The concept of the 'mobilization of bias' is a product of the community power debate in political science and has not played a prominent part in the debate on organizational power. Bachrach and Baratz discuss the 'mobilization of bias' by noting, 'when the dominant values, the accepted rules of the game, the existing power relations among groups, and the instruments of force singly or in combination, effectively prevent certain grievances from developing into full-fledged issues which call for decisions, it can be said that a non-decision-making situation exists'.[29] This is similar to the perspective of Lukes, earlier discussed, and indeed Lukes and others[30] utilize this perspective in their own work.

Parry and Morris[31] argue that a clear distinction should be made between different kinds of decisions, for instance, whether they be 'key issues' or routine administrative decisions, and, for each type of decision, between the types of power involved. Three types of power are discussed, the power to initiate a routine; the power by which the routine is maintained; and the distribution of power following from the performance of a routine. The focus on routines, and the values and power distribution sustaining them, is vital to the analysis of local government decision-making and this too has been ignored by researchers with some rare exceptions.

Garrard, in his recent historical studies of the power relations inside local governments, has raised the problem of the empirical investigation of non-decisions. He claims, 'non-decisions, involving as they do discrete inactivity, are necessarily hard, if not definitionally impossible to identify. It is very difficult to establish whether those who benefit do so intentionally (and thus as the result of some clear extension of power) or inadvertently, in a situation where power is less clearly involved'.[32] Nevertheless, Garrard believes that any analysis of power in nineteenth and twentieth century urban society is incomplete without such a category as non-decisions. First, it draws attention to the way in which local governments serve the interests of the socially and economically dominant classes by 'routines and routine administration' as Parry and Morris argued. Such routine administration is and was a pivot of 'system maintenance'. Secondly, the concept of non-decisions draws attention to important areas of local government where, though a problem was recognised, no action was taken due to the 'reputation for power' possessed by members of elites or elite groups. Garrard gives examples with regard to industrial pollution. Here regulations might never be produced at all, or more frequently, they were produced but not enforced, or framed so loosely as to make enforcement impossible. This was sometimes the result of explicit negotiations, but was more often produced by political inactivity.[33] In a critique of organizational theory, Clegg[34] has distinguished between power, rules and domination, arguing that pluralist theory has focused on the surface manifestations of power, i.e. participation in key issues. He argues for an analysis of the rules supporting and constraining such participation and for an analysis of the structure of domination which supports the rules. This still has not been carried out by either the local government research or the specific discourses on organizational theory.

A further application on non-decisions in local governments can be found in the conceptualizations of the borders between political and social life. Categories of social control and hegemony focus on the important fact that power has to be analyzed in much more than political terms. Gramsci, the Italian Marxist, favoured by Lukes, utilized a number of interlocked categories in which the dominant social classes and their ideologies structured a 'world view' of 'common sense' for subordinated social categories. Gwyn Williams has described such a hegemonic world view as 'diffused throughout society in all its institutional and private manifestations informing with its spirit all taste, morality, customs, religious and political principles, and all social relationships, particularly in their intellectual and moral connotations'.[35] This is an ideology of 'common sense' (in Gramsci's words) which is articulated in day-to-day social practices. It may be noted that inside a mode of hegemonic cultural and political domination, whether within a total society or a particular sub-unit, negotiations may well take place which both consolidate the overall hegemony and also allow a shift in power and concessions between the power groups.

Radical organizational theory, while recognizing the category of 'hegemony' in the work of Gramsci and others, has treated it with some superficiality.[36] Historians have gone deeper. Two social historians, Eley and Nield, state 'hegemony is not a fixed and immutable condition, more or less permanent until totally displaced ... but is an institutionally negotiable process'.[37] In this negotiation, consent by subordinated classes and groups is reworked and reconstructed, and the boundaries of 'common sense' shift with a new hegemony emerging. Historians of local governments, such as Garrard,[38] document this reconstruction of hegemony by dominant classes which allows space for the representation of subordinate social groups and recognizes the rise to bureaucratic authority and decision-making power of new professional elites organically tied to the local government system. Hennock,[39] too, has pointed out that in the nineteenth century 'reactionary' popular movements in urban governments, based on small capitalists whose income was derived primarily from rents, often opposed with success the plans for fiscal expansion supported by the large capitalists at the apex of local government and advocated by the professionals. An empirical recognition of the negotiations inside a hegemonic order, which in its turn raises the problem of the conceptualization of dominance, still has to be carried out in the field of local government studies.

Urban historians, examining local governments and power, have shown no hesitation in looking at conflicts over policy and control over, for example, the tax base of local governments. Some political scientists,[40] arguing that local governments politics are constrained by structural factors beyond the local level, point out, however, that individual actors retain the ability to make choices and pursue strategies within such limits. Other political scientists[41] have argued that, in spite of their dependency on central government financial grants, local governments should be treated as political systems; they have their own specific political cultures and characteristic approach to the resolution of disputes. Smith has concluded from a survey of the research literature in this area that 'local political variables do affect the way in which needs are perceived and met ... many of the social characteristics of the population which appear to be directly related to policy outputs have proved, on closer inspection, to be a function of intervening variables measuring some aspect of 'political decision-making'.[42] CIPFA statistics tend to confirm this perspective on decision-making.

In an interesting explanation of these variations, Rhodes[43] has argued that the concept of 'dependency' in studying local–central government relations is ambiguous, as financial dependency has not been automatically translated into policy construction dependency. In the field of intergovernmental relations, Rhodes suggests that local governments have political, ideological and organizational resources with which they may seek to influence the direction of central government policies, and even resist or defy such policies. The former unwillingness of central and local governments to break from a corporatist bargaining process meant that a number of corporatist structures existed which gave local governments some representational power.

Rhodes' model of intergovernmental relations implies that interactions are a process of exchange. Participants employ a variety of strategies, including coalition, co-option, disruption, confrontation and assertion of authority. The process is conducted within a set of 'rules of the game'. Rhodes also calls attention to the role of personalities and the possibilities for variation in the degree of discretion available to the decision-makers according to the policy field.

A counter argument can be made: if an analysis looks for evidence of bargaining at any level such evidences will be found. That does not count as evidence that a state or an organization is pluralist unless this has been assumed *a priori* beforehand. It is easy to observe the detailed process of exchange among the actors in the public sector, and then to exaggerate the importance of the observed differences and to conclude finally that the state or the organization is indeed a pluralist one.

Another problematic feature of the Rhodes' framework is the concept of the 'rules of the game' which set the approximate limits within which discretionary behaviour takes place. As Saunders comments, those 'who make the decisions also make the rules according to which their decisions are taken'.[44] To analyze only decisions taken within the framework of rules may eliminate important decisions of power, including the whole area of non-decisions, the modelling of bias and the rule-making process itself.

However, events in recent years have shown an inequality of bargaining power between central and local governments, as Rhodes himself recently admitted. The basic strength of central government is that it can change unilaterally the 'rules of the game' if it so desires as the constraints are cultural and ideological rather than constitutional. Indeed, Burgess and Travers[45] argue that local autonomy over policy decision-making is nowadays all but extinguished, as the formal shell of structure has little representative democratic content. The new legislation on the spending of grants has, they argue, narrowed the options on resource allocation and transformed the political process into mere administration of central government's decisions.

This perspective of the 'death of local government' is widespread and does correspond to significant shifts in the form and content of intergovernmental relationships. The degree to which the changed power balance constrains, and is perceived to constrain, the elites of actors inside local government has not been sufficiently empirically tested through fieldwork studies. Rhodes' earlier model would suggest, in opposition to Burgess and Travers, that power is relative and likely to remain so even in the contemporary period. Rhodes' insistence on a multi-faceted and complex network of relationships was a legitimate reaction to the sterility of the previous model of the agent/partner dichotomy but it may, in the 1980's, be seen as an over-reaction. A new reformulation is required of local-central governmental relations.

Central government in the 1970's made a sustained effort to introduce a type of corporatism into its relations with local governments. The main innovation was to try to incorporate the powerful local government associations into a 'social contract' on spending. This was done, for example, by establishing an important structure called the Consultative Council on Local Government Finance,[46] which brought together representatives of the Treasury and the associations in face-to-face, if unequal, bargaining relationships. It was an attempt to integrate the planning of local spending into a national system for projecting public expenditure five years ahead. There has also been a suggestion that it was 'an attempt within local government to shift power away from service-orientated councillors and officers . . . and towards local politicians and finance directors more concerned with corporate planning, increased the efficiency and financial soundness . . . in order that they would be better able to control the rest of the local government system in return for consultation'.[47]

Foster and colleagues have noted, in opposition to Taylor, that the Consultative Council was 'a powerful engine through which central government persuaded local governments to do what it wanted. But there was a price to be paid for such an arrangement . . . Corporatism in the relations between central and local government has reduced central government's freedom to introduce reforms.[48] However, no evidence is offered to support this argument.

A dominant contemporary analysis is to treat processes inside the Consultative Council as formal and technical in the sense that financial grant totals are largely non-negotiable but determined on professional and technical criteria. To emphasize this formal aspect may be somewhat misleading. While there exists a number of sub-groups working on a variety of technical systems such as need assessment, the formal aspect was linked in the past years to bargaining which reflects real conflicts between central and local governments. The history of the rate support grant is a history of conflict over both the total and the distribution of grant. However, whilst bargaining does take place, it must not be overstated, and it must be placed in a conjunctural context which allows such space.

Central government, since 1979, seems to have less commitment to consultation mechanisms and still less to corporatist devices, though they still function with decreasing authority and conviction. The Consultative Council on Local Government Finance is, it is argued, increasingly converted into a structure in which little or no bargaining takes place and where central government representatives announce 'hard and fast' decisions to unavailing protests by the local government representatives. Paradoxically, the response of many Labour Party controlled local governments is to adopt a stronger adversary response to this new balance and to attempt to evade the new imposed regulations by seeking out loopholes and ambiguities. Cooper and Stewart[49] suggest that the differences in spending patterns between Conservative and Labour councils widened dramatically in the 1980's, with nearly half the Labour local governments over-spending in 1981-82, and over half the Conservative councils underspending more than 6 per cent below their central government target levels.

The limits to the power of central government over local governments is mediated by resources and ideology even in the 1980's and to that extent Rhodes' early analysis carries some weight. Central government departments do not in themselves have the staff or the operational knowledge to run local services even if they desired it. Indeed, central government does not still have enough staff to police the full range of controls they formally have over local governments. In the past, central departments have not found it easy to manipulate much of the funding to control local governments. Over four-fifths of centrally allocated finance is paid over in a general or block grant which is not directly linked to particular services. Within their grant total it has, in the past, been relatively easy for local governments to distribute money between services as they wish, even in a manner which may frustrate central government policy. Thus, local governments had the option to protect one service from centrally imposed cuts by reducing spending elsewhere in their budgets and then utilizing these savings to preserve the threatened service's funding.

The power of local governments at the inter-governmental level is circumscribed by the 'rules of the game', which are imposed on them but quite often they have some negative power which permits them to do nothing or to delay implementing central government policies for a considerable period, or simply to be half-hearted about doing something they dislike. Thus, central government's attempt to force local government to sell council housing stock in the 1980's found that numbers of Labour councils claimed that they had not the staff to process sales quickly. Generally they made it as difficult and slow as they could (within the law) for the tenants to purchase council houses. Finally, however, councils complied with the formal legislatory authority.

Power is not distributed equally between central and local governments as the 'rules of the game' are set by the central governments but, inside the given rules, local governments in the past have attempted to negotiate meanings and consequences to some degree. In addition, local governments can be elected on specific mandates dealing with services and, by reference back to the mandate, can try to manipulate electoral legitimacy, in any blocking attempt by central government. The Greater London Council, controlled by Labour, stated in its manifesto in 1981 that they would, if elected, among other things, discontinue expenditure on civil defence and reduce fares on London Transport by increasing its subsidies from the rates. In the case of civil defence, the Greater London Council faced the probability that central government would declare such a policy in default of its statutory obligations – it would be disobeying the law. In the case of London Transport, central government in 1983 was introducing legislation which would take away control by the GLC of the public transport system, and thus, would impose changes in the 'rules of the game'. By 1986, the GLC was itself abolished.[50]

The power relationships between local governments as a system and central government, in the years between the introduction of the rate support grant in 1967 and 1980, were mediated by a procedure whereby central governments set overall financial targets for local government expenditure as already implied. Individual local governments then made their own spending and ruling decisions, having paid whatever attention they considered appropriate to the advice and guidelines which they received from central government departments and their ministers. Alexander argues 'on the face of it, in terms of national economic planning and the control of public expenditure, this was a rough and ready, hit or miss mechanism, but in every financial year but one (1974-75, the expensive year of reorganisation) the eventual out-turn of expenditure was within 2 per cent of government's targets'.[51]

Central government may well be seen as utilizing a symbolic language of stigmatizing local government as 'overspenders' and 'irresponsible' and which is largely contradicted by empirical reality. The language may well hold captive key political actors in central government and is an important legitimization for a policy of tighter control over local government decision-making. It can be argued that, for the purposes of national economic planning, central government does not need to control the aggregate of local government spending, much less the spending of individual local governments. Jones[52] has argued that central government only needs to control the level of the grant it pays, an objective attainable by the device of cash limits.

In analyzing power relations between central and local governments there is substantial evidence to show that the frequent expression by politicans, for a policy of removing controls, is deceptive. Elcock argues that, since 1979, central government has shown some signs that outside the financial sphere they would increase the autonomy of local government. The 1980 Education Act restored the power to support pupils at private schools, as well as allowing local governments to supply school meals or not, and to charge whatever price they think fit. 'Many minor central controls were abolished in the government's early days and the number of circulars sent to local authorities was considerably reduced ... the government is also wavering in its determination to make local authorities conform to its monetarist policies ... In 1982 the government is seeking to restrict local authorities' freedom to levy supplementary rates'.[53]

The 1980 Local Government, Planning and Land Act demonstrates the dialectic of control and decontrol in central government politics. It narrows local autonomy; for example, a local government, which under the old systemm could have financed, say, a new project of a headquarters from its revenue income rather than by raising a loan, will no longer have the freedom to do this. The removal of controls, in this Act, in practice means the removal of procedural controls, rather than political and substantive ones. This Act abolished about 300 controls exercised by central government over local governments, whilst increasing other controls. It is difficult to find any supposed freedom that materially affects the decision-making autonomy of local governments or which noticeably retards the process of the potential increase of central government control.

It is not advisable to construct a myth of a local government golden age in which central government intervention was insignificant and to situate the present increased controls against the 'golden age'. Cycles of control or attempted control can be found in earlier periods, especially when local governments came under control of supposedly 'radical' politicians who desired to utilize the partial autonomy of local government to carry out reforms.

In the late nineteenth century the 'progressives' on the London County Council were suspected by the parties and their supportive social elites who controlled national government of wanting to use local taxes and rates to subsidize controversial projects. As Yearley points out

> the Council was deprived of many general powers which a provincial town may exercise as they see fit. It was barred from spending a penny on any inquiries or negotiations ... any public interest and service outside of the Council's statutory work. Even with that statutory work, it was subjected to picayune harassment; for instance, when it resolved on one occasion to examine the utility of labour bureaus for the metropolis, the Council was forbidden to spend for translations for a Paris report on such agencies'.[54]

The resistance of the elites of rural aristocracy and gentry, who, Ashford claims, ran the government system until 1888, to democratic practices that would threaten their tax base was a main ingredient in central government control politics of local finance.[55]

Essentially one major response in the twentieth century has been to give the professional chief officers greater bureaucratic power vis-a-vis the politicians, as in the Bains Report. Another is to take important functions out of local government control and to establish non-accountable structures to administrate them. Hospitals, unemployment assistance, trunk roads, etc. were all taken away from local government with a consequent weakening of its power base as a system and its increased subordination as a junior partner.

It is useful to locate the power relationships between central and local governments as possible contests, conflicts, negotiations and pseudo-negotiations between two unequal power blocks, which can themselves be both united and also internally divided. In central government, in the past, it has not been uncommon to find that central government departments had conflicting interests and lacked the available agencies to co-ordinate between themselves fiscal and administrative procedures and policies. Such an apparent fragmentation in the past allowed local governments to utilize this gap to bargain for resources and to play off one department and its interests against another. The internal competition for influencce among central government departments at Whitehall has to some extent been shaped by their dependents' 'clients'. This, in recent years, has been weakened to some extent but is not totally dead. Captive clients can still influence the mechanism of control through the control mechanism itself. Strong earlier forms of corporatism showed this tendency clearly, with a marked decline in the 1980's.

Unity between local governments and their associations can be both fragile and strong. Whilst nearly all local governments have an interest in maximizing their power base and diminishing the controls exercised by central government (at least at a rhetorical level), in practice the picture is not clear cut. Some local governments, who are favoured in the process of grant allocation, may feel little solidarity with those who are less favoured; other local governments, whilst in public objecting to specific central government guidelines and policies, may have groups of influential officers and politicians who are, to a degree in sympathy with the 'enemy' and thus been 'turned', and so support is highly conditional if it exists at all. Thus, if directors of education believe they have lost influence and resources by the political process internal to local government, they may also believe that they, as an elite, can gain if their service is taken out of the control of local government decision-making.

Local governments may be united on the need for a general autonomy from central government encroachments, but, as a system, it is often deeply divided. In the operation of the financial relationship, it is a fragmented collectivity of competing interests, and each interest is confined to one class of authority. This lessens the overall power resource base of the national local government system in its attempt to gain some advantage from the initiatives of central government.

Local governments are represented in their bargaining at national level by four separate associations. Central government, in 1981, was able to neutralize the opposition of the Association of County Councils to its legislation to tighten controls by informally offering 'benefits'. Even before the 1974 reorganization of local government, central government noted and perhaps used the tensions and conflicts between different types of local governments. Crossman, the minister on whose initiative the reforming

Redcliffe-Maud Commission, was appointed, recognized that a state of 'war' existed between the county councils and the county borough authorities. This was fought over three central concerns of local government – territory, tax base and status. Whilst technocrats and 'reformers' in central government disliked the structures that produced these conflicts, on the other hand these conflicts allowed politicians and civil servants to act as arbitrators and mediators. Local government, as a system, lost in this process as different types of local government became clients of patrons in the various parts of governmental apparatuses. If one department in Whitehall lost influence and power, its clients could also lose.

Sub-units of local governments were also affected. The education service in local governments is a notable example. This was tied to the Ministry of Education and the rise and fall of the influence of the Ministry was of vital significance to the internal bargaining mechanisms over resources inside local government. In a period of expansion, an education service or personal social services could use a circular or recommendation from a specific Whitehall department to support a particular bid for resources, and, even under contraction, to change an existing policy practice at local level. Local government is thus fragmented into a series of interests, as professionals and politicians utilize their dependencies to compete within the local government system. Rhodes infers that these dependencies in turn, to some extent, limit the innovating power of central government strategic actors. More cautiously he finds that, in the past, bargaining over the form and content of specific policies was common and the fact of bargaining did not support a hierarchical interpretation of the relationship.[56]

As emphasized previously, bargaining potential should not be equated with equality of bargaining power, since institutional resources (as levers) are unequal rather than otherwise. Rhodes admits, in his later work, that bargaining is structured and limited by agreement over the 'rules of the game' and that the quality and type of bargaining over issues, when a fundamental lack of consensus exists, is radically different to the bargaining that takes place inside such consensus, which is not imposed upon the weaker actors. Non-decisions become part of this fabric normally when central government departments in their 'common sense' practices eliminate, without debate, certain options from the process of negotiating and bargaining. In intergovernmental relations, it is central government which normally eliminates such options by its location in an unequal power relation but local government can also, in practice, utilize resources so that non-decisions may be arrived at. This has been observed in the manner in which incrementalism has structured the fiscal base of local government budgets. However, a weakening of incrementalism is normally tied to a stronger political input by central government actors rather than new initiatives by local government actors.

It can also be argued that whilst strong bargainers are to some extent dependent on the co-operation of weaker partners, this does not automatically mean they welcome the weakness in this position in every context. Reaction to uncertainty can and does take the form of attempting to maximize control. Grants to services represent money that Whitehall departments have fought hard to obtain, sometimes against the Treasury and other departments with rival programmes. Heclo and Wildavsky[57] have noted that the Treasury has both informal and formal mechanisms of monitoring grants, though these may be determined finally by particularistic cultural variables. Uncertainty over the manner in which government grants are utilized or the manner in which local governments allocate resources has a tendency to push Whitehall departments, which have patron client ties to services, into welcoming the possibility of greater control over their weaker partners, who may have the potential power to damage the reputations and interests of central government actors with which the supposed weaker partners are in 'partnership'. Local government actors, whilst abstractly, and in many cases, personally committed to the defence of the autonomy of local government, by accepting a conceptualization of the power relationship as 'partnership', may find it difficult to resist their Whitehall partners.[58] The rhetoric of supposedly common values, in the form of value for money, undercuts resistance over means to goals and leaves goals unquestioned in many instances. Pluralist models of power, which argue against the hegemony of one group over another by stressing both the possibility of bargaining and the spread of power as resources, tend to ignore this question of the 'mobilization' of bias.

As already noted, local governments have articulated with central government departments through a tendency towards corporatist mechanisms. Such mechanisms represent the interests of the various layers of local governments as a system and the values and policy recommendations of the elite professionals, who manage the services but who have a legal status as the 'mere servants of the council'. The policy impact of the professionals has been studied unfortunately, 'only at the implementation interface, the point of contact with citizens or "clients"'.[59] The generalists who form Heclo and Wildavsky's [60] 'village community' in central government are unified through both a structural interlocking of senior roles and through a dense 'informal' culture. The power to shape collectively central government decision-making at certain levels (though not at others), and to allow and pursue internal mechanisms of negotiation over goals and means is integral to this 'village community'. Heclo and Wildavsky point out that, while it has no formal legitimacy in national corporate management, it is rather more than an accumulation of mere occupational values, though it includes these. The gap between the generalists who form the senior civil service and their political masters is eliminated by an acceptance (which benefits especially the civil servants) that both are political administrators.

The top professionals who manage the services in local governments have role identities as both specialists and managers. In the past they were able to mobilize professional support among high status members outside local governments, political administrators, and their professional dependents and clients inside central government. Such a mobilization has normally been a consistent historical trend which pulls back professional work from a too close monitoring by public representatives. The alliances between Whitehall, national professional communities, and local government specialists have been conjunctural but have also been central to a process whereby a relatively 'invisible' and unresearched group of professional elites have risen to bureaucratic authority and, in practice, power inside local governments. Such alliances, among other things, set standards which were sometimes legally enforceable, disseminated information about approved practices in a promotional manner and attempted to bring the more 'backward' (and stubborn) local governments into line with national trends, which, perhaps, the elites themselves had underwritten by policies originating in the very conjunctural alliance networks which bridged both central and local governments. In education, for example, the inspectorate employed by the DES has historically been significant in this process.[61] Other services have similar network linkages to actors who can play innovative or broker roles between different levels of intergovernmental power; Cohen suggests that issue networks are not necessary politically active coalitions though they can become so.[62] Whilst most elite professionals can enjoy a degree of discretion through which they are able to influence the implementation of policy, specific members of issue networks can become advocates. Thus, the role of education inspectors in bridging the DES and LEA allows them an active input into policy formation and implementation. Rhodes has also drawn attention to the importance of the inter-organizational networks as a unit of analysis which has been under research, and this in turn may draw attention to the variety of 'central-local' government power relationships.[63] Issue networks should perhaps be distinguished from those which are patterned and stable. Issue networks are relatively fluid in membership with no permanent dominant actors who subordinate others. They are composed of policy activists who know each other through the issue and draw for membership on only the upper layers of the local government professional categories. Information is the main integrating mechanism and common values in specific policy areas are a further bond between such roles.

Dunleavy has argued that elite professionals should not be analyzed in just localist roles but often as power actors in a 'national local government system'. In some of his empirical case studies he demonstrates that an articulation of private firms, local government professionals and actors in central government, at various levels of administration, can allow the private sector of the national economy to influence actively and determine policy formation. Thus, significant sections of the design professions in local government were activated in favour of high rise technology by 'professional ideologies' which entwined with inputs from the construction industry.[64]

It has been noted that specific to local governments is a partial separation of particular professions from external practices and the growth of highly specialized bodies of techniques and knowledge. Unlike doctors, architects, planners, etc., who can easily move into work roles outside local governments, lawyers, accountants, administrators, etc. are more circumscribed in their training and have been closely tied to particularistic practices and loyalties.

It has already been noted that the apex of the professions have a strong orientation to a 'national community' of the most senior professionals who have pressure group structures at their disposal, which link them to both central government departments and the national associations of local government. Whilst elite professionals may be promoted within a particular local government, it is customary for most chief officers to move, usually upwards, between local governments. Patronage ties and career alliances form another network/reference group which is not formally structured or orientated to policy issues but may be significant in status and career terms. At one and the same time, the occupants of roles at the apex of each profession have to be 'localist' and also 'cosmopolitan' and draw authority and status from each level.

If Weber's belief in the 'hidden dictatorship of the official' has any validity in local governments, it is because professionals can normally control not merely techniques and information but the variety of structured and unstructured networks which mushroom and grow out of a corporatist consensus. Attempts by councillors to control the interface of the implementation of policy are perhaps a weak substitute. As previously hinted 'non-decisions' are often the result of an accumulation of day-to-day administrative practices in which networks and coalitions, consciously and subconsciously, eliminate some items from the agenda and give legitimacy (supported by councillors) to others.

The research carried out into central-local power relationships by the public administration tradition focuses mainly on professional discretion and linkages, decision-making, inter-organizational relations, professionalism, party political and local government association links. It ranges over a wide variety of substantive policy areas. Whilst, for example, financial dependency and detailed control remain themes, debate has moved beyond 'top down' models of policy implementation to an interest in unravelling the 'complexity, ambiguity and confusion' which Rhodes identifies as characterizing current perspectives. There are few connections between this work on central-local power relationships and the analysis of local politics and community power grounded in radical social theory.

Dunleavy asserts that since the currency of professional debate on substantive policy issues is ideas, knowledge and techniques, and since individual professionals have a large level of discretionary power in implementing policy, then it is relatively easy for fluctuating intra-professional debates or paradigm shifts to be 'reflected in sudden, large scale, relatively intense and, at times, cyclical policy changes often carried out in a quite unplanned and decentralised way by individual professionals'. Furthermore, 'since a policy system ostensibly based on rational arguments places no special virtue on compromises, stressing instead the one best solution, situations of ideological disequilibrium tend to produce a polarisation of professionals around rival solutions'.[65] The chief officers who form the apex of the local government professional hierarchy can themselves be somewhat sympathetic to 'purist' value positions but may also find the adopting of such positions can weaken the political process of consensus construction inside service departments and between them. Elcock has noted that 'their preoccupation with their own special fields means that in an issue involving several departments, officers may have great difficulty in presenting members with a coherent set of recommendations'. Local governments have, therefore, tended to 'remain in essence loose confederations of semi-autonomous empires' even those which have a nominal corporate management system superimposed.[66]

The stress by critics of the traditional literature on central government subordination through the law, finance, networks, etc. of the local government system has tended to overlap with an emphasis which stresses the diversity in relationships. This is a useful amendment to the neo-functionalism of Cockburn's 'local state' model. Martlew[67] has documented the degree of diversity which exists between the interests displayed by different apparatuses and levels of central government. In an important attempt to integrate different models of analysis, he emphasizes the importance of vertical linkages which exist between national and local levels of decision-making and the difficulties historically faced by central government in pursuing coherent long-term strategies in local finance. Thus, spending departments in Whitehall often have party client relationships in local governments which unify against the Treasury, as well as allowing the Treasury to utilize Whitehall spending departments to control.

Central government controls in the past have been mediated through such mechanisms as statutory legislation. The effect of these obligations has been uneven but they can often weaken the scope of discretion over policy choice by local government actors. Between 80 and 90 per cent of an education or social service department's budget can be committed to expenditure which the relevant committee and its politicians has no choice but to undertake. Only within the remaining 10 to 20 per cent of the departmental budget of education and especially of social services can local government actors make choices. While statutory obligations confer chief officers with additional safeguards vis-a-vis local pressures, the discretionary areas are more difficult to protect in a period of retrenchment and cuts.

It should not be assumed that service chief officers are automatic supporters of the autonomy of local decision-making. Their own values and the central government institutional support for particular services may push them in other paths. One director of education told Kogan and Van Der Eyken that 'I believe that political decisions should be made nationally. I don't see why they should be made again locally and sometimes at several levels locally'.[68] The networks linking chief officers to central government can confer professional and service protection against local pressures. On the other hand, if the network linkages offer little but negative controls then conjunctural alliances in this context are possible between chief officers and other local government actors. Such alliances strengthen the bargaining hands of professionals to a great extent and politicans to a lesser extent. The elite professional normally seeks to pursue alliances simultaneously with sectors of central government and with influential members of local elites entwined to the council. In a situation where the 'partnership' ideology between local and central government is being questioned, the issue networks which link professionals to agents of central government can still confer some degree of protection and control. If councillors challenge the networks which link the professionals to central government, they will find that some of the most influential local politicans vis-a-vis the committee system automatically support the 'right' of the professionals to participate in corporatist networks. However, this type of conflict is extremely rare and the 'mobilization of bias' normally functions in favour of the continuation of such corporatist mechanisms.

Statutory legislation protects areas of departmental budgets at local government level; it also has the tendency to reinforce incrementalism; but such legislation does not cover the whole of a departmental budget. These margins of budgets can be of extreme importance, both symbolically, and in relation to policy changes. A head of department and his or her committee allies can stake his or her professional reputation and influence by policy decisions made over such budget margins. These minority percentages may, therefore, symbolically represent rather more than just the financial percentage of the total. They can allow innovations which can be noticed and judged by fellow professionals and politicans in the local government in which they take place. They are also noticed by specific reference groups and networks of professionals in the 'national local government system'. Reputations can be won and lost and won again and stakes are high in professional terms. Alternatively the head of a service department may choose not to gamble with the resources in such an arena. Or, if the gamble is likely to fail, he or she may argue that the service committee instructed that the resources to be committed by such activities. Such role distancing has its price and costs. A professional running a service department can lose even more reputational status by such an admission.

Elite professionals are expected by their significant others to be able to influence significantly policy formation, 'as statesmen in disguise', as well as to implement it and not to be the rubberstamp of even stronger committee chairperson. The margins of budgets then allow and encourage reputations to both expand and contract. If statutory legislation does become weaker or even totally withdrawn from significant activities, the formerly frozen ritual of incrementalism will perhaps be replaced by new political patterns which encourage significant innovations. It may well be the 'mood' among many strategic professional actors in the local political system, that the withdrawal of statutory legislation from some activities rather than others increases the potential control over policy by local political forces and ensures that budget negotiations become less ritualistic and more dangerous. The search for professional autonomy is thus relative rather than absolute.

Significant sectors of elite professionals and their representatives may then recoil in fear from this freedom. In the name of their clients and services, they may well take the option of attempting to utilize for defensive purposes the existing network linkages to the Whitehall 'technocracy'. The ministers in charge of central departments could then be pulled into contradictory positions as the balances inside central government shift.

Central governments and local governments have had major differences over policy in the past and on occasions such differences have been heard through the courts. To a large extent such differences of policy were softened, if not eliminated, by the ability to secure compliance through the provision of extra money. However, in the 1970's, a relative contraction of grant to local governments became economic policy. By the years 1980-81, the aggregate exchequer grant was worth in real terms almost 14 per cent less than in 1975-76.[69] Less money for local governments also increased the tendency for the stakes in the process of negotiation between services to be higher. Weak departments with little political protection could appeal to Whitehall or to those local roles such as Chief Executives as well as influential politicans who were not committed totally to the larger and more powerful departments. Patrons in large departments who formerly had given limited but real protection to weak clients in an era of contraction could turn cool or even hostile as budget stress continued. The corporate management system, which has never eliminated the older political system of the alliance between chairperson and elite professional 'guarding' departmental interests, is now faced by new uncertainties. In some local governments the strength of party groups allowed yet other inputs into the attempt to control resource allocation. Professional power is never untested and free from contests.

Pahl, an urban sociologist, wrote in a text on the city: 'I am arguing that resources are allocated in all advanced societies through a system of managerial bargaining . . . the allocations are made by agents in organizations'.[70] Saunders writes: 'the fact remains that the ecological, political and economic constraints on urban managers serve only to narrow the scope of decision-making; they do not determine it'.[71] Both allow a significant autonomy from central government, at certain levels of decision-making, to local strategic actors. Johnston[72] quotes studies which tend to argue that the power of 'urban managers' in local governments is not of the same degree between different elite professions and between local governments. He argues that in local governments, housing officers, for example, are located in contexts where some tenants have more power over the managers than others in securing allocations to the types of property and areas that they define as desirable. The most powerful are those living in homes scheduled for demolition under slum clearance programmes. These can hold out for a desirable property and/or estate before they are prepared to move. The managers are required to rehouse all these people by statutory legislation which allows their clients some control over policy implementation. Immediately below them, in terms of power, are those with support from a medical professional for a transfer or a new allocation. The least powerful are those on the council waiting list without special qualifications and the homeless, who must take what is offered.

It has been further noted in the literature that 'urban managers' can accept bargaining between an individual client and their department as legitimate and part of the 'rules of the game'. They are, however, strongly hostile to any attempt by clients to organize collectively and bargain collectively. In this they are often supported by local politicians who may see their representative role threatened, though some exceptions to this do occur. Hampton noted that even some Labour-controlled local governments were 'suspicious of spontaneous leadership'[73] by tenants collectively organized in associations.

The planning profession in local government is more insulated than others from bargaining politics with individual clients. Blowers[74] has analyzed the Bedfordshire structure plan and its implications for a sociology of professional power. A joint committee of elected politicans and professional planners drew up the brief for the plan. The generality and vagueness of aims could and was interpreted in a wide variety of ways in the preparation of detailed plans. This task was undertaken entirely by the planning professionals who came up with seven separate strategies, five of which were chosen by the politicans for detailed consideration. This involved other actors, including central government departments and other local governments, plus pressure groups. The result of this process leads Blowers to the conclusion that power over policy making in planning is concentrated whereas that over implementation is more dispersed. This occurs because the professionals, in concert with a few influential politicans, usually committee chairpersons, define the terms of reference for the aims of the plan which constrain the range of choices offered to the formal decision makers. Implementation requires local political action, and, in the case of a county structure plan, involved winning the support of a number of separate actors.

The role of chief executive, which formerly, before the 1974 reorganization, was linked to the role of town clerk, is a key role in the potential control of the agenda in local governments. The strength of this is illuminated through Harloe's study of Swindon,[75] which emphasizes the potentiality of role authority if the occupant desires to expand such authority.

The Town Development Act of 1952 gave Swindon some bargaining power with central government over allowing new industries to be built. Harloe argues that Swindon's use of the Act was very much the result of the actions of the town clerk who pursued a single-minded growth policy for twenty years. He maintained the support of the Labour majority on the town council and the respect councillors had for his ability meant that 'the ready acceptance of his reports was almost a foregone conclusion'.[76] Such a large expansion scheme was likely to generate conflict, but, by the careful control of the flow of information to the council, the town clerk was able to get the policies adopted quickly without much debate in public. This is a typical example of an influential, indeed powerful, elite professional who operated through the elected council of local politicans, but in such a manner that he had very close control over the formal decision-making process of which he was supposed to be merely the implementer. Too great an open independence from the politicians could have forced the council members to clash openly with a town clerk which could, in turn, threaten their representational legitimacy; but a skilful chief officer will back off from openly undercutting the symbolism of the politicans.

The emphasis on the managerialist models of government of Pahl's urban managers could be more accurately modified to a conceptualization of relative or semi-autonomy rather than autonomy. A number of sets of relationships constrain 'urban managers' as gatekeepers in the allocation of resources. Ecological factors such as the different geographical distribution of population from inner city, to suburbia, to rural village, structure the distribution of resources. In the same way that housing is less expensive to construct in some areas than in others, police resources, for example, are easiest to supply when distances are short and the human terrain favourable. It has already been noted that a political relation qualifies the autonomy of most elite professionals in local government and they cannot deny its legitimacy openly. Thus, the freedom of housing managers to determine allocation policy is a relative freedom. They cannot contravene too markedly the boundaries set by legislation and politics. In a similar manner, chief police officers, who operational independence is greater by far than other managers in local government, may deny policy explanations to their police committees and may thus temporarily frustrate the local political relations but at a cost. The ability to balance and play the Home Office as a strategic actor against the local police authority has been noted in the literature. However, even the ability to frustrate the police committee in the short run has certain consequences in the ideological field of legitimization and local budget construction.[77]

Pahl has argued that managerial ideology (in the sense of the system of ideas through which the urban managers determine priorities and organize decisions) decides resource provisions. These professional elites, in judgements over the appropriation and allocation of resources, are an independent or quasi-independent variable and a legitimate focus of independent research. Policy-making, for Pahl, and to a degree for Saunders, is defined by a distinction between the influence of 'internal' factors and 'external' factors, the internal factors being relatively unconstrained by environmental factors outside the local government.

If an historical dimension is introduced, however, the internal/external distinction can no longer have the same meaning. It could be argued that what are 'internal' determinants today represent the outcome of past 'external' determinants. What seems to be 'independent' strategies of actors may in fact merely represent a reaction to earlier 'external' determinants. For example, if urban managers in local governments anticipate external constraints and determinants (the two are not conceptually the same) on the internal decision-making process by specific decisions or non-decisions, this may be taken as reflecting a situation in which 'environmental' determinants (whether strong or weak) have become incorporated within local government as internal factors. This can be significant in the analysis of councillor and professional ideologies.[78]

In Pahl's work and the usage of the category of urban managers to define the elite professionals, the links and articulation between these groups as actors and the macro-structures is unproblematic. Pahl later shifted his analysis of the actors as an independent variable to an analysis that conceptualizes such actors as one type of intervening variable that mediates between contradictory pressures. This shift in analysis also allowed a diffferentiation to take place theoretically between elite professionals by a comparative examination of their occupational potentiality in power. A chief of police in the UK (unlike a housing manager) acquires his authority not just from his mode of professional expertise but also from a legal relation. The legal relation

85

is permissive in form and discretion is mandatory in its exercise. While the chief police officer may be conceived of as being restrained by ecological factors, the local political relations and the economic structure of the revenue base, he has, in his legal relation, a striking degree of autonomy in real terms. Unlike housing managers and the elite professionals employed by local governments, chief police officers have a legal autonomy from local political control and direction, and they have the right to make decisions which can contravene the expressed wishes of the council and authority.

Pahl's final position is that local or central governmental politics do not always or necessarily reflect the interests of capital, as Cockburn argues, but are rather the outcome of 'managerial bargaining' between agents representing different types of organization.[79] Like Weber, therefore, he is concerned to stress, first that political power is not simply a reflection or derivation from economic power and, secondly, that such power has ultimately to be analyzed as a function of relationships between individuals. Analysis of political outcomes must therefore begin with the goals, values and practical 'common sense' purposes of those individual actors who control access to key resources. Furthermore, an attempt should be made to identify the constraints that limit the potential scope of their actions.

That local government professionals enjoy some autonomy from the dictates of central government and the constraints of the economy are axiomatic. The question is how far and in what situations does this autonomy extend. Pahl's answer appears to be that this is simply an empirical question. Saunders argues, against Pahl, that such an answer is inadequate given that empirical research, even if conducted comparatively across different types of local government, will be unable to identify the sources of particular politics, unless it is grounded, he argues, in a theoretical framework that specifies the sort of situations and contexts in which different strategic actors are able to exercise discretion as opposed to those in which they cannot.[80]

Dunleavy's work on the impact of important client groups, i.e. the construction industry, stresses how it may influence a profession such as architecture. He concludes that where a profession relies heavily on the patronage of a particular group, it is bound to take the latter's preference and demands into account.[81] Thus external determinants may become transformed into internal practices. The work of Malpass[82] on architects and Ravetz[83] on town planning illustrate, however, why the actions of signifcant sectors of such professions may not simply reflect external determinants, even those from past conjunctures. Malpass acknowledges the important constraints of external 'environmental' factors but he stresses the way that local government architects are more than just reflectors of such contraints. Malpass uses a case study to describe how, by employing complex and technical 'professional' arguments, the architects were able to remove the influence of local politicans and other potential interest groups from policy making over housing. He, unlike Blowers, argues that the power of professional elites will tend to increase when they can resist the potential influence of a number of diverse external pressure groups by claiming to represent the 'general will' rather than the particular interest of any one client or pressure group. The potentiality for brokerage roles also can be strengthened by a relative plurality of external pressures. In local government, brokerage roles between different levels of government and inside a particular local government are respected as the ability to accumulate power and to gain significant autonomies.

Ravetz's comments on the planning and architectural professions tend to reinforce those of Malpass. She suggests that professional authority leads to professions involved to resist actively other professional claims and external pressures. The strategy was that 'the importance of the material environment was at first exaggerated, to make it a proper field for professional control; then, as this was imposed, the effect was actually to increase the importance of the environment'.[84]

This further suggests that, while macro-determinants can be influential, they normally only form the context within which elite professionals seek to maximise control inside local government. As already stated the significance of professionalism as an intra-departmental determinant on policy making has also been neglected in the existing literature. The lack of research into the variety of power balances in the relationships between the professionals and their supposed political masters, has, Dunleavy claims, 'disguised our complete ignorance of the intra-departmental policy process', which is part of the entrenched institutional myth 'that all departmental proposals originate from the Chief Officer'.[85] The search for hierachy is thus a way of seeing and a way of non-seeing in the existing literature.

It must be stressed yet again that within the 'national local government system', professionalism is the dominant ideological form of the policy-making levels of the bureaucracy. This results in a paradox, as the apex of the service departments is composed of managers who, as its natural guardians, must defend professionalism. They themselves, however, are rarely able to keep up a personal fieldwork professional identity with clients other than in the most symbolic manner. The apex is now formed by political managers, whose skills are weighted in the direction of negotiating consensus and to this extent who experience 'grass roots' alienation from subordinates and their occupational culture. Professionalism has been highly fragmented internally into different work specializations and this has been legitimated by 'traditions', along departmental lines. This fragmentation has recently been reduced by the amalgamation of service departments into large directorates, though it still persists as an underlying reality, unacknowledged but massively unshaken. The particularism of certain occupational roles also has important consequences for departmental power and decision-making.

The highly specialized but narrow professional training of officers can increase the possibility for difficulties in the co-ordination of proposals between departments. The recent amalgamation of service departments into large directorates tends to shift the strain into the internal decision-making system of the directorates themselves rather than eliminate it altogether.

Local government as a system is in contrast with central government, where the senior civil servants are normally 'generalist' political administrators who are preoccupied with ensuring the smooth working of the machinery of government. These generalists may be influenced, at the margins, by support staff which is professionalized, but they are dependent on their patrons who are not specialists.[86] Co-ordination in local government is made more difficult by the lower status of such generalist administrators as do exist in local governments. Whereas in central government the generalists occupy the top policy making points, in local government generalists will be, normally, junior officers in administration departments responsible for committee administration and with little power and they are inferior in status and authority to other specialist groups.

Traditionally – and traditions are part of the cement of local government relationships – the highest point to which most officers aspire is to become chief officers in their own professions, in charge of a department and responsible for it to a committee and its chairperson. Only the lawyers, and to a lesser extent, accountants, can hope for still higher status and authority by becoming a chief executive of a local government and, as such, head of the entire professional hierarchy. In 1977, Lomer found that 80 per cent of chief executives were lawyers and 15 per cent accountants.[87] The expertise of law and finance in local government allows a certain primacy to these categories as the fabric of intergovernmental relations mainly revolves around these two points. Interpretation of legislation by such specialists strengthen their group claims to be the guardians of the system and not merely influential professionals.

In interactions with local politicians and between local government departments, the culture of professionalism provides and draws upon customs and rules which systematically stress bureaucratic autonomy. This is reinforced in those local governments which are controlled by the Conservative Party regimes by an ideology of the 'right and duty' of managers to manage. This claim is less readily accepted in those local governments controlled by the Labour Party.

Control over information as a power resource is protected by such rules. Green, a councillor, has noted that, in a Labour-controlled urban authority, backbench councillors were denied systematic access to budgetary information and inputs into policies.[88] The culture of professionalism, while political in a non-party manner, places emphasis on the avoidance of 'political' involvements and formally holds to an ethic of non-interference by professionals in other departments' affairs. This can, and is, pragmatically modified when the boundaries of activities of one or more departments mesh together.

Professionalism is a central ideology of the intergovernmental relationship, and also an expression of the belief of many 'traditional' elites in local government. The past belief of such elites that they are involved in the business of administration rather than mere politics, can still count on broad support structures. It reinforces the tendency for a considerable degree of 'natural' support to exist between a variety of officers and departments against the threat of encroachment on professional authority by elected local (and national) politicans. This factor does not eliminate the sets of alliances over issues and overall policy, which unify the values and interests of particular local politicans and professionals, in the local arena.

The development of policy planning systems in those policy areas which involve central and local governments is becoming increasingly prevalent. Houlihan[89] has argued that this tendency and the increased professionalization of the policy areas has not been to strengthen directly central government's control over local policy making, but rather to dilute the power of local governments and consequently their resource ability to withstand external 'environmental' pressure.

It has never been sufficient for central government to rely solely on political force, legal power or financial control as techniques for obtaining compliance at local government level. While the bureaucratic form of administration, along Weberian lines, has been the most common form of 'rational' control, Houlihan suggests that central government is now consciously replacing bureaucracy in local government as the main form of control, by the use of specialized professionals who can make judgements based on technical grounds of efficiency.

The weakness of bureaucratic control is its relative inflexibility and the difficulty of rapid intervention. The establishment of policy-planning systems provides a mechanism whereby the agents of central government can short-circuit bureaucratic relationships by providing direct access for rapid intervention in a number of policy areas which are often only peripherally linked to local processes. Professionals in local government can gain and lose in this type of intervention, as has already been emphasized. Such planning systems determine, in hidden and explicit ways, what potential goals are and what problems have the chance to appear on the agenda.[90] In such planning systems decision-making is a technocratic rather than an open political process, with an implicit devaluation of non-quantitative inputs.

It has been a theme of this chapter that one of the significant changes in central-local government power relations has been 'vertical' coalitions between specialists in central and local governments. These can share similar responses to specific issues, which leads to a degree of predictability in terms of local government decision-making.[91] Wilding emphasizes the elite representation on government structures and that the favourable report of the Seebohm committee on the professional claims of social workers came from a body on which the profession had a number of influential representatives. He dryly observes that 'non-social work members were less organised, less convinced of what should be done and were therefore easily carried along in the rush for social services departments'.[92] These types of determinants lead to possible consequences for the development of a possible service 'professionalism'.

Such professionalism is both tied to the older concept of a local government service and yet finds strong links with departments in central government and through such links, with colleagues in other local governments. The possible close interactions with committees and colleagues in other departments in a specific local government are interwoven with these other levels of intergovernmental relations. A differentiation among local government elites is noticeable as reference groups do not all have the same weight as significant others. Thus, Houlihan, in a comparison of housing officers and planners, points out that planners had a clearer conception of the notion of a professional community at national level, compared with housing officers who were more likely to take their values and normative cues from the culture of the local government in which they served and the significant others inside it. Interestingly he remarks,

> in a number of inter-departmental conflicts this proved to be the strength of the housing department and the achilles heel of the planners ... In local governments where one-party control was fairly permanent the degree to which some housing departments accept a party political definition of housing policy proved to be a very great asset in withstanding challenges from the planning profession'.[93]

Too great a dependency by one professional category on political resources provided by politicans may, however, weaken the strength of the claim to professional status which implies a degree of autonomy. The local versus cosmopolitan continuum inside local government professions is not always clear cut but sometimes complex and multi-faceted. Linkages and alliances unify and divide inside and across local governments and power is the property of such simplicities and complexities. The weight of such relationships and nuances can vary significantly between local governments. In some councils the political support given to housing departments allowed them a successful expansion of their authority from being primarily a council home management department to being the fulcrum of housing strategy thereby relegating the professionals in the planning architects' department to a client and subordinate status. In other local governments the role of strategic policy-making in housing had been taken over by the professionals in the planning departments and their allies. The planning professionals as 'cosmopolitans' rather than mere 'locals' had closer network links to influentials in important central government departments and this gave them the potential to occupy the crucial and controlling 'neutral' roles in the unfolding of housing policy programmes. Frequently, this was the group that gained the responsibility of overseeing the work of other local government professionals in such areas as rehabilitation, physical housing and surveys. If these areas of control are negotiated rather than merely imposed by superior links, the negotiations are at the margins, with one group of professionals able to resist only at specific points rather than totally as the network weight is massively against them.

Central-local government relationships are structural relationships, power relationships and agent relationships. Professionals play important personal and representational roles in decision-making and implementation and, although this fact has been formally recognised, it has been under-researched or neglected.

Inside local governments power contests and conflicts are governed by folklore customs and common sense symbols of 'fairness' as well as more brutal exercises in the imposition of authority. The local 'game' of power is both entwined and coupled with the intergovernmental game of power but also, in certain conjunctures, relatively autonomous. The supposed 'game' of politics, though, is not just about scoring goals. Even more important are the questions of who controls the referees, who frames the 'rules of the game', how many should play, and even what constitutes a goal. It may be true that in politics the name of the game is to avoid playing for high stakes unless you have the referee in your pocket, or can frame the rules to suit your own game, or have twice as many players as the opposition. At other times, rules are apparently negotiated with some 'fairness' though rarely through individual altruism.

It may be that the balances in a social order can produce and sustain the 'non-decisions' that allow both pseudo and more authentic negotiations to take place between strategic actors. Hill has argued that bargaining politics is typical of US local governments. The fragmentation of power is balanced 'by a degree of informal centralization. Such a goal can only be achieved by a very extensive bargaining process ... Such collective action as it achieved will come about as a result of deals and reciprocal commitments rather than as a consequence of shared ideals'.[94] Hill, however, denies that bargaining politics exist to any significant extent in UK local governments. He argues:

> formal power is very largely distributed in such a way that there are very few competing jurisdictions ... Conflict eventually takes the form of what will be called administrative politics rather than bargaining politics in that conflict is largely kept private and appeals are rarely made to the general public for support in such cases. This fact must be attributed partly to an absence of constitutional devices which would enable interorganisational differences to be fought out in public ... but perhaps more significantly by an elitist approach to government.[95]

A study of the city in the UK by Elliott and McCrone argues that the tilt towards an increase of the power of elite professionals is counterbalanced by client resistance, by the attempts by local political parties to reverse the situation by close political imposition of goals, and by the fact 'that in Britain local government is relatively formalised and tightly structured in that it is difficult for protest or interest groups to bargain directly with officials ... the American system offers a great deal of scope for bargaining and local bureaucrats are frequently drawn into acting as 'brokers', a fact which gives them a great deal of power. In Britain more unified formal structures, together with the considerable degree of central governmental control makes it harder for the bureaucrats to engage in 'bargaining' politics'.[96] This is a less categorical denial of the possibility of bargaining politics than that made by Hill, in so far as it recognizes that bargaining is difficult rather than impossible. It fails to recognize, however, that even in the UK where the elites in government and civil society are relatively tightly integrated, disjunctions and lacunae exist inside and between each level of government, and in this space agents interact and construct policy within the limits set by other agents.

The secrecy of the process of interaction and bargaining protects from both research and public awareness. The state is a broker state as well as a Hegelian totality which refuses to recognize that internal structures have internal political systems. It is perhaps significant that one of the few important studies of the specific governmental cultures and politics which underpin the negotiations over resources between departments in Whitehall, *The Private Government of Public Money*,[97] was written by an

American political scientist and an Englishman matured on American political analysis. A specifically English public administration mode of analysis may well have either denied the importance of negotiations or reduced the determinants to technocratic variables.

Resource allocation analysis then becomes depoliticized and the actors inside invisible, thus emphasizing the sacred over the secular reality. It has also been argued earlier that corporatist mechanism and structures are important impositions of control, and inside the control of dialectic allows subordinate groups some power to negotiate and bargain the terms of formal subordination. It may be objected that this is a form of pseudo-negotiation but even negotiations at the so-called margins of social life can be of some considerable symbolic significance. It is an empirical problem which cannot be resolved without reference back to some mode of what Rhodes dryly called 'barefooted empiricism'. But a map is needed of the agents of government at central and local level, the nuances of the professionalism and other ideologies that sustain them in their collective and individual attempt to work the knots which tie administrative structures together.

NOTES AND REFERENCES

1 Rhodes, R. A.W. *Control and power in central-local government relations*, 1981, 1 & 34.
2 Dearlove, J. *The re-organization of British local government*, 1979, 3.
3 Foucault, M. *The archaeology of knowledge*, 1972. An original and convincing use of discourse theory is put forward by Said, E. W. *Orientalism*, 1978.
4 Hampton, W. *Democracy and community*, 1970.
5 Hill, D. M. *Democratic theory and local government*, 1974, 230. A more recent example of the pragmatic passion of an academic, who believes in local democracy, is Stewart, J. *Local government*, 1983, 6. He claims, on little empirical evidence, 'a local authority lies closer to the governed than can ever be true of central government. Those who make decisions in the local authority, whether councillors or officers, will have a greater likelihood of personal knowledge and contact with the circumstances surrounding a decision'.
6 Dunleavy, P. *Urban political analysis*, 1980, 9.
7 *Ibid.*, 18.
8 Wolin, S. S. *Politics and vision*, 1961, 352-435.
9 Benington, J. *Local government becomes big business*, 1976, 26.
10 Cockburn, C. *The local state*, 1977. Contains an analysis of the practice of corporate management in Lambeth Council. For another perspective of corporate management in Lambeth, see Maslen, A. T. J. The politics of administration reform, *Local Government Studies*, 1983, May/June, 45-65.
11 Clapham, D. Rational planning and politics. *Policy and Politics*, 1984, 12(1), 31-52.
12 Di Maggio, P. J. and Powell, W. W. The iron cage revisited. *American Sociological Review*, 1983, 48, 147-60.
13 Meyer, J. W. and Rowan, B. Institutionalized organizations. *American Journal of Sociology*, 1977, 83(2), 340-63.
14 Mouzelis, N. P. *Organisation and bureaucray*, 1967.
15 Dearlove, J. *The politics of policy in local government*, 1973, 229.
16 Rhodes, R. A. W. The lost world of British local politics? *Local Government Studies*, 1975, 1(3),

39-60. Lee, J. M. *Social leaders and public persons*, 1963, 212-14. This valuable pre-reorganization study of county government in Cheshire noted 'the leading councillors were those who learned the art of understanding discussions at "officer level" and who thereby gained the confidence of the chief officers. Such men, if they were also respected by the organizations of the political parties, and had the necessary ability to grasp the intricacies of the administrative detail involved, constituted a ministerial party ... promotion into the inner ring depended upon making an impression upon not only one's immediate colleagues, but also upon the chief officers and the chairmen'. The approach of this book makes it a rarity in studies of decision-makers in local governments.

17 Saunders, P. *Urban politics*, 1980.

18 Kogan, M. with W. Van Der Eyken. *County hall*, 1973. Bush, T. and Kogan, M. *Directors of Education*, 1982.

19 Dunleavy, *op. cit.*, p. 119.

20 Hinings, C. R. and Greenwood, R. Research into local government reorganisation. *Public Administration Bulletin*, 1973, 15, 21-38.

21 Lukes, S. *Power*, 1974. For a critique of Lukes, see Benton, T.Objective interests and the sociology of power. *Sociology*, 1981, 15(2), 161-84.

22 Benton, K. Realism, power and objective interests. In Graham,K. (ed.). *Contemporary political philosophy*, 1982, 7-33.

23 Pfeffer, J. *Power in organisations*, 1981.

24 *Ibid.*, 2.

25 Crozier, M. *The bureaucratic phenomenon*, 1964, 145. However, note his comment (147) 'that most interactionists have preferred to study interactions ... without taking into account the hierarchical system of domination. They can explain the emergence of spontaneous leadership but not the impact of an authority imposed from the top down and of the concomitant struggle for power'. For further comments see Hindess, B. Power, interests and the outcomes of struggles. *Sociology*, 1982, 16(4), 498-511.

26 Greenwood, R., Hinings, C. R. and Ranson, S. The politics of the budgetary process in English local government. *Political Studies*, 1977, 25(1), 27. Recently a sharp reaction to this type of environmentalist determinism has emerged amongst INLOGOV writers, but it has not yet affected their contemporary writing on the UK local governments. The new approach is illustrated in Ranson, S., Hinings, C. R. and Greenwood, R. The structuring of organisational structures. *Administrative Science Quarterly*, 1980, 25, 1-17.

27 Pugh, D. S. and Hickson, D. J. *Organisational structure in its context, 1976.*

28 Lawrence, P. R. and Lorsch, J. W. *Organisation and environment*, 1967.

29 Bachrach, P. and Baratz, M. S. Decisions and non-decisions. *American Political Science Review*, 1963, 57, 632-42.

30 For example Gaventa, J. *Power and powerlessness*, 1980.

31 Parry, G. and Morris, P. When is a decision not a decision? In Crewe, I. (ed.). *British Political Sociology Yearbook*, 1974.

32 Garrard, J. A. Social history, political history and political science. *Journal of Social History*, 1983, 16 (3), 113. Critiques of advocacy of 'non-decision' research are numerous, for example Wolfinger, R. E. Non-decisions and the study of local politics. *American Political Science Review*, 1971, 65(4), 1063-80.

33 Garrard, J. A. *Leadership and power in Victorian industrial towns, 1830-1880*, 1983.

34 Clegg, S. *Power, rule and domination*, 1975.

35 Williams, G. A. The concept of 'Egomania' in the thought of Antonio Gramsci. *J. History of Ideas*, 1960, 21(4), 589.

36 For example Burrell, G. and Morgan, G.*Sociological paradigms and organization analysis*, 1979, 288-90 and Clegg, S. and Dunkerley, D.*Organisation, class and control*, 1980, 106-13.

37 Eley, G. and Neild, K. Why does social history ignore politics? *Social History*, 1980, 5, May, 249-71. This problem is also faced, though not satisfactorily answered, by Miliband, R. *Capitalist democracy in Britain*, 1982.

38 Garrard, *op. cit.*

39 Hennock, E. P. Finance and politics in urban local government, 1835-1900. *Historical Journal*, 1963, 6(2), 212-25.

40 Saunders, P. *Social theory and the urban question*, 1981.

41 Stanyer, J. *Understanding local government*, 1976. Stewart, J. *Local government: the conditions of local choice*, 1983.

42 Smith, B. C. *Policy making in British Government*, 1976, 123.

43 Rhodes, R. A. W. *Control and power in central-local government relations*, 1981.

44 Saunders, P. They make the rules. *Policy and Politics*, 1975, 4, 31-58.

45 Burgess, T. and Travers, T. *Ten billion pounds*, 1980.

46 Taylor J. A. The Consultative Council on Local Government Finance. *Local Government Studies*, 1979, May/June, 7-35. Taylor emphasizes that the rules of the game were not themselves on the agenda for negotiation.

47 Dunleavy, P. and Rhodes, R. A. W. Beyond Whitehall. In Drucker, H. (ed.). *Developments in British politics*. Revised edition, 1984, 126.

48 Faster, C. D., Jackman, R. A. and Perlman, M. *Local government finance in a unitary state*, 1980, 3.

49 Cooper, N. and Stewart, J. Local government budgets closer to targets. *Public Finance and Accountancy*, 1982, 9, June, 17-21.

50 Thrasher, M. and Dunkerley, D. *Inter-governmental exchange relations*. 1981. Mimeo. In an application of social exchange theory to analysis of central-local government relations in Britain, this paper argued that there are 'considerable hidden costs to central government extending its power and control over local government'. It concludes that, in May 1981, central government 'increased dependence upon local government to the extent that the administrative costs of reorganisation and dislocation have become prohibitive'. (17). The inability of social exchange theory to contemplate basic changes in the 'rules of the game' and the inability to comprehend the 'conviction' politics of the Thatcher type are both evident.

51 Alexander, A. *The politics of local government in the United Kingdom*, 1982, 104-5.

52 Jones, G. W. How to save local government. In Institute of Economic Affairs. *Town hall power or Whitehall pawn?*, 1980, 129-41.

53 Elcock, H. *Local government*, 1982, 290-1.

54 Yearley, C. K. The 'Provincial Party' and the megapolises. *Compative Stud. Society and History*, 1973, 15(1), 51-88.

55 Ashford, D. E. A Victorian drama. In his *Financing urban government in the welfare state*, 1980, 71-96.

56 Rhodes, R. A. W. Analyzing intergovernmental relations. *European Journal of Political Research*, 1980, 8, 289-322. However, he modifies his model significantly in *'Corporate bias' in central-local relations*, 1982.

57 Heclo, H. H. and Wildavsky, A. *The private government of public money*, 1974.

58 Thrasher, M. The concept of central-local government partnership. *Policy and Politics*, 1981, 9(4), 455-70. He argues that the partnership model has been overstretched and advocates either a more rigorous definition or an abolition of the term altogether.

59 Dunleavy, P. Professions and policy change. *Public Administration Bulletin*, 1981, 36, 3-16.

60 Heclo and Wildavsky *op. cit.*

61 Regan, D. E. *Local government and education*, 1977.

62 Cohen, G. Issue networks in the analysis of intergovernmental relations. *Policy and Politics*, 1982, 10 (2), 217-237. See also Metcalfe, J. L. Organizational strategies and interorganizational networks. *Human Relations*, 1976, 29(4), 327-43.

63 Rhodes, 1981. *op. cit.*

64 Dunleavy, P. *The politics of mass housing in Britain, 1945-1975*, 1981.

65 Dunleavy, P. Professionals and policy change. *Public Administration Bulletin*, 1981, 36, 3-16.

66 Elcock, *op. cit.*, 94.

67 Martlew, C. The state and local government finance. *Public Administration*, 1983, 61, 127-47.

68 Kogan, *op. cit.*, 89.

69 Greenwood, R. Pressures from Whitehall. In Rose, R. and Page, E. (eds.). *Fiscal stress in cities*, 1982, 44-76.

70 Pahl, R. E. Socio-political factors in resource allocation. In Herbert, D. T. and Smith, D. M. (eds.). *Social problems and the city*, 1979, 33-46.

71 Saunders, P. *Urban politics*, 1980, 146.

72 Johnston, R. J. *Geography and the state*, 1982, 226.

73 Hampton, W. *Democracy and community*, 1970, 219.

74 Blowers, A. *The limits of power*, 1980.

75 Harloe, M. *Swindon,* 1975.

76 *Ibid.*, 229.

77 Brogden, M. In Police authority. *Sociological Review*, 1977, 25(2), 325-49, and *The police*, 1982. Both give excellent discussions of the relative autonomy of chief police officers.

78 Harrington, T. Explaining state policy-making. *International Journal of Urban and Regional Research*, 1983, 7(2), 202-18.

79 Pahl, R. Socio-political Factors in Resource Allocation, in Herbert, D. T. and Smith, D. M. (eds.). *Social Problems and the City*, 1979, 33-46

80 Saunders, P. *Social theory and the urban question*, 1981, 134.

81 Dunleavy, P. *The politics of mass housing in Britain, 1945-1975*, 1981.

82 Malpass, P. Professionalism and the role of architects in local authority housing. *RIBA Journal*, 1975, 82(6), 6-29.

83 Ravetz, A. *Remaking cities*, 1980.

84 *Ibid.*, 229.

85 Dunleavy, P. *Urban political analysis*, 1980, 119.

86 Kellner, P. and Lord Crowther-Hunt. *The civil servants*, 1980. They discuss how the technocrats are subordinated to the 'generalist mandarins'.

87 Lomer, M. The chief executive in local government, 1974-1976. *Local Government Studies*, 1977, 3 (4), 17-40.

88 Green, D. G. *Power and party in an English city*, 1981.

89 Houlihan, B. The professionalisation of housing policy making. *Public Administration Bulletin*, 1983, 41, 14-31.

90 Ranson, S., B. Hinings, S. Leach & C. Skelcher. *Domination and distribution in policy planning networks*, 1980.

91 Page, E. Grant consolidation and the development of intergovernmental relations in the USA and the UK. *Politics*, 1981, 1.

92 Wilding, P. *Professional power and social welfare*, 1982, 22.

93 Houlihan, *op. cit.*, 23.

94 Hill, M. J. *The sociology of public administration*, 1972, 217.

95 *Ibid.*, 222.

96 Elliott, B. and McCrone, D. *The city*, 1982, 20.

97 Heclo and Wildavsky, *op. cit.*

CHAPTER FOUR

Organizational theory, politics, local government and retrenchment

There seems to be little consensus in organizational sociology on the relationships between what is termed the 'environment' and organizations.[1] There is even less consensus on how such relationships should be either conceptualized or measured. This could be read either as a sign of health or as a sign of severe illness. It can be noted that such perspectives in organization theory in the context of local government are concerned with a depolicized 'efficiency' and may reflect a fear of ungovernability. Such strength as does exist in organization theory usefulness can be most easily recognized in the inter-governmental bargaining model of Rhodes which situates relationships between central and local governments in a context of strategies, skills, resource bargaining and rules of the game.[2] In a critique of the loose manner in which the environment has been conceptualized in organizational theory generally Salaman has argued that 'to the extent that the outside world does impinge on the structure and functionalising of organizations it is conceptualised not as a source of interacts, values, class loyalties, ideologies, market development, etc., but as the organization's "environment"'.[3]

Recently it has become increasingly common to regard local governments as political systems, with their own political cultures and characteristics approaches to the resolution of disputes and the discharge of their functions.[4] This stress on at least the semi-autonomy of local governments from central governments has been built upon research conducted over the last two decades. Instead of regarding local governments as a mere extension and subordinate part of central government, this perspective emphasized their autonomy in the field of inter-governmental relations, through possessing their own resources with which they may seek to influence the course, resist or even openly defy central government policies. However, events in the recent years have shown the inequality of bargaining power between local and central governments and the ability of central governmment to change unilaterally the rules of the game. Indeed Burgess and Travers[5] argue that local autonomy since 1980 is all but extinguished. This perspective is not totally accepted by myself but some shift in the form and content of relationships has taken place. The degree to which it constrains and is perceived to constrain the strategically significant actors inside local governments has not been tested empirically through fieldwork studies. Rhodes' model would suggest, in opposition to

Burgess and Travers, that power is relative and likely to remain so even in the contemporary period.

Cockburn[6] states that local government political systems mainly reflect the needs of capital accumulation and that decision-making essentially by politicans and professionals is set by the determinants of the tempo of the private sector. Dunleavy,[7] who also adopts a structuralist model, suggests that the national corporate process of central government national networks of professionals and the industries and firms in the private sector establishes the boundaries of decisions on important processes in relation to consumption. He tends to discount the variations in political cultures as ultimately not being of major importance on such issues as are given by the external 'environment'. The range of decisions he examined were set outside the reach even of significant local influentials in local governments. However, the resource allocation systems internal to the local authorities did show a significant and interesting variation between local governments. The party variable and the administrative structure variable all had some significance in this spread of choices between local governments at certain levels of decisions.

Jones[8] noted that the Conservative and Labour Parties 'differ in their attitudes' to what is prudent spending, and over priorities, the pace of development of services and who should receive what benefits. Alt[9] found that the expenditure of urban local governments, when associated with control by the Conservative Party, was linked to higher expenditure on law and order issues than Labour-controlled councils who gave greater priorities to educational spending. Boaden's study[10] reached similar conclusions on the significance of party on expenditure. However, Danziger's demographic study[11] reported that party differentiation was only moderately related to levels of service provisions while party competitiveness had virtually no systematic relationship with any measure of resource allocation. Karran[12] argues that in spite of the complexity and diversity of the local government decision-making process, the political variables chosen for inclusion in most studies are remarkable for their paucity and lack of sophistication. He draws attention to the interplay of the administrative system of each type of local government and the diverse impact of party. He suggests that the degree and type of control granted to chief officers in policy construction is set by the pattern of social representation on each council and the pattern of the rules of the game established in each local government. The question of the specific balance of organizational, political and ideological, as well as personal forces arises and organizational theory, is ill-equipped to help in theory building on such matters.

Jones[13] argues that the balance between politicians and professionals varies not only between local governments but also within a local government depending largely on the authority of the professionals and of influential politicians. Influence and power is not a static eternal verity but can be won, lost and regained in the arena of local bargaining. Generalizations then about the uniformity of impact of both the administrative and the political variable are tentative, thus giving the diversity of practices. Karran[14] suggests that rural counties, in the past prior to reorganization in 1974, had a tradition of allowing crucial decisions to be affected by the idiosyncratic practices of politicans whilst permitting a greater degree of discretion and authority than in the boroughs to the professionals. The relative absence of a strong partisan system in the rural counties strengthened this tendency. Lee's study of county government in Cheshire[15] suggests that in this county the leading professionals constituted a permanent body of chief ministers who had almost complete control over the information system. As Pettigrew[16] demonstrates, information control is a power resource in every type of organization. Lee argues that the influential politicians were those who had learnt to acquire the art of working with the professionals and understanding their presentations of publicity. Lee's study establishes a category of the 'public person' with which leading politicans and professionals are both identified and which makes the task of role differentiation more difficult. Lee's study also hints at a model of specificity of practices which cannot be easily generalized into a universal model.

Aiken and Bacharach[17] following Karpik have put forward a useful series of hypotheses within which a specific local government can be accepted as a historically specific form. They emphasize institutional specificity and this differentiates them from the bulk of the organizational theory literature on the 'environment', which attempts to develop general concepts that are applicable to most or all organizations under most or all conditions. Aiken and Bacharach suggest that organizations are best conceived of as political systems both internally and in their external relationships with the actors who have their own needs, objectives and strategies to achieve those objectives. Coalitions of actors emerge in organizations and they devise collective objects and strategies to achieve those objectives. They are constrained by organizational structures, techniques, the existing rules of the game and ideologies. The dominant coalition is the one which controls the authority structure and resources at a given point in time.

Most organizational theorists, whilst acknowledging the effects of exogenous contingencies and internal uncertainties, often fail to explain the mechanisms whereby the organization's 'environment' produces contingencies or uncertainties. It may be suggested that a concept like uncertainty remains nebulous unless the structures and mechanisms producing uncertainties are examined and specified. It can also be argued that the contingencies for different kinds of organizations, such as private sector firms, schools and local governments, are likely to vary and hence the factors producing contingencies and uncertainties for one type of organization may not be generalizable to another type. It is thus of vital importance to understand the specificities of organization 'environments' in addition to their generalizable features. This chapter examines the process of retrenchment of resources in a number of English local governments from this perspective. It examines cases which illuminate the essential political nature of organizations, emphasizing both the internal political process as well as the political process whereby the dominant coalition engages the organization in political relationships with its 'environment'. The variables of party and administrative structure will be examined as determining aspects of these processes.

In a context of the contraction of resources for most local governments, choices and options take on a sharper focus than in the previous period when resources were relatively plentiful. Stewart[18] has attempted to pinpoint this important difference and its impact on organizational structure. He suggests that in an era of an expansion of resources the expectations around growth, while not formally written down, were built into the procedures and local governments' 'rules of the game'. The era of growth allowed working compromises to be built between potentially antagonistic spending departments and their political allies and within spending departments between different functional sectors. In an expansionist era it was not necessary for the 'rules of the game' in the internal resource allocation system to take the form of one sector of professionals and politicians challenging the bids of another department, so that open and potentially dangerous confrontations between departments were not likely to happen or were ruled out completely. This situation is overturned when resources either decline or reach a standstill with potentially disruptive consequences for organizational relationships. Stewart argues that concessions in one year by a spending department's representatives in an expansionist era are not seen as permanent but as tactical and temporary to be recovered in successive years.

The organizational literature on the consequences of fiscal contraction in the USA is more empirically based than the UK literature on retrenchment. Rubin, Levine and others [19] note the severity of tax base erosion in urban city local governments. They argue that the type and nature of the political control from the local community is the key factor in explaining the internal processes which determine retrenchment. In these local governments politicians have had to make a series of difficult decisions to close the widening gap between revenue and expenditure. Political forces seem to be overwhelmingly in favour of either raising new resources or denying the existence of a gap while deficits begin to build up and budgetary practices become less cautious. It seems that once a strategy of obfuscation takes place, it becomes more difficult to know how large or important deficits are. As long as political community pressure groups support obfuscation there is little motivation for politicans to return to more conservative balanced budgets.

It may be the case that the relative lack of control by the Federal government over local governments in the USA compared to the tight controls on spending in the UK allows local politicians and elected officials greater control over all areas of the budget. Faced with unyielding demands for resources from strongly represented interest groups and a relative fragmenting of authority, elected officials have often been unable to cut back expenditure. Instead of cutting back, elected officials have been forced to deny the severity of the fiscal crises, engage in excessive short-term borrowing and hide deficits while hoping for an early increase in revenue. Despite such hopes, revenues have continued to decline while deficits have increased causing severe cash flow problems, defaults on bonds or notes. The strong pluralist interest group model on which urban local governments operate in the USA implicitly assumes expanding resources so that local-based interests can bargain over increments without fearing that their established expenditure base will be threatened. Growth in resources, allows bargaining to take place as Stewart recognizes in the UK as well. It also allows a relative integration of community interest groups and their professional allies and spokesmen and women inside local governments. Those who have no strong representational voice and who are not awarded legitimacy have no place in their bargaining politics. Resource decline in the USA endangers this process as public officials and politicians lose the slack resources necessary to maintain bargaining among established coalitions or to satisfy the demands of new interest groups. The US experience according to a series of empirical studies conducted by Rubin, Levine and Wolohojian is likely to force local governments into a volatile process of helpless indecision marked by episodes of conflict produced by the linked problems of resource decline and increased potentiality for political fragmentations.[20]

The writers on the impact of a contraction of resources in English local government have been strongly influenced by a type of organizational theory which predicts possible outcomes. It is extremely different from the model of institutional specificity advocated by Aiken and Bacharach and outlined earlier in this chapter. It should be admitted that organizational theory is not very satisfactory when analyzing retrenchment moments in the life of an organization. The lack of a relevant literature becomes salient when viewed from a perspective which asks whether there are any structural aspects of organizations that increase their ability to adapt when resource levels decline. The literature on organizational decline can be categorized perhaps in three general models. The first is a homeostatic model in which retrenchment triggers adaptive processes.[21] The second is a model of decline in which the organization becomes rigid as it grows and is unable to cope with retrenchment.[22] The third model is a contingency model which argues that the degree of flexibility in the organization at the time when the 'environment' becomes threatening determines the survival capacity of the organization.[23] The third model asks the profitable question when or under what circumstances will the organization be able to adapt, and this is the dominant model utilized by Greenwood, Walsh, Hinings and Ranson who are highly influential in dictating the research strategy on UK local governments. Thus a recent text uses contingency theory to explore how far structural variation and change exist in English local government and the extent to which that variation and change may be explained by the situational circumstances (or contingencies) of the local authority.[24]

Underlying contingency theory is the assumption that the 'congruence between structures and contingencies matter'. The four theorists from INLOGOV also admit in their recent book that they are left with the puzzling conclusion that the same contingency works in different ways in different types of local governments. They accept and indeed further admit that this model seeks to explain the nature of organizational structures and practices in terms of environmental and organizational characteristics. They admit to a mechanistic form of explanation that eliminates the role played by organizational actors. 'The argument of contingency theory is that for an organization to perform effectively its structure must "fit" its circumstances but the degree of "fit" manifestly varies'. They state 'some consideration must be given to the politics or organizational behaviour ... people within an organization can influence its structure and processes. It is they who have to understand which contingencies are creating stresses and strains and it is they who have to make choices as to what might be an appropriate organization'.[25]

This plea to bring the men and the women back into the social processes of organizations in general and local governments in particular may be blocked by the method of social research favoured by contingency theory itself. A qualitative fieldwork practice, the obvious alternative method, which examines the politics of organizations and which can examine how strategic actors make particular choices, is not advocated by them.

Contingency theorists are politically opposed to the attempt to narrow the options on fiscal policy choice and object to recent legislation from 1979 onwards which threatens local governments. Greenwood delicately warns of the erosion of local government authority and the possibility that local government may become no more than local administration.[26] This is a widespread and legitimate fear among many writers on local government, who argue that in the new legislation central government has powers to influence not just the total of public expenditure but the expenditure of individual local governments. Greenwood and his fellow contingency theorists, along with other writers, have noted the additional problem which the volatility of significant institutional factors in the external 'environment' of local government imposes on local governments. Between May 1979 and the middle of 1981 local governments had to work with four different financial frameworks: the rate support grant system as it existed until 1980: the transitional arrangements introduced by the Secretary of State for the Environment between the publication of the 1980 legislation and its enactment; the block grant settlement and the arbitrary setting of grant-related expenditure assessments; and the threat or imposition of financial penalties on local governments that 'overspent' on targets set by central government.[27]

If inter-governmental relations are traditionally bargaining relations as well as power relations, representatives of local government noted in a letter of protest, their lack of control on their external environment: 'it (the government) has introduced five changes in the grant system in the last two and a half years ... (it) changes the rules as the sides are in play'.[28] The fifth change was that contained in the Local Government Finance Bill of November 1981.

The contingency theorists have not yet built into their model the importance of the increased volatility in the external inputs from the 'environment' of central government though they have registered them. Greenwood has argued that, in a period of contraction and cuts in local government services by central government, it would be difficult for central government to allow substantial discretion. Writers from the perspective of contingency theory tend to be antagonistic to the recent legislation which threatens the traditional semi-autonomy of the local government system. Yet they also argue that financial retrenchment or standstill will or could probably bring on increased rationality in budgetary processes as it will weaken both the element of incrementalism and the political determinants on the budget. Other defenders of local government as a system of articulated relationships, which are being unnecessarily complicated and weakened, have also taken this position. Hepworth, the Director of CIPFA, states, for example: 'A halt to growth means that the only way of meeting new marginal needs is to review the distribution of existing resources. To that extent such a change can have beneficial purgative effects. And on the whole this is what has happened in local governments'.[29]

In a number of significant papers the contingency theorists, Greenwood, Hinings, Ranson and Walsh,[30] have distinguished four ways in which local governments have responded to financial constraints:

1 Politically inspired retreats from corporate management.
2 Managerially inspired retreats from corporate management.
3 Centralization of policy planning.
4 A decentralized or corporate 'matrix' approach. In this scenario a group of professionals will produce policy programmes for different client groups to be protected as far as possible against the cuts.

In their empirically based sampling of local governments the contingency theorists noted that most fell into the last category. They adapted the hypothesis that less resources will make local governments adopt a more 'rational' review of the budget base and produced a rationality index which lists a number of budgetary and analytical procedures which constitute in their view a rational mode of procedure for organizations under financial strain. These include a strategic analysis of expenditure with a classification of estimates into base-committed growth items, manpower forecasts, a strategic analysis of demands for services, an explicit statement of objectives, and policy or issue analysis.

They conclude that in the mid-1970's most local governments acted in ways in which, by the indices above, are seen as 'rational' and hence that: 'A contraction in the supply of resources widens the parameters of budgetary review and introduces a greater measure of rationality . . . budgetary famine, a least for a time, decreases the likelihood of incremental budgeting'.[31]

The emphasis on rationality is widespread throughout the literature on organizational theory. The imposition of the category of a universal abstract rationality has its obvious dangers when attempting to analyze the internal organization and politics of local governments and the diversity of determinants on fiscal processess. In a perceptive comment on budget politics in a Swedish city, Jönsson[32] argues that fiscal processes are not characterized by one scientific rationality but by a multitude of different and competing 'rationalities'. The allocation of resources between spending departments and programmes is compounded by an absence of a consensus on acceptable measurement of 'output' and a disjunction in knowledge on how means are related to ends. Jönsson remarks that budgeting in Swedish local government takes place in an ambiguous internal and external 'environment' where there are very few fixed points to which 'rational' behaviour can be anchored. A number of studies of budgetary behaviour and fiscal retrenchment exist but these leave the internal realities of the budgetary process and its politics largely unexplained. An underlying theme of this chapter is to suggest that the whole antithesis between more or less rationality is not merely unhelpful but positively misleading. It may be of greater use to chart the diversity of the different rationalities of actors and their representatives in local governments. Actors may even carry more than one rationality depending on the nature of the issue at stake and the conjunctural politics of the history of the local government. This is loosely coupled with the determinants set by the political party variable, the administrative system and its culture and the idiosyncratic practices of local politicians.

In an early paper, the contingency theorists, Hinings, Greenwood and Ranson state that a sociology of local government fiscal processes would have to be based 'Upon the political features of organizational life, rather than upon the cognitive deficiencies of decision actors'.[33]

In a more recent paper the contingency theorists emphasize the importance of the meanings which organizational members attach to their actions: of the aims, purposes, and intentions which they bring to bear upon situations in order to shape their probable course. These are seen as: 'Sources of organizational cleavage ... setting actors at odds with each other and frequently bringing them into conflict. Analytical attention then shifts to the political prowess in organizations'.[34] However, this informal recognition is negated by the failure to document and situate such processes.

Stewart[35] implicitly moves away from the perspective of the contingency theorists on the possibility of increased rationality in decision processes inside local governments within a period of retrenchment. He emphasizes the possibility of a dominant political dimension which could possibly even increase in significance. This is partly supported by a number of other highly tentative studies.

Glennerster[36] argues that the social planning systems that emerged in the 1970's allowed some *modus vivendi* between the different rationalities and interests in the resource allocation process as resources were available. In a period of contraction and standstill, affected and amplified by tight cash limits. Glennerster notes the likelihood of increasing conflicts over the allocation of resources. He points to a growing incompatibility between the different forms of 'rationality' and postulates that which one dominates will depend on the power relations in particular contexts; he suggests from his data tentatively that the politicization process is likely to overwhelm all structures and processes which attempt to move above (and below) it.

Bebbington and Ferlie[37] suggest that it is possible that the contraction and uncertainty in the external environment could lead to a partial or total collapse of budgetary systems and the emergence of unstructured forms of confrontation as a consequence. Some of the fieldwork data they present also questions the assumption in the rationality model of the contingency theorists that fiscal stress would lead to a restructuring of services on a more cost-effective basis. The social service department they examined showed little sign of this. In addition they found that the majority of local governments had an organizational response which actually slowed down the rate of innovation and limited the ability to switch resources. Thus schemes aimed at promoting more cost effective alternatives to residential care ironically have themselves fallen victim to the search for economies. Spending departments may be scutinizing more carefully their base budgets in response to fiscal stress but they conclude that the apparent rationality in corporate management merely reflects political inputs. 'Local governments' still called for blanket cuts . . . and such prioritization as extended was based on local political preferences rather than analysis of needs. They found that in those few local governments which allowed the reallocation of resources to new projects the crucial variable in decision-making was the political bargaining between politicans and between politicans and officers rather than an abstract corporate rationality.

In another survey, Ferlie and Judge[38] report that little new growth has taken place in budgeting. They found, for example, in Berkshire which was cut by 8.8 per cent, that the budgets provided for net cuts of £1,281,000 and provision for growth of just £5,000. They also insist on the dominant political dimension in deciding how the cuts should be allocated and, therefore, take issue with the contingency model which predicts that the budgetary process will, after a period of fiscal restraint, be more fluenced by corporate rational analysis. For example, Devon decided to protect its reputation in education by calling for a 3 per cent cut in education and 5 per cent cuts elsewhere. They conclude that the size of the budget is determined by central guidelines, political stances, national policies and rate fixing. The slicing of the budget cake is often dependent on the outcome of structured confrontations between treasurers and each chief officer. They observed that, in a number of local governments controlled by the same political party as in power at Westminster, local politicians used the budget to express a symbolic forum for cuts which met with diverse forms of resistance from chief officers who attempted to 'fudge' demands for cuts.

Rhodes has commented on the lack of studies of the impact of chief officers on policy construction and execution as follows: 'One of the major actors in this decision-making process is noticeable for his absence from studies in local politics. Policy construction cannot be unambiguously distinguished in local governments from implementation and administration of particular decisions'.[39] Studies of local government politics have often drawn attention to the evolution of unwritten 'rules of the game' which routinely shape, direct and give meaning to the interaction of the actors in local governments; the studies in the main concentrate on politicians.[40]

Formal institutionalized rules are significant in regulating behaviour in all organizations to a greater or lesser extent but they can and often do coexist with less cohesive and less explicit recognized rules and procedures. Albrow[41] has suggested that organizational structures can best be viewed as the outcome of negotiations between the different groups that exist within an organization. The formal rules which regulate these negotiations are the public face of local governments and reflect the dominant legalism in the ideology. They intermesh with other rules which as hinted are generally tacit, implicit and 'informal' and these are the projects of specific institutional relationships which may be shaped in different ways in different local governments. Some studies of organizations seem to find that these tacit rules can be stretched or 'fudged' by actors pursuing their own interests.[42] In local governments such actions, by either chief officers or politicians are possible but the legitimacy which is attached to such actions is weak. Short-run gains can be undercut by the long-term risks incurred by offending these powerful implicit agreements which are so central to coalition formation and decision-making.

Informal 'rules of the game' are thus responsive to politicans and professional interests and may facilitate the adaptation of regularized patterns of interface politics which owe relatively little for formalized expectations of behaviour. The 'rules' regulate contexts and conflicts over resources, policy and authority. In an era of resource contraction these rules become potentially more unstable as the interpretations of the working out of rules are increasingly open to challenges by professionals and politicians. If an actor has a reason to look for it, both vagueness and ambiguity can be discovered. It should not be assumed that such challenges entail a total overthrow of the existing consensus or set of consensuses among organizational actors. Rather they allow the existing rules to be modified and renegotiated. The tempo of fiscal stress is likely to have such an impact on crucial aspects of existing rules of the game in local governments.

Each actor attempts not merely to work within the existing rules of the game but to achieve a tactical and strategic advantage by controlling the rules. In the post-Bains[43] era, the new rules, formal and informal, strengthened the control roles of treasurer and chief executive rather more than other chief officers. These two roles, especially the treasureship role, can be of extreme importance in the choice of an apparent neutral technology of budgeting. In a contraction or standstill era the negotiations inside the internal resource allocation system between a treasurer who constructs – both formally and informally – the 'neutral' financial rules of the game to a greater degree than any other chief officer is not normally seen as a bargaining between equals in other than the most formal sense. It is not merely the chief officers debating, it is about two different sets of ideological and structural relationships which distribute power inside local government organizations. The influence over the apparently neutral choice of budget technology also allows a treasurer to steer resource allocation politics away from an open clash for diminishing resources between spending departments.

Greenwood argues that the 'extended percentage pool' technology offers the key members of the budgetary elite, the dominant coalition, the opportunity to be able to switch resources from one service to another by comparing and choosing between potential fiscal cuts.[44] To the dominant coalition inside the party regime and among the chief officers, this budget technology could be more useful than the 'simple percentage pool' system whose characteristic is a relative lack of flexibility in the allocation of resources across spending departments. The choice of an apparently neutral technology of budget construction by the dominant coalition allows them to determine what 'rules of the game' operate. Such rules structure the representation allowed to spending departments in their bids for resources and command over policy. The control over the construction of these rules allows members of the dominant coalition an input into interface politics inside the negotiating process and also allows a control over the very terrain in which such negotiations are carried out.

Since the reorganization of local governments many more councils are internally organized on party political lines. The increased partisanship is linked to the problems encountered in the adoption of the forms and prescriptions of corporate management in local governments. Hill[45] suggested in the early 1970's that two types of local council existed. These he termed 'ideological', which he equated with the strength of party commitment and 'administrative', which pushed formal party inputs to the margins or eliminated them. In the last he suggested that policy construction was bereft of a formal and articulated party ideology. In the last type of local government there would be a tendency for chief officers to be allowed significantly more authority over policy construction and administration than in the other type of local government, where politicians would tend to be wary of chief officers openly involved in the construction of decisions. In the type of local government where ideological politics dominate, studies have shown that councillors have weakened or destroyed strong corporate management systems on the ground that such systems weaken political roles and are 'unnecessary'. There is evidence that the reduction of the powers of committees and departments is unwelcome to politicians of all parties in all types of local governments and are viewed equivocally by those professionals who manage spending departments. Corporate management also creates tensions between backbench councillors and a party regime leadership by sometimes excluding backbenchers from any more than a symbolic influence on policy.

The contribution of party values to the process of policy making is often reactive rather than initiative and this makes the process similar to that of local governments who value supposedly pragmatic administration over 'ideology'. Hill argues that in councils where administration is the norm the chief officers will be involved in relationships both within the local government and external to it. These relationships have an element of bargaining, negotiation and consultation in a manner than has traditionally been regarded as 'political'. He further suggests that chief officers will, from time to time, be forced to legitimate their own actions by what is termed 'democratic devices'. In councils dominated by an administration style, a manageralist consensus is constructed within which conflicts of interests are seen as pathological. Policy options become 'obvious' for if everyone is on the same side the task of politicans and professionals becomes merely the search for the most expenditious means of implementing a 'non political' consensus on what is taken to be the public interest. Important questions relating to decisions can be taken out of politics, and no longer seriously debated from different and conflicting perspectives. Those who ignore the informal and tacit 'rules of the game' of this organizational culture by raising contentious issues for public debate are generally dismissed as politically motivated.[46]

It can easily be argued that the practice of pragmatic administration in these local governments does not mean that there was no general ideological framework tied to specific social interests nor that the professionals were not very well aware of it. Haywood[47] (he was a councillor) documents in his observational study of a 'non political' regime that a number of policy issues arose in which a fragmented group of politicians disregarded the advice of the chief officers. Inputs from politicans plus what chief officers knew to be sensitive issues for councillors, coalesced to provide what he calls a 'pseudo-ideological' framework for decision-making within the council. Haywood describes how this framework was strongly conservative in its concern to keep down rates and conflicted with the aspirations of some professionals who wanted to improve services. Haywood documented a meeting where, in spite of the dire warnings of the chief executive, the establishment was cut by 10 per cent. It seems that the influence of these councillors did not end with the determination of broad strategies. Their 'predispositions' also influenced the enthusiasm with which professionals administered controversial politics given by the external 'environment' of central government.

Haywood admits that, in this local government, whilst councillors had a considerable influence in establishing the context in which decisions were made, they failed to have much influence on the detailed programming of agreed policies. Cuts in committee budgets were decided by councillors with no recommendation of the strategy to be adopted. The management team of chief officers produced a lot of suggestions for each committee to consider and their suggestions were accepted. In this case retrenchment did not fall evenly and, in the absence of a significant input from politicians, it was the chief officers who looked at the total picture and then made specific suggestions. Since their strategy was the only available to councillors, its overall shape was unchallenged. Haywood suggests, however, that the professionals privately knew the 'articulated reactions' of councillors and this stock of knowledge was used to set the boundaries of their internal bargaining inside the management team.

In rural-based local government before the 1974 reorganization, it was common to find an administrative culture which believed that national party politics should not be significant in local decision-making. A survey of the literature shows that the strength of this viewpoint even incorporated oppositional political forces on the council. Marshall quotes the leader of the Labour Party on the council of the old county of Lancashire who was of the opinion that politics as such did not and should not enter into county council work, which could be said to be purely administrative.[48] A study conducted of a rural southern county, Suffolk, in the mid-1970's showed the continued strength of this tradition even among Labour Councillors.[49] Similar concepts of local governments can be found in other Western European societies.[50]

Chief officers in local governments do not automatically flow into apparent power vacuums in organizational relationships. There is some evidence that Labour-controlled councils would resent this expansion of professional authority as it threatens their mandate and their psychological perceptions of role rather more than the Conservatives. It may be as Newton concluded, from the study of Birmingham, that in general 'the relationship between elected representatives and appointed officials is rather more equal than dictatorship of the official' prophecy suggests.[51] However, Alexander, Green and others show in their work that the fear of such a dictatorship is still determinant on the interface politics at work in relationships between politicians and professionals.[52]

In a context of political fragmentation with no pattern of consistent policy carried out by an acknowledged leadership, it has been known for chief officers to attempt to carry through policy construction by mechanisms of bargaining internal to their management team. This solution, which openly rejects the symbolic status of the chief officers as the mere 'servants' of the council, exposes the chief officers to possible problems of legitimization even in the eyes of the chief officers themselves. Elcock has documented such difficulties by describing how, in Liverpool after the 1979 municipal elections, no party was in overall control and no agreements between parties over committees could be made and kept. The chief officers found that even if a chairperson got policies through committee, there was no guarantee they would also get through the full council. In this context the strains in the composition of the council meant that chief officers retreated from implementing committee decisions which might be reversed.[53]

Very few studies of chief officers' inputs into policy making exist. Blowers' study[54] of decision-making without overall party control in Bedfordshire is unusual. Decisions could only be made by a long process of negotiations amongst party politicians and at each stage the outcome could be uncertain, with numerous instances of policies approved by committees being rejected by council or of conflicting recommendations by committees which reflected different political balances. It is well known that the origins of corporate management, at least in part, have been located in attempts to improve the quality of the budgetary process and to give the budgetary elite of influential politicians and chief officers greater control over the uncertainties in the environment of decision-making. Blowers documents the dissatisfaction felt in Bedfordshire with the traditional methods in which each committee made bids for resources leaving the internal political process inside the full council to arbitrate competing claims. This method led to what the budgetary elite believed to be inconsistencies given the balances inside and between parties which could vary significantly at different stages of the budgetary process. Thus a proposal by one party to have target budgeting, on the basis of which a main committee set the levels of expenditure and then allocated resources to the committees, was seen by another party to be a device to restrict expenditure since it did not start from agreed levels of service provision. A third political party's budget proposals were rejected by the other two. Chief officers reacted to this uncertainty in a manner which amplified the weaknesses in the 'trust' relationships with politicians.

Self has pointed out that politicians are the ultimate controllers of administrative systems and one of their chief problems is to demonstrate and maintain the reality of their control.[55] The symbolic aspects of this, a ritual performance which professionals normally accept (no matter what their real authority is in decision-making) is part of the fabric of the 'rules of the game'. All parties normally benefit from the ritual whereby politicians are allowed to demonstrate their formal control and this element has probably increased since the nationalization of local politics following reorganization. Any threat to this ritualist element is disliked by politicans of all parties and independents. Kogan's study gives examples of chief officers, before reorganization, openly blocking and thwarting any change, major and minor, sought by their committee politicians.[56] Whilst corporate management may attempt to give greater influence to professionals in decision-making, as Dearlove has hinted, by the curbing of political inputs which the central government and the local professionals define to be outside the new 'rules of the game' it is by no means always certain that this will be the actual result of its introduction.[57]

Blowers documents the frustration felt by politicans of all parties at their inability to exercise any effective control over the chief officers. The symbols of deference seemed to be increasingly hollow. Working groups set up to review expenditure and organizational structure met with resistance when they attempted to alter establishments and cut expenditure. After a number of years politicians reacted by establishing an all party policy review group to try and agree on policies which the council as a whole could support and which would then become mandatory upon the professionals. This led to a further major overhaul of the council's organizational structure, which was strongly supported by the chief executive who considered that he was more isolated and less well informed than the council had intended. Other chief officers had less to gain from such a review. The strength in the alliances between chief officers and the nature of the resistance delayed these proposals for several years. This was reinforced by the lack of overall control in the council, despite councillors' efforts to find ways of strengthening their control.[58]

It is frequently argued that the possibility of policy initiation by chief officers and the general element of discretion taken or allocated to them has been significantly reduced following the introduction of party politics. Before reorganization and especially in the rural counties, in the absence of any clearly defined policies, chief officers could exercise a primary role in determining policy. The Maud Committee Report identified a common pattern of politicians on committees dealing with so much of the everyday details of work and services that the formulation of policy was often ignored. Chief officers would find themselves formulating policy as well as implementing it because of the unwillingness and inability of politicans to do so.[59] Alexander and others have noted the importance of the rise of the party in shifting the locus of decision-making to the party group rather than basing it entirely in the hands of chairpersons and the committee. An increase in tension between officers and politicans has been documented in some local governments with councillors fearing that a chief management team would constitute a competing centre of decision-making to the politicians themselves. However, relatively few local governments have politicians who actually initiate policy. Although it is common in some local governments for decisions to be taken inside a dominant party group rather than a committee, politicans still seem to accept the link of chief officer to chairperson and dislike those aspects of corporate management which seek to weaken the significance of this relationship. In a situation of fiscal retrenchment such relationships, plus the dominance of the party group, can allow a political leadership to accept bargaining politics as a means of deciding on cuts. Strong corporate management systems ideally would eliminate or weaken this element of internal division and weaken both politicans and service department chief officers. Chief officers such as the treasurer and to a lesser extent the chief executive are more favourable to strong corporate management systems, while acknowledging the power of the dominant alliances between politicians and professionals to hinder or block such a development.[60]

The arrival in some local governments of councillors who are effectively full-time in their commitment to local government has led to important modifications, since not only does the orthodox distinction between chief officers, who are professionals and councillors, who are supposedly part-time politicans lost its force, but the information gap is also reduced. However, a differentiation between those councillors who become effectively full-time and form the core of the 'influentials' and the part-time councillors who form the bulk of backbenchers, is still of significance in understanding the balances inside parties in decision-making. Lee,[61] in his pre-reorganization study of county government in Cheshire, noted even then that leading members and chief officers formed a natural alliance which he saw as being weighted in favour of the professionals. What distinguished the 'inner ring' of members was their ability to keep professionals informed of possible difficulties and their control of party and special networks in the county. Lee suggested that leading members of the council and the chief officers formed a kind of ministerial party which was required to take action against some of their own councillors. The influential members obtained and kept their prominence by practicing broker roles inside the county. If these influentials in county governments also have a tendency, at least in part, to become effectively full-time councillors, the nature of the dominant alliance alters as the professionals lose some of their exclusive knowledge of the administrative machine. Newton,[62] in his study of Birmingham noted that a small group of councillors, both Conservative and Labour, were effectively full-time. Alexander has speculated that the tighter alliances in local governments exist where the level of partisanship and of party competitiveness are highest, because a change in political control is, in itself, a pressure towards close co-operation between chief officers and professionals.[63] However, this closeness results in professionals consistently becoming the subordinate junior partners with resulting legitimization problems in the eyes of the oppositional parties which especially cause strains in the transition to a new regime. Jones in a study of the dominant Labour group on Durham County Council suggests that, in local governments where the political pendulum does not swing regularly, the influential politicians in a dominant alliance may feel less interest in ensuring swift implementation because their re-election is not in doubt.[64] In such local government the professionals may be allocated more authority and their subordination to an active political will amongst councillors may be less obvious.

The greater influence of chief officers on policy in those rural and semi-rural counties in England, which are now strongly Conservative one-party authorities in the main, may have an elective affinity with two factors. The first factor is that, inside one-party states, processes are not strongly linked to partisanship between parties. The security felt by the dominant party allows a loose reign on party discipline which, in turn, encourages factions and coalitions to be formed which are attuned to specific issues and personalities rather than party programmes. Chief officers, in a wide variety of local governments, accept at best with reluctance the introduction of a partisan politics as it decreases the legitimate boundaries of the 'rules of the game' under which they, as an administrative category, can negotiate and bargain *vis-a-vis* their local politicians. Partisan politics, which is not always the same thing as party politics, sets sharp limits to the amount and type of influence they can bring to bear on specific issues.

A second factor, which could act to strengthen chief officers in their relationship with the politicians, is located inside a socially conservative ideology. Many formerly 'independent' councillors, now located in the Conservative Party as well as Conservative ideology generally, emphasize the right of managers to manage without external interference. In practice, councillors in the one-party states, whilst, at times, ambivalent on the *de facto* authority of chief officers and strongly hostile to any open challenge to their symbolic roles as controllers, normally allow the professionals great authority. This is strengthened by the ties in the trust relationships between chief officers and chairpersons which exist in every local government. Challenges by backbench councillors to chief officers on the right of professionals to manage are normally blocked, because such challenges are also a legitimization problem for the council leadership. A common tradition in local governments is that politicians should not criticize chief officers in open council in personal terms, since they have no automatic right of reply, as the mere 'servants of the council'. Hostility by backbenchers, publicized in the mass media, would lessen the chances of the backbencher gaining promotion inside the council hierarchy. Criticism inside a committee is given a certain degree of acceptance by the council leadership, if it does not threaten the dominant alliance inside the council. Only if a number of influentials feel threatened by chief officers is there any danger of a major upheaval in the normal 'rules of the game'. Alexander noted how the antagonism of councillors to the chief officers' management team in one authority has led to its formal abolition. In Cumbria County Council in 1977 it was abolished and replaced by a new institution called the joint management team, consisting of senior chief officers and senior councillors, and this became the centre of decision-making.[65]

Many councillors are themselves located in professional occupations. Whilst they may have the necessary confidence to scrutinize the practice of chief officers and their subordinate professionals, it is seemingly rare for councillors to question the way professionals work even when supported by a democratic mandate. It seems it is possible to occupy a political role, yet also sympathetically to identify with professionals and their claim to the right to manage. This right allows an ideological claim not merely to policy implementation but also policy contruction inside the trust relationships with influential politicans. This is especially the case if the dominant alliance defines these processes as 'non political' and thus takes them out of the political arena. The local 'rules of the game' will then work this right to manage into its fabric of implicit as well as explicit understandings.

Unfortunately studies of budgetary processes noticeably fail to take into account the specificity of the balance between roles in each local government. It is perhaps the case that different spending departments and their chief officers will adopt different priorities on expenditure. The extent to which such professional personnel will effect expenditure priorities is largely dependent on the type and degree of control exercized by the influential politicans who are themselves dependent to some degree on their professional servants. Karran concludes from a use of causal path analysis that the method of decision-making process in the counties contrasted with the decision-making process in county boroughs. In the boroughs the impact of party, although muted, was nevertheless apparent. In the counties, party conflicts had a negligible effect on the decision-making process which was dominated by an administrative system and by a policy to develop in an ad-hoc manner untainted by party programmes.[66] The evidence is taken from studies sometimes conducted prior to the 1974 reorganization and, whilst some of the exceptional features of the counties may have been transformed in the early 1980's through feeling the bite of national party programmes, the organizational structures still retain some of the older divergencies. Interestingly, the committee structures operating in rural county council governments tend to increase rather than diminish the scope for policy initiation by professionals. County council committees meet usually about four or five times a year, whereas in the boroughs they normally meet between ten or twelve times. This infrequency of meetings means that chief officers are more likely to make policy decisions if important issues crop up between meetings.[67] Politicians may also, unless in practice they work full-time in their roles, find it difficult to challenge the recommendations of the professionals if the interactions between officers and councillors are few, especially as the professionals control and filter the dissemination of information. The professional is both guardian and gatekeeper of the local government's information system. A study of an urban Labour-controlled local government, Newcastle, by a backbench councillor claimed that: 'Some chairpersons and chief officers tended to release only information which demonstrated the rightness of the policy they constructed ... attempts to obtain additional information were often vigorously resisted'.[68]

Newton in his study of Birmingham noted how chief officers could use their gatekeepers' role over information to increase their influence as brokers *vis-a-vis* external pressure groups.[69] Thus even in urban local governments chief officers had organizational power which checked, to some degree, the impact of pragmatic party politics. Committee chairpersons – with a greater possible access to information in a variety of different local governments – were able to have potentially greater control than backbenchers on *de facto* decision-making, if they themselves saw their role as permitting it and were able to impose themselves on such processes.

Under conditions of fiscal contraction and standstill, organizational power holders become subject to a variety of pressures and cross pressures. Power is both located in institutional roles and in the product of the interplay of roles. Thus, in retrenchment contexts, the organizational structures may have to modify certain practices while finding it necessary to produce others. Particularly since the mid-1970's the Rate Support Grant and Block Grant Systems have assumed an overwhelming importance in the budget cycle of local governments. While, as Rhodes has argued, the intergovernmental relationships between central government and local governments should not be seen only in terms of centralization and financial dependency, the bargaining base of the two are increasingly unequal. This has important effects on the planning systems of local governments as increasingly they find the external 'environment' out of their control or even influence. This lack of control sets into motion changes in role relationships and role politics, which lead to new ways of handling both the level of uncertainty or, at least, containing its decriptive effects on each local governmental system and on mechanisms for handling reductions in expenditures. The internal 'rules of the game' and the dominant alliances are forced to meet the tensions of possible increased competition for less resources between spending departments and their political allies and of reducing the general level of uncertainty in the external environment so that muddling through decisions can still be taken. Perhaps, in a number of local governments, it my even be possible to find an increased corporate awareness going beyond departmentalism as the INLOGOV writers suggest. Equally, it may well be the case that the existence of the hidden strength of departmentalism, which is deeply rooted even in normal corporate management systems, may be emphasized more under these conditions.

Many local governments in the past have attempted to reduce the level of uncertainty in external environmental factors by obediently following central government guidelines on the rates of expenditure for particular services. The Chartered Institute of Public Finance and Accountancy statistics for the early 1980's, however, still show, as in Table 1, important variations on expenditure between local government on identical services. This implies that the level of service provision is still substantially a matter for local decision. It is not possible to tell whether the variations were the result of different needs in different local governments or of political decisions by the members of their councils. They do indicate that the amount of money spent on local services, like education and policing, varies considerably in different areas, even if these services are carried out with central control through finance inspectorates and legislation. Many of the services are prescribed by legislation passed by central government and the effect of these statutory obligations is to set the boundaries on the discretion of local governments over the level of services to be provided. It can be estimated that the two largest spenders among the services, education and social services, find that between 80 and 90 per cent of the departmental budget has been committed to expenditure which the dominant alliance in every local government has no choice but to undertake. Only the remaining 10 or 20 per cent covers activities where the local government has a choice whether to support or not. Perhaps these areas of discretion tend to suffer the most when central government demands cuts in expenditure by changing the fiscal rules of the game. While the 1979 Conservative Government has relieved local government of some of their statutory duties, so they can reduce expenditure by ceasing to undertake them; it has not by such actions simplified fiscal politics.

The contingency theorists at INLOGOV identified four main stages in the budgetary process. The initial bids on resources, the level of the supply of resources, the allocation of resources between departments and the process of matching the initial bids with the available resources. Greenwood, Hinings, Ranson and Walsh comment that the financial retrenchment on expenditure since the 1970's has brought with it a tendency to reverse the first two stages.[70] It is normal to assume that proposals for expenditure exceed the available resources. The dominant alliance in each local government can utilize a number of options. The first alternative involves the increase of the rate levy or dipping into resources or a combination of the two, while a second option means that important decisions must be taken about which services the council regards as having the highest priority. Greenwood *et al.* identified four methods used by the diverse local governments they studied to make cuts. The first was the voluntary pool in which departments and their committees were asked to compile lists of the cuts they would be prepared to see made, but no target for cuts was set and no overall priorities between services established. Other local governments used a percentage pool system whereby each department and its committee were instructed to reduce spending

Table 1
Expenditure of non-metropolitan county councils on main services per head of population, 1980–81

Service	Highest spender	Average spending figures in % per head of population	Lowest spender
Education	176.74 (Cleveland)	146.64	119.70 (West Sussex)
Libraries	5.14 (Bedfordshire)	4.05	3.18 (Berkshire)
Social Services	29.49 (Cleveland)	23.04	17.79 (Shropshire)
Police	30.19 (Cumbria)	25.92	20.32 (Isle of Wight)
Fire	10.42 (Cleveland)	6.85	4.92 (Northants)
Administration of Justice	4.38 (Nottinghire)	3.13	2.24 (Essex)
Highways and Transport	24.95 (Northumberland)	19.71	16.34 (Bedfordshire)
Town and Country Planning	3.37 (Derbyshire)	1.52	0.96 (Avon)
Refuse Collection and Disposal	4.82 (Berkshire)	2.38	1.12 (Cambridgeshire)

Source: The Chartered Institute of Public Finance and Accountancy, Financial, General and Rating Statistics 1980–81, 87–8.

by a given percentage, which might be the same for all committees or be varied in accordance with political judgements made about priorities. Thirdly, cuts can be centrally directed possibly by the chief executive in alliance with the treasurer and then presented for consideration to the chief officers' management team. Finally, a number of local governments asked departments to analyze their programmes and recommend policy options to the party politicians. The last entails a careful examination of the budget base which is not necessary for the voluntary pool system and to a lesser degree for the central office direction system.

Local governments have two alternatives in making cuts: to raise the rate levels or to finance expenditure by reducing the balances. It is difficult for a local government to save 'for a rainy day' by increasing balances as a District Audit can instruct that excessive balances be returned to the rate-payers by reducing the rate levy.

The writings of Greenwood, Hinings, Ranson and Walsh in the late 1970's do not recognize the possibility of a partial or total breakdown of the budget cycle if the external environment arbitrarily changes the 'rules of the game' not once but a number of times in quick succession. The political actors, councillors and chief officers, in practice begin to accept that the model of forward planning is increasingly unreal as the new situation forces a different tempo. Thus from 1979 onwards the sudden change to the Rate Support Grant by central government in terms both of percentages and penalties upset the budgetary cycle as a process in most local governments. An open increase of politics rather than a subordination of political inputs to a corporate process is the outcome of changes in the environment of central-local governmental relationships which strengthens rather than suppresses the political processes at work. The adapting of either modified incrementalism or a modified form of zero-based budgeting is dependent at least in part on the values and balances inside the dominant coalition inside every local government, as the research on retrenchment in US municipal governments earlier reviewed seemed to suggest.

My own interviews with influential politicians and chief officers illustrate some of the resources in role relationships in periods of retrenchment in a number of local governments. Inside a retrenchment context, alliances between spending departments can persist when interests are not competing. A social service director could create an alliance with the housing director because the bulk of housing expenditure is on the capital account; the alliance would be directed against education expenditure on staff.

In a county government of a one-party type, where partisanship is almost totally ineffective, retrenchment politics were confused in 1979-81 by the inability to build a consensus on cuts strategy by the party leadership. A distaste for their national party goals in local government by some formerly independent councillors, now influential Conservatives, complicated consensus construction. This was amplified by a general unwillingness among influential chairmen and women to make large cuts even though they were also unable to defy national party policy. The lingering traditions of county administration were also a barrier to the thrust from central government to cut expenditure. The volatility in the external environment whereby uncertainty was created about the level of funding which the county would receive amplified strains. In this context some influential councillors psychologically wanted an early decision they could stick with to reduce the level of uncertainty, whilst others seemed to withdraw from playing active roles in the political arena; still others felt some points of identity with services they felt unable to defend in a committed manner. The cross pressures on political roles increased the instability in the 'trust' relationships on the committees, as chief officers felt they could no longer automatically count on their chairpersons and committees for advocacy roles. This was a strong tendency, for, although counter-balanced by swings back to the old role playing, the 'trust' relationship seemed no longer one of unqualified trust. In this county government, the response of the chief officers, led by the Chief Executive and Treasurer, was to attempt to smooth out the volatility of the political masters of the council by strengthening the alliances between the chief officers, so that the collective weight of the professionals could have a significant impact on financial decisions. Yet these alliances between chief officers were nuanced with important strains as well as solidarities.

The Chief Executive and the Treasurer were both linked to the chief officers as heads of spending departments themselves and to the political regime as the leading central administration heads. Both had strong views on how they should play their roles, individually and collectively, and both expanded the range of authority of their institutional roles in this retrenchment crisis. The confidence felt by influential politicians of all factions allowed these roles to be of increased significance as brokers. Actors in organizations accumulate power through a number of factors but an increase in the level of uncertainty in the 'environment' can be of importance to those alliances in local government whose power depends upon their ability to limit or control such uncertainties. If the leading local politicians could have acted as important brokers *vis-a-vis* their party in power in central government and stabilized the external environment, they too would have strengthened their claim to organizational power and authority. Their failure to gain significant representation among national government politicians helped to produce a crisis of internal confidence in their own ranks as they were unable to play significant brokerage roles. In France, the rigidities in the inter-governmental relations between central and local governments force the local mayors into brokerage roles and failure to succeed creates internal organizational and political problems *vis-a-vis* the other local significant actors.[71]

In this local government, the Chief Executive and the Treasurer were both conscious of their roles as heads of spending departments in a retrenchment era and the constraints on their merely acting as heads of spending departments. Who guards the guardians in these contexts? Nothing except the delicate balances inside the expectation of the 'rules of the game' that one chief officer does not benefit from the misery of other chief officers. This should not be merely seen as a question of ethics but of organizational consequences, as the treasurer role stands to lose as well as to gain if his professional judgement is supported by the dominant alliance among the influential politicians against the feeling of the collectivity of chief officers. The Chief Executive in the local government also made his bid for resources in the following manner: 'I have already worked out the percentage cut for my department. I don't think I will have to make anyone redundant but it's getting very difficult. In 1976 I had 135 staff and now I'm down to 110 and I have to reduce still further by wastage'.

Another chief officer of a spending department in the same local government was sharply aware that the duality of roles as controllers of expenditure and users of expenditure of treasurers and chief executive had the potential to increase the inequality of bargaining power inside the chief officers' management team. He stated:

> It's becoming difficult inside the chief officers' group at times. In my department cuts involve loss of middle management staff. I am very aware that the Treasurer is cutting 3 clerical staff and also that he is attempting to fill 2 middle management vacancies. When you look at my department I have a department where the Principal Officers' grade is only 2 per cent while in the Treasury it is 22 per cent. If I cut, I cut into a small valuable management cadre. I feel that other departments in practice are cutting clerical grades as well as administrative staff. So I'm not convinced that the central departments are taking a fair percentage of cuts. The Finance Committee does not adopt the same critical attitude to Treasury staffing as they do to me. They don't say to the Treasurer, 'you are being asked to identify in relative priority the effects of making further cuts'. I'm aware the Chief Executive's department has been reduced since reorganization, but I'm still worried about credibility in how cuts are given out. We don't really have the corporate mechanism to deal with such situations. It depends upon mutual fairness and trust.

Behind the official structures of corporate management imposed since the Bains report by nearly all local governments, dwells the older political system built around the links between departmental chief officers and politicians. However, the super-imposition of the new corporate management structures has modified in varying degrees the significance of the interactions between chief officers and between politicians. The balances and relationships between the older political system and the newer corporate structures vary considerably between local governments. While few openly decide to reject the new structures even fewer adopted them whole-heartedly. Even the professionals, who might have gained by the full adoption of corporate management which tilted the balance in theory to the officer side of the 'trust' relationship with politicians, remained ambiguous at the weakening of departmental ties with politicians through committees. Even under conditions of retrenchment, and perhaps even more so under these conditions, the interplay of political relationships can be more dominant than a process of corporate rationality. A deputy chief officer from the same county local government stated:

> I still remember when the Chairman of Finance went behind my back to my Chairman to say how much do you really want? Is it half a million? All the objective arguments given earlier to the Finance Committee and to my own committee, in a situation where the officers had attempted to move away from merely defending their own corner went by the board. However objective the exercise, the informal understandings between political colleagues depending upon their respective influence with, the party group, was still very important and determined what happened. In that case it was to the benfit of my service

that, without any more attempted objective analysis, a Chairman of Finance said well let's give them half a million.

In this local government the chief officers of six of the most powerful service departments met every week with the Treasurer and County Executive. These meetings were increasingly felt to be necessary since the volatility among the politicians, who were thus responding to the uncertainty in the external 'environment' of central government's financial policy, created tensions in inter-departmental relations. Not only do the spending departments' chief officers mobilize committee allies, but they in turn can be dragged behind the 'moods' and sharp turns of their political allies. The increasing uncertainty increased the stakes in the internal debates inside the weekly meetings of the chief officers' group.

The majority of chief officers, who managed smaller and less important spending departments, met together with the most influential chief officers, the Treasurer and the Chief Executive, once a month. It was felt by some of them that the exclusion from the weekly meetings weakened the departments not represented though they had access to the agenda and could attempt to request the Chief Executive on specific matters. However, the creation of an inner and outer ring of chief officers meant a production of inequality of influences when it came to negotiation over policy and resources. The Bains report tentatively proposed that the ideal size of the management team should be about six and accepted the possibility that 'if the management team's activities are not made known to those chief officers who are not members, distrust and suspicion are bound to be created'.[72]

In a period of financial expansion the most powerful spending department can adopt the role of patron to the weaker departments who may not have influential politicians on the relevant committees. Sometimes it has been the case that some spending departments have not had their own committees but were grouped under the umbrella of the committee for high spending departments. The alliance then between these departments is one of dependence rather than equality with the stronger departments playing a role which weakens as well as strengthens the smaller departments. In a situation of retrenchment, the limited protection provided may decline in significance or even disappear altogether if resources which were formerly seen as relatively marginal become more significant to the major spending departments. In such a context, the chief executive and treasurer roles become even more valued if they can offer protection to the weaker departments, especially if the 'rules of the game' in the internal resource allocation system become bent in the favour of the larger department. It may also be in the corporate interest as well as in the role interest of the chief officer and treasurer to attempt to give some protection to the weaker departments and to devise 'rules of the game' which don't sacrifice their interests. Spending departments with low budgets normally have committees (if they have committees at all), with low ranking politicians on them, who may carry less weight than politicians who sit on those committees which are attached to the big spenders.

Even if an influential politician has a place on the committee of a small department, his or her loyalty may be given to his or her position on a more influential committee. Education and social services which form the greatest spenders normally have the most influential politicians on them.

It is politically simple for party regime to advocate cuts across the board as it lessens the possibility of strong conflicts between the major departments and their political allies. However, such a consensus strategy could damage the budget of a small department to a greater extent than a larger department. A chief officer in charge of a small department in the local government under discussion explained the option open to him:

> I have been very uneasy. We had a meeting of chief officers and it was agreed that we should suggest to the Finance Committee that an extra half per cent cut be levied on all departments to give help to smaller departments. We have the smallest budgets and it's much more difficult to make substantial cuts when you've got a small budget. There is less room for manoeuvre and flexibility. This was agreed in the monthly meeting where all chief officers came together but it was subsequently overthrown at a small meeting of the most influential chief officers. This incensed us, the chief officers of the smaller departments, and we used our committees to appeal to the Finance Committee and also the Chief Executive.

This was coupled with an appeal to the goodwill of influential councillors and this goodwill has its limits. Certain councillors, who are linked to county administrators as a whole, even though they are strongly based in the major committees, give some protection as part of a total cuts strategy.

The Treasurer in this local government argued that the smaller departments as a whole might believe they were at a crippling disadvantage in gaining political support but there were a number of internal rivalries which limited the potential unity they could offer. This fragmentation meant that such alliances as existed between the smaller departments were weak and limited to temporary issues.

> Some of the smaller departments tried to hide behind and seek protection from larger departments in order to protect themselves. I doubt if they will succeed even if some larger departmental chief officers are personally sympathetic. Why should they give them shelter from the storm in the present economic climate?

A chief officer of a small department emphasized the lack of protection felt by a small department in a retrenchment era:

> I have got the Chairman of our Committee on the important Policy and Resources Committee. That is very good, but only if he is also a Vice-Chairman of Education who I look upon as my biggest rival. It's a real disadvantage working 11 miles from County Hall with less chance to see the councillors. We are in difficulties because we run a library service used by school teachers, with project material and books for children, and that's paid for by the Education Committee and in the past all they do is hand over the appropriate sum of money to me each year. We employ the staff and work out the programme. Education now tell me that in order to achieve their economies next year

119

they are proposing to cut out any further payment towards the school library service. It's an invidious position because the staff are mine and I don't want to sack them but I have no money to keep them . . . it's a situation where one committee can make a financial decision which can totally upset the working of another committee. I have support on the Education Committee but I don't know what will happen. It's now got to the Finance Committee. Until recently my service came under Education. In the past they represented my service. When I was appointed, I wanted a committee independent from Education and the Education Chief Officer agreed. I did not think Education would have protected me in a crunch from severe cuts.

The smaller departments ruled out the possibility of attempting to organize and indirectly lead pressure groups in the county. In this rural county government, unlike the metropolitan boroughs, councillors could be both indifferent or hostile to pressure groups, if they felt the pressure group was attempting to pull them in a direction which threatened the dignity of their role as political representatives. They, in practice, in a manner similar to the politicians of Kensington and Chelsea in Dearlove's study, divided pressure groups into two: those who were given strong or weak legitimacy as reputable interest groups, and those who were seen as irresponsible.[73] Chief officers involved in mobilizing a constituency, outside the formal processes and informal understandings of the council, could find that the anti-populist culture of the politicians will fuel increased coolness and even antagonism to those chief officers suspected of having strong links to threatening local pressure groups. Paradoxically, the larger spending departments rarely need the support of active pressure groups in bargaining with politicians. They can have greater authority inside the deference culture, if they do not threaten councillors who must seem to be in control even if they cannot often formulate policy independently of the chief officers. In other local governments, however, legitimacy is given to broad-based pressure groups and this is linked to the politics of the local government. In Sheffield, the Trades Council, unions, social worker activities and the unemployed were not only sympathetically heard by the councillors but were allowed to place pressure on certain chief officers whom they were challenging on budgetary issues. The alliances between chief officers and councillors were thus weakened by the legitimacy given to some pressure groups who were able to utilize party and non-party networks to influence policy openly. Inside a Conservative-dominated rural county, where my main research was conducted, these types of pressure groups would be more harshly treated and the politicians' alliances with officers would be tighter in a defensive reaction.

In retrenchment contexts it is hypothesized that a spending department may hope to unload difficult or expensive activities onto another spending department. In an era of financial expansion the imperialist claims of spending departments on those areas which overlap between services are eagerly upheld. Under standstill and contraction contexts, if these areas of activity are considered to be peripheral to the traditional professional core of the service, they can be unloaded. The professionals can be differentially cross-pressured, as those at the top who play senior management roles can respond more fully to the pressures to unload them on other services, while disliking such a solution as much as their subordinate professionals. In harsh times, organizational or professional altruism tends to become more fragile. Corporate mechanisms to resolve these decolonization moves by formerly imperialist spending departments are not equipped to resolve resulting tensions. In an era of expansion, corporate management accepted the claims by professionals to work, space and client group and, in an era of retrenchment, the professionals have the power still to redefine their core professional tasks and possible clients.

In a situation of the past when a spending department, such as the social services, and local health authorities both claimed responsibility for such clients as the elderly, the handicapped and the disabled, joint funding becomes uncertain. The political regime in control of the local government may become more reluctant to accept short-term gains through joint funding if they carry long-term additional costs to their budgets. Interactions on these issues between chief officers and politicians produces strains in their alliances. Subordinate professionals may be critical of their chief officers' decision of a partial or total withdrawal from those tasks which are not laid down by statutory legislation. Such a move away from formerly assumed and taken for granted work roles, while functional for organizational survival becomes dysfunctional for clients and can cause legitimization problems for personnel.

Chief officers serving local governments, normally Labour Party controlled, which are potentially clashing with the demands for cuts in expenditure by central government, sometimes believe they should attempt to maintain some distance from the party regime. This is a new nuance in the professional-political relationship given the existing 'rules of the game' practiced through the committees and introduced new complexities into professional and politicians 'trust' relationships. In these situations some treasurers and chief executives decide sometimes to 'go public' and articulate their fears of a loss in grant from central government if local politicians do not cut expenditure to the extent demanded by central government. Other reactions can be seen as even more threatening by council members. One prominent Labour leader of a council has written: 'The words surcharge and fiduciary duty have become commonplace in local government circles. The natural caution of paid officers has increased, spreading to a whole range of hitherto perfectly acceptable areas of activity. The tendency to ensure maximum personal protection ... has been strengthened'.[74]

In South Yorkshire County Council, the Chief Executive began the procedure of obtaining an opinion (without being directed by the politicians) from a nationally known law firm. This indicated to the politicians that their nominal 'servant' thought he had the duty and the right to protect himself and other chief officers against possible legal action.

Similar steps seem to be taken in other local governments with the chief officers, rather than the councillors, deciding what questions should be asked and what lawyers consulted. This has an impact on retrenchment politics. If lawyers are asked for their interpretation of a current ruling, rather than asked for advice on how an actual court case might go, the area of space in which politicians can take options is significantly diminished. As news about lawyers' doubts circulates in local governments, it is normal for existing tensions inside the dominant party to grow with some resentment also of chief officers. However, other chief officers identify either personally with resistance to retrenchment strategies by local governments and feel professionally that their duty to the council should not include such tactics as may narrow its options.

Much of contingency theory concentrates primarily not on power but on the structural characteristics of organizations. The literature is diverse but its major contention is that organizational structure will be contingent on a number of factors: in particular, the environment, the technology it uses and its size. Relationships are established between organizational structure and situational variables, with the underlying assumptions that the level of organizational performance is related to the fit between structure and situational circumstances. Child has noted that, whilst establishing statistically the presence of associatons between organizational characteristics, contingency theory usually leaves the underlying processes to be inferred. An obsession with constraints, argues Child, implies that 'Organizational behaviour can best be understood with regard to functional imperatives rather than political action'.[75]

Contingency theory, according to Child, ignores the political process whereby power holders in organizations decide upon courses of strategy and action. In contingency theory, the actors are phased out of the system; behaviour, action, values and perceptions all have a secondary role. In Child's argument the thrust behind environmental forces may not precipitate change but will be assessed by organizational decision-makers, attempting to take positive steps to define and manipulate their corner of the environment. Greenwood, Hinings, Ranson and Walsh have modified contingency theory by acknowledging the distribution of power and influence between groups in local government structures and organizations. They conclude that socio-demographic and environmental variables are filtered by an organization whose output and performance is a function of the power and influence within it. However, lack of comparative fieldwork studies of local governments as political systems with 'rules of the game' which have particularistic aspects as well as more general characteristics, and the lack of weight given to an examination of the ideological variables, all illustrate the lacunas in this era of research. It would be accurate to argue that such determinations on the internal resource allocation system in a period of retrenchment, as Newton and Sharpe pointed out, 'Would include local administrative traditions, the calibre of councillors, the degree of professionalisation of the bureaucracy, the dispositions of both councillors and bureaucrats and the effectiveness of their mutual interaction'.[76] However, they also argue, 'It would be futile to pretend that even if it was possible to obtain all this information about the internal decision-making process, it could all be rendered into measurable indices, although it is possible that some features could be'.[76]

It would be both symbolic and sad if the writings on the impact of the fiscal crisis on organizational forms and processes, which are so integral to state and society in the UK, fail to meet the level of public needs.

NOTES AND REFERENCES

1 Karpik, L. (ed.). *Organization and environment*, 1978. Includes a number of attempts to resolve this issue.

2 Rhodes, R. A. W. *Control and power in central-local government relations*, 1981.

3 Salaman, G. Towards a sociology of organisational structure. *Sociological Review*, 1978, 26(3), 519-54.

4 Stanyer, J. *Understanding local government*, 1976.

5 Burgess, T. & Travers, T. *Ten billion pounds*, 1980.

6 Cockburn, C. *The local state*, 1977.

7 Dunleavy, P. *Urban political analysis*, 1980. Dunleavy, P. *The politics of mass housing in Britain, 1945-1975*, 1981.

8 Jones, G. W. Varieties of local politics. *Local Government Studies*, 1979 1(2), 17-32.

9 Alt, J. E. Some social and economic correlates of county borough expenditure. *British Journal of Political Science*, 1971, 1(1), 49-62.

10 Boaden, N. *Urban policy making*, 1971.

11 Danziger, J. N. *Making budgets*, 1978.

12 Karran, T. 'Borough politics' and 'county government'. *Policy and Politics*, 1982, 10(3), 317-42.

13 Jones, *op. cit.*

14 Karran, *op. cit.*

15 Lee, J. M. *Social leaders and public persons*, 1963.

16 Pettigrew, A. M. Information control as a power resource. *Sociology*, 1972, 6 (2), 187-204.

17 Aiken, M. and Bacharach, S. The urban system, politics and bureaucratic structure. In Karpik, L. (ed.). *Organization and environment*, 1978, 199-251.

18 Stewart, J. From growth to standstill. In Wright, M. (ed.). *Public spending decisions*, 1980, 9-24.

19 Levine, C. H. and Rubin, I. S. (eds.). *Fiscal stress and public policy*, 1980.

20 Levine, C. H., Rubin, I. S. and Wolohojian, G. G. Resource scarcity and the reform model. *Public Administration Review*, 1981, Nov.-Dec., 619-28.

21 Cyert, R. M. and March, J. G. *A behavioural theory of the firm*, 1963.

22 Merton, R. K. Bureaucratic structure and personality. In his *Social theory and social structure*, Enl. ed., 1968, 249-60.

23 Pugh, D. S. (ed.). *Organization theory*, 1971.

24 Greenwood, R. *et al. Patterns of management in local government*, 1980.

25 *Ibid.*, 76-7.

26 Greenwood, R. Pressures from Whitehall. In Rose, R. and Page, E. (eds.). *Fiscal stress in cities*, 1982.

27 Alexander, A. *The politics of local government in the United Kingdom*, 1982.

28 Quoted in: *Ibid.*, 123.

29 Hepworth, N. P. Local authority expenditure. *Three Banks Review*, 1980, 127, 3-24.

30 Hinings, C. R., Greenwood, R., Ranson, S. and Walsh, K. The organisational consequences of financial restraint in local government and Greenwood, R., Hinings, C. R., Ranson, S. and Walsh, K. Incremental budgeting and the assumption of growth. Both in Wright, M. (ed.). *Public spending decisions*, 1980, 49-67 and 25-48. See also Greenwood, R. Fiscal pressure and local government in England and Wales. In Hood, C. and Wright, M. (eds.). *Big government in hard times*, 1981, 77-79.

31 Hinings *et al., op. cit.*, 67.

32 Jönsson, S. *A city administration facing stagnation*, 1982.

33 Greenwood, R., Hinings, C. R. and Ranson, S. The politics of the budgetary process in English local government. *Political Studies*, 1977, 25(1), 27. A footnote insists that 'our treatment is consistent with ... treatment of the policy process as a bargaining process'.

34 Ranson, S., Hinings, B., Greenwood, R. and Walsh, K. Values and the organization of local governments. In Dunkerley, D. and Salaman, G. (eds.). *Internal yearbook of organisational studies, 1980*, 1981, Ch. 11, 197-221.

35 Stewart, *op. cit.*

36 Glennerster, H. Prime cuts. *Policy and Politics*, 1980, 8(4), 367-82.

37 Bebbington, A. and Ferlie, E. *Budgeting and planning in the social services departments in the face of cutbacks*, 1980.

38 Ferlie, E. and Judge, K. Retrenchment and rationality in the personal social services. *Policy and Politics*, 1981, 9(3), 311-30.

39 Rhodes, R. A. W. The lost world of British local politics? Local Government Studies, 1975, 1(3), 39-60. A similar point is made in Collins, C. A., Hinings, C. R. and Walsh, K. The officer and the councillor in local government. *Public Administration Bulletin*, 1978, 28, 34-50.

40 Saunders, P. They make the rules. *Policy and Politics*, 1975, 4, 31-58.

41 Albrow, M. *The study of organisations – objectivity or bias?*, 1968.

42 Zimmerman, D. Record keeping and the intake process in a public welfare agency. In Wheeler, S. (ed.). *On record*, 319-54.

43 Study Group on Local Authority Management Structures. *The New Local Authorities: Management and Structure* (Bains Report), 1972.

44 Greenwood, R. The local authority budgetary process. In Both, T. A. (ed.). *Planning for welfare*, 1979, 78-96.

45 Hill, M. J. *The sociology of public administration*, 1972.

46 This argument is also discussed in Newby, H., Bell, C., Rose, D. and Saunders, P. *Property paternalism and power*, 1978. See also Grant, W. P. Local councils, conflict and 'rules of the game'. *British Journal of Political Science*, 1971, 1(2) 253-6.

47 Haywood, S. Decision-making in local government. *Local Government Studies*, 1977, Oct., 41-55.

48 Marshall, J. (ed.). *The history of Lancashire County Council*, 1977, 183.

49 Newby *et al., op. cit.*, 252-6.

50 Kesselman, M. *The ambiguous consensus*, 1967, 136. and Grant, W. P. Non-partisanship in British local politics. *Policy and Politics*, 1973, 1(3), 241-54.

51 Newton, K. *Second city politics*, 1976.

52 Green, D. G. Inside local government. *Local Government Studies*, 1980, 6(1), 33-49. See also Alexander, A. *Local government in Britain since reorganisation*, 1982.

53 Elcock, H. *Local government*, 1982, 85.

54 Blowers, A. Checks and balances. *Public Administration*, 1977, 55, 305-16.

55 Self, P. *Administrative theories and politics*, 1972, 161.

56 Kogan, M. with W. Van Der Eyken. *County hall*, 1973, 47.

57 Dearlove, J. *The re-organization of British local government*, 1979.

58 Blowers, *op. cit.*

59 Heclo, H. H. The councillor's job. *Public Administration*, 1969, 47, 185-202. One councillor told Heclo that 'policy and administration have actually been reversed. The officer formulates the policy and the committee argues about the technicalities of administering it'.

60 Keith-Lucas, B. and Richards, P. G. *A history of local government in the 20th century*, 1978, 184. They state that 'there can be little doubt about the growth of disciplined party groups inhibited Clerks and Treasurers'.

61 Lee, *op. cit.*

62 Newton, *op. cit.*

63 Alexander, *op. cit.* 104.

64 Jones, A. *The politics of educational planning in County Durham*, 1979. Mimeo.

65 Alexander, *op. cit.*, 113.

66 Karran, *op. cit.*

67 *Ibid.*, 337.

68 Green, D. G. *Power and party in an English city*, 1981, 119.

69 Newton, *op. cit.*, 163.

70 Greenwood, R. *et al. In pursuit of corporate rationality*, 1976.

71 Becquart-Leclerq, J. Rational power and systemic articulation in French local polity. In Karpik, L. (ed.). *Organization and environment*, 1978, 253-92.

72 The recommendations of the Bain's report are given in Alexander, A. *Local government in Britain since reorganisation*, 1982, 82-6.

73 Dearlove, J. *The politics of policy in local government*, 1973. Saunders, P. *Urban politics*, 1980.

74 Blunkett, D. A truly public transport. *New Statesman*, 1982, 19 Feb., 8-9.

75 Child, J. Organisational structure, environment and performance. *Sociology*, 6, 1-22.

76 Newton, K. and Sharpe, L. J. Local outputs research: some reflections and proposals. *Policy and Politics*, 1977, 5, 61-82.

CHAPTER FIVE

Professionals, the politics of role and finance: resource allocation inside local government

The rise to a position of bureaucratic authority of elite professionals in local government in the nineteenth and twentieth centuries has not been studied nationally or on a comparative basis between local governments. However, a body of historical and social science knowledge on the social background of local politicans, their values and impact on policy is in existence. Furthermore, under what radicals called 'old corruption', municipal office was regarded as a form of property and a respect for such 'rights' acted as a barrier against bureaucratic reform. The absence of a bureaucratic history has meant, as Rhodes states 'that one of the major actors in the decision-making process is noticeable primarily for his absence from studies of local politics'.[2]

This silence in the literature is in dramatic contrast to the numerous studies of leading civil servants who placed their stamp and occupational values on so much of nineteenth and twentieth century central government legislation. Lambert, for example, stated that civil servants 'acted as statesmen in disguise, using personal influences, public pressures, exploiting laconic discretions, to achieve their ends. More importantly, it marks the advent to power in government of a particularly potent type of civil servant'.[3]

Nor was the potency of expertise a purely central phenomenon. Hennock quotes Lovell's 1908 text which argued that the position of professional experts in local government was so central to the whole process that the excellence of municipal government was roughly proportional to the amount of influence that the salaried officials were allowed to exercise. According to Lovell the main motivating force behind municipal government was to be found largely in these professionals.[4] The lack of research into the rise and consolidation of this social category is still unfortunately coupled with a lack of research into the significance of contemporary professionals in the budget process and other areas of policy.

Any contemporary study of the location of the professionals in finance politics must also penetrate deeper than the contemporary moment. The barriers which check and balance professional authority and legitimacy at the local level have a singular history which is, as has been earlier remarked, unexplored. Professions and role relationships in local government have been shaped by the networks of social and political relationships which sometimes have had complex histories and influenced local traditions in local government. It may be also tentatively argued that, while the local government system today has strikingly less financial autonomy from central government than the nineteenth-century local government system, role relationships between professionals and politicians may have some similarities in structural nuances as well as important differences. The establishment of local government created professional roles and gave them a density beyond any individual occupant's history.

Recently Dearlove has pointed out that:

> The policy-administration dichotomy is a quite inadequate way to describe the ... division of labour between elected and official participants ... the issue is not whether officials have power, but to what extent they have power ... it is not possible to generalise over time, place and issue as to the relationship between councillors and officers ... it is important to try to specify the variables which will have a bearing on the impact of the different participants.[5]

The very weakness of bureaucratic authority *vis-a-vis* the local politicans in the nineteenth century is significantly different from the post-Bain era.

A historian, Fraser, in a study of urban politics in Victorian England, made a number of useful comments on the structural position of professionals in municipal politics. He noted how the professionals were a legitimate part of the local social networks and how this tended to diminish professional neutrality in policy construction in local government. Central government in this period had not the strength or inclination to force through statutory legislation, which would loosen the subordination of the professionals to the interplay of functional and political strife inside the urban elites. Indeed many professionals themselves may have resisted legislation that give them bureaucratic autonomy. After all, positions in local government administration were seen as part of a mechanism by which spoils were rewards for the visitors: 'In Leeds the old town clerk was manoeuvred into resignation and replaced by ... who had acted for the Liberals as agent ...'

In Liverpool, the treasurer was appointed at least as much for his significance as a Liberal activist as for his financial skills. 'Attorneys naturally looked to town clerkships and bankers to treasureships'.[6]

It may be speculated that, if they were successful and influential professionals and bankers in the municipalities, they could potentially transfer part of their social authority to their professional roles inside local government. However, their dependency on factional patron-client relationships increased their professional vulnerability if the political wheel of fortune turned. In addition, many of these local government roles could be filled by occupants on a part-time basis. Briggs notes that in Birmingham from 1869 'there was a tradition that the Town Clerk carried on his private business as a solicitor as well'.[7] Briggs also noted that the municipal reform programme of Chamberlain 'could not have carried out its increasingly complicated work had it not been for the assistance of a growing City Treasurer's department ... in 1867 when W. R. Hughes became City Treasurer of Birmingham he was assisted by a book-keeper and a youth: in 1898 there were twenty clerks and a Deputy'.[8]

In local government in the late nineteenth century, unlike today, the key professionals were not dependent solely on the authority and status of local government for their status and income in their local communities. Very often they were influential professionals who were roughly equal in social position to the members of the town or county council. In one sense it could be argued that they owed their social authority to the new roles they played inside the local government system. Even much later Maud and Finer remarked on the then comparatively recent total full-time commitment of the key elite professionals on the status, power and authority of the councils for their role authority.[9] The relative autonomy of the earlier professionals from council bureaucratic control has been summed up thus: 'The convention of appointing solicitors as part-time clerks (or bankers, as part-time treasurers) gave them a peculiar position; as professional men they tended to regard the councils as clients rather than as employers, and to regard themselves as bound by their professional ethnics and conventions rather than by the orders of the local authority'.[10]

The great differences in salary and role authority among professionals in comparable positions in different local authorities perhaps was closely linked to the dominance of local particularisms and specific patron-client relations.

In recent times it has been part of a 'conventional wisdom' that chief officers, the supposed servants of a local authority, encroach on policy making to the point where they can in fact, if not in theory, be the senior partners to their political masters. In the nineteenth century, and for a large part of the twentieth century, it was the other way around with politicians 'encroaching' on the work space and authority of the officers though the politicians did not think of it in that light and indeed regarded the encroachment as a legitimate part of the political role. This aspect of the role played by the elected members for a very long period was particularly marked in the crucial area of finance. Hennock said:

> Until 1855 the Leeds borough treasurer had been little more than a cashier receiving and paying out money as he was told while the whole burden of drawing up estimates fell to the chairman of the finance committee. In Birmingham in the late 1860's it was the chairman of the finance committee who devised a new system of accounts as well as cheaper method of raising loans ... For another generation powerful chairmen of the finance committee, drawn from the circles of big businessmen continued to control the municipal finances in great detail'.[11]

The comparative lack of professional authority and the surprising strength of professional subordination to patron-client relationships had long-term consequences. It could be argued that it was only the partial withdrawal of the formerly dominant economic and social notables in local government which created the political space which allowed the professional experts to rise to bureaucratic power in alliance with politicians from the subordinated social layers in the margins of formerly dominant elites. This alliance according to one important study of county administration[12] was consolidated by the passing of the 1929 Local Government Act by central government.

It is suggestive that relatively recent studies of Birmingham, Newcastle-under-Lyne and Bristol[13] failed to trace any but a weak connection between council politicians and the local social-economic notables. On the other hand, a recent study of Croydon by Saunders[14] found a strong business representation on the council. However, whatever the social composition of a council, the alliance between elite professionals and politicians who represent a variety of interest groups and social categories is the corner-stone of local government politics. Though the professionals are formally only the servants of the council, it could be argued that in practice collectively they institutionally represent the strongest potential limitation on the power of the politicians for they initiate discussions (often as a result of central government or internal departmental stimuli, but also sometimes in response to politicans' own suggestions). They are also collectively involved in the role of actively resolving policy 'problems'. The close relationship between an elite professional in charge of a spending department has been often compared to a double-edged sword, for if the politician uses the expertise of the professional, it is also the case that the former can influence the latter through the information he (or she) chooses to make available and the way options are presented. As Heclo points out, information and expertise constitute crucial power resources in the increasingly complex world of local government.[15] Or as Weber observed, 'The question is always who controls the existing bureaucratic machinery. And such control is possible only in a very limited degree to persons who are not technical specialists'.[16]

Local government is both a bureaucratic organization and the kind of organization whereby elite professionals modify its Weberian functionality and transform it into a professional organization with the dominant characteristics of professional controls and culture.[17]

Today's fiscal crisis of local government has altered not merely the important financial relationships between local government and central government. The crisis has, in an uneven manner, the potential to force a number of important as well as marginal readjustments to the organizational cultures of local government. The role relationships of the elite professionals can flow into new as well as familiar patterns. The impact of the fiscal crisis on the elite professionals at the top of the hierarchy both at the level of policy, but also at the level of the social organisation of authority, is subject to new strains.

To trace this impact of the fiscal crisis further may be of service as it allows the study of the world-taken-for-granted in which all the major actors are situated. Stewart and others have speculated that the move from the growth budget base to one of standstill and actual decline has the potential radically to alter and shake up the expectations around growth which, while not written down, are written into the procedures and structure of local government in the sense that those procedures and structures take the assumptions for granted. An occupational strain, perhaps even a value crisis, for those elite professionals who run spending departments, is the enforced recognition that growth has been halted and that partial contraction is a strong possibility.

In the past, the alliance between officers and politicians was built on growth insofar as growth has allowed a network of compromise understandings to exist between potentially antagonistic sectors of local government. In a growth situation all recognize that a relatively small change becomes of great significance if there is an expectation of continuing small changes. Stewart has argued that, in such situations 'disjointed incrementalism can become jointed incrementalism on the assumption of continuing growth'.[18]

The contest over the allocation of growth came to be seen in this period as the key decision by all of the major actors in the budgetary process. Both traditional budget procedures and newly developed corporate planning procedures focused on the increment of growth as the vital issue in the resource allocation process and as the main mechanism for inputs of political decisions on significant changes in spending patterns.

Both professionals and politicians recognized the central importance of the increment of growth and took its strengthening of censensus politics for granted. It was not necessary, for example, for one alliance of officers and councillors centred around a spending department to challenge all the bids of another spending department, or for the major monitoring roles of chief executive and treasurer to impose a strict financial control with no possibility of movement on expenditure items. For example, it is useful to see virement packages as forming part of the bargaining process. It must be emphasized that the increment of growth tended to provide the means of buying consensus: bargaining was easier inside corporate management since present concessions by one spending department could compensate in the future by another. Growth allowed diluted forms of relatively weak departmentalism to become acceptable and this formed the basis for what passed as corporate management in many local governments. Fieldwork research tentatively hints at significant changes in organizational relationships. One treasurer stated:

> I don't know what is going on outside but there is less co-operation than there has ever been simply because pressures are so great that each Chief Officer is obliged to defend his corner whether he wants to or not. The only corporate decision we are likely to get is the corporate decision on the distribution of the latest batch of unpleasantness. In practice, corporate decisions are no more than a collective decision to protect that particular individual. While we probably never had a strong corporate system we never quite had these pressures on us. Politicians on committees are also clashing amongst themselves and dragging in Chief Officers or you could argue that Chief Officers are dragging them in.[19]

Because of the centrality of the increment of growth and of the internal discourses about its allocation, bidding strategies emerged in numerous local government units, through which alliances built round spending departments made claims upon the increment. The norms and standards produced by central government departments were significant guidelines, and statutory requirements for local government services in a growth era could be used by spending departments as the basis for bids for the increment of growth. Thus it was common for personal social services departments to look to the ten-year social services plan required of local government units by the

Department of Health and Social Services in 1972. The norms for service provision embedded in these guidelines represented increases in manpower two or three times greater than the existing levels. Such norms were strong cards, as they meant the possibility of national government political support for such elite professionals as the Directors of Personal Social Service Departments. These national plans also created linkages and alliances between senior civil servants who acted as brokers and the spending department's professionals and political allies.

> On certain issues professionals will attempt to persuade central government to give local authorities discretionary powers in the belief that their members will enjoy increased discretion while on other issues they will attempt to persuade central government to make measures statutorily binding on local authorities similarly in the belief that the hands of their colleagues will strengthen within their local authorities.[20]

Part of the rise to power and authority of local government experts can after all be explained in relationship to the charter and protection given the professionals by senior civil servants in central government, who desired some checks on the latest possibility of a serious contradiction between central and local government, if a right or left radical political input totally dominated local policy. The central government desired a neutral body of influential professionals. Until recently the assumption of growth allowed a weakening of the traditional fears and distrust of central governments by the elite professionals and their political 'masters' and strengthened the assertion of a neutral harmony of interests' ideology.

Role relationships in the present period have the potentiality to operate on a relatively different set of assumptions. In a situation of standstill or relative decline in financial resources, bidding strategies have no immediately obvious role. Local governments can be expected to give a very much reduced role to those national standards and guidelines that require for their implementation a growth in resources. A possible weakening of statutory legislation may also withdraw some of the cards which elite professionals and their political allies could use in the past to obtain resources from both local and central government. One Chief Officer commented;

> In the last 18 months, central government has not given a single statement or indication of what its policies are. We have had statements about spending guidelines and only euphemisms about protecting those in greatest need: a total retreat from a clear statement of policy which could commit resources. On one hand DHSS continues to increase the amount of money available for joint finance and the Department of Environment tells me to reduce expenditure in absolute terms. In the past we have sometimes gained from contradictory policy in central government but now we lose. In the past we used guidelines which were convenient to your argument and rejected those which went against it. Sometimes it would discredit me to argue for those guidelines.

It may well be argued that a weakening of statutory legislation may formally allow the heads of spending departments in local authorities more space in innovating specific programmes whilst cutting back others. However, in a period of standstill or relative decline of financial resources, it may well be the case that chief officers perceive a weakening of statutory legislation as a threat to vital areas of their services. In a similar manner it is possible that, with a standstill or a relative decline in resources, the elite professionals now have mixed feelings about capital programmes they have welcomed in the past and been allocated by central government and may even tactically advise their politicians to reject them if such programmes imply a commitment at some later stage to assume direct financial responsibilities for such a project. In a context where further growth was automatically assumed, the basic assumption in such a situation was that the resources would be there, over time, to meet these commitments. It is a possible irony that joint financing, which previously used to be a strong card chief officers held in gaining in the internal resource allocation process, could be now a possible threat to the defence of existing expenditure. A number of policy possibilities arise, which have not been tested in fieldwork research, with regard to how corporate management in local government units will meet the cold wind blowing in from the external environment. It may well be that a weakening of consensus politics may emerge with a wide variety of nuances. Stewart has speculated that one possibly obvious reaction is to strengthen the lines of authority and control and accept a weakening of those elements dependent upon a consensus culture, with all the unquestioned informal and formal agreements which oil it.

It is also possible to anticipate a relative decline in the chief officer's management team as an expression of the consensus culture and a strengthening of the central political and finance roles of chief executive and treasurer. Where the chief officer does not seek a crucial expansion of role authority, the role of the treasurer may well emerge in a yet stronger position. If this is the case, it could be expected that an increase in the authority of the politicians on the finance committee and such central control committees as the policy and resources committee could also follow as well.[21] However, it must be emphasized that few case studies exist of the impact of the present financial situation on role relationships and organizational forms in local government units. Those case studies which do exist are not empirically based on the current internal bargaining policies of local government but emphasize the final set of local decisions.[22]

In an era of growth, alliances between spending departments and their respective politicians are probably relatively consistent. In a period of contraction or even standstill new strains may enter these notional alliances, especially if departments compete for resources. In a context where no competition basically takes place an alliance can persist. Thus in one Metropolitan authority a chief officer stated:

> My alliances here are with the housing department. Our interests do not clash. His budget is almost entirely capital and my budget is almost entirely revenue. In the Chief Officers' Group he will not challenge me for recovering things on revenue and if he get away with something on capital it does not affect me much. Also neither of us like the education department as we feel they have too much money anyway.

In a county authority, the chief officers of education and social services were both extremely conscious of the strains in their alliance of professional interests when financial resources came into the picture. It is important to emphasize that personal relations were extremely good and the two chief officers felt that their private and professional values meant that they had similar views on many issues. The Chief Education Officer could state: 'I welcomed the new social service department when it was formed and my department works closely with his. For example, I accept their social service workers inside my service instead of having our own education welfare officers'.

He argued that this was not a recent phenomenon but it went further back into the early years of the 1970's:

> I became conscious of social services eating into my budget from about late 1973 when it began to be of importance. Before then, while none of us claimed we had enough money for all the things we wanted to do, we were expanding. I remember sitting, from late 1973, in meeting after meeting and what I saw was that four or five of us were actually challenging the bids of our colleagues in order to defend our corner. In relation to social services I found I was asking whether it was really necessary to estimate the provisions for the elderly at quite the rate at which it was estimated ... In 1976 and 1977 education was hard hit because I was being asked to trim my primary school teaching budget because of falling rolls. It's very difficult to trim proportionately with the fall in school rolls. At precisely that time the social services were expanding their manpower very quickly.

It is ironic that, while the guardianship element in the roles of the central monitoring and administration departments should be taken for granted by the textbooks in local government administration, all chief officers in the local authority were quite conscious that the Treasurer and the Chief Executive were also heads of spending departments. In a context of cuts, such organizational strains in relationships became apparent. Whilst it has been tentatively argued by some INLOGOV theorists that standstill and contraction bring a possibility of an increased rational budget construction with the possible elimination of subjective and political inputs, it may be that the opposite is taking place. A deputy chief officer from the same local authority stated:

> I still remember when the Chairman of Finance went behind my back to my Chairman to say how much do you really want? Is it half a million? All the objective arguments given earlier to the finance committee and my committee, in a context where officers had attempted to move away from merely defending their own corner, went by the board. However objective the exercise, the informal understandings between political colleagues, depending upon their respective influence within the party group, were still very important and determined what happened. In that case it was to the benfit of my service that without any more attempted objective analysis a chairman said well let's give them half a million.

Any exploration of the resource allocation processes in local governments must illuminate the possible patterns of interface interactions between certain chief officers and influential politicians who form the core of what Danziger called the 'budgetary elite'. However, while the relationship of politician to professional is of crucial importance and has been recognized as such in the liberal democratic theory of local government, the inter-organizational relationships between the chief officers themselves has more rarely, if ever, been noticed. Perhaps an influential legalism which officially noted these professionals only in relations of subordination to politicians or to the head of the bureaucratic apex, the chief executive, is responsible for the invisibility of these important actors. It could also be true, as earlier stated, that the local government literature too readily assumes that the problem areas have already been mapped out.[23]

It is quite possible that in the resource allocation process role relationships in the context of bids on expenditure are circumscribed by the more or less dominant incrementalism in budget construction. However, the options for bargaining on the significant margins of the budget remain. Also the technology of one budget construction model over another allows for a possible choice even in a context of standstill or relative decline in fiscal resources from central government. Thus, as Greenwood acknowledges, the 'extended percentage pool' offers the budgetary elite the ability to switch resources from one service to another by 'comparing and choosing cuts'.[24] This technology could be at times more useful to the budgetary elite than the simple percentage pool whose characteristic is a lack of the flexibility which does not allow for the switching of resources across services. On the other hand, it may well be a decision of keeping expenditure tied down to the existing service categories by a non-decision which retains the technology of the simple percentage pool system. Such a choice weakens the possibility of new political contests over resource allocation. The finance professionals' expertise in such a situation allows them greater authority *vis-a-vis* the politicans in the appropriate, apparently neutral, choice of budgetary technology. Other factors in the choice of budget technology can be subjective. One chief executive said:

> One of the reasons we went over to the target budgeting system is that about twelve years ago we used to have a councillor who would always spring up at the rate levying meetings and propose a penny off here and a few hundred pounds off there ... as a result practically everybody, members and officers, got fed up with him and wanted some other system of doing the rates which did not involve a sweating process and that was one good reason we went over to target budgeting.

In an era where central governments's new statutory legislation could lessen the partial autonomy of local government or even transform the situation into what Burgess and Travers[25] argue is a Whitehall takeover of the town halls, it would be unwise to equate the loss of power to make significant choices by local politicians with a significant loss of professional power. Indeed, any collapse of political power over the administering of services by local politicians may well be inherited by the collective body of professionals, whose roles will not only make them dependent on the strata of political administrators at Whitehall, but also make central government vulnerable by its increased dependency on the local elite professionals. In such a situation 'even if one partner appears completely to dominate the other, the dependence remains reciprocal'.[26] Bargaining and negotiations would not be excluded from the authority given and taken by the collective communities of elite professionals. This does not negate the strong commitment to the partial autonomy of local government in the value systems of many individual professionals. Indeed, in some respects, they collectively are amongst the more consistent defenders of localism as a legitimate and efficient balance in liberal democracy. To qualify this, one county treasurer commented:

> Quite a lot of professionals I think would be perfectly happy to be an extended arm of Whitehall. Their professional perception of their role is comparatively clear and I think they could accept a disappearance of the local political input with almost total equanimity. They are not concerned with local government as such; they are concerned very much with a particular service. Among Treasurers there has been a certain politicisation of their roles and an increased consciousness that they help to defend local government. Treasurers' strongest alliances are inside local government rather than outside.

However, an emerging corporatism has integrated them through a network of integrative ideological bargaining processes into the structure of central government. This type of corporatism, as Rhodes, Winkler and Panitch[27] have argued, organizes the core activities of central government and allows subordinate social categories significant inputs into national state policy. The Consultative Council on Local Government Finance, established in 1976, is one obvious political and organizational mechanism which allows a certain bargaining pattern between different sectors of government represented by professionals whose cultures are interlocked. This alliance, between civil servants from central government and local professionals, sealed in the mechanism of corporatism, can be examined for example in a report which was part of the local government expenditure review and which argued that the social services budget was unrealistically inadequate, even before recent planned reductions.[28] It can also be argued that the relative loss in authority over recent central government policy by such corporatist bodies may explain why a confidential report was leaked to a national newspaper in the possible hope of strengthening the bargaining power of the alliance of civil servants and local government professionals who prepared the report. The dilemmas produced by corporatism were articulated by one treasurer: 'CIPFA is interested in the defence of local government, but paradoxically they have agreed to help build a new audit system which will be the arm of central government. They don't expect to get professional control but I think they hope they can influence it fairly substantially'. Research on the resource allocation system in one local authority, a county, supplemented by selected interviews in others, have established that obvious, as well as less obvious, patterns emerge in a budget contraction period. As one influential former treasurer stated in a textbook: 'Some check on departments is essential ... for those responsible for the services have every incentive to expand them, and at the same time are not subject to a profits incentive, or an automatic test of efficiency'.

Quoting a government report, Marshall supported the Haldane Committee's argument: 'on the whole, experience seems to show that the interests of the taxpayer cannot be left to the spending departments'.[29] Evidence presented earlier in this chapter implied that the roles of guardianship are political and technical and the spending departments recognize this even if the central administration department's chief officers are ambivalent. The neutrality of the guardians is not abstract but shaped by political conjunctures and contexts, as well as professional ideologies and personal values. The role of revenue guardian is integral to the institutional relationships and roles inside the Treasury, both in local government and central government, though the internal organizational strains and determinations in both are not identical. Those elite professionals who manage spending departments accept the formal logic implicit in the controlling and monitoring roles of treasurers and chief executives who, in turn, also accept that the logic of those non-finance professionals is to 'fight their own corner' in the allocation of resources. However, the guardianship role of the treasurer allows an intervention and support for one department against another. One treasurer stated: 'Education cut, from their budget, youth projects, and they then tried to swing that cut to another committee with a separate funding arrangement. I opposed them at committees. It was only £17,000 but it creates difficult tensions'.

This arena of action inside the corporate management system can thus integrate a significant input from local politicians which can vary between parties and inside parties. Significant determinants on resource allocation are difficult, if not impossible, to analyze in a hierarchy of determinations but, as Newton and Sharpe point out, other empirical data presented implies that determinations 'would include local administrative traditions, the calibre of councillors, the degree of professionalisation of the bureaucracy, the disposition of both councillors and bureaucrats, and the effectiveness of their mutual interaction'. However, as Newton and Sharpe also argue: 'It would be futile to pretend that, even if it was possible to obtain all this information about the internal decision-making process, it could all be rendered into measurable indices, although it is possible that some features could be'.[30]

Work culture and the political culture of the specific local authority are inter-locked with the internal 'traditions' of interface negotiations between local politicians and professionals and between different professionals. It is the failure of Danziger[31] to explore the arenas of administration interface politics and the macro-determinations on the micro-processes that makes his largely positivistic methodology one-dimensional. His limited use of qualitative data still gives his work some superiority over the typical resource allocation study. As Newton and Sharpe dryly remark: 'The typical output study seems to be ... more and more elegant with analytical techniques being applied to poorer and poorer data ... the poorer the data the more elegant the theoretical model'.[32]

Inside every local government corporate management system – no matter what its real relationship to departmentalism or the peculiarity of its local political traditions – professionals who manage spending and control departments are interdependent on each other. The quotation already given from Marshall, however, also does not rule out sharp differences, even bitter contests, over policy authority and resources as empirical data demonstrates. Spending departments face control departments in a consistent and legitimate struggle to carry out projects. To examine the patterns of contestations and those 'rules of the game' which establish the boundaries of such conflicts is an obvious task of any study. The 'rules of the game' are partly given by the occupational culture of the professionals, the local political inputs and the overall general economic climate. A dramatic change in the economic climate can signal that a period of contraction of money is likely to modify and even transform the meaning of the existing rules as Stewart has speculated. It is instructive to note that one study of cuts in spending inside central government in the 1960s remarked on how 'Cuts . . . were done in ways totally contrary to the rules of the game. Undertakings entered into in a proper way with the Treasury were broken. Cutting was done by horse trading, plus political push and pull'.[33]

Rules which emerged from a period of expansion have to be unlearnt or modified by professionals or else they undercut the search for a new strategic strength in a reworking of existing institutional relationships. The very success of a spending department in the past in gaining resources can be a barrier to learning the new mechanisms for safeguarding existing resources.

The culture of elite professionals is and has been based on mutual 'trust' by chief officers who know they will have to continue to reach agreements with each other year after year on issue after issue. In a similar manner to the political administrators studied by Heclo and Wildavsky, they collectively believe that if professionalism means anything it means knowing how to treat members of one's own group. The system recognizes mutual dependence even, indeed especially, in the midst of conflict. Such mutual trust only retains its dynamic when relations of near equality are the norm among elite professionals. Unevenness in power between departments can weaken trust and trade-offs since bargaining is unequal. Trust and interdependence is based on the assumption that chief officers can sway and influence the councillors who sit on the committees and this in turn feeds back into the resource allocation system. In a similar manner to processes in central government, the informal mechanisms of a telephone call, lunch, or the chance meeting, provide the occasion to negotiate differences and arrive at solutions even before they reach the committee or the chief officers' group. Decisions, then, are very often worked out in early, bilateral consultations between departments on a face-to-face basis. Normally, the senior finance professionals based in the treasury exercise control over spending departments' expenditure by not always giving flat 'no's' to departmental proposals. If it did, it would strikingly reduce the space for negotiations and risk the spending departments using their collective political strength to put pressure on the finance committee to overturn the finance professionals' decision. A consistent 'no' by the treasury and its finance committee runs the long-term risk of a total politicization of the various degrees of corporate management even if in the short run it can be forced through; it also implies a collective long-term reduction of professional authority even if in the short run some professionals may gain. It is obvious that the interdependence between finance professionals based on the treasury and the professionals who manage the spending departments is always subject to strains and even important crisis in a cuts era. To the treasury, financial institutional security denotes being protected against surprise by sudden expenditures. To the spending departments, being secure means they can go ahead with long-term projects, confident that the money will not suddenly be pulled away. There are real conflicts built into this situation which cannot be dismissed as merely failures of communication. However, the oil of good working relations can and does deaden the impact of these conflicts and allows space for compromises to be negotiated, though these compromises depend on enough money being available as well as the reproduction of the organizational culture. One ex-treasurer, now a chief executive, stated:

> I remember a real dust up in the committee with the previous Chief Education Oficer because he put something forward I didn't agree with and he had not consulted me beforehand. Actually, tactically he did it very well though I opposed the proposal. He could have squashed me completely because then I was quite junior and he an officer of some stature. However, he said it looks as if this had not been properly discussed so we must withdraw the proposal from committee. The present Treasurer and myself may have differences of opinion but we try to make sure we both have similar positions before we go to committee. If we don't the council members will not see it as just two points of view but a choice in backing one of us against the other. We both think it better, if differences exist, to put up a range of options and not let the members know which of us is supporting which option.

Spending departments' alliances materialize normally when they find a common interest in assaulting financial regulations that affect them all adversely or another department. However, while there are few active alliances among departments, this is not to say departments fail to act in unison. Co-operation among the professionals who manage departments is still a powerful cultural integrative mechanism and takes the passive form of never violently cutting each other down in front of the chief executive and treasurer at a formal chief officers' meeting, no matter what may be said in private. Bids can be discussed and criticized and that is acceptable. Departments do not usually, in public, offer up each other's projects to solve a common cause and offer no gratuitous aid to the treasury by publicly criticizing each other, as it can make the search for future allies more difficult. The lack of comparability between some spending departments' budget-base helps this realization of interdependence as does the realization that once competition and conflicts over resources go too far, short-term gains for an individual professional can be wiped out the next time round with permanent damage to the existing balances inside working relationships. However, it is unwise to ignore the strong external financial pressures on informal culture agreements. Willingness to co-operate has its obvious and not so obvious limits. As one chief officer stated, looking back at nearly two years of organizing contraction in financial resources:

> I feel it has become more difficult to behave with the same respect for existing relationships with council members and chief officers. We have planning exercises where we are asked by members and the Treasurer and Chief Executive to think about the unthinkable while we hope our supporters among the members can turn it into an abstract exercise which will not be too painful. Our confidence in our existing relationships with

council members is not very high at times as they are volatile in the range of responses they make. One day they say further cuts are not possible; the next they vote for further cuts. Over the past year several times I've been asked to prepare options for cuts. Each time I've prepared a list and the first part is taken and the second part is rejected. The next time I start with the second part and the third line so that ultimately you get to the point where you would become wary of writing down the options. Past experiences tell you that, whilst this time round that's unlikely to happen, the next time you've written it down as an option it's only a matter of time before it becomes acceptable to council members.

It is the lack of consistency among the local politicans in the majority party and the weakening of the potential to influence members that forced the elite professionals to retreat to the terrain of corporate management and interdependence on each other, to protect their collective authority and their service. When the known political environment at the local level, as well as at a national level, becomes uncontrollable as well as unpredictable the common agreements among officers sometimes reveal possible new strengths as well as new weaknesses. Each chief officer estimates the potential strength of his or her alliances in the local community and the relevant social soil and builds a bidding strategy on to that while realizing that potential community support, contrary to pluralist theory, is not always transformed into significant political input. One chief officer explained differences in tactics and strategy in the following manner:

> I suspect my attitude and the attitude of the Education Chief Officer is fundamentally different both in this local authority and nationally. If the Education Department is asked to spell out in a seminar on further cuts, Education's reaction nowadays is to take a very broad brush approach and to portray a situation where, for example, you are making massive cuts in the 16 to 19 year old education facilities, the possible withdrawal of school meals, etc. Horrifying and dramatic issues in which many people in the local authority would be directly affected. Education politically can afford to gamble knowing how much local public opinion would be affected. Special Services budgets are not under such global heads as Education and that is significant as it means I can't use such a strategy. So when in the last analysis I have been instructed to make cuts to an amount of money, I must be certain those are the things which would go. Also my internal departmental structure and ethos is different from Education and that has a significance for my cut strategy. Small but important cuts are just barely acceptable though demoralizing. We bleed from many small wounds while Education can dramatically bleed from one or two large ones and hope to get them reversed or modified.

The different services have different budget structures, different support networks and different strategies forced on them in a cut and contraction era. Some departments propose offsetting savings which they hope their political allies can put back. Some departments can agree to offer compensatory savings but choose items which can become politically damaging to local council members. If the members then disagree where savings are to be gained they may instruct the chief executive, the treasurer and the chief officers to find counter economies; this is when bargaining takes on a new reality as it leaves the initiative in the hands of the professionals. This is especially so

139

when local politicians find the easiest option is to attempt to make the cuts a neutral, technical exercise. The attempt to depoliticize cuts, however, is rarely manageable, but it does allow the professionals some space in controlling a fluid, standstill, or contracting environment. Thus the competition for resources may still be a contest, but it is far from being a free-for-all.

It is perhaps significant that if cuts have to be made in local government, it is the elite professionals at the apex of bureaucratic authority who feel their authority diminished if they themselves do not in practice point to the areas to be safeguarded and those which may be weakened. In such a context, a revolt against Whitehall and County Hall by the dominant elite of professionals is highly unlikely. Corporatism still wins skirmishes and battles by allocating authority to elite professionals, even in a conjunctural national situation where the governing party sometimes claims to be engaged in a war with both local state and overspending and corporatist state practices.

NOTES AND REFERENCES

1 In Birmingham, faced with a demand for a steep increase in the rate, the ratepayers revolted in 1855 ... they inaugurated their regime by dismissing the Borough Engineer whose roads had given him a national reputation and replaced him by his assistant at half the salary. The quarrelled with their Town Clerk and ruled for over ten years with great inefficiency.[9]

2 Rhodes, R. A. W. The lost world of British local politics? *Local Government Studies*, 1975, 1(3), 39-60.

3 Lambert, R. J. A Victorian national health service. *Historical Journal*, 1962, 5 (1), 16.

4 Hennock, E. P. *Fit and proper persons*, 1973, 7.

5 Dearlove, J. *The re-organization of British local government*, 1979, 54.

6 Fraser, D. *Urban politics in Victorian England*, 1976, 147-8.

7 Briggs, A. *Victorian cities*. New edition, 1968, 238.

8 Briggs, A. *Op. cit.*, 238.

9 Maud, J. and Finer, S. E. *Local government in England and Wales*, 1953, 132.

10 Keith Lucas, B. and Richards, P. *A History of Local Government in the Twentieth Century*, 1978, 25.

11 Hennock, *op. cit.*, 8.

12 Lee, J. M. *Social leaders and public persons*, 1963.

13 Newton, K. *Second city politics*, 1976. (On Birmingham). Bealey, F., Blondel, J. and McCann, W. P. *Constituency politics*, 1965 (On Newcastle-under-Lyme). Clements, R. V. *Local notables and the city council*, 1969. (On Bristol).

14 Saunders, P. *Urban politics*, 1980.

15 Heclo, H. H. The councillor's job. *Public Administration*, 1969, 47, 185-202.

16 Weber, M. *The theory of social and economic organization*, 1969, 338.

17 Bucher, R. and Stelling, J. Characteristics of professional organisations. *Journal of Health and Social Behaviour*, 1969, 10(1), 3-15. It could be argued that the less status professionals have in local government, the more it functions as a typical bureaucratic structure. However, at the top, the elite professionals use their location as heads of bureaucracies to erect the culture of professionalism.

18 Stewart, J. From growth to standstill. In Wright, M. (ed.). *Public spending decisions*, 1980, 9-24.

19 This quotation and those which follow arise from the author's fieldwork, mainly undertaken

in one local authority (a largely rural county) but checked through interviews with a number of other elite professionals in local authorities in different parts of the UK.

20 Laffin, M. Professionalism in central-local relations. In Jones, G. W. (ed.). *New approaches to the study of central-local government relationships*, 1980, 19.

21 This interesting argument is put forward by Stewart, *op. cit*. Similar arguments can be found in Greenwood, R., Hinings, C. R., Ranson, S. and Walsh, K. Incremental budgeting and the assumption of growth. In Wright, M. (ed.). *Public spending decisions*, 1980, 25-48. However, the latter writers believe in a strong possibility that, in a standstill era, budget construction is likely to approach a technocratic rational model, whilst Stewart obviously doubts this possibility.

22 For example Greenwood, R. Fiscal pressure and local government in England and Wales. In Hood, C. and Wright, M. (eds.). *Big government in hard times*, 1981, 77-9.

23 The following statement exemplifies this view: 'It is ... a relatively easy system to study because things are pretty well what they purport to be. It is not necessary to keep saying that such is the law or the theory or that is what is supposed to happen, whereas the reality is quite different. There are few matters where such divergences exist'. Jackson, R. R. *The machinery of local government*. 2nd edition, 1965, 8.

24 Greenwood, R. The local authority budgetary process. In Booth, T. A. (ed.). *Planning for welfare*, 1979, 78-96.

25 Burgess, T. and Travers, T. *Ten billion pounds*, 1980. An excellent technical account of the changes in central government funding and the long-term implications for the partial autonomy of local government.

26 Crozier, M. and Thoenig, J. C. The regulations of complex organised systems. *Administrative Science Quarterly*, 1976, 21, 547-70. Midwinter and Page comment 'Officials and ministers in central departments responsible for particular services are naturally anxious to defend such services and will tend to encourage local government. Guardians of particular functional services may even see the ability of local authorities to raise income through local taxes and other changes ... as a second line of defence against the Treasury axe'. Midwinter, A. and Page, E. (eds.). Cutting local spending. In Hood, C. and Wright, M. (eds.). *Big government in hard times*, 1981, 56-76.

27 Rhodes, R. A. W. *Control and power in central-local government relations*, 1981. Winkler, J. T. Corporatism. *European Journal of Sociology*, 1976, 17 (1), 100-136. Panitch, L. Trade unions and the state. *New Left Review*, 1981, 125, 21-43.

28 *The Guardian*, 1981, 23 Oct., Friday, published an article on this report.

29 Marshall, A. H. *Financial administration in local government*, 1960, 33.

30 Newton, K. and Sharpe, L. J. Local outputs research. *Policy and Politics*, 1977, 5, 68-9.

31 Danziger, J. N. *Making budgets*, 1978.

32 Newton and Sharpe. *Op. cit.*, 69.

33 Heclo, H. H. and Wildavsky, A. *The private government of public money*, 1974, 212.

CHAPTER SIX

Professional authority and resource allocation: treasurers and politics in UK local government

Before the rise of professional power in bureaucratic structures, professionals, or rather the occupants of municipal office in local governments, possessed significant differences from those of the reformed system of late Victorian society. In the old unreformed system a treasurer was allowed, and even expected, to hold a plurality of positions from which he drew revenue and income. As already suggested, the position of the treasurer was a type of property which could be passed down in specific families from father to son or even grandson. In the rural counties, where gentry had a strong dominance, and in the towns, where self-employed tradesmen and merchants dominated, these local notables, often negotiated with the incumbents of the treasureship over the amount of income to be drawn from such office holding, Keith-Lucas has noted that was acceptable for those occupying treasurers' roles in the counties to utilize the balances to make a personal profit by lending them out at interest.

While the negotiated official salary was often quite small, such control over funds was highly prized. Keith-Lucas documents a Surrey County treasurer having a salary of only £150 a year, but being able to make another £450 by lending funds at interest. In Wiltshire, the treasurer lent money to the banks at 5 per cent per annum.[1] The power of office as property and the protection offered by traditional patron-client relationships underpinned such practices. Keith-Lucas quotes Cobbett in *Rural Rides* on the consequences of such a system. The Treasurer of Hampshire, 'a Mr Hollis, who has for many years been under Sheriff as well as Treasurer of the County, and holds several other offices, and who has besides large pecuniary transactions with his bankers, has for years had his accounts so blended that he has not known how this money belonging to the County has stood. His own statement shows it was all a mass of confusion'. Doig comments on the unreformed municipal corporation of Ipswich. 'The treasurers did not produce accounts, public monies passed through private accounts ... 'I do not know by whom or for what purpose', said one treasurer when £1,500 was found in the bank under his name'.[2] Keith-Lucas further notes that the treasurers of many different trusts came, not only from the self-employed professions, but also, for instance, from the clergy, the peerage and members of parliament.

Garrard has noted that in the transition between the unreformed system and the beginnings of the new system, nineteenth-century municipal officers were different from their successors. Corporate officials could become social leaders and even compete for local prestige with their employers. Indeed, some were successful local notables before acquiring their posts. The town clerk was often a leading solicitor and remained so after appointment.[3] Similarly, Briggs noted that in Birmingham from 1869, 'there was a tradition that the town clerk carried on his private business as a solicitor as well'.[4] To a certain extent, therefore, their influence was derived from the same source as that of the councillors and they could be seen as a legitimate part of the local elite of notables rather than its rivals. Party disputes often incorporated these professionals as patronage was dispersed through such mechanisms. In Liverpool the treasurer was appointed at least as much for his significance as a Liberal activist as for his financial skills. Fraser comments that 'attorneys naturally looked to clerkships and bankers to treasureships'.[5] If these professionals were regarded as successful and influential in the municipalities, it was possible for them to transfer part of their social authority to their roles inside local governments. However, a too great dependency on factional patron-client relationships could increase their vulnerability if the political wheel of fortune turned.

In contemporary times, it has been part of a 'conventional wisdom' that chief officers, supposedly the mere servants of the council, have encroached on policy making to the point where they can, in fact, if not in theory, become the dominant force in the relationships to their political 'masters'. While, in an earlier period, folklore has given the impression of a golden age of the politician, a little king of a municipal castle, historical reality may be somewhat different. Waller argues that the boundary between professional advice and policy making in the late nineteenth century was admitted to be fluid in local government. 'Officers were expected to be creative figures, not simply agents obeying orders and executing routine work'. Waller gives evidence of the town clerks of Manchester and Liverpool, 'actively participating in council meetings: not just neutrally elucidating a complex point of law, but forcefully intervening to check councillors who, in their view, advocated wanton or mistaken policies'.[6] Hennock quotes the American Lovell's 1908 book which stresses that 'the excellence of municipal government was roughly proportionate to the amount of influence that the salaried officials were allowed to exercise'.[7] According to Lovell the main innovating force behind municipal government was to be found largely in these professionals, yet it would be a mistake to see the ostensible political masters as the mere dummies to the ventriloquism of their professional 'servants'. In the crucial area of finance, elected members could and did play a vital role. Hennock himself found that:

> until 1953 the Leeds Borough Treasurer had been little more than a cashier receiving and paying out money as he was told, while the whole burden of drawing up estimates fell to the chairman of the finance committee. In Birmingham, in the late 1860's, it was the chairman of the finance committee who devised a new system of accounts as well as a cheaper method of raising loans ... for another generation powerful chairmen of the finance committee, drawn from the circles of big businessmen, continued to control the municipal finances in great detail.[8]

Other councils perhaps had less financial expertise at their disposal. Bolton in 1858, when the Treasurer Wolfenden retired, elected him to the council and within three months he had taken over as Chairman of the Finance Committee.[9] Two decades later, in spite of the respect payed in Bolton to financial expertise, the borough treasurer was blamed for the whole system of accounting which was 'defective in system and slovenly and inaccurate in execution'. In turn, the treasurer laid the responsibility on the finance committee.[10] Bolton at that time appeared to have a financial system that no one controlled; still less co-ordinated. Other councils have similar histories.

Not only were professional accounting systems crude and often non-existent in practice, but the audit in this period was equally defective. Even in the 1900's, the borough audit, which was supported by central government, was well known to be greatly defective. Waller quotes a one-time City Treasurer of Birmingham as stating 'borough auditors' reports were more spectacular than practical. Items which disclose any incidents of civic feasting or expenses paid to members of the council were emphasized, whilst important matters, such as the adequacy of reserves or depreciation allowances, are seldom dealt with'.[11]

There are comparatively few studies of the modern institutional role of local government treasurers.[12] A number of political science-based studies throw some light on the political relationships of treasurers within their localities. In Liverpool, the Labour Party machine 'boss', Braddock, combined the Chairmanship of the Finance and General Purpose Committee with the leadership of the council. Elcock states the annual estimates were worked out by Braddock in collaboration with the city treasurer and the bulk of councillors had no effective part to play.[13] In a study of Cheshire county government before reorganization, Lee noted the importance of the alliance between the county treasurer and the chairman of the finance committee. Rate-fixing was a process of informal negotiations mainly between these two role occupants.[14] A later study of Cheshire between 1961-1974 inferred that the county treasurer was an influential chief officer who initiated financial policy and did not merely carry out a policy set by the politicians.[15] A recent study of Newcastle implies that the recommendations of the city treasurer and the finance committee varied in authority and acceptability. In one year, a budget went through party and committee in a context where most councillors had little time to weigh up proposals or to obtain detailed information. This was in a period where the dominant party had an autocratic leadership in alliance with the treasurer. An increase in financial information and the mobilization of internal opposition among councillors during the next budget year produced significant modifications to budget patterns. Green's conclusions were that the influence of the treasurer was considerable but it was checked and balanced by new councillors 'learning the ropes' and in time gaining in potential authority.[16]

A few further studies have commented on the socialization of treasurers into the values of financial markets. Dunleavy has argued, for instance, that the processes of borrowing money and servicing debt by treasurers and their advisors who normally are brokers or bankers, socialize a treasurer and his staff in a specific manner.[17] Sbragia argues that an acceptance of market rationality by treasurers in capital expenditure was not particularly evident in other facets of local finance. Thus, Sbragia found that several strongly questioned the concept of 'value for money', a concept at least implicitly linked to market criteria in areas other than lending. She states, however, 'yet in the area of lending the market's criteria were accepted unquestioningly'.[18]

Greenwood, Hining, and Ranson have argued that any sociology of local government budgeting would have to be based 'upon the political features of organizational life, rather than upon the cognitive deficiencies of decision makers'.[19] In this paper and others, they suggest that the treasurer role is pivotal in the traditional pre-corporate planning budget system where the internal debates centred on resource inputs and neglected policy outputs. In these systems the built-in conflict between service chief officers and the role of treasurer is dominant and resource allocation is assumed to be highly incremental. Thus, they suggest that in corporate systems when the power of the treasurer goes down, that of the majority party goes up. This is problematic and probably ignores the variety of relationships which create a diversity of power bases for a treasurer who has learnt political skills. From the evidence presented by Greenwood *et al.*, it could be argued that the power of the treasurer is virtually unrelated to the commitment to corporate planning or even the power of a chief executive.

Danziger himself has commented that the institutional treasurer role has a more crucial impact on budget making that what Greenwood *et al.* imply. He argues in reply that a treasurer 'seems to have a power base that is not zero sum with that of the majority party or of corporate planning structures'.[20] Danziger argues that he found in his own research that treasurers and their senior officers were often important actors in the budgetary process even when 'rational' techniques and corporate planning systems were instituted. Danziger implies that within these boundaries the allocation of resources was mainly influenced by the treasurer, guided by policy advice from service chief officers and from the majority party leadership. Danziger insists that in his study he found that it was the treasurer's role whose behaviour embodied corporate planning while making the necessary political concessions to the spending departments. He states that 'it was not simply the case that the Treasurer would allocate incremental shares to all spending departments'.[21] In the context of an alliance with the role of chief executive, the treasurer would have a distinctive input into resource allocation. This would be 'contingent upon each Treasurer's reading of national policy, local decisions and his own assessment of local needs'. Hence, a system with a powerful treasurer and few corporate management characteristics could produce a system of highly non-incremental budgetary outputs. Danziger, Greenwood, Hinings and Ranson stress that intra-organizational configurations of power have a significant input into resource allocation decisions. Danziger argues, correctly, that research should be 'sensitive to the continuing importance of the Treasurer's office and to the complex set of roles and alternative values that might be manifest in that office ... ideally the ... analytic framework needs to incorporate variables that measure the agenda and roles of the

Treasurer most fully, so that the relationship between this important factor and budgetary outputs can be specified'.[22] Greenwood, Hinings and Ranson concede in replying to Danziger 'that the role of the Treasurer within alternative budgetary systems is more subtle and complex than is given credit'.[23] They also correctly argue that 'Danziger himself fails to offer any alternative explanation' in his text *Making Budgets*.

Authority and power in institutional roles should be analyzed primarily as a product of structural relationships and not merely as an extension of attributes of individuals who occupy roles. The role of the treasurer could be usefully studied by an attempt to understand these relationships and the nuances which can develop from them. Otherwise, 'the absence of an adequate sociology of financial management and executive roles in local government literature allows a prescriptive formalism to exist in financial management textbooks'.[24]

The methodology which is utilized in this chapter follows the path that Danziger suggested though he did not adequately follow it himself. He has argued that: 'Configurative approaches at the individual level remain attractive because they provide a rich descriptive data from which to generate stories as explanations and because they capture more of the texture of politics than system level or organisational level approaches'.[25]

A treasurer has strategic influence and power in both an era of growth and an era of contraction. Nevertheless, fiscal contraction has the potential to accentuate a number of readjustments to the organizational cultures of local government. Stewart especially has speculated that the move from growth to standstill and actual decline radically shakes and alters the expectations around growth, which, while not written down, are written into the organizational procedures and alliances.[26] This world, which is taken for granted in an era of expansion, allowed a network of compromise understandings to exist between potentially competing professional interests inside local governments. Consensus politics were relatively easy for a treasurer and a chief executive to manage. It was not necessary, for example, for one alliance of officers and councillors based on a spending department to challenge all the bids of another spending department or for the administrative role of the treasurer to impose a regime of tight financial control with no possibility of movement on expenditure items. It is useful to see 'virement packages' which a treasurer would allow as forming part of an internal bargaining process. In such a context of growth, present concessions by one spending department could be balanced and compensated in the future by gains made by another spending department.

While it could be argued that a weakening of statutory legislation may allow formally more space in innovating specific programmes while cutting back others, in a standstill or contraction of resources era, other rationalities may develop. Treasurers especially can develop mixed feelings about capital programmes they have been allocated by central government. They may even advise their politicians to reject them tactfully if such programmes implied a commitment at some later stage to assume direct financial responsibilities for such projects. In a past context where further growth was automatically assumed, the basic assumption in such a situation was that resources would be available, over time, to meet such commitments.

The treasureship role seems to be closely linked to a defence of local government as a 'natural', relatively autonomous, unit in central-local governmental relationships. Sbragia has noted that treasurers who have 'entrepreneurial' attitudes 'saw themselves as leading the fight for local autonomy'.[27] The retreat to a strong advocacy position has meant that earlier conceptions of central-local relations as a partnership have become significantly weakened. This can have an impact on role behaviour. In one local government where the leader of the council was a party leader of the same party in power in central government, and where the role of chief executive was occupied by an officer who was not able to influence strongly the leader, the following situation was described by a treasurer:

> The leader was tight on financial resources. I though too tight and we had some fairly strong arguments behind closed doors. I remember arguing a financial point which had considerable significance for the services. When we prepared the budget last year there was the question of the rate of inflation which was the key to a lot of problems. The government cash limits would indicate that next year we should only provide sixteen millions and my calculations indicated it should be nearer nineteen millions. The difference between those two assumptions in inflation was greater than the sum of all of those cuts we had made. I had three very prolonged meetings with the leader because in the report he wanted to follow the government line on inflation. I told him I could not agree. I'm the county Treasurer and I've got to advise the council what I think inflation would be and the impact on services. The government figures are too low but as a professional officer I can't accept it. In the end, after a lot of argument, we struck a compromise and he went a long way towards my estimate.

In this local government, it was the networks of party and government (the leader was recently awarded a knighthood) that allowed this council leader to subordinate the authority of fellow party councillors to his own. Other chief officers seemed to be unable to resist strongly his authority even when it conflicted with professional judgements. In such a context, the expansion of influence of the treasurer's role had significance as the occupant was forced to take a strong advocacy position. The respect given to the 'non-political' professional as head of the major financial control system often allowed him to be the informal spokesman for the suppressed collectivity of chief officers. The role of chief executive which is much more directly tied to political relationships and dependence seemed to be more vulnerable. The Treasurer noted:

> The budget of each committee would be determined in discussion. The Chief Executive used to sit in but it was mainly a dialogue between myself and the leader ... the main areas where we had problems were on the Community Leisure and Public Protection Committees. Community Leisure were given their allocation and it was up to the Chairman of that committee to decide whether it wanted to spend more on libraries and less on youth, etc. The Chairman was given the authority to decide what would be the allocation between departments. On the Public Protection Committee we had a number of small departments under one umbrella and for a number of years, the Chief Officers inside that committee wanted me to use my authority to give a sub-allocation within the

total allocation to various departments. The Committee members also wanted me to do this. I refused and pointed out it would make less flexibility for the committee. They wanted me to take political decisions and I drew back and refused.

In the next local election, the formerly dominant party and its leader lost control of the council. The Treasurer's role playing altered. Under the old regime he was a critic of local underspending policies and a spokesman for selective increasing spending by service departments. His professional reluctance to accept Whitehall's estimation of the inflation rate was linked to a perception of Whitehall as a place to be circumvented when possible. Under the new regime which came to power on a programme to restore former cuts in expenditure and which opposed the attempts to monitor closely local expenditure by central government, the Treasurer relearned vital political skills. The new administration had no autocratic leader and indeed a number of influential councillors did not want such a leader. The budget brought in by the new regime was seen by the Treasurer as less subject to his professional authority. He states:

> This year we have got what they call a continuation budget. In my view it's not working properly because it is an invitation to everyone to shove in as many bids on resources as they can. My Chairman of Finance who is an accountant can see the dangers of this. We discussed it and I said if we go for a continuation budget we will set down very clearly the rules for preparing the budget, because it we don't set down the rules, then the Committees' Chairmen will start crying 'foul' . . . I was able to say to everyone this is what the Finance Committee has decided should be the rules we are playing by.

The Vice-Chairman of the Finance Committee in this local government when interviewed admitted that some councillors of his party probably assumed that the Treasurer was antagonistic to their policies. The Treasurer's known influence in the last regime on the leader undercut the early development of a new 'trust' relationship based upon a supposed professional neutrality. The Treasurer's dislike of central government's new legislation to tighten controls on local governments helped to change councillors' perceptions. In addition, the Treasurer was able to demonstrate his use as a loyal 'servant' of the council on financial grounds and policy grounds generally. The Vice-Chairman of Finance states:

> The first thing was to establish at the outset that we wanted to prepare the budget on a continuation or no cuts basis. Politically it was very important to establish with the chief officers what was going to be our starting point because we were not going to have cuts in any circumstances. The Treasurer's department were worried because a continuation budget allowed limited growth. What we want the Treasurer to do is to ensure that financial regulations relating to virement and other things are very strictly adhered to because although we are allowing a modest expansion in parts of our budget we have to make sure that certain rules and regulations are abided by. One important spending department was showing reluctance to conform to procedure and we supported the Treasurer in trying to get that chief officer to keep to the rules. The Treasurer's views are very similar to the Chairman of Finance on our policies but at the end of the day the overall budget was determined very firmly within our political group. The Chairman of Finance and perhaps the Treasurer did say that if we planned for an extra £12 million

instead of £2 million that would be wrong but a majority of the group had already come to that conclusion.

It was in the professional interest of the Treasurer to establish the new rules of the financial game and to gain the support of the new regime in consolidating them. While in the old regime the Treasurer stressed his representational role on behalf of other chief officers, in the new regime a modification of role behaviour seems to have occurred. One consequence was a close monitoring of financial deviations in the new situation where the heads of the service departments were allowed greater authority by the leader. In a series of conflicts with other chief officers, the Treasurer, as the principal finance officer, was seen to be not merely demonstrating a professional judgement, but was also claiming to be the guardian of the new 'rules of the game'. The Vice-Chairman of Finance recalled:

> Recently the education department wanted a project and received the support of the education committee of which I am also a member. The Treasurer had informed the education department that as the project was not in the education budget virement must be found if it was needed. The Education budget is £200 million and the Chief Officer objected and said we can't find the money. At the education committee we had a very public and unseemly dispute between the representatives of the Treasurer and the Chief Officer. As Vice-Chairman of Finance I supported the Treasurer as he was applying our regulations and rules. Inside the committee there was some argument between the Chairman and myself but we sorted it out and we are now united in feeling it was the education department and not the Treasurer who was at fault.

The new regime seemed to be interested in actually extending the authority of the Treasurer in those areas where overall financial policy seemed to be threatened by service departments, while resisting the Treasurer's advice when it contradicted party programmes. Other chief officers were dependent on the support of the Treasurer while attempting to lessen and check the authority of the Treasurer through collective pressure inside a corporate management system which was weak and formerly had been even weaker. Unlike the previous regime with its autocratic leader, decision-making had to take into account the lack of automatic compliance with its policies on finance. The Vice-Chairman of the Education Committee gave the following example:

> We on the finance and education committees want joint financial reports between the education department and the Treasurer on projects. The education department seems to be resisting this. Perhaps they see the Treasurer as our arm and believe it will increase his department's influence over education, but we are worried about the education department's financial planning and trust the Treasury.

The Treasurer saw some of the differences in role performance as being structured by the differences between the two regimes in control of the council. In the old regime one of his major problems was the underspending politics of the budget and he attempted, as earlier described, to use his professional influence to correct this tendency by presenting a number of financial options. He saw the difficulties in this as follows:

> The leader of the last administration felt vulnerable if financial facts were put on the table as arguments because he felt his political opponents could pick these things up. That's what made giving professional advice so difficult. I had to insist that I was not happy with the government's estimates on inflation and cash limits and wanted to whole council to know. What I was saying was you choose the government's figures or mine or something in between but you should be clearly aware that choices have to be made.

The Treasurer was extremely conscious of the problems posed by the elimination of possible strategic options from decision making by not according them legitimacy. In this context, the limiting of a range of options to be openly discussed as real possibilities was seen by him as a threat to his conception of professionalism. However, even this Treasurer may not have accepted the legitimacy of economic or social policies in the extremes of political discourse, as part of the normality of local government decision making which is defined as being both pragmatic administration and 'non ideological'. The pressure on the treasury role is not linked to any deep empathy with the new central government legislation. However, while 'creative accounting' to outwit central government is often seen as an integral part of the treasurer's role, the occupant still has almost to overplay the new possible penalties.

The Treasurer from the same local government described the situation thus:

> Whereas in the old days I would try to actually encourage the administration to spend and I disliked their underspending, nowadays I'm faced with a new administration with a manifesto they want to implement. Basically they want no cuts in expenditure at all, which I can understand, but I'm worried about the County being penalised by the allocation given to us in the rate support grant. So now I play a different role. I don't know yet how the rate support grant will come out but I have to warn the administration that if they don't want to face an increase of x per cent in the rates you have to consider making selective reductions. The later the administration leaves the possibility of reductions the more difficult and expensive it may be to cut expenditures. I make sense to some of the councillors but others are resistant and I see their point of view. If I'm right, of course I expect I will gain more influence when we discuss next year's budget.

Another interview with treasurers emphasizes the problems faced in an era of fiscal contraction where leading politicians resent the potential for decision making in treasury roles. In one metropolitan city borough, the leader, on the resignation of the chief executive, refused to appoint to refill the role. He was seen as being a full-time chief officer himself with the added strength which was provided by his political base. In addition, he attempted to form new alliances which gave him access to organizational information and power. One chief officer stated:

> The leader forms relationships with officers below chief officer level. For example, there is a talented officer at third tier level and he spends a great deal of time with him and he will cut out the chief officer and the deputy. He has even done that in practice to the Treasurer himself. By doing this he creates an atmosphere of uncertainty among the chief officers.

This leader was primarily responsible for recruiting ten more accountants to the treasury. Their role was to increase the day-to-day financial monitoring of the service departments and to lessen the managerial autonomy of service department chief officers. The refusal to appoint a chief executive and the weakness of a corporate management structure did not significantly increase the role authority of this Treasurer though the treasury personnel collectively grew in influence. The Treasurer himself while not insignificant, did not overshadow the collective influence of the staff who fed the leader information and power and in return were awarded status. One officer in the treasury remarked:

> The leader is very involved in all the financial processes. He recruited ten extra accountants to tightened up the financial controls within the spending departments. He is not just interested in the overall budget but in the details. To give you some idea, one of his tactics is to go through the budgets of departments, examining the provision in the original estimates for the current financial year, then he would go down line by line of the management budget and he would say how much have you spent on that. You've got £400 in there and you've only spent £150, we are in the seventh month of the year so I'm knocking £200 out of it ... He relies very much on the resources of the finance department.

The power to filter information as a resource in organizational relationships is highly prized.[28] It would be misleading to infer that this leader did not offer chief officers the occasional carrot on budget issues. A certain degree of reciprocity had to be given to form dependencies. Also a leader can't afford to alienate totally a treasurer by too much open encroachment on his work space. If such disputes are made public the oppositional parties could form conjunctural alliances with chief officers and even a strong leader's own internal political base may be shaken. To mollify service chief officers does not, however, automatically help a treasurer whose advice may not always be taken. But a leader can increasingly take on the political skills of a treasurer. In this local government, for instance:

> The leader told the departments that if they co-operate with the accountants on their budget exercises any money which would be saved they can have back. He will not allow the Treasurer to claw it back. In effect he's saying, you can build your own growth into the budget by exercising economies in areas where there is a surplus and utilizing the money for developments in the service elsewhere. Of course, it's too good an offer for them to turn down and say, well we won't co-operate even if they resent the level of financial monitoring by the accountants.

Nevertheless, while it is possible for local politicans to circumscribe tightly individual treasurers, the overall picture from interviews is rather different. The emphases on value for money and close financial monitoring have increased the potential in the role even if the occupant himself is reluctant to utilize such potential. The formal subordination of the role and its 'traditionalism' and 'constitutionalism' hold in check the encroachment of the role on other political and organizational roles. Indeed, a treasurer can actually gain in the 'trust' which is awarded to him by such careful distancing from open encroachment as it safeguards the diverse 'rules of the game' which underpin the legitimacy of the system as a whole. One treasurer pointed out how his 'constitutionalism' affected other roles:

151

It is most important to find an acceptable role for the Chief Executive starting from the assumption that the main points of a budget would be summarized and the document will be written by myself. I've consciously withdrawn from some, but not all, of the longer range planning of money resources but I have held on very tightly to the actual summary of the budget. If I exercise my right to summarize all the financial issues arising from corporate planning then it's my experience that the councillors will always work to that document because it reduces the various options and problems to a series of relatively simple points.

Treasurers value, even overvalue, the organizational culture in which they live, survive and flourish. The natural alliance between the roles of chief executive and treasurer is also highly prized even by the supposed junior partner, who is formally under the authority of the chief executive. Both roles act as the guardians of the existing balances, keeping back spending departments from openly overplaying their hands yet representing the spending department in contests with local politicians. Both roles are 'go betweens' with influence accumulated through such a multiplicity of representations. A treasurer, who was interviewed, supported a statement of the previously quoted Treasurer and displayed a similar political sensitivity to possible strains:

I deliberately do not come in too early into policy discussions. I leave the Chief Executive and the Chief Officers a lot of time to talk in non-financial terms about policy issues. I don't draw out financial implications until that process has gone on for some time. I suspect many officers in fact would prefer me to get involved earlier. Some are glad of my support, others wary. Some feel they ought to be able to supply their own financial expertise and I have encouraged departments to be, in part, self-sufficient in financial personnel.

Treasurers can encourage service departments to hire accountants at fairly senior levels. Some of those interviewed who have done so have reported obvious organizational consequences. It enables a service department chief officer to make a 'fundamental' comment on finance at committee meetings on the basis of the briefing given by departmental senior accountants. To the extent that he learns financial skills he can respond to the anxiety and worries of a treasurer. The accountant in the employment of a service department can tighten up expenditure controls and lesson the vulnerability of a service department to external critics. Both a departmental manager and a treasurer would welcome this new input. However, the potential of a service department to negotiate on more equal terms over such items as inflation rates, financial regulations and potential ambiguities are not always welcomed by treasury personnel who can see a situation of a 'gamekeeper becoming a poacher'. A new power balance in negotiations could be then established and resistance to such a situation could make a treasurer a semi-captive of the culture of his subordinates with a subsequent loss to the apparent autonomy of the treasurer's role. In the interviews there was a variety of responses by treasurers to such a situation.

It has already been argued that treasurers can hold back from expanding the boundaries of role influence on decision-making. This is especially true if the boundaries become blurred and politicians wish for greater protection. While unpopular decisions can never be popular, politicians can present treasurers with open political problems.

When politicians of all parties have to make reductions of expenditure on services, it is a temptation for them not to attempt to manoeuvre the chief officers into presenting the cuts as being determined solely by non-political technical criteria as it strengthens the management of public discontent. The chief officers are normally aware of this and if they manage services they are placed in a difficult position as they don't want to abdicate from deciding which programmes shall be cut and which areas will be given protection. The treasurer's role as the chief accountant can become a smoke-screen for highly political decisions, which are taken as mere accounting technical decisions. A treasurer remarked:

> In the old administration because I am the Treasurer some councillors who wanted to cut expenditure seemed to expect me to take the initiative. They wanted me to say you have no alternative but to stop doing this. It would be implied I should have been tougher over expenditure. They wanted me to stand up in committee and say, in my opinion, this project or that project is most unwise and that would have been enough to influence the bulk of the councillors. Some councillors implied it was my professional duty but I thought that type of hard advice is essentially political advice. In a sense, they wanted to use me to justify their support for them following national government policies to cut expenditure. It's very helpful for them if the Treasurer comes along and says that government has said you must do this without looking closely at the small print. I've always taken the line that they must take their own decisions because they must be held responsible.

All the treasurers interviewed realized that supposedly professional advice had strong political implications. In negotiations with central government over finance, the treasurer can sometimes be of crucial importance. A significant part of the negotiations rests on his professional competence in building a financial brief, even if he personally does not conduct them at interface level. His technical ability as a manager and as a presenter of financial information are interlocked and his credibility can be of strategic importance. Authority in the treasury role depends upon the ability to bring 'home the bacon'.

The reputation and presumed ability of past occupants of the role are part of an invisible network of reference points in which he judges himself, and is judged by his professional peers in other local governments. The occupational community of treasurers, while small, is very self-conscious and integrated. Frequent meetings at regional and national level allow a consistent evaluation of each treasurer's role performance. The work ideology is just as determined by such a national occupational culture as by the more obvious organizational culture of the local government in which treasurers are based. This can complicate their advocacy role of local government against the dominance of central goverment. One treasurer remarked: 'CIPFA is interested in the defence of local government, but paradoxically they have agreed to help build a new audit system which will be the arm of central government. They don't expect to get professional control, but I think they hope they can influence it fairly substantially'.

The organizational strength a treasurer can draw from both intergovernmental relations and the national occupational culture can sometimes be translated, though not automatically, into increased authority within local government. However, it is possible for treasurers, like other chief officers, to find the opposite is the case. A great deal of time which is spent on national committees and affairs can even weaken a local political base. While treasurers are not directly linked to Whitehall in the manner which education and social services managers are, and see themselves as the 'guardians' of local democracy, the increased respect which is given to accounting evaluations by central government does benefit the status and centrality of the role and the national occupation community in general. However, the lack of direct contact with the Whitehall 'village' networks possibly gives some service departments a greater credibility with local politicans. Unlike local state professions such as social services, housing or education, accountants feel the lack of occupational representation in the governmental apparatuses.

Sbragia rather convincingly notes in her sample from Scotland that 'many officials saw the Treasury as filled with theoretically oriented economists and felt that both the Treasury and the DoE lacked accountants, professionals with the kind of background to which local finance officers could relate. They felt they had no one to talk to'.[29] Data drawn from English treasurers tends to confirm this pattern. The lack of intimate contact of nearly all treasurers with Whitehall 'village' communities forces them to depend on CIPFA for representation and information. Yet CIPFA for representation and information. Yet CIPFA is at least a semi-corporatist institution with an interest in marginalizing potential conflict areas between central and local government. In a situation where central government is unwilling to allow 'go betweens' too much negotiating power, CIPFA is subject to opposing strains with a tendency to want to satisfy all parties and finds it difficult, if not impossible, to do so.

Differences in role perceptions as well as differences in value attitudes to specific aspects of local government were not uncommon. One metropolitan county treasurer emphasized to a greater extent than others the accountability of politicians to the local electorate as a key to understanding the essential strength of local government. This treasurer expressed strong concern that many of his fellow chief officers had a relatively blind relief in themselves as 'non-political' professionals and refused to scrutinize the recommendations on the possible options which they gave politicians:

> In this local authority chief officers don't recognize the problems in the advice they sometimes give. Many don't realize that even when they discuss resource allocations their advice has a social edge to it. There have been suggestions that money should be spent in the Highways budget, and a certain balance worked at between road construction and support for the bus services. In fact I pointed out that the highways construction programmes benefited some sectors more than others and public bus services benefited

more than others. Chief officers attempted to present it as a totally professional decision and it was correctly recognized by members as a highly sensitive political issue. The chief officers concerned could not basically accept that. One of the reasons I'm negotiating with the bus companies at the moment is because there is a disagreement between the surveyors here, the bus company and the council and I'm acceptable as an honest broker.

It is very possible that another occupant of the role of treasurer might not have decided to play out the role in this manner. It is also possible that another occupant could have decided to accept his fellow chief officer's self definition of professionalism and not even consciously thought of challenging it. He could lose as well as gain by linking his role authority on these issues to the challenges made by councillors, after all. This Treasurer believed most councillors accepted the fact that he acted as an 'honest broker' and therefore occupied political space with their tacit consent, but they rationalized this by saying that the treasurer 'can't really' be taking on political roles. In practice then, because of the particular trust relationships established, this Treasurer can seem to be allowed to float in the area which is artificially separated between politics and professionalism, precisely because of the personal trust given as well as the institutional role trust in the Treasurer's advice as a technical expert.

While a chief executive draws his authority from representing service departments to the politicians and *vice versa* (as well as balancing between the claims of different service departments), he can be more vulnerable than a treasurer, precisely because his political relationships are integral to the authority of the role. The role strength of a chief executive is also its potential weakness. The strength of any competent and politically skilled treasurer is that his institutional role allows him to take part in policy construction without an automatic challenge by councillors that he is talking politics.

This Treasurer explained that he was usually able to decide the type of intervention he would make by examining the particular balances between both chief officers and politicians in the relationship to general long-term goals. He gave the following example:

> Immediately after the last local elections, the Minister made a perfectly clear threat that if we did not cut £10 million off our budget we would lose grant to the amount of £6.3 million. The new administration did not want to make these cuts but they did not want to be seen as taking an extreme stand based on an overt political philosophy. Initially I was brought into council discussions on the Minister's threat. I did not suggest they should make cuts but merely suggested they should consider what the effects of the cuts would be. My logic at that time was that they were a new council and they had to play a public role of being reasonable and responsible and the most likely way of doing that was to actually examine the effects of cuts on services.

The Treasurer was interested in supporting the new council by the use of specific tactics of negotiating with the relevant central government departments and politicians, and demonstrating that pragmatic administration was the dynamic of this local government. This sensitivity to the ideological level was coupled with a desire to win to the council's policies as much across the board support as possible in the local community as well as local and national newspaper support. The Treasurer stated:

> We monitor our unit costs closely and the County has a good track record. We compare very well with other metropolitan counties who, on the whole, have the same problems. It was obvious that the exercise would lead to the realization that cuts in expenditure would have fairly damaging effects on the services. The council were able to say to the Minister that they had considered cuts. They were even supported by the local newspapers who normally dislike high spending on rates for obvious reasons.

The Treasurer considered that without the skilful use of public presentation of technical arguments, this local government would have been forced to make severe cuts and the axe would have fallen on those departments with the weakest (in political relationships) chief officers. He saw his 'trust relationship' with councillors as having a strategic and important consequences in inter-departmental relationships, and while often critical and opposing other chief officers' judgements on specific issues, he also saw himself as the 'guardian' of spending departments in a context of an unstable environment. This 'natural' guardianship element of the role was linked to an ability to support councillors, at other times, against chief officers.

In another metropolitan district an exceptionally strong chief executive attempted, after the reorganization of local government, to eliminate as far as possible all external political inputs into the corporate process. In this city, perhaps more than any other, the possibility of increased rationality in a climate of financial contraction, should be taken as given. The Treasurer of this local authority was interviewed and stated he believed that chief officers would adhere to a strong corporate system only when it was in their interests and when the relative weakness of their political relationships forced them to compensate by increased dependency on the Treasury and the Chief Executive. He commented:

> The weaker departments such as libraries, museums, recreation do better out of corporate management but the larger ones will support it only as far as they gain. If chief officers think they will be able to get political support for projects they will be less cooperative. The Director of Housing has now got a separate housing committee and that has increased his hand in making bids.

In this local authority it was common for the strong Chief Executive and his junior partner, the Treasurer, to dominate, within limits, the influential politicians in one of the major parties and to have considerable influence on a number of senior politicians in the other major parties. The coming to power of the Labour Party, on a manifesto of resistance to cuts in services, made the Treasurer's input into policy more difficult as a significant minority of members wanted no cuts and many of the others were prepared to allow cuts to be made elsewhere than in particular departments they gave political priority. Forward planning, according to this Treasurer, had broken down as it was not possible to control the external resource environment over a number of years. He argued that he and other treasurers, therefore, tended to operate more than ever before on a year-to-year basis while still attempting to make financial plans and recommendations. This Treasurer described last year's budget in a context when large cuts had to be discussed and agreed upon by the council:

> We decided to take £4.8 million from the education budget. It was possible politically to do this because the education budget has, after all, around 70 per cent of our resources and because the education department never learnt the necessary political skills to justify its keeping all its budget. He depended on the size and importance of his committee to get protection and his chairwoman was not very able in her political relationships. The Chief Executive and myself decided that they should learn a few lessons. So we did not intervene in their favour.

It is significant that this Treasurer was not automatically allied to the spending department with the largest budget. It is also significant that he saw a learning process as integral to the management of a budget with penalties, as well as rewards, being imposed. This particular Treasurer expected to be able to have a definite influence on party policy and perhaps had less doubts than other treasurers about openly attempting to narrow the policy options which were presented to council members. He believed that the local authority had a tradition of openly strong officers and the council members would be lost if they failed to get definite advice. A presentation of all options would not in every issue be justified and would lessen administrative efficiency. He saw his role behaviour as legitimately crossing the grey boundaries of professionalism and politics and sanctified by the local 'rules of the game':

> I wrote the budget speech for the last leader. With the change in power on the council I have just written a speech which condemned the budget. It's just professionalism. Budgets are electoral devices. I do intervene when I feel it necessary. The new administration started off with a target of 20 per cent rate increase and at the end ended up with 13.2. I had a head-on collision with the deputy leader. He said I had too much in contingencies. I had £2½ million and he said we are going to reduce that by a penny in the rates. I said in my professional judgement that contingencies were likely to be under, rather than over, provided. He eventually accepted that. It was underprovided too, by £2 million.

All the treasurers interviewed expected to be consulted and to have a significant influence on council policy over the rates. It is rare for a treasurer to be able to step back on this issue from maximising his role authority as the issue is so intimately related to the current debates on local government employment initiatives and closely entwined to expectations, which are held by politicians and chief officers, of a treasurer's inputs. Furthermore, as already argued on finance issues, the treasurer is the only chief officer who can give financial advice which is translated out of technical professionalism, but who does not feel exposed to political attack by members on his role legitimacy. On these issues the chief executive and other chief officers can find that their alliance with the treasurer is then, at times, potentially unstable. A Treasurer argued that he had to balance professionally, in his policy calculations on rates, between his personal perceptions of what local industrialists and self employed would stand without public outcry and also against the felt needs of service departments and their political allies. He suggested that it was also possible that in his local authority several councillors adopted, on the Finance Committee or their equivalents, an advocate role for local firms and enterprises. This is especially important for policy of regimes which are based on the Liberal or the Conservative Party, and if councillors are also on service department committees they could also experience various degrees of role conflict.

Councillors saw their role in local government politics as primarily to reduce expenditure, and loyalty to service department committees was relatively nominal rather than otherwise, though if central government funding would increase, this could change. He pointed out that the CBI were encouraging their membership to enter the local political arena as councillors and mentioned one councillor on the Finance Committee in his local authority who was, in his opinion, the 'CBI's representative'. The Treasurer, he thought, cannot afford not to register such pressures and allow them a legitimate weight in his calculations. His professional advice rests upon such variables as his professional influence in the politics of the council as a whole, the 'trust' relationships built up around his role and his estimation of the balances between political forces at a particular conjuncture.

Advice from a treasurer can be seen as reasonable by councillors in one conjuncture and rejected in another. It is part of the treasurer's role to recognise that there may be a significant variation between parties, and even inside parties, among councillors on their attitudes to rates and this variation can lead to differential inputs into negotiations between councillors before a consensus is created for what the public want, or will stand, on the rate level. Treasurers can tell councillors what the services need and tell the services what the politicians think the public will accept without a political backlash automatically taking place.

Another treasurer had some doubts about the too clear advocacy of a rates policy. He thought it important not to be over precise:

> I have influence because of the way I put things over. For example, to get them to see sense on the rate levy I told the elected member about a large mail order firm who had already publicly stated that they were going to reduce their employment by one thousand. This company at the moment had to pay £505,000 in rates. If the rates went up by the figures the politicians wanted, they would pay £625,000. If they were asked to pay an additional £125,000 they may increase the numbers they could make redundant. I won my case.

The Treasurer in his financial calculations was heavily affected by what he thought could be the direct result of a political desire to raise rates. Whether or not he had a personal intimate knowledge, through his Finance Committee, of the local self-employed's attitudes and the attitudes of large and small firms to increases in the rates, he became their advocate rather than the advocate of the spending departments in the corporate process. This area of role authority of the treasurer could potentially be translated into a significant political capital to be used according to professional and personal judgements. As the 'go-between', the broker, the mediator of resource bids on the budget by spending departments and their committees, the 'neutrality' of the treasurer role offers significant political and organizational power. If he sees himself as a spokesman for an 'invisible' constituency of ratepayers, a treasurer can play, in some circumstances, a more significant role in the context of financial policy than even a chief executive. The last role, while also a broker role, is set by the necessity to be closely attuned to building consensus agreements inside a local authority. A chief executive would normally find it difficult, if not impossible, to advocate, in isolation from the treasurer, controversial positions on finance.

Interviews with both a sample of treasurers and chairmen of finance and policy resources committees present a picture whereby those who have a 'localist' ideology favour the general grant system, which in 1958 replaced grants which were specifically tied to expenditure on individual services. The 1958 system both increased the space of discretion and strengthened the local internal resource allocation system. These actors on the local stage now face Whitehall departments and politicians, who desire to transform the Rate Support Grant so it becomes weighted in the direction of an aggregate of specific grants strongly tied to particular services. Their perceptions are in striking contrast to other important actors on the local government stage. In contrast to treasurers, the chief officers of spending departments such as education may value, to some degree, the semi-autonomy of local government, yet not to be automatically hostile to attempts by central government to tie more strongly services to specific areas of grant. Thus, they do not always feel the same straightforward antagonism, as their committee politicians and treasurers, to these changes which may reduce the level of internal competition (it depends on the value and perceptions of each director of education). The natural alliance between politicians on an education committee, who gain from the semi-autonomy of local governments, and chief officers, who do not gain in the same way as heads of spending departments, is strained by such nuances. The lack of such ambiguity among treasurers was in contrast to that of education chief officers. One county treasurer stated:

> Quite a lot of our professionals, I believe, would be reasonably happy to be an extended arm of Whitehall. Their professional perception of their work is comparatively clear and I think they could accept the disappearance of the local political input into policy making with almost complete equanimity as they have always distrusted it. They are less concerned with local government as a system than they are with their own particular service. Treasurers, on the other hand, have felt a certain politicization of their role and an increased consciousness of the need to defend local government as a system. Treasurers like myself feel that our alliances are inside local government nowadays and in no way can we gain in a comparable sense by allowing it to go under.

Stewart, Stanyer and other writers have insisted that local governments are local political systems and show a range of diversities in the cultures which bind and bond the actors inside them.[30] The treasurer's role is significant in every local government as its technical core is a common base line of influence and authority. The degree to which additional factors become important in expanding or contracting the influence of the formal role depends upon such factors as the values of the occupant, the balances inside party political and professional 'interests' of the local government system, and the ability of the treasurer to function as a political 'non-political' accountant. A 'book-keeper' in the formal role may find himself rejected if he attempts to deny the politician in the role, while overstressing the accountant. Thus, the role is not above or below politics. It is shaped by politics and in turn shapes the politics in which it is located. All the treasurers interviewed acknowledged this as a fact of organizational life. Unfortunately, such facts of life are not easily accepted and analyzed in the existing body of normative prescriptive literature.

NOTES AND REFERENCES

1 Keith-Lucas, B. *The Unreformed Local Government System*, 1980, 61–63; Rubenstein, W. D. The end of old corruption in Britain 1780–1860. *Past and Present*, 1983, 101, 55–86.
2 Doig, A. *Corruption and Misconduct in Contemporary British Politics*, 1984, 62.
3 Garrard, J. *Leadership and power in Victorian industrial towns, 1830–1880*, 1983, 81.
4 Briggs, A. *Victorian cities*, 1968, 238.
5 Fraser, D. *Urban politics in Victorian England*, 1979, 148.
6 Waller, P. J. *Town, City and Nation England 1850–1914*, 1983, 282–3.
7 Hennock, E. P. *Fit and Proper Persons*, 1973, 7.
8 Hennock, *op. cit.*, 8.
9 Garrard, *op. cit.*, 73.
10 Garrard, *op. cit.*, 81.
11 Waller, *op. cit.*, 308.
12 See comments in Chapter 8.
13 Elcock, H. Tradition and change in Labour Party politics, *Political Studies*, 1981, 24(1).
14 Lee, J. M. *Social Leaders and Public Persons*, 1963, 145–6.
15 Lee, J. M. *et al. The Scope of Local Initiative*, 1974, 4.
16 Green, D. E. *Power and Party in an English City*, 1981.
17 Dunleavy, P. *Urban Political Analysis*, 1980, 126–7.
18 Sbragia, A. *Capital Markers and Central-Local Politics in Britain: the Double Game*, Centre for Study of Public Policy (Studies in Public Policy 109), 1983, 314–5.
19 Greenwood, R. *et al.* The Politics of the Budgetary Process in English Local Government, *Political Studies*, 1977, 25(1), 27.
20 Danziger, J. N. A comment on the politics of budgetary process, *Political Studies*, 1978, 26(1), 112.
21 *Ibid.*
22 Danziger, *op. cit.*, 113.
23 Greenwood, R. *et al.* A rejoinder to Danziger's comment, *Political Studies*, 1978, 26(1), 116–18.
24 See Chapter 8.
25 Danziger, J. N. *Making Budgets*, 1978, 205.
26 Stewart, J. From growth to standstill. In Wright, M. (ed.). *Public Spending Decisions*, 1980.
27 Sbragia, A. *op. cit.*, 314–15.

28 Pettigrew, A. Information control as a power resource. *Sociology*, 6 (2), 1982.

29 Sbragia, A. *op. cit., 38.*

30 Stanyer, J. *Understanding local government*, 1976; Stewart, J. *Local government: the conditions of local choice*, 1983.

CHAPTER SEVEN

The languages of role:
treasurers in UK local government

> Local policy makers for the most part act as if their localities were self contained. They perceive their environment as bounded though not of course as impermeable. It is for them a field of vision, expectation and action.[1]

The 'assumptive worlds' of local government strategic actors have been noted and recognized but rarely studied. Young has argued that the roots of these tactics to manage the interorganizational environment and the complementary local policy nexus are located in the local policy makers' understanding of their local worlds and multiple realities.[2] This chapter is an attempt to investigate particular aspects of the 'assumptive worlds' of treasurers and their organizational relationships with politicians and chief officers. Empirical data taken from relatively unstructured interviews with treasurers in a variety of local authorities will be selectively used to illustrate the multi-faceted realities of such officers and the relationship this has to the emerging policy process. The language or languages of treasurers are both pragmatic and symbolic – both levels will be noted.

Dunleavy is one of the very few political scientists to comment on the socialization and role politics of treasurers. He has argued that the very process of borrowing money and servicing debt has forced treasurers to internalize the culture and language of their advisers who are normally brokers and bankers. This is, Dunleavy implies, the dominant reality of such professionals. 'Such actors take on the role of market operators, participating in and acting on market signals and are likely to share the ideological outlook involved in such behaviour'.[3] Dunleavy stresses the integration of local governments into the mechanisms of the market via borrowing and investments. The treasurer in this model has a shadow existence in his local authority and his reality there is the mere reflection of the external market. Dunleavy further suggests that this involvement in the financial markets' 'notoriously variable and exaggerated and partisan view of the realities of the economic situation is likely to explain to some extent the irrationalities in local governments' budgetary behaviour'. Dunleavy believes that this ideological socialization, like that of other supposed strategic actors in the local government system, both undercuts the primacy of local politics and drains the content from the formal shell of local policy-making. To see treasurers as the natural guardians of local government interests in this perspective is misleading as their guardianship is of the type that opens the front door to the external enemy. The language of markets is assumed to be the language of local government accounting with the emphasis on value for money, etc., dominating the political and professional agendas.

Evidence does indeed suggest that treasurers and their supporting staff have a strong affinity to the cultural and ideological values of financial markets. However, other writers have argued indirectly rather than directly that treasurers have more than one reality and language, and it is difficult to argue that market rationality dominates in every context and conjuncture. Midwinter, Keating and Taylor suggest from Scottish evidence that in a context of fiscal contraction the loyalty and dominant reality of treasurers, when faced by 'irrational' central government legislation, allows the primacy of local political goals over narrow accounting values.[4]

Sbragia notes that the 'chief loan officer of an English metropolitan district or Scottish regional or district council is in charge of borrowing anywhere from £1 million to £15 million a day'; the officers involved in borrowing usually have the sense that they are involved in work which is largely incomprehensible to those involved in other aspects of local finance (including sometimes the authority's treasurer).[5] The work is then sometimes delegated to an officer who is recruited from outside local government who has developed the reputation of being a successful market operator. The larger an authority's debt the more attractive 'turning it over' is in career terms. However, treasurers who are thought to be particularly well versed in market operations, upon retirement are almost routinely hired as consultants by the major houses of brokers. Sbragia found that the influence of the market is pervasive on the treasurer's role in the area of capital expenditure where the discipline of the market is accepted as a legitimate one for the treasurer to impose on the local government's activities. However, she also noted that several treasurers when interviewed complained about the use by auditors of the concept of 'value for money'. They argued that auditors were trying to impose an essentially political decision, camouflaged as an economic calculation. While in the area of lending the market's criteria were accepted unquestioningly, the treasurers interviewed by Sbragia in Scotland were usually unwilling to attempt to impose a strict market test in other areas of their work. The languages of role are contextual with no language eliminating the other. In a similar manner, accountants from the treasury, who are seconded to spending departments and even employed by such departments, learn and use in their negotiations a language based upon the 'soft' values of the spending department in order to ensure effectiveness and credibility while, at the same time, maintaining a 'hard' professional language of book-keeping.[6]

Rose and Page state that:

> Instability is chronic in local government today because the conditions necessary to promote persisting regularity are not present. Budgets cannot be made in a closed world

> impervious to changes in the larger economic environment. Nor for that matter can budgets be made in a set of bargains between one single group of decision-makers. The openness of the system makes it uncontrollable.[7]

All treasurers recognize that 53 per cent of revenue and 83 per cent of expenditure is principally determined externally. However, this does not normally mean that the occupants of senior finance roles abdicate their subjectivity and declare themselves to be mere puppets. As Californian surfers attempt to ride the waves and breakers, finance professionals invest their professional capital in both interpreting the national and world economic currents and attempting to ride them with skill if not careless grace.

Interviews with treasurers illustrated a variety of strategies which treasurers utilized to maximize their constitutionalist weight in decision making. One Treasurer in a non-metropolitan southern county argued that an attempt by a legitimate pressure group, the local CBI, to influence the politicians had contradictory influences on his role authority:

> Two years ago just before the council met to decide on the rate level, the CBI placed a full page advert in the local paper. They knocked two pence off the rate that had been agreed upon by the Policy and Resources Committee. The members refused to listen to me when this pressure was on. However, it left them in a very difficult financial situation and special meetings a few months later had to make further cuts.

This Treasurer felt that in the long run his professional authority was not shaken. He had provided the necessary information, the decision makers had admitted its validity. Two years later, the CBI attempted the same tactic of using the local press to win rate cuts and the tactic backfired. Encouraged by the Treasurer and the Chief Executive, the council refused to break the informal agreements arrived at on the level of rates. In a Conservative county the CBI found that it was not able to override the cohesion of the party group and the weight of technical advice given by the chief officers. In a Conservative 'one-party state' even the CBI met strong resistance to an attempt to mount a populist movement that would overwhelm a political culture and relationships which are highly institutionalized and elitist.[8] The alternative CBI strategy of encouraging its members to become councillors was seen as a more legitimate tactic by the Treasurer and other strategic actors. The Treasurer stated:

> Last year my advice was not taken, this year the council's financial circumstances are making the point for me. I think I'm the only Treasurer in a county who presents the budget to the council and that was a consequence of the CBI intervention last year. The Leader took the view that there had been so much trouble among members that it was in my statutory responsibility to advise members. So I put the case to all members I had put privately to him and the committee chairman. I have been presenting the budget ever since.

In this context a fragmented political party which was not always able to control its backbenchers actually asked a professional to increase the scope of his role authority as a mechanism of cohesion. The very size of the majority of members of the dominant party, fifty-eight to three, encouraged the formation of factions and challenges to the regime's leadership. The Treasurer found himself a 'constitutionalist' and ambiguous about the expansion of his role influence and its possible consequences: 'I go highly visible when I present the budget. Perhaps it's overdoing it. I don't want to have too much influence in that sense, it could backfire at a later date. I only want members to understand what my advice means.'

The language of such professionalism was highly constititionalist in saying that traditional relationships and nuances are weakened by a chief officer taking on a public 'advisory' role which could cross, or be seen to cross the boundaries between politics and professionalism. It is a mistake to assume that occupants of highly traditional roles automatically desire to expand their influence on policy whether openly or in private. Some obviously do and some obviously don't. The 'assumptive worlds' of treasurers, as Young remarks in his general comments, provide strategic actors 'not just with their audience backcloth and other props but also the stage directions, lines and cues'.[9] Treasurers are aware that other chief officers as well as politicians may become uneasy about the implications of an increased expansion of the role authority of finance personnel. Script and lines are given and read in terms of co-operating actors and any actor who also desires to produce and direct a play may find the collective co-operation of a team turned against him. Pragmatic fears and worries are supported by highly ritualistic rewards and punishments.

The Treasurer who was interviewed was highly conscious of the theatrical nature of his public role playing: 'We tend to have fairly outspoken council meetings. Often I turn my coat about my own particular prejudice. I might make a provocative statement about certain services which I think are sacrificial lambs. If I don't attempt to do this my views get watered down.'

In an era where cuts in service departments' budgets are expected, except for the police that is, the Treasurer felt his organizational relationship with other chief officers was both one of co-operation and one of conflict and tensions. He alone had to speak the language of accountancy and 'real cuts' in those chief officers' meetings in which other officers were protesting and speaking another language of services and clients:

> I have to assess whether a spending cut is 'cosmetic' or not. Education has a shrinking school population. We expect to have to make some teachers redundant. So in our calculations we take the savings in salaries less the redundancy payments. Last year it happened that the Education department was particularly successful in redeploying teachers. So redundancy payments were not called in often and the provision was above the need. Education trotted out this budget head, redundancy, and told us they were going to reduce it. It was not a reduction, it's a one off figure that related to that particular year. Not a very complicated trick but I had to oppose it as cosmetic.

It was noticeable that even the largest spending department, education, with its strong political allies, was not able to challenge successfully the Treasurer's professional judgements on issues relating to the way 'cuts' were evaluated. The Treasurer, however, was not in the business of supporting the total elimination of services. On occasion the role occupant would intervene and use his financial status to support a service, providing such support did not weaken his claim to professional competence. He stated: 'I encouraged a costing system that showed that if we got rid of the architects (as some members seemed to want) private fees would cost us far more than the salaries of the architects we have at present.'

While the small departments are apparently politically weaker than the big spenders, the Treasurer believed that this was not always accurate. He felt he did not have to intervene when some members thought 'the library service had outstayed its welcome', as the library lobby inside the recreation and leisure committee was powerful with a high degree of legitimacy awarded to it by the most important politicians.

The Treasurer attempted a comparison between his role playing and authority in the era where high cuts were not sought after and the present period:

> In the past the main target for my attention was growth, the margin, and I was invited and expected to give my opinions. We spent most of the time on capital development and some revenue. So I had influence on those margins. Whereas today I advise the council on how to apply cash limits. This brings me into the policy area much more and early on. I have to be much more involved in the whole of departmental budgets. All the information to review budgets necessary for sub-committees and committees I have to provide so I, or rather my department, has a bigger work load.

To gain the increased co-operation of those spending departments and to be able to monitor expenditure with their goodwill the Treasurer was able to offer the occasional carrot. It was in his power to grant virement requests and to inform the finance committee after the event. Authority, which was delegated to and from him, was necessary if the machinery of obtaining agreements was oiled.

Another Treasurer in a London borough explained his attitude to any such carrots as were offered:

> The Director of Social Services came to see me and said he wanted to reorganize the meals on wheels service. He also said he would resent it if I took money from him so we came to a private deal. He saved £70,000 on his reorganization and I took £30,000 and gave him back £40,000 to develop the mental health service. If I took it all the Chief Officer would resent it and remember it. Even a Treasurer needs friends.

The Treasurer in this borough noted the importance of a strong minority opposition. Even writing reports was structured by his perception of the difficulties they could cause if their party and personal values challenged assumptions in his reports:

> If I write a report on pension fund policy I have to remember that the Labour opposition has strong views on investments in South Africa. As part of the cuts exercise I have offered to close down two of my branch cash offices. The opposition gave me a rough time by claiming I was depriving ratepayers. The majority party supported me but I took the flak.

Policy over investments could cause problems for a treasurer within the majority party:

I had a young chairman, a chartered accountant, who was anxious to change the pattern of superannuation investments. The management of the superannuation fund investments was put in the hands of two firms of merchant bankers. Incidentally, one firm had a partner who was related to the chairman of the Finance Committee – which did not make me very happy.

The Treasurer realized that he was not politically strong enough to oppose directly this policy but he could perhaps weaken it in the committee as a whole where the opposition had a presence. He used the opposition to check his chairman: 'In the end the majority party went along with my compromise, which was that the council should keep the old brokers they used for one part of the superannuation fund and one firm of merchant bankers for the other part. It was a very delicate situation.'

In his first year as treasurer (he had moved to the post from another authority), he found that his chairman was determined to bend him and his professional opinions in a manner which he considered to be dangerous:

The chairman came to my office before I prepared an important report and told me he would not present it to the Finance Committee or support it. In effect he was blackmailing me by saying 'you may get the Finance Committee to agree with you but I shall make it clear I am at variance with the views of the committee'. So I withdrew totally. Two years later I might have behaved differently.

It was a difficult if not impossible relationship. While the Treasurer had the relatively normal respect for value for money held by accountants, he found his chairman had stronger views that he did on the necessity to cut expenditure even further.

We had cut our services down to the bone already and the majority of the government party knew this. But my chairman and one or two others wanted even harsher cuts and he controlled the Finance Committee. We were strongly attacked by the minority party and by a number of chairmen of spending service committees. The most difficult thing I had to do was to publicly support him while privately dissenting. But I had my duty to do.

The Treasurer felt his doubts were known and in several meetings where cuts were being opposed his authority was appealed to by the members:

At a meeting on staff reductions I took the line that given a number of months would elapse before the beginning of the year, given the fact that there was then a year in which certain sections of the labour force could have a high wastage rate, why press for redundancies? The majority party wanted a direct cut there and then. It would have poisoned industrial relations. The opposition and several chairmen supported me and in the end they adopted my line.

A number of times the Treasurer found a strong opposition of importance in the strategies he used. He had no close relationship with the Chief Executive who was institutionally weak and the lack of a 'natural alliance' with such a role emphasized his own political weakness.

167

While treasurers are expected to give adequate financial information to members and their self-image regards the provision of such information as a legitimation of their 'natural' professionalism, unexpected departures from the practice can occur. A Treasurer in a northern metropolitan borough implied that guarding the local authority's balances could contradict the practice of providing adequate information to members. He stated:

> On balances I put in my report that they ought to retain £4 million. When the Conservatives, now the opposition, went out of office I had only £900,000. I could not argue against £3 million really. You see I've got £1 million in my back pocket which they don't know about. I calculated the Rate Support Grant this year on a lower basis and it worked out about £101 million. I have played it carefully and only disclosed £100 million to members. It's my job to help the controlling party group as much as I can and in the long run I do that by building up adequate balances.

The Treasurer obviously felt short-term deceptions were in the financial long-term interests of the local government. Few treasurers expressed this attitude with the same force though all had a 'guardianship' ideology.

The same Treasurer commented on the 'natural' alliance of the institutional role with that of the chief executive and the careful subordination of the treasurer's roles, 'I transmitted through the chief executive whose role is normally more managerial in a broad and highly political sense with little or no technical core to it by comparison with a treasurer'.

A Treasurer in a district commented on how his alliance operated:

> The Chief Executive and myself arrived at a number of personal value judgements on how cuts in expenditure should operate. We had always felt the council spent too much on their park and open spaces with no value for money. A lot of projects were put forward for show. It was only a question of us putting objects to members and the members saying 'right'.

The Chief Executive had occupied the role in this authority for three decades and was defined by the Treasurer as a 'highly political animal' with close ties to the leaders of the council who are normally from the same political party from election to election. The Treasurer noted that the Chief Executive, an engineer by professional background, took a 'harder line' on attempting to cut expenditure than he himself would do. The Chief Executive influenced the members by suggesting they should instruct him to carry out a public opinion poll on projects he thought might be too costly. In spite of the joint influence of both roles it was one of the few occasions when the majority party resisted advice:

> They said they had been elected on a platform of providing better facilities. The turning point came when members appreciated there was no hope of financing the project except through their own capital allocations and they were totally inadequate. The estimated cost had risen from £4 million to £8 million. If the public poll which allowed public opposition to be more vocal had not taken place they would still have felt they were committed. Finally it was deferred but I think there is no longer any strong political will to bring it out of mothballs.

The closeness of the relationship and the manner in which role playing was jointly carried out was illustrated as follows:

> Just before we presented the final report to committee I gave the Chief Executive a ring. It was all in my report but he said 'fine'. In the committee meeting he led for quite a long time on that specific point. If I had tried to do it all it would have been too much. Equally it would have been wrong if the Chief Executive (in my opinion) had done it all and tried to cover the whole budget.

A treasurer in a metropolitan county found that he was institutionally stronger than his chief executive who had lost the confidence of senior local politicians. He found that his interventions sometimes had to cover areas in which the Chief Executive ought to have prime responsibility. In a 'natural' alliance he became the senior partner but at a certain cost, the partial alienation of the Chief Executive who recently resigned. Inside the chief officer's group he did not publicly subscribe to a value for money, private market ideology and indeed was interested in distancing himself from such an identification. This did not mean a relaxation of accounting controls, but merely a certain scepticism on whether financial expertise should dominate policy formation:

> I recently intervened. I worked out that all departments had just enough capital resources to manage except Highways whose allocation only allowed half its programme to be carried out. I deliberately concentrated the members' attention on Highways almost to the exclusion of the rest of the capital budget. I suggested to the Chief Officer of the Highways, the Surveyor, that he put forward a list of what he wanted to do if he could get more money. His first list simply coincided with the amount of money he thought he could get.

The Treasurer discussed the list with the Chief Executive and others and decided it was worth supporting. Instead of encouraging the Surveyor to cut expenditure, the Treasurer decided he would push for an increase in expenditure:

> I went back to the Surveyor and told him that instead of asking to replace lamp posts and that sort of thing he should bring into his first list two major projects. One should be a by-pass for one of our county towns. If he wanted support he should include items that would carry political weight. I knew I could get the Minister to accept that package while one that concentrated on 200 yards of pavement straightened out would be very difficult to push.

Yet the Treasurer voiced a reluctance to expand his role authority and invade political ground no matter how inviting it was. In that sense he too was a 'constitutionalist'. He defined his role playing as related to issues: 'My strength in this authority, such as it is, depends on how far I can make members and officers concentrate on what are the real issues not what they think are the real issues'.

Reality definition is rather more impressive than keeping money for the balances in a 'back pocket' or the other tactics and strategies utilized by treasurers. The Treasurer was faced with a situation in the last regime where the majority party had on certain issues little internal cohesion. Chief officers found that such fragmentation made 'reality' definition even more difficult:

> I found that often policy would be worked out by a chairman which elected members as individuals would not support. Sometimes committee attendances would be low and they would find they could not carry their backbenchers. The leader, who is in favour of cutting expenditure further than I would, can't carry his chairmen and they in turn could not often carry their committees.

In such a context, policy-making becomes volatile and a tendency exists for chief officers to be pulled into making decisions that should have been made by politicians. The 'constitutionalism' inside the occupational cultures of these professionals resisted. Also the consequences of an open de-legitimation of political roles in the long run could provoke the possibility of a backlash. The Treasurer noted:

> Sometimes I had to insist it's up to elected members to take decisions on unpopular cuts. We would be vulnerable the next time the opposition came to power otherwise. I told the majority group, after a meeting where they had decided to cut by £3 million, that it was OK with me. I also said, however, in my budget report that you cut by £4 million and you will have to state publicly that you are not taking my advice. They thought that was fair. Now they have taken their decision I will defend it.

In the new regime which took over, the Treasurer kept insisting on using his reports to state professional opinions even if they were not acceptable or accepted:

> I have just come from a party group meeting of members. I had to go over with them the present financial situation. I told them they were spending £20 million more than we have got. They did not like that advice but they are going to get it in writing, and get it publicly. They will almost certainly decide against making major cuts. I'm more pessimistic than they are of what Whitehall will do.

The Treasurer felt that members believed he had the right to say what his professional opinions were. Many members are themselves professionals and thus award him the licence and mandate (to use E. C. Hughes'[10] categories) to express such opinions. The Treasurer attempted to describe his problem:

> The subtlety of my position is I have to maintain my right to professional opinions without actually taking too much advantage of it. If I take advantage of it too much then the essential relationship with the controlling party, as distinct from the council as a whole, would be damaged. They would feel all the time I was reserving my position, reserving my right to say something public that would embarrass them. Then there would be a limit to what I could contribute to private discussion. But, nevertheless, I have got to claim the right to independence and I have got to convince them that it's normal that I should have it. Because when I do need it I need it badly.

A treasurer in a non-metropolitan county in the south-west described the difficulties he faced. He felt that the changes in rapid succession by Whitehall of the financial 'rules of the game' complicated his normal relationship with politicans as it increased a level of volatility in 'mood' and decision-making. Handling such an environment and the resentments of spending departments' chief officers placed new burdens and strains on his organizational relationships. The management of cuts was to a significant extent left to the Chief Executive (an ex-treasurer in the same authority) and the Treasurer to organize:

> I led the service Chief Officers in an important seminar before all the members – the first time we have had a teach-in on finance. It's a terrible responsibility to cut £5 million from the budget. I wanted to make certain that members understood the pros and cons I had gone through. If they did not like what arguments I had been using, I wanted them to say so. I wanted to describe exactly why we were overspent.

Another chief officer commented on the exercise led by the Treasurer: 'The Treasurer summed up the implications of the cuts in making reductions in services. His recommendations in the morning were clear. That they should take £2.3 million, which was the amount of the cut we had adjusted the budget by earlier in the year, and do nothing more until they know what the Rate Support Grant would be'. The Treasurer and the Chief Executive, two professionals who were normally given high credibility and trust, found that their 'trust' relationships were suddenly rather weak: 'In the morning's meeting, the members applauded the Treasurer's advice to wait and in the afternoon in the Finance Committee the same members rejected it and organized another exercise in looking for further cuts, which in the morning they had rejected'. The members were cross-pressured by service department committees and strong party and pro-cut allegiances who also felt a vote for further cuts was a symbol of strong support for their party in power at Westminster. The normally influential party leadership which ruled by consensus lacked the cohesion in this context to support the Treasurer and the Chief Executive. However, the Treasurer was still regarded as highly influential:

> In this economic climate where finance is dominant I am very reluctant to take on any Chief Officer in front of the Finance Committee, my committee. I will automatically normally win. Just this morning I had to see the Chief Probation Officer on a report he had written to which I strongly objected. I almost threatened him that if he did not withdraw it I would get him at the Finance Committee. He knew how strongly I felt and he withdrew the report.

A treasurer is in an institutional position to make like difficult for chief officers, but sometimes his opposition would only be nominal: 'Education had a certain cut in their budget, youth projects, and they then tried to swing that cut to another committee with a separate funding arrangement. I opposed them and lost. It was only £12,000 and my opposition was half-hearted'.

Sometimes a treasurer would approve but expect to find a combination of influential chairpersons against him so a compromise of some type would occur. A treasurer would only have strength against a particular chairperson if other chairpersons stayed neutral:

> My committee has to hold back the chairman of the spending committees and also hold

back those hard men and women among members who want further cuts. That's why I told chairmen no more virement, no more supplementary estimates. Only one chairman has gone over our heads to the Policy and Resources Committee. He frequently spends money allocated for one project on something else, then wants it a second time.

The Treasurer's strategy of allowing chairpersons the freedom to manoeuvre meant that it was difficult to monitor particular chairpersons' strategy closely and thus to check them in time. A powerful chairperson could attempt to use his political influence and his alliance to overrule the finance committee: 'We can say no to a request in Finance and then lose it in Policy and Resources where other chairmen may support his bid'.

Departmentalism was still the name of the game, with corporate management more shell than substance at least as far as the chairpersons of the committee are concerned: 'The Finance Committee's report which called for a halt to all capital projects was defeated in Policy and Resources. The chairman of Finance knew he would be defeated partly because it is impossible to stop this year's capital programme but he wanted to clear the decks for next year. It was stage managed'. However, such organizational theatre also expressed a real conflict between the chairpersons who all sit on the dominant Policy and Resources Committee and the Finance Committee.

Stewart has argued that local authorities accept a myth of statutory constraints by Whitehall.[11] The general and frequently imprecise terminology allows both ambiguity and local interpretation of needs. The Treasurer won a victory over local influential chief officers and politicians by local evaluation of need: 'The Department of Education and Science told us we could spend £3½ million on education buildings next year. I and the Finance Committee took the bull by the horns and said we can only afford to spend £500,000. That's the first time we have done this and it has caused no end of friction with Education'. Battles with influential departments and politicans could be won and lost. In one year, the Rate Support Grant benefited the county council rather more than the Treasurer expected. He was then faced by a strong alliance of Education and Social Services demanding money to be restored from the previous cuts in departmental budgets:

> Education and Social Services asked for £1 million to be returned but I held them off to £500,000. The Library service asked for £15,000 to retain a mobile library, but got nothing. I had an agreement with Education and Social Services, but I was partly resisting as I felt we should keep up our balances. Anyway the deal went through.

The Treasurer had to give strong departments something but saw no reason to encourage small departments who had less political support. In addition, the Chief Executive and the Treasurer saw themselves as the guardians of the smaller departments and had earlier acted to give them protection from the impact of a cross-the-board percentage cuts, which would hit them especially hard on a smaller budget base: 'I did not want other departments like Libraries to ask for money back, so I played a hard line. It was no use opposing totally Education and Social Services together as too many important members sat on their committees and most members now wanted to give them some of the money back'. The Treasurer also discovered that his ally the Chief Executive had already sympathetically heard the Education and Social Services chief officers when they informed the Treasurer of their claims. If the Chief Executive could not be counted as a strong supporter of a hard line the Treasurer had to seek a compromise.

The alliance with the Chief Executive was of key importance. In a context where members could make contradictory decisions on financial matters regarding services within the same week, a common strategy was not only sensible but imperative. The other chief officers were not able to act on their own without such a lead and their political relationships seemed to be turning against them rather than working for them: 'Members were saying we had to cut by £5 million, which would be impossible. The Chief Executive and myself worked out a list of acceptable cuts at £2.6 million. What we did was to pick items which could cause less public outcry and thus help the politicians. It was highly political and frankly subjective'.

The right of chief officers as managers was underlined by such action and the politicians were given some protection by highly conscious political management: 'In Education we were aware that the closing of small village schools would lead to an outcry so we left those out of cuts on the capital budget list'. The Treasurer and Chief Executive saw each chief officer and departmental accountant privately and left members completely out of decision-making though the leader knew what the role incumbents were doing and gave approval. The chairman of Finance also knew: 'Each Chief Officer knew what could happen to his department and yielded up cuts but each chief officer did not know until much later what he had asked of other officers. We got agreements worked out at the chief officers' group by keeping strictly to the options chief officers had presented'.

Politically, the chief officers were anxious to avoid forced redundancies which would mean trouble with unions and sour internal departmental relations. Options which guarded labour power were taken. Criteria utilized in making cuts were to allow chief officers to decide on options using where possible national average statistics and political conceptions of 'fairness':

> We found some smaller departments had well above average performance costs so we tended to be somewhat harder on these and they took their full percentage cuts this time. The Education department presented us with the options of protecting the post-16 year olds or nursery education. With rising rates of unemployment in the county we chose to protect the post-16 year olds. We were always very conscious of the unions' professional opinions and the local rate-payer.

While the Treasurer was closely linked to the chairman of finance, the Chief Executive was not and was often strongly critical of the chairman's tactics. It seemed to be accepted that the Chief Executive could cross swords with the chairman of finance without directly involving the Treasurer. The Chief Executive stated about one committee meeting already mentioned:

> I realized that the Finance Committee was going to try to halt all capital projects. The proposal from the chairman was daft and mainly a political gesture as he knew some projects we could not stop as it would be too costly. I told the Leader of the council I was going to speak against the complete chopping of the capital programme. I did not think it would get through but I could not run the risk that it might with members being so flighty. I could not expect the Treasurer to speak out against his chairman as it might have soured the relationship.

The Treasurer and the Chief Executive could be said to be 'double agents' in the sense that while they were not engaged in double-cross organizational politics it was to their institutional advantage to act as brokers. They could act as representatives of the political leadership to chief officers and could, in turn, represent officers to politicians. Such role playing could result in considerable role strains, but it also offered considerable rewards to skilful brokers. Patching up agreements and negotiating settlements could result more or less in a recasting of the balance of power inside a local government. If brokers' roles were combined with a reluctance to dictate crudely policy to fellow chief officers and a traditional respect for nuances and customs, rituals of respect and deference, the long-term effect could be significant. The 'constitutionalism' of a treasurer should not be dismissed as a surface manifestation with no deep roots in his values and occupational culture. The very strength of a broker role is located precisely in the traditionalism of a role actor:

> As Treasurer I sometimes want my people to have more weight in the service departments but how can I say this to the head of an indepedent department in an organization which is not structured properly? I can, and do, intervene if the standard of financial management is poor and the other Chief Officers do not openly object. So I knew the Surveyor's finance management was bad. I took a report to the Finance Committee about it. I called in external auditors to bring in a new integrated costing system. I tried to use my organizational strength to tell the department 'you will do this'.

The Treasurer, to some extent, was able to change the financial 'rules of the game'. The rules for virement in past years had been mutually agreed between officers and committees with the Treasurer diplomatically allowing sums of money allocated under one budget sub-head to be swiched to another. This, in practice, also encouraged savings and was in line with a vague but influential local version of 'value for money'. This year the Treasurer decided to change the virement rules and was supported by the Finance Committee:

> I try to be fair with departments who have voluntarily made savings. In the past, they could keep all the money but this year I'm trying also to be fair to the rate-payers so a sizable percentage, perhaps half, of departmental savings are going to remain with me. This new rule has been made by me without fuss. If I formally present it as a change in regulations to the Policy and Resource Committee the chairman on it would have reversed it or weakened it.

The Treasurer realized he could not take back all the savings as it would have eliminated the initiative of chief officers to search out savings and members associated with spending departments would have resisted strongly: 'I picked on Education first as the biggest spender. I let them have some savings back but I kept some to build up my balances. I took that as a precedent for the other departments. If Education agrees the smaller departments would find it difficult to dissent.'

The Treasurer emphasized that few strategic actors apart from the leader and members of the Finance Committee were interested in building up county balances. Many members of the Finance Committee also sat on spending department committees and when they did so the Treasurer was not certain that they were still his 'people'. They could be 'turned' by the spending departments into becoming the advocates of that department even on the Finance Committee itself. Only the chairman and perhaps the vice chairman were immune to being 'turned'. And the Treasurer was vulnerable. He was a departmental chief officer:

> Don't forget I head a department. Like every other Chief Officer, I'm taking a 5 per cent cut and I don't like it. I can't cut off an area of activity and I can argue that the overall cuts create more work for my department. I should have argued for special exemption in the Chief Officers' group, but can you imagine what the other Chief Officers would have said? I believe I can only cut by 3 per cent not 5 per cent.

The Treasurer recognized that his dual role as head of a spending department and also the head of a financial monitoring system could have its dangers for the council: 'I could start to give council advice that cuts should only be 3 per cent and put reasons for doing so simply because I did not want to cut my department by more than 3 per cent. That could cost the council several million pounds'.

The initial cut across-the-board strategy which equalized pain for all departments was an openly political strategy to reduce the possibility of powerful chairmen claiming exemption for their departments. The chances of successful alliances against an equal cuts strategy were practically nil. This did not mean that the Treasurer and key politicans, who were not directly liked to the protection of spending departments as a top priority, could not see the advantages of a different strategy. Government guidelines on spending were becoming less precise since 1980 with the exception of a recommendation that 'law and order' services should have a high priority. While the police budget benefited from Whitehall recommendations it caused further problems as the heads of service departments, not normally associated with law and order, claimed exemption from cuts on the grounds that part of their departments' professional activities could be claimed for 'law and order':

> Whitehall papers tell us law and order should receive high priority. In this authority the Fire Brigade argues his service counts as law and order so the Fire Brigade is doing better than other services. The Director of Social Services publicity stated that he is responsible for children in care and that activity should be included under law and order. I think he has convinced the Leader though not me to that degree.

The history of the treasurer's role goes back into the time of the unreformed local government system and has always been prized, though not always influential. The steady growth of the role influence and authority in the twentieth century has been both striking and significant and there is no reason to believe that its institutional authority will not further expand – sometimes in spite of the subjective desires of its occupants. To be a good treasurer is to sometimes be a bad accountant but an effective street politician. If a treasurer insisted on imposing the language and codes of accounting as the rational and dominant language of local government, he will have taken on a new and perhaps dangerous project. Such a project would seek to recast not only other professional languages and to subordinate them to its own logic, but would threaten those rituals and symbols built into the supposed pragmatic common sense of the organizational structures. Inside these rituals and symbols strategic actors bind themselves to meet, talk and decide and are, in turn, made captive. The rationality of an accounting language even when articulated as a guide to efficiency and effectiveness need not be welcomed by such willing captives.

NOTES AND REFERENCES

1 Young, K. and Kramer, J. *Strategy and Conflict in Metropolitan housing*, 1978, 228.
2 Young, K. Values in the policy process. *Policy and Politics*, 1977, 5(3).
3 Dunleavy, P. *Urban political analysis*, 1980, 126-7.
4 Midwinter, A. *et. al.* Excessive and unreasonable: the politics of the Scottish hit list. *Political Studies*, 1983, 31.
5 Sbragia, A. *Capital markets and central-local politics in Britain: the double dilemma*, Centre for the Study of Public Policy (Studies in Public Policy, 109), 1983, 12-13.
6 Rosenberg, D. *et. al.*, A work role perspective of accountants in local government service departments. *Accountancy, Organisations and Society*, 1982, 7(2).
7 Rose, R. and Page E. Chronic instability in fiscal systems. In Rose, R. and Page, E. (eds.), *Fiscal Stress in Cities*, 1983, 221.
8 See Danziger, J. N. *Making Budgets*, 1978, 226: 'These systems are controlled by competent and benevolent technocrats, but the situation invites concern about the limits upon democratic citizen involvement'; also see Dearlove, J. *The Politics of Policy in Local Government*, 1973, 155-74 for local politicians' ideologies of pressure groups' legitimacy.
9 Young, K. *Op. cit.*, 5.
10 Hughes, E. C. The humble and the proud: the comparative study of occupations. *Sociological Quarterly*, 1970, 11 (2), 147-56.
11 Stewart, J. *Local government: the conditions of local choice*, 1983, 146-50.

CHAPTER EIGHT

The role set of treasurers in their relationships to chief executives

Newton[1] has claimed with justification that no systematic or comprehensive attempt to study the actual role orientations and behaviour of elected representatives in British local politics exists. Rhodes[2] accepted this claim and further asked why research on the authority and power of the key professional elites in local government had also been generally avoided in local government studies. The answer must be located in the general poverty of theory and fieldwork practice in research. The absence of case studies of senior local government officers in comparison with case studies of the role relationships of teachers and social workers is significant. Dennis and Davies are among the exceptions in this situation.[3]

A ROLE THEORY PERSPECTIVE

Role theory has a number of weaknesses. The two most important weaknesses are a lack of concern with the historical processes of the organization and the external historical dynamics which determine the organization. The second weakness in role theory is linked to the past domination of structural functionalism in organizational theory. This theory limited the possibilities of the actor in choosing different options in role presentation and identity. Nevertheless roll theory can pragmatically help develop a model of elite professionals in local government structures and also resolve gaps in the literature on the politics of the budgetary process. It is a vehicle in which power relationships can be explored and the implications of the power relationships for organizations investigated. A weak rather than a strong use of the role category will structure this chapter. This chapter accepts Salaman's position that: 'It is highly likely that members of organizations may be exposed to more than one body of expectations ... the relative weight of relevant expectations can very enormously'.[4]

Power is inherently unquantifiable in this mode of analysis. This is partly because it is not a unilinear phenomenon and partly because it cannot simply be reduced to an individual's attributes or personality; though these may have an input. Power is analyzed as a quality of social relationships rather than an extension of attributes of individuals alone. Research on the power of elite professionals may also be linked with the stress placed on their 'neutrality' and the trust that other major actors have in what is seen as an independent source of expertise.

This paper follows the path Danziger took for a brief moment in an attempt to explore and evaluate the ideas and values of the main actors in the process of budget construction. He has argued that: 'configurative approaches at the individual level remain attractive because they provide a rich descriptive data base from which to generate stores as explanations and because they capture more of the texture of politics than system-level or organization-level approaches'.[5]

He does not, however, provide the data to support such a statement. The absence of an adequate sociology of financial management and executive roles in local government literature allows a prescriptive formalism to exist in financial management textbooks. Yet the interplay between the roles of treasurer, chief executive, chief officers and public representatives in decision-making is of obvious vital importance in the analysis of policy construction.[6]

The literature (where it exists) on the treasurer's role is sparse and unsatisfactory. Thus a recent study by Hinings *et al.* mentions the leading role of the head of the financial control system in one brief sentence: 'The formal position of a Treasurer is no different from that of a surveyor, but because of the resources he commands and his strategic position in the organization he can wield potentially considerably influence'.[7] This hardly advances any theory of power in local government. An earlier study by the same authors did give one example of the strains on the treasurer's role in budget politics, but went no further.[8] The impression left is that these authors believe that contingency theory in the analysis of organizations is an adequate substitute for a sociology of power and role relationships. The fieldwork research in this chapter may indirectly bypass the *cul-de-sac* problems posed by contingency theory.

The increasing professional and technical influence of the treasurer's role, as well as other elite professional roles, is recognized by Stanyer, who observed a recent tendency in local government to reduce the number of departments and chief officers. The rationality behind this, in his analysis, was that this restructuring was done 'partly to promote co-ordination between what are believed to be closely related services. Its consequence is to create overlords ... and thus introduce a more formal status system within the relations between chief officers. This process of differentiation shows how different professions have been valued in local government'.[9] He acknowledges that the treasurer has tended to increase the potentiality in his power role aspect by emerging as an overlord of financial administration. Stanyer hints that it is the breadth of issues to which a treasurer can contribute which allows such an expansion of influence. It may well be that it is the very breadth of the issues and the treasurer's acceptable legitimacy, given by other key elites, in linking these issues which explains the possible expansion of authority in the treasurer's role. Stanyer explains that these 'two horizontal departments ... the Clerk's and the Treasurer's ... are much more organizationally oriented than many others and they have played crucial functional roles ... they have frequent contacts with all other departments and with all committees whereas many of the others are operationally more self contained'.[10]

HISTORICAL, LEGAL AND CULTURAL ASPECTS OF THE TREASURER'S ROLE

While elite professionals may be social influentials in their local authorities, their influence today stems from their position in local government. Maud and Finer state the orthodox position: 'Local government officers ... (with some exceptons) are servants of the local council, deriving from it their powers and functions, and their tenure of office is at the mercy of a single resolution of the council, or perhaps in practice the decision of a single committee'.[11] The treasurer's role, like that of other professionals, is structured by the legal theory of a master-servant relationship between council members and officers. A certain ambiguity can exist and generate role strain and affect performance. Thus, in the old boroughs before reorganization, the treasurer's role related to the legal fact that the corporate body was not the council, but the whole body of ratepayers, the burgesses. Legally the treasurer had a duty and a responsibility not merely to the narrow body of aldermen and councillors, but to the ratepayers of the town or city as a whole. The analogy can be drawn with a company director who owes a duty not only to the board of directors, but to the whole body of shareholders. In the counties the legal position of the treasurer was somewhat different. County officers such as the county treasurer existed long before county councils and had established professional traditions based on their relationship with the Quarter Sessions.[12]

The ambiguity in the role set of the treasurer was underlined in the legal judgement given in the case of the Attorney General *versus* De Winton in 1906. The court held that a borough treasurer must disobey an order from the council that calls for an illegal payment. This legal input into the treasurer's role is very rarely consciously used by a treasurer as it would signal a breakdown in working relationships with the public representatives and weaken the treasurer's role in the very instant of its use. Richards has argued: 'If a treasurer refused to carry out an instruction from the council because of doubts about its legality, it would still be open to the council, at least in theory, to dismiss their treasurer. If ever a dispute threatened to reach this stage, public opinion would be aroused and play a large part in deciding the issue'.[13] A former treasurer, Marshall, states:

> The mere existence of a responsibility independent of the council can create a delicate situation, and few treasurers can relish those occasions upon which they have to remind their councils of the position. That major conflicts are so rare is attributable to the good sense of the local authorities who shrink from pursuing courses which force their officers to decline to follow their instructions and to the sense of balance which treasurers, in general, show in exercising the personal responsibilities of their office.[14]

One treasurer who was interviewed in this study saw his duty as mainly being responsible to the ratepayers of the local authority; in fact he was suspended from office for too rigorous a pursuit of this aim, although he was later reinstated.

Both Richards and Marshall infer that the treasurer's role has a potential in role authority which is rare in local government and this is a product of the guardianship occupational ideology, and the respect given to a 'non-political' professional like a treasurer can be translated into political support in a clash with the local politicans who are legally his masters. At the very least neither the public representatives nor the treasurer would win for, in conflict over policy, the trust relationship is weakened. In addition, such a clash allows the possibility of external political interventions. Danziger has hinted that the 'budgetary elite' prefers a closed system of decision making since it serves to 'simplify the pressures of resource allocation on the major budgetary decision makers. The budgetary elite prefers an efficient, unencumbered problem-solving system to a system which facilitates participation and open communication'.[15] A clash between a treasurer and public representatives would then potentially allow a further political input from the public and interested groups which may not be managed or controlled.

In the organizational charts of local government the role of treasurer, like all chief officers, is subordinated to the new role of chief executive. Local government research literature suggests that the chief executive role draws some of its authority from what are essentially political rather than professional relationships. In contrast, the core characteristics of the treasurer's role are linked to the technical professionalism of financial management with a low external and visible political input. Roles of both the chief executive and the treasurer are played by officers who can make political calculations, but the authority base of each role is radically different. The volatility in authority and power of a chief executive, the potential for the expansion and contraction of influence, is mainly geared to the political inputs of the public representatives. Chief executives can be and are dismissed by their councils with some regularity, unlike treasurers. The very tightness of a financial role, its 'neutral' professionalism, allows greater potential in resisting certain types of political input.

Role relationships in local government are both clear and ambiguous and the ambiguity is an element in the culture which allows for a variety of expected and unexpected patterns. Ambiguities can thus be functional rather than dysfunctional. Role relationships are structured an another level by trust and distrust; co-operation and unwillingness to yield too much in the process of co-operation. While the consensus building in the culture attempts to allow everyone to win at least once, in a situation of contracting resources some of the actors cannot always win and a few rarely win. A treasurer is a powerful ally even for a chief executive and if the chief executive loses the trust and authority given to him by the councillors the treasurer may inherit at least part of the authority. Haynes documents the example of Birmingham in 1977 when 'it was announced that the chief executive was to lose his employment altogether, and that his duties, including that of overall co-ordination, were to be taken over by the City Treasurer'.[16]

In Somerset, the chief executive was dismissed and the role could possibly have been abolished. The council then decided to promote the treasurer to the post of chief executive. In the city of Oxford, it was decided by the council that the city treasurer should also fill the role of chief executive at the same time. In a number of crises in which chief executives were challenged by public representatives it was the holder of the treasurer's role who inherited some of the authority of the chief executive. It is rather unlikely that a chief executive would be able to eat into the professional components of the treasurer's role to the same extent. The acceptance by public representatives of the claims to value neutrality and technical competence by key finance professionals allows them credibility in filling the space left by a weakened or dismissed chief executive. Some, at least, of the sample of treasurers interviewed were aware of this aspect of their role relationships with other members of the local authority.

In the post-Bains era, after the reorganization of local government, a certain standardization of the treasurer's role seems to have taken place. Before this, differences in authority allowed in the role set could be as significant as the similarities. Marshall himself hints at the 'startling contrasts in the position accorded the chief financial officer in different localities. In some places ... he plays a weighty and effective part: in others he is little more than a book-keeper ... In between these two extremes almost every possible variation is to be found'.[17] In the absence of written provisions the boundaries of the role are set by such variables as the personality of the treasurer and the specific local authority traditions. These traditions may actually have a brief history, but they mesh into the local system of social relationships and, in turn, are shaped by them. In researching a variety of different local authorities, Grant has established the existence of local political frameworks which allow conflicts to take place and compromises to be established.[18] These local rules of the game have been noted at the level of party politics though not at the level of relationships between elite professionals and politicians. The totality of these local rules of the game form the parameters within which local government decision-making takes place.

One of the very few studies of county administration argues that the withdrawal of the local gentry, the traditional 'social leaders', from occupying dominant active positions on the county council, has resulted, since the 1929 Local Government Act, in a new alliance filling the vacant space. The rise of state corporatism has in this context led to a structural alliance arising out of the increase of collective authority by the elite professionals, supported by central government working in harness with a relatively new political layer, a stratum who, while often 'well to do', cannot always be easily located as a tight social oligarchy. The importance of this stratum is in the social articulation with all factions of the significant local social classes, and their collective ability to act as brokers between local and central government through the national party system and between different local and national interest groups. This particular study acknowledges that while the gentry decline in political importance inside county government, professionals, owners of capital, local industrialists, and farmers continued to be significant power holders.[19] This awareness of social relationships in the local authority becomes a common-sense, pragmatic realism and determines policy options in decision-making.

A treasurer, just as much as any other chief officer, attempts to maximize his influence and to sidestep potential problems which may weaken the authority at his command. He has to learn to master the nuances of these specific local social relationships if he wants to predict the determinants operating on the public representatives, his masters, in council policy. The success or failure of this learning process expands or contracts the power, influence and authority of all key elite professionals. Thus in Lee's study of Cheshire, the treasurer's role was strong enough to play a significant part in rate-fixing negotiations between the chairman of the finance committee and the treasurer. Lee's study implies that the significance of the treasurer's role was openly recognized as a vital element in the local political establishment and his name was closely linked to the most influential local politicians. The role boundaries between professional advice and power over policy supposedly held by the elected members is blurred in such contexts. Any sociology of the master-servant relationship in local government will show that the concept of servant hides as well as reveals the contours of power.

The importance of political skills which allow an accurate reading of the social relationships by elite professionals including the treasurer, and the importance of being able to predict their consequences for policy, is shown in a recent study of an urban local authority. Saunders, in his case study of Croydon, contrasts the failure by the professionals in the education department to predict a revolt by the local middle class against the introduction of comprehensive education, with the calculations of the Director of Finance and his deputy.[20] The relative decline in Croydon's Rate Support Grant produced another middle-class revolt against a raising of the rates, and the local politicians and finance professionals used this revolt in their bargaining with the London County Council and central government. Saunders documents a number of statements showing some professional sympathy with the rate revolt.

These brief notes taken from the sparse literature in local government studies are not a substitute for a total historical sociology of the treasurer's role. They are the tentative first steps in the location of the role inside a patterned system of relationships which sometimes has the temporary permanence of a kaleidoscope. The last section of the chapter will probe the nature of alliances, tensions and strains inside the alliances between the elite professionals who control the central monitoring departments. The making, breaking and rebuilding of organizational life through tight or loose alliances is a common feature in local government decision making. It may be helpful to utilize a language of political processes which emphasizes negotiations and contests over policy and resources. In the exploration of role relationships between the key positions in the hierarchy held by the roles of chief executive and the treasurer, Greenwood *et al.* point out that 'A more adequate theory of budgeting, in other words, will have to be based on the political features of organizational life, rather than upon the cognitive deficiencies of decision actors'.[21] To this end, attention will now be turned to an analysis of the observational and interview data of this research. It must be emphasized that nearly all the evidence on role relationships stems from observations of only one of the major actors, but it is argued that, while this is a weakness, it does not undercut and invalidate the general interpretative thrust of the argument.

182

THE RELATIVE INFLUENCE AND POWER OF CHIEF
EXECUTIVES AND TREASURERS

The 'trust' relationship between elite professionals, as well as between professionals and politicians, is composed of formal and informal understandings. It is a particular balance of power and authority in decision-making and a subtle form of influence which is rarely static. Trust can be lost and trust has to be won on a day-to-day basis grounded in the routines of the organization. It is a relationship which tests the credibility of each partner and as such can be both surprisingly strong while in other situations fragile. A number of examples will be given which emphasize the context over authority in the working relationship between treasurer and chief executive which is normally termed one of trust.

> When I was Deputy Treasurer here we had a new Chief Executive who wanted more safeguards and additional powers written into standing orders on where he would stand in relationship to budgetary control. He wanted to be in on it from the start. The Treasurer and myself were both upset, but the politicians supported him. Still, though these powers are still in standing orders, I believe it has not made much difference. I don't feel limited in my authority over the budget. I suppose it gave the Chief Executive the comfort that he would automatically be sent all important financial information straight away. I inherited the situation and though I don't like it, I have learnt to live with it.

The comparatively gentle assertion of authority by the chief executive in this case had both an aspect of symbolism in the formal strengthening of the role in standing orders and a strong recognition that information, especially financial information, is power in local government organizations. Limited access to information weakens the role's potential to intervene in the construction of finance policy at an early stage.

Another treasurer saw the negotiations over authority in role relationships as being rather one-sided. His description of the somewhat brutal assertion of authority between roles is quite clear:

> Our Chief Executive is, in theory at least, committed to corporate planning and the existence of a finance committee. The treasurer before me, however, was a very powerful officer. In fact, in everything except name he was also the chief executive. In those days the present chief executive was the deputy town clerk. He sat in the wings, watched and listened. He was obviously determined that in no way was he going to have another treasurer competing with him as a town clerk or chief executive. One way of doing so was to reduce the power and influence of the finance department and he partly did this by abolishing the finance committee. So now I have not got a chairman and I have got to go and share the Leader of the council with the chief executive and when I go to the Leader it is normally through the chief executive. Of course I am very loyal and careful. Getting rid of the finance committee was deliberate policy because the main opposition to the chief executive's effectiveness could only really come from the treasurer who also runs a central service ... At reorganization the chief executive also pushed through a new internal structure of the finance department so that we now have two treasurers. I was still the director of finance and therefore head of the finance department, but the day-to-day running of the office was placed in the hands of a chief finance officer who was very powerful.

183

The loss of a structured relationship, independent of the chief executive, to influential council members is linked to a decrease in potential political support in any inter-organizational clash over policy and authority. While political ties between council members and elite professionals are not automatically translated into leverage inside the organization in contests with other professionals, the loss does weaken bargaining power over policy and authority issues. Like the treasurer in the first example, the political input is often a major input into the differential power resource base of professionals. The creation of two treasurers in the place of one, while it may help the technical functioning of the finance department, may also be seen as an organizational weapon to weaken the control of the director of finance over the department from which he draws his authority and influence. These are two examples of chief executives' success in defining the trust relationship as relationships of subordination as well as partnership. A third example below demonstrates a less extreme variation of the subordination of a treasurer by a chief executive through external policies.

> The chairman of the finance committee who was politically very shrewd and probably the most financially aware councillor is no longer on the council. He would consult me and the chief executive but he could and did carry the day with no problems on issues which we may not have agreed. The weakness of the majority party is that they now no longer have the financial awareness they used to have. They are, therefore, more dependent on the chief executive and myself for advice. Even when the financial advice comes from him it originates from me. He has his own idea about where he would like to make cuts, but I'm the only one who knows in practice what the result will be ... So now there is more joint action between us. He can't influence the finance review working party unless he gets information and advice from me and therefore I know now what he is getting up to ... if the chief executive supports me when estimates come in, then, if I don't go along with the departmental bid, I can get it rejected. If he does not support I normally lose ... The chief executive is very much an autocrat ... with very close ties to the members. I have my links with the finance chairman, but his ties with all key members are much stronger. This strengthens his autocratic hand and his control over the chief officers. At times I do not find this acceptable, but I can gain influence through the chief executive.

However, a conflict or loss of trust between a treasurer and council member can also have a major impact on the chief executive as well as other chief officers. The erosion of one key trust relationship penetrates all others and the loss of credibility with politicians weakens even a treasurer with a strong personality. A treasurer in a borough was first suspended and then reinstated. While he refused to be interviewed, a chairman of an important spending committee in the same local authority attempted to describe the breakdown of the working relationship in these terms:

> I think the Treasurer felt his traditional role was being eroded. We thought increased expenditure was necessary and he did not ... When he looked at the long term he correctly saw the longer you leave the reduction of the budget the deeper the cuts have to be. The increased support we gave the service chief officers in the traditional conflict with the treasury meant we felt we wanted to improve the service regardless of the financial consequences ... We also have a comparatively weak chief executive and a forceful director of finance. Our chief executive backed away from acting as a compromisor

between us council members and the treasurer. What precipitated his suspension was a sharp disagreement between the treasurer and the chief executive on the question, to be blunt, on how far they should try and force the members in the direction they did not want to go. The chief executive took the usual view that at the end of the day the politicians were responsible for the decisions. The treasurer has increasingly stepped outside that position. He believes he is granted in law a responsibility to the borough's ratepayers. He sees himself as a representative of the ratepayers in a role that may partly be mentioned in statutory legislation. That basically puts him outside the traditional conception of who does what.

This council member documented the problems posed for role relationships if a treasurer decided to activate the ambiguity in the legal theory of the master-servant relation. The imbalance between chief executive and the treasurer also meant that the treasurer could look for no support from other chief officers in his challenge to council policy. The chairman further noted the strategy of the treasurer was one in which the threat by central government of surcharging individual councillors was used by the treasurer on a number of occasions. He further added:

> He told us if we did not make certain cuts the district audit will get the council. He used the art of advising and warning us on the dangers of surcharging. It does not always work. An issue came up, the renewal of the bank account. This came up after we had revised standing orders in order to say we will not place contracts or accept tenders from businesses with South African connections. We banked with Barclays but got a tender from the Co-operative Bank which came in £15,000 higher than Barclays. We said the gap is reasonable we are going to give the contract to the Co-operative Bank. Then the treasurer brought out the surcharge threat yet again, but this time we ignored it.

The attempt then by the treasurer to assert his role responsibilities to the ratepayers which he saw as legitimate forced him into an open political role with respect to the councillors. At the same time he intruded into the work space and authority of other elite professionals in a manner which alienated him from them. Both the chief executive and the solicitor strongly dissented from his interpretation of council policy.

It is equally difficult for the normal functioning of local government politics if the chief executive role becomes alienated from that of other chief officers, including the role of treasurer. If the chief executive also simultaneously loses the rapport and confidence of the politicians, he is in an untenable, indeed impossible, position. The role is much more determined by political inputs than the treasurer's, and yet cannot use devices such as surcharging as an organizational weapon in a contest over authority. The role is not strongly linked to central government mechanisms to monitor local government and cannot claim a responsibility beyond the composition of the council. Treasurers in conflict with local politicians are more difficult to eliminate than chief executives. A chief officer remarked on the normal potential strength of the role of treasurer if it is coupled with the confidence of the politicians in the occupant of the role:

> Our last chief executive lost the confidence and trust of the council over both his personal and administrative conduct. This was in the very early days of a change to the corporate

> management system recommended by Bains. It suited us in one way to have a chief executive who did not have the trust of his members as we felt little confidence in him. We benefited because we were able to get on with the job of managing our services without hindrance. When the chief executive was dismissed I know that some of the council members wanted to abolish or weaken the post. The then treasurer was known and trusted and he was given the job. He played a low profile for a couple of years and was prepared to retreat if it seemed prudent and he was obviously eager to conciliate.

In this crisis of trust, confidence was borrowed from both the treasurer's role and the personal attributes of the professional in order to rebuild the chief executive role. The rebuilding of credibility in the chief executive role through such a transfer of trust cemented a new relationship between politicians and chief executive. Though some councillors were themselves professionals in different sectors of the private economy, they faced the crisis of confidence in an elite professional as a crisis in a political rather than as a professional relationship. In other contexts, it is possible that such councillors could relate to local government professionals both as politicians and as professionals.

In this context another elite professional transferring between roles was able to translate professional-technical authority into political resources in his council relationships. The rebuilding of credibility, after the authority claims of the new chief executive role had been shaken, was seen as a lengthly process with many contradictory nuances. Trust in organizational relationships is not a static quality in a manner similar to some routinized interpersonal private relations and can be in constant negotiation. As this chapter has already hinted, trust can be surprisingly weak because once questioned, even on a relatively minor issue, it can lead to a lengthy chain reaction and undermine role authority even in a context where such authority apparently has been accepted for a lengthy period. Reinterpretation of the past can be a crucial element in any contemporary crisis.

A treasurer discussed this aspect of role relationships in the following words:

> The previous chief executive's relationship with me weakened and life just became extremely difficult. Council members began to use me as a vehicle of communication with him. He had just reached retirement age when this crisis occurred and I was glad, frankly, when he retired. Otherwise I felt I would have to resign. The crisis arose out of his attempt to formulate a tight corporate budget. While the members had initially accepted it, they failed to realize some of its implications and, when they did, they felt tied down and their options narrowed. It was over-constraining. So the councillors had a private meeting and then instructed me to prepare a traditional incremental budget. The chief executive was away and I had to tell him when he returned. Perhaps not unnaturally he felt I had initiated the whole process though I had not. It was a difficult time as senior colleagues began to communicate policies and ideas through myself and other chief officers and completely by-passed the chief executive.

The paradoxes of dependency, interdependency, autonomy and bargaining in role relationships between elite professionals are nearly always related to policy issues and work space issues. A treasurer who has few strong links with key politicians (as this chapter has already stressed) has fewer cards to use in negotiations and is forced into a 'junior' partnership, sometimes a very junior partnership, with the chief executive.

A treasurer in this position has some similarities with the treasurer in the third example. He stated:

> My links to the council are not very strong. I have been the treasurer here for two years and the leader of the council has never once been inside my office. The chairman of finance comes in, but that is normal for pre-committee meetings and routine. I have perhaps once or twice been called by the chief executive to see the Leader in his office. But the Leader has never talked to me about financial matters independently ... I was able to argue the council into a new policy of differential percentage cuts for the services. The first year I was here they did not want to accept it but this year they did ... I did not work at all closely on this issue with the chief executive, but he did not oppose me ... If he had shown himself to be very much against, that would have meant we would have had the old policy of equal percentage cuts straight across the board ... We do collectively sign the resource allocation reports and he sees a draft ... If I was closer to the chief executive we could informally discuss ideas about basic changes I think are needed, but chief officers very rarely see each other. We have a meeting for one hour every six weeks in the chief executive's office ... the most that happens is that you occasionally see each other in the lifts, but there is very little contact at the informal level and that level is very important indeed.

The treasurer who was last quoted asserted the obvious organizational strength of a natural alliance between the chief executive and treasurer roles. His present alliance seemed to be relatively weak and it is inferred that the chief executive needs it, politically, rather less than he does, though a technical, functional relationship is always integral to both roles. The balance and boundaries of the alliance are not constant, but shift as issues come and go. It may be the case that a relatively new occupant of a strategic role may need the input given by an alliance rather less as he or she (though few women are chief officers in local government) grows in authority and credibility. Even when a deputy treasurer who is familiar with the personalities and local politics inherits the treasureship in the same local authority, the problems of role influence and authority do not vanish, as to a great extent the role is both consistent in the job and work specification context and inconsistent in role authority, power and influence.

The treasurer quoted last complained of the lack of contact between himself, the chief executive and other chief officers. However, it may be argued that a lack of regular interactions is interlocked with a weak system of corporate management. In such a situation council members have a far greater sway over policy construction and, to a certain extent, the chief executive's role benefits from this as his role, more than that of others, is linked to all of the most influential members. In a strong system of corporate management not only is the weight of backbench council members diminished in practice, if not in theory, but the possibility also arises of potential checks to the chief executive role by an alliance between the other chief officers.

Even when an ex-treasurer becomes a new chief executive in the same local authority, it should not be assumed that the new occupants of chief executive and treasurer roles will form a natural political alliance in addition to the technical alliance of control and monitoring departments *versus* the spending departments and politicians. While on some issues a similar finance background can lead to a similar value orientation to goals, it may be less significant than other determinants of roles. It must be emphasized again that the chie͏ᶠ executive role, far more than that of the treasurer, is strategically tied not only to council members and their political inputs but to the need for acceptable consensus-building politics between and across spending departments. The strains on the natural alliance between treasurer and chief executive roles are produced by such variables. A treasurer may, for example, assert the prime importance to the council of keeping up his balances, etc., and he will sometimes discover that he will not in practice be able to carry with him the chief executive whose role must incorporate not only this goal but others.

Another treasurer asserted:

> A lot of chief executives are now ex-treasurers. When they are they have to bend over backwards to convince the chief officers and the politicians that they are still not treasurers at heart. They have to be conscious of finance, but in a different way from the way I am ... A chief executive, as an ex-treasurer, will rather go against you rather than be for you so that no one can accuse him of being half a treasurer. I have found it extremely useful to develop close relations with council members on the finance committee and outside it.

This treasurer asserted that even when an accountant was chief executive and no longer a treasurer, the claim to a professional identity was still strong and co-existed with the open political aspects of the chief executive's role. This allowed the chief executive both to support and openly to question the professional judgement of the treasurer.

The alliance between chief executive and treasurer roles is possibly strengthened in a budget contraction situation where cuts have to be made, but even there the different nuances in role set emerges. The same treasurer also stated:

> The chief executive and myself went to the spending departments ... and together we drew up a list of possible cuts. Both of us kept this list confidential from all but the Leader of the council and the chairman of finance. In the chief officers' group we then worked out with the other chief officers tactics whereby officers collectively could manage to hold the political line on the cuts and bring in the influential members to support them. We did not speak to members about it until late in the day. We had to keep it secret as it could have been interpreted by members as an infringement of their council authority ... later I found that the chief executive and myself did not have the same line on other matters ... He gave back nearly half a million to the two largest spending departments when they asked, but they did have a lot of political clout behind them. On the face of it, we had done relatively well from the Rate Support Grant, but I wanted to keep healthy balances. The chief executive, however, on this occasion thought the clawback demand was legitimate. On such an occasion I feel very much the treasurer and I noticed that the relationship between some spending departments' chief officers and the chief executive is far closer than between himself and myself.

While, as a by-product of budget contraction, the influence of finance may have grown as chief officers have had to learn financial management skills, it is not so easy to argue that the treasurer's role in every local authority has significantly grown in influence. It may well be that treasurers themselves, for a number of reasons, including subjective occupational values, are reluctant to use the role potential as it could force a reshaping of the old organizational relationship. The culture of local government is, like most cultures, conservative and the informal gentlemen's agreements which oil the system are highly valued.

IMPLICATIONS FOR IMPROVING OUR UNDERSTANDING OF FINANCIAL CONTROL IN LOCAL GOVERNMENT

Political scientists and organizational theorists have begun to ask questions about the 'rules of the game', and how these rules become the ideological boundaries of local policies. Perhaps if more attention were paid to the budgetary elite, the awareness that budgets are the outcome of clashes between entrenched interests may take on a new dimension of meaning.[22]

However, much more fieldwork into decision-making should be carried out before such a proposition is accepted or rejected. A substantial research effort on the alliance between the key roles of chief executive and the treasurer may shed further light into the closed system of the budget process. Danziger suggests that the budget process is 'controlled by competent and benevolent technocrats, but the situation invites concern about the limits upon "democratic citizen involvement".'[23] The liberal democratic theory and practice of accountability in local government should be checked by studies of accountants and other elite professionals and their organizational behaviour in the arena of local government.

In their study of the culture of senior civil servants and politicians in power inside central government, Heclo and Wildavsky tend to suggest that both civil servants and politicians can be described as political administrators unified by bonds of common kinship and modes of understanding. The professional element in the role of such senior civil servants is subordinated to the element of political adminstrator in the role.[24] As no studies of local government financial politics have a comparable degree of rich fieldwork research, all research interventions by academics tend to take on an unreal and unsatisfactory appearance and to be either formalistic or polemical and sometimes both. The theoretical field of local government may well benefit from being dissolved as a 'given' and then reconstructed.

NOTES AND REFERENCES

1 Newton, K. Role orientations and their sources among elected representatives in English local politics. *Journal of Politics*, 36, 1974.

2 Rhodes, R. *Control and Power in Central-Local Government Relations*, 1981. Also R. Rhodes, The Lost World of British Local Politics. *Local Government Studies*, 1(3), 1975.

3 Davies, J. *The Evangelistic Bureaucrat*, 1972; Dennis, N. *Public Participation and Planners' Blight*, 1972.
4 Salaman, G. *Work Organizations*, 1979, 169.
5 Danziger, J. N. *Making Budgets*, 1978, 205.
6 *Ibid.*, 226.
7 Hinings, B., *et. al. Management Systems in Local Government*, 1980, 18.
8 Greenwood, R. *In Pursuit of Corporate Rationality*, 1979.
9 Stanyer, J. *Understanding Local Government*, 1976, 123.
10 *Ibid.*, 159.
11 Maud, J. and Finer, S. E.. *Local and Government in England and Wales*, 1953, 136.
12 Keith-Lucas, B. and Richards, P. *A History of Local Government in the Twentieth Century*, 1978, 26.
13 Richards, P. *The Reformed Local Government System*, 1973, 125-6.
14 Marshall, A. H. *Financial Administration in Local Government*, 1960, 61.
15 Danziger, J. N. *Op. cit.*, 226.
16 Haynes, R. *Organization Theory and Local Government*, 1980, 185.
17 Marshall, A. H. *Op. cit.*, 56.
18 Grant, W. Local Councils, Conflict and the Rules of the Game. *British Journal of Political Science*, 1971, 1(2).
19 Lee, J. M. *Social Leaders and Public Persons*, 1963.
20 Saunders, P. *Urban Politics*, 1980.
21 Greenwood, R. *et. al.*, The Politics of Budgetary Process in English Local Government. *Political Studies*, 1977, 25-7.
22 *Ibid.*, 33.
23 Danziger, J. N. *Op. cit.*, 226.
24 Heclo, H. and Wildavsky, A. *The Private Government of Public Money*, 1974.

CHAPTER NINE

The assumptive worlds of managers of personal social services in UK local government

A lacuna exists in the absence of studies of the role politics of social service directors in the resource allocation process. This is perhaps surprising as other strategic elites in the 'local state' such as managers of housing and education services have been studied.[1] The emphasis by political scientists on studying local governments as political systems which are highly diverse, as well as uniform, has still emphasized the local politician to the exclusion of the elite professionals. Their occupational cultures have been noted but what Young has called their 'assumptive worlds' have not been adequately examined. However, the relationship between particular assumptive world categories and particular policy outcomes are, at present, a matter for speculation. In another context, Barry has warned against the difficulty of using values to explain phenomena.[2] However, if the multiple realities of the major actors in the political systems of local government are not comprehended then an important component of analysis is lost,[3] as this chapter emphasizes.

This chapter uses relatively unstructured interviewing across a sample of local governments to construct a picture of how some managers of personal social services perceive their work in the present era of fiscal retrenchment. It is assumed that the values of such agents can determine not merely the end results of resource allocation, but the very mechanisms which help to establish the 'rules of the game' of the allocation process. To an extent it questions Dunleavy's argument that such agents have little or no actual autonomy in decision making, as he believes the national corporate structures tend to produce and direct resource allocation options irrespective of the values of the party in power in each local government, or of the values of the actors.[4] Dunleavy argues that the invisible socialization process of the national local government system is dominant in the 'assumptive worlds' of local elites.

Nevertheless, variations between and inside local governments have a certain importance. Jones found, when reviewing the variations in local political systems, that political parties differ in attitudes 'as to what is prudent spending, over priorities, the pace of development of services and over who should receive what benefits'.[5] A study before the reorganization of local government on the provision of children's services found that specific political inputs had a definite effect on expenditure, with the Labour

Party generally more favourable to social services' expenditure.[6] Alt found that the dominance of the Conservative Party was associated with higher expenditure on 'law and order' services than the Labour Party which gave greater priority to educational and social welfare expenditure.[7] As indicated in Chapter 4, in the 1980s it has been found that significant variations in the allocation of resources to the same service in different local governments still persist. This may relate in part to the calculations of need imposed by Whitehall, but it may also relate to different political decisions on resource allocation by strategic actors. In 1981, CIPFA statistics show that the expenditure per head in the counties on social services was between £29.49 per head of population in Cleveland and £17.79 per head of population in Shropshire with a national average of £23.04.[8]

Past studies of social expenditure have drawn attention to these variations but the decision-making process itself has not been the object of study, merely the end result. Yet, Lewis has argued that the failure to study decision making as a political process has drained the literature of much of its significance.[9]

It is possible to acknowledge the weight of Dunleavy's argument that the internal resource allocation system of local governments in certain crucial policy areas of decisions, such as the provision of public housing, is of marginal significance in practice.[10] It may well also be accurate to argue that certain activities of personal social service departments are statutory and enforceable by central government, and resources linked to those activities are committed in advance by central-local relationships. Nevertheless, local state managers are recognized by Glennerster as playing a vital part in those areas in which expenditure is not already committed by central government. Thus, he notes the importance of decisions taken through inter-committee bargaining in local governments. He further recognizes:

> It is important to seek to find how far priorities are determined in an explicit way and how far they have emerged entirely unrecognised . . . the fact that resources are allocated in an explicit way does not necessarily mean that knowledge on which decisions are taken are published or open to public debate . . . it is also helpful to ask how far resource choices are made on technical and professional grounds and how far they are left to the interplay of political forces.[11]

The political skills and relationships of personal social services directors have become of great importance in the present era of fiscal retrenchment. In an era of expansion, the incrementalism in the policy process made such skills and relationships less strategic, though still important, in the internal resource allocation system. In the 1980s professional opinion points to the growing mismatch between needs and resources; DHSS evidence to the House of Commons' Social Services Committee in 1981 revealed that ten out of one hundred and eight local governments experienced absolute cuts in real net expenditure in 1979-80 compared with 1978-79. A further fifteen local governments secured less than the 2 per cent growth needed to meet the increasing needs arising from demographic trends and other changes. In all, therefore, twenty-five or a quarter of local governmments failed in 1979-80 to obtain the growth rate which the DHSS calculated was necessary to maintain service levels against increases in need. The corresponding figure for 1980-81 was 44 per cent and it is estimated at 67 per cent for 1981-82. Thus, comment Webb and Wistow, despite significant real increases in current expenditure, absolute levels of services are not being maintained in all local governments.[12]

This new context in the 1980s places a new emphasis on the performing of political skills in formal roles. The awareness of the managers of personal social service departments that, under contraction, political skills are as important as more purely administrative ones, has probably increased. It is possible that the scope for initiatives by senior officers is highest in those local governments where 'administrative politics'[13] is the norm, i.e. where party political conflict is absent or muted. Yet even where party, and party values, are strongly emphasized in the programme of a local government such chief officers as directors of personal social services can play key roles in assessing resource allocation priorities. Such managers may not be powerful in the sense of being able to dominate decision making even in the face of low political saliency and councillor deference. They can, however, still be influential by virtue of strategic positions at the axis point of a number of conflicting parties, individuals and interests. Dunleavy has argued that because such elite professionals are nationally organized and orientated they will be resistant to excessive local control and will encourage the fragmentation of local administration into professional chiefdoms. Such elite professionals would seek initiatives from national trends in their occupations rather than localist sources.[14] However, this perspective in turn may underestimate the brokerage element at the local level in the formation of policy in local governments, and underestimate the accumulation of power and authority from not only national relationships, but also highly specific and conjunctural local factors. The Seebohm Committee's recommendations for the appointment of directors ensured that suitable legislation would exist to give social service managers sufficient authority in the local corporate management system to compete adequately with other heads of spending departments.

Such 'localist' political factors can at times be of primary importance to personal social services directors and can establish a pattern wherely the successful manager is also a successful politician. Weber insisted on a dichotomy among politicians between those who live 'for' politics and those who live 'off' politics.[15] Failure by a chief officer managing social services to make politics his or her internal life (to utilize Weber's words) undercuts those political relationships which allow the chief officer, as head of a bureaucracy, to live 'off' politics. Judge has demonstrated how many directors of social services, in reaction to an allocation of capital resources by the DHSS which they regard as a thoroughly 'irrational' process, have developed highly conscious political strategies as a line of defence.[16] Overbidding, and developing close working relationships with DHSS regional offices in the hope of converting them into advocates, were common strategies documented in the 1970s. Perceived irrationality was not met by an increase of rationality but by a managerial politics which attempted to utilize the apparent internal contradictions and irrationalities to win concessions. It was not in the individual or even collective power of local state managers to overturn an allocation system imposed by Whitehall. Non-compliance, even with an 'irrational' system, would have imposed costs and penalties. Such costs could also weaken their professional reputations, both among their peers in the national community of directors of social services and inside their local governments. The political culture and skills of such managers is tied to the weight and nuances of relationships, which both confers protection and narrows options for action. To that extent the national and central-local networks of relationships bind them captive. Yet personal social service directors see themselves, and are perceived, as the apex of a service of specialist professionals dealing with a Whitehall structure where generalists and politicians impose policies on local state professionals.

The assumptive worlds of Whitehall and Town Hall actors can and do both meet and clash as the multiple realities impose their sometimes conflicting definitions of the situation. If a policy from Whitehall is defined as 'contradictory' or 'irrational' by those occupational cultures and communities which are influential in forming local state practices, its lack of legitimacy will allow the policy to be challenged, though rarely overthrown. Alliances as well as contests between managers are an aspect of attempts to impose a counter-rationality, based upon a supposed negotiated professionalism, to such Whitehall policies which can threaten as well as guide. Linkages with social work advisers at Whitehall or the regions, representation at the national level through the local government associations, can all be mobilized with varying degrees of failure and success. In the contest of resource allocation, control over data and data interpretations allows a challenge to be articulated and to gain possible legitimacy with sections of the elite publics. Data and information given to the Social Services Committee of the House of Commons can also act as a professional check on the activities of the DHSS if used with care and political skill by the Association of Directors and individual officers. In local governments, the ability to master political skills and relationships are of crucial importance in the 1980s. Professional managerial skills incorporate such a political dimension.

The rest of this chapter is an attempt to illustrate how the 'assumptive worlds' of directors incorporate a political set of skills which can weaken or strengthen a particular chief officer in his bargaining practices over resources and policy. The local governments from which interview data was gathered ranged from semi-rural and rural county councils dominated in the main by strong Conservative regimes (with one exception) to metropolitan boroughs controlled by Labour regimes. It is significant that no director denied that his role-playing incorporated such political skills, while other more junior managers tended to stress their professional social work ties and loyalties.

One social services chief officer in a rural county suggested in an interview that what Glennerster has called 'beggar thy neighbour'[17] is a common response to a financial squeeze on resources. He stated: 'We shifted the responsibility for handicraft instruction into the voluntary sector and we shifted the responsibility for organising holidays for the elderly from ourselves to the voluntary sector. We have not cut services as such.'

It can be argued that, where resources are contracting, a department's strategy could be to unload its difficult or expensive cases and projects onto another agency, especially if they are considered peripheral to the traditional professional core of that service. In an era of financial contraction, organizational or professional altruism tends to decline. This chief officer also noted an increasingly open scrutiny of the projects and budgets of other departments:

> What has happened in the Chief Officer's Group in the management team is that I will challenge Education and Highways, the big spenders, as well as the small spenders like Libraries. I have said to the Chief County Librarian, you are going to expand the number of large type books for the partially sighted. Fair enough, but I have to equate the demands of a deaf officer in the south of the county with a more sophisticated library service. Of course my arguments are aimed more at the Chief Executive and the Treasurer than the Chief Librarian and he knows it. Libraries kept their money but while in 1981 and 1982 I was asked to take 2.8% out of my budget, when it finally came to Committee it was 1.1%. In fact, I got the money mainly off Highways which, while it is a big spender does not have the same protection as a little spender like Libraries seems to have.

This chief officer was not only aware of the balances inside the Chief Officers' Group but also the balances inside the party regime which ran the county council. Knowledge of these balances allows a possible strategy to emerge which will have to be cut and tailored to the interests and perceptions of key politicians and chief officers:

> I thought about my own budget and that of other chief officers and I asked myself 'Where do I dig my heels in and fight?' I thought a total cut of £285,000 was unreasonable, but I could not get away with less than £100,000. Anything smaller would have hit the small services – museums, public health, consumer protection – very hard, and some of the politicians would not have accepted that. My chairwoman thought she could get my cut down to £50,000, but I advised her against fighting that hard. In this council Social Services needs friends, and what we win in the short run we can more than lose in the long run.

The relationship between chief officer and chairperson is partly built on a joint knowledge of the existing balances. The chief officer believed that the very real authority of the chairperson could be weakened if the political incumbent bends too openly in the service department's interests and offends or disturbs other chairpersons. The local 'rules of the game' can be, and normally are, highly nuanced:

> My chairwoman could have got it through the Social Services Committee which we control, but it would have faced stiff opposition in the Finance Committee and in the Policy Committee. She normally knows when to concede. She was even, despite the £100,000 we had to find, prepared to offer £30,000 to the Education Service for handicapped school leavers: I thought it a good idea as you have a massive Education budget which is weak on the special education/handicapped side. We made friends by the offer, and tactically it made great sense. It was corporate and rational, but it also benefited us when we have more financial problems.

While the education budget is normally the greatest commitment of resources, it can also be highly vulnerable. Nevertheless, education can be an important ally, as well as an opponent, for a social services department. The chief officer stated:

There is a very substantial maintenance element in the Highways budget and there have been voices raised who have argued that maybe we have to get used to a rather different standard on the minor and unclassified roads, which normally have a very high standard anyway. The Education Department and Social Services are attempting to persuade the Highways that they ought to take a different line on road maintenance. This could release money, if they will agree, up to £500,000. Those departments who have been arguing a case of protection (including by own) could benefit. It would also block the larger departments complaining that the smaller departments are not taking their fair share of the cuts.

Social services and education together were, and are, the largest spending departments, and normally the most influential. Since the formation of social services as advocated by Seebohm, a tendency has existed in local governments for education to lose a relatively small percentage of the budget to the bids of social services. The borders of professional activities between these departments at the client interface can both create ties of dependency, co-operation and also conflict. The chief officer noted:

In the Chief Officers' Group, when we were discussing cuts, I informed them of a departmental reorganization which hit top and middle-level management especially, very hard. We did this to protect out service delivery people, like social workers, day service, and domiciliary workers. I wanted to show openly where my commitments were. The sums saved were fairly small but the Education and other departments accepted the cuts and reorganization as acceptable. This helped to limit the cut to £100,000, as the politicians in turn went along with the service chief officers.

The closeness of the chief officer and chairperson relationship comes from a process of joint learning and dependency, itself a form of politics:

When the chairwoman and I first started, we agreed that on the relevant committee days she will be in my office at 9 o'clock in the morning. It's symbolic but also more than that. Committee meetings are often like one act plays, so you have to know your lines and your brief and not contradict each other. We both agree on many areas but we have to go through the issues on the agenda and assess problems before they arise and how we can meet them. I think we both have learned how to encourage our backbenchers on the Social Service Committee. I can act as a sort of speaker. If I want to encourage a backbencher I will scribble a note to the chairwoman sitting next to me saying 'Ask Mrs So-and-So to speak.' She knows my technique.

When the chief officer-chairperson relationship breaks down or is weakened then an organizational crisis is manifest. In another local government, a county, the social services director admitted that the party regime not only did not consult him but also ignored his chairperson:

The Leader by-passed my and the Social Services Committee. Appointments to my department have been given to the Personnel Department to handle, who then notify me. They, the Leader and his friends on the council, also blocked my reports. I felt, sooner or later, there would be some appalling scandal, so I wrote to the Leaders of the Council and Opposition. Then I went public in the local press. The people who act as chairs of the programme committees have little influence and the Chief Executive seems not to want to fight the Leader. The Leader has very close ties to the government, so I can't use the regional DHSS office either, as it would be ignored. If the other party was in power in Whitehall I might be more successful.

Corporate management existed in name only, as little corporate collective influence existed. Since the 1974 reorganization, no strong traditions of professional autonomy from open political intervention existed in this local government. The internal Chief Officers' Group was itself fragmented, with no traditions of strong professional cohesion:

I had several meetings with the Director of Personnel about staff and manpower issues. We would agree at the meetings and prepare a joint report. It would go to Social Services Committee and be passed. It would then go to the Personnel Committe and he would alter it and contradict it. He had obviously got some political instructions to kill it. And we would do a joint report and the day before the report was due to go out he would phone up and say he was not signing it. You knew then it would not go through.

The Director, in desperation, attempted to use the local press to gain support. He appealed to the 'public' and faced the danger of an open political challenge to the regime's legitimacy. The Director argued that the blocking and alteration of his reports undercut his authority as a manager and a professional.[18] Nevertheless, he could expect no open support from fellow chief officers and even the Opposition, and such a move itself demonstrated his institutional weakness. It seemed he faced a very real danger of being forced to resign when the dominant party lost control of the council in the local elections. In their manifesto, the opposition party pledged increased accountability and this, in turn, strengthened the Director by increasing the authority of chairperson and committee. However, the new regime also presented problems. He noted: 'The new committee is very closely aligned with the unions which means a real bias against middle and top management on a number of issues. We did not want the cuts forced on us and neither did the unions, but they looked upon us as the instruments of the cuts. I suppose they thought I had more influence than I did.'

It is a mistake to believe that social service directors have a total opposition to the cuts in social expenditure forced on services. Total opposition would seem to be 'unrealistic', especially in local governments where the party regime would not be strongly supportive of such a stance. This Director further argued that under the old regime he could use the possible options on cuts to obtain managerial goals:

You can use cuts because it allows you to cut services you would never be able to touch otherwise. The ... Training School had nine Social Service Committee members who were also on the governing management committee there. The decisions they agreed at the Social Services Committe they would resist at the Management Committee and *vice versa*. The training school should have been closed three years ago, but the cuts provided the only way.

A social services director who worked for a metropolitan borough which has normally resisted cuts explained his strategy and role politics:

> The Leader of the Council was formerly our Chairman. It helps far more than anything I can do myself. Last year the Treasurer asked for a 2 per cent savings, a cut, from all departments. I prepared a number of options and presented them to my Chairman and his deputy. They rejected nearly all of them, though I felt some were genuine possibilities, and said 'No, it's not politically acceptable to do this'. The package which went forward was far less than 2 per cent. When it went to Budget Sub-committee, the Leader spoke quite strongly against Education for not having achieved a savings, but did not mention Social Services. My influence is not that great, but support for the department is very strong.

This Director openly recognized and utilized local interest and pressure groups. In Conservative Party dominated counties some of these pressure groups and tactics may weaken, rather than strengthen, the departmental position, as their legitimacy may not be recognized by the party regime:

> A lot of open lobbying goes on. They go direct to the politicians and have a significant influence in the City Labour Party. One-parent family associations, feminists, parents for mentally handicapped, MIND, ethnic minority representatives. A lot of my staff are politically active and they too will lobby directly. Some chief officers think all communications from councillors should go only through only the chief officer. I don't think that's realistic in this city, and if it helps departmental services I can live with it. Inside the department we have a pressure group called 'Client Participation' and it openly sells a slightly subversive journal. Some of my divisional managers are unhappy but I have to work with these activities.

In this local government the politicians succeeded in their attempts to marginalize corporate management as a threat to their overall political authority. The support of the Leader and the elite of local politicians then became all important. Total identification with the goals of politicians and an open declaration of support with few reservations is not a usual professional response of directors. However, this director believed his close identification with supposedly left-wing Labour goals was a crucial advantage to his department. More traditional chief officers who attempted to keep their distance from too close an identification lost on a number of policy issues by keeping such a distance, and social services gained.

In another county in the extreme south west, the survival of an independent political tradition and the lack of a strong party machine gave the director of social services a number of unusual problems:

> There does not seem to be any party caucus which dominates at all. Votes on the council can often be very unpredictable. None of the most senior members seem to worry about it. The lack of a network of strong county families such as you have in the county next door means that politics are extremely parochial and it's extremely difficult to help formulate policy for the county as a whole.

The 'nationalization' effect on local politics, which normally has the affect of establishing strong party systems and forcing council regimes to represent both the national and local interests, had shallow roots in this county.[19] The weakness of party structure meant that the director had to gain influence and credibility by emphasizing, even more than usual, traditional strategies of co-opting local interests:

We have two aims. We flatter the parochial view and take advantage of it, sometimes very effectively. Members will identify strongly when a new training centre or an old people's home is being planned for their particular locality. We also aid those members who want to gain a coherent county plan and have not the political support to push it through automatically. We encourage a county ethos among members by emphasizing over and over again that social expenditure is much lower than the national average. When the cuts were inflicted, that insistent educational pressure on members meant that we were spared the 2.5 per cent other departments were forced to give. In fact, at the end of the day we were given an extra 2 per cent.

The history of a low level of social expenditure also allowed the director to gain resources in a manner which was more common in the early 1970's than the 1980's:

Last year we had a political commitment to build a large old people's home costing £1,000,000. It's been half financed by the Authority and half through the joint finance system. The year before I could not play the card of white paper guidelines, but last year I was allowed to. Our joint funding allocation now runs at about £700,000 per annum for the next three years. The members have supported it and that was a real gain. We had to strike a bargain by putting together a package which was such a good deal the Area Health Authority could not refuse it.

The importance of informal mechanisms was emphasized by the weakness of party politics. The relative lack of cohesion meant that the individual political skills of both chief officers and chairpersons could gain significant rewards in reading the 'silences' of members correctly. This skill normally is of importance in local governments, in which the majority has a party system, which established internal cohesion and social roots. It is of even greater importance in those very few contexts where this had not happened:

The previous chairwoman neither enabled the department to gain or lose ground. The department compensated before me in having a director who was extremely able in judging the appropriate tactics. We had a dilapidated old people's home. He was able to take advantage of joint funding to replace it. The Area Health Authority gave 90 per cent and effectively replaced the council's own resources. It served their interests but on paper it's very unusual. The previous director was able to create and sustain a professional atmosphere which made it acceptable. Almost by slight-of-hand really. He set the stage and we all spoke his lines.

The present director thought that as the county was spending only 75 per cent of the national average on social expenditure even in a Whitehall atmosphere of cuts his department could claim and obtain protection. He believed in both going direct to the DHSS in London and also using the regional office:

While I sometimes go direct to a senior civil servant at Whitehall, I don't show publicly that I have not time for the regional advisers. They are very competent professionals and they can sometimes be useful. Not just in gaining resources and support for new projects either. On one occasion we used their credibility to persuade the DHSS to say no to a local project which had been developed some years back. I could not block it on the council. It was coming to the point of tendering and actually starting on the ground. It was a relief when we got the Ministry to reject it.

Utilizing national guidelines to increase financial resources in a county where members have traditionally had very low rates is by no means always successful. A local authority in the past has not been tightly bound by guidelines, and members can choose to ignore guidelines. In a parochial council, a policy by chief officers and their political allies to gain resources and increase spending can only win if specific local interests and personalities seem to benefit even more than is expected in 'normal' regimes. The lack of a political machine to sustain the formal structures forced officers to play one localist interest off against another in a style of politics which would not be necessary in a regime dominated by a strong county network of party figures.

Another director, in a neighbouring county, was not himself impressed by the usefulness of the regional office. He argued:

> I have always tended to by-pass them because they can be a block between me and the relevant Ministry. If you subscribe to the view that you don't go to the DHSS until you have consulted the regional office you lay yourself open to relatively junior civil servants getting an input into how you think things should be done. Then the DHSS begins to see that as a way of side-stepping or delaying.

However, this particular director, unlike the previous one quoted above, was a well-known and powerful actor in the national professional and local government context. He admitted:

> In terms of the DHSS in London I've always had the advantage of not only being a director in a very large authority but I have also had national appointments as an ACC adviser. I'm very much involved in negotiations between the local authority associations and the government which gives me access to ministers. Previously I was Secretary of the Association of Directors of Social Services. So again I had a very intimate relationship with the head of office in not only the DHSS but the DES, Home Office and others. This can help. I don't often use my contacts as too much use can turn against you. I save them for emergencies. Normally my reputation does the trick.

This director believed that it was possible to translate national reputation into a local county political capital. However, this was a possibility rather than a certainty, and in such cases too much national involvement could mean a weakness. In addition, it may go against the necessary 'localist' skill which would enable an officer to read the local balance of forces correctly. This Director felt his reputation at both local and national level allowed him to remain undamaged by political currents which could cause difficulties to other chief officers. In one sense his national involvement with governmental negotiations stressed his supposed professional neutrality:

> I have always been pleased that in 1974, and even after, I was asked by all three political parties to write drafts on the key issues of social services they should provide. It's easy to do because the issues are the same irrespective of politics. All the parties knew the others were asking, but they knew they would get an informed professional opinion. In the event, the manifestos said practically the same thing. This gives me a peculiar freedom. I can strongly criticize Conservative ministers today without the local political party (which dominates the council) attempting to shut me up. I tell the Chairman of my committee

first what I'm going to say before I address a public meeting. It's accepted by the party politicians I'm not playing party politics. If I'm seen to be doing so I would be dead in County Hall within a week. I'm against BASWA affiliating directly to the TUC and the Labour Party as it is supposed to promote the professional point of view. If it is tied to one party it weakens me.

While pursuing national governmental relationships the director acknowledged how the adoption of a supposed local ethos was a necessary tactic. Councils are composed of members who can have a 'cosmopolitan' reference group, but 'localists' are very strong. The belief that local government is specifically 'local' is given lip service and complete public deference, even by chief officers who pride themselves on their membership of those national networks which help to tug into line too great localist deviations. The director stated:

> I have the advantage of being born in the county and I went to the local university. I had the greater advantage that my first appointment in a children's department and then the welfare department was in the county. Until I came back as Director much later, my career was outside the county. I'm accepted as a native and I kept up my knowledge of what was going on in the county when I was away. It certainly helps. If I speak in my professional field it is more acceptable if I can get them to accept me as county. I take advantage by slipping into the vernacular if I want to make a particular point or I feel there is tension. It always produces a laugh and is very useful.

While members respect and value and reward managerial skills and professionalism in general, the conflicts between each level of local government and national government has meant that chief officers are expected to demonstrate symbolically supposedly local loyalties first and sometimes last. Professionalism is respected, but a ritual symbolic identification with localist elites and goals brings rewards; failure brings punishments. Yet promotion is normally gained through a career structure where he or she learns a national occupational culture. The same director commented: 'I was appointed as deputy director by a clerk who told me, "I want you for three years but not longer, because we will bleed you dry in that time". I was only 27. He sat on the Seebohm Committee which founded the modern personal social services. It suited me as I knew that promotions come only by moving about.' So, while assistant and deputy directors are allowed to be without deep roots in the local governments they serve, directors, who can be categorized as 'locals' or given pseudo-localist identities, are preferred by members. Yet members expect directors to be able to manipulate 'cosmopolitan' national networks in their interests without giving those networks their primary loyalty. Even a modern Prince advised by Machiavelli might lack sufficient political skill in such contexts.

The directors stated that with less financial resources for social service departments, statutory legislation still committed resources. In those grey areas which gave local managers and politicians power whether or not to commit resources, the situation was more complex. Clashes between departments arise when changes in policy occur which affect others: 'The Education Department has been quite deliberately cutting back on special places for children in maladjusted schools, residential places, etc., which could hit a large number of children who need those facilities who are under the care of Social Services. These have previously been paid out of the Education budget. Now they want Social Services to pay.'

The overlap of professional activities creates alliances and tensions between such 'natural' allies as education and social services. In a northern metropolitan borough where, since the Bains Report, the chief officers have often publicly claimed (without reprisal from members) policy making power as well as policy implementing power, the alliance was actively being broken by social services. Education competes with social services for recurrent expenditure on staff costs whereas housing expenditure, for instance, is on the capital account. One director acknowledged openly the importance of organizational politics *vis-à-vis* other chief officers and politicians. Both sets of power reference groups were to be used and manipulated without one excluding the other, and both have different ideological determinants:

> When I have a weak Chairman I use the corporate process to strengthen me. At the moment I have a strong Chairman. Before the last local elections my department had decided to make a big cut by closing a home for the elderly which would have meant the possible loss of 60 jobs. The Opposition fought it and at election time they came to power. The new Leader told me he did not want it closed. I gave him through my committee two papers, one on closure, the other showing how we can keep it open. It also said if we did so we would need at least £200,000 capital to maintain it. I think it was politically very difficult after the local papers had come out against closure to close it. I asked them, 'Did government want a big reduction of home helps?', knowing it was a cut they would reject. So I was able to safeguard 50 per cent of my expenditure.

This did not mean a neglect of important officers in the corporate process altogether, merely because of a temporary strong political input:

> We are still closely involved with the Treasury people. We negotiate our budget at base where it matters very carefully at a very senior level and we are allowed at times to get away with blue murder. Negotiations on our margins can be as significant as arguments about growth. You could gain or lose up to 2 per cent just like that. For example, if you have 100 staff and they are each paid £1 a year, you use £100 to pay them. Now obviously for reasons like turnover etc. you need only £93 or £96 to pay those staff. We pay considerable attention to this and we have managed to get Finance to allow up to 98 per cent of the theoretical money whereas we probably need only 96 per cent. We can put into recruitment control 2 per cent to pay for growth. Now I don't need to do any recruitment control so that 2 per cent is going begging and never even showed as growth. I kept it a secret from other departments and other departments don't use such tactics.

The director went on to admit that even with a new favourable climate his department was weaker than the education department. These very strong departments are not forced by political weakness into learning such manoeuvres and would not be very sympathetic to them if they were informed of them. It is not that they would disdain additional money; it is merely that as yet education does not have to fight for more money like social services.

The chief executive of this borough commented on the particular strategy of the social services manager:

> The Director is clever. When he has had fairly weak Chairmen who will not be able to get him very much, he stresses links with me and the Treasurer. We are the most influential officers. Now he has got a very influential Chairman he feel he can go his own way more. Corporate management can be defined for him as whatever suits him at a particular moment.

The chief executive noted the alliance against education but he did not think he should automatically act to counter-balance it. The department with most committed resources should learn the necessary political skills to defend its budget. The costs of learning such lessons was revenue partly gained by social services and housing. In 1980, the budget was unexpectedly better than anticipated and £7 million was gained by the Authority in clawback. The Treasurer described what happened: 'The Housing Chairman supported by the Social Services Chairman passed a resolution which gave £4 million to Education, £2 million to Housing and nearly £1 million to Social Services. They knew that they had to offer that much and together they could block the smaller departments from getting away with bids.' The arrival of a new regime with politicians who wanted more control over policy and had a manifesto commitment to social services gave the director new strong cards he could play. The treasurer explained:

> The new council came to power on a basis of resisting the cuts and making social services and housing their top priority. When we had cuts the chief officers agreed it would be the same percentage for all departments. I thought Social Services had agreed but at a party group meeting their Chairman made an unexpected intervention and argued that Social Services should be cut by 1 per cent less than the other departments. And he got away with it. I was not pleased and neither was the chief executive.

The Chairman of Social Services when interviewed declared: John (the Director) was not in favour of my success in getting the departmental cut reduced by 1 per cent. He thought it would be defeated and he would make unnecessary enemies. But I won and we gained £168,000. It meant we could keep the Family Service Unit going as well as others'. The Director himself explained his changing strategy:

> When I was first appointed as director I looked at my political strength and I found that the Authority had little commitment at that time to personal social services, so I was weak. Instead of attacking the corporate structure, which other chief officers did, I decided to support it, because in supporting it I could manipulate it. I knew the basic demographic trends should give us more resources, and the more the Authority recognized them, as was corporately rational, the more it worked in our favour. Thus in 1977 we had a high number of children in care. I presented a package which involved a central foster unit and other items and we sold it on a cost benefit approach. We used the official commitment to a rational method of management to present them with a case they could not turn down. We gained another £140,000 that way.

Dependency on a corporate system heavily influenced by a chief executive allowed protection to be given against the weakness of the older chairman of committee. The ineffectiveness of the old chairman also forced the director into paths he basically thought were dubious, as they crossed the boundary between professionalism and party politics, and members recognized such an invasion of their territory: 'The opposition was out to get me because they saw me as a right-wing Tory. A situation I got into because I had to rescue and defend a weak chairman who could not handle oppositional attacks. Somewhat late in the day, I attempted to pull back and run for cover.' Changes in party control of the council and its committees could have made the director very vulnerable. His attempt to reassert professional neutrality was probably open to question. The current chairman gave an example of the director's vulnerability:

> On one occasion the Conservatives were so embarrassed by the decision reached in the Sub-committee that they voted with us against it in full Committee. The only disagreement came from the Director who in standing orders had the power to move it up. He did so, the first time it had been done in six years, and there was considerable political feeling about it, as we felt a paid officer should not push it.

In the new regime the enthusiasm of the chairman of social services and his obvious party authority quickly cemented a new alliance which was strongly against a corporate strategy. The dominant party leadership was unable to override the political strength of particular chairmen. It was striking how the chairman, an unemployed man from a local political dynasty, was incorporated into the departmentalism of the social services staff and had little interest in a corporate strategy. His personal as well as party values had an influence in such areas as the discretionary grants to voluntary societies, and the director did not attempt to kill the goose which was laying such spendid eggs:

> We cut grants to the ... Flower Fund Homes, strictly upper class in the way it operates. We stopped the grant to the Abbeyfield Society. They will not get money unless the type of service to the community they offer is in line with our political philosophy. Gingerbread (which is an active pressure group) is different, but I don't want to support their new community programme for three extra workers this year, but I might next year.

Booth found in a study of Calderdale that the ruling party group and its leaders had been unsympathetic to the aims of the Social Services Committee which they have regarded pejoratively as a 'give-away committee'. As a result, the Chairman was not a member of the inner caucus, nor did he exercise any political clout within the ruling group.[20] Only one local government in the sample studied in this chapter had a similar experience which was then reversed when the opposition party came to power. Nevertheless, social services directors can and do feel vulnerable to accusations that their departments are not good money managers, and both symbolically and pragmatically they believe it is important to convince members and the various lay publics otherwise. The symbolism attached to supposedly pragmatic policies was heavily emphasized by all directors who were interviewed. As previously hinted, the style and political sensitivity of directors varied. A lack of political skills in reading the changing balances inside the council members and the chief officers could also mean a weakening of the professional authority formally given by central governmental legislation. Since formal and actual authority can be and sometimes are, strikingly different, the disjunction can allow a skilful director to be a major power in the authority. A director lacking the necessary skills, though having adequate technical qualifications, can be a 'rubber stamp' determined by external events and unable to intervene and change the existing balances of forces in a favourable direction. At such levels in a formal bureaucracy, claims of managerialism and professionalism are not opposed to conscious political role-playing. Indeed, it is an organic element in the claim by a director to be both a professional and a manager.

A Director of Social Services in another county now saw the policy-making in Whitehall in these terms:

> In the last year we have had statements which only are euphemisms about protecting those in greatest need. A total retreat from a clear statement of policy that could commit resources. On one hand the DHSS still continues to increase the amount of money available for joint finance, and the Department of the Environment tells us to reduce expenditure in absolute terms. In the past, we have sometimes gained from contradictory policies in central government, but I believe we lose now.

In a 'policy muddle' of this type inside a contraction of real resources, directors are sometimes told that a weakening of statutory legislation can allow them as managers to innovate new programmes while cutting back on others. Such an apparent freedom may also be perceived as a threat to services not covered by statute. Directors can even have mixed or ambiguous feelings about capital programmes they have been allocated and welcomed in the past. It is now the case that sometimes they advise their committees to reject them, if such programmes imply a strong financial commitment in the future which will narrow down possible options.

In this county government, the directors of both the social services and education departments were both extremely conscious of the strains in their organizational relationship when financial resources came into the picture. It is important to note that personal relations were extremely good. The Chief Education Officer stated: 'I welcomed the new Social Service Department when it was formed and my department still works closely with Social Services. For example, I accept Social Service workers inside my service instead of having my own Education Welfare Officers.' However, he was extremely conscious of competing for similar resources:

> I watch Social Services very closely. In the capital budget field there is no argument because our programmes are quite separate. However, staffing is a key area. I remember one example from a recent Chief Officers' meeting. A main control is on manpower. In the last three years on the continuation budget, social services show an increase of 130 staff. This is of crucial importance to me. The compensatory savings in manpower will have to be made up from somewhere, so I must at least ask for an investigation of that growth.

The Chief Education Officer emphasized that his sensitivity to social services expansion was not a recent phenomenon, but went back to the 1970s:

I became conscious of Social Services eating into my budget from about late 1973. Before then, while none of us claimed we had enough money, our services were expanding. I remember sitting from late 1973 in meeting after meeting and saw we were challenging the bids of our colleagues in order to defend out own corner. I was asking Social Services whether it was really necessary to estimate the provisions for the elderly at quite the rate it was estimated. In 1976 and 1977 Education was hard hit because I was asked to trim my primary school teaching budget because of falling rolls. It's very difficult to trim proportionately with the fall in school rolls. At precisely that time Social Services were expanding their manpower.

The Social Services Director argued that his department's lack of a strong county pressure group meant a different strategy from education had to be followed *vis-à-vis* the politicians. Education, with over 70 per cent of the budget and a large group of influential members tied to the department, followed a public pressure group strategy involving the mobilization of teachers and parents. Social services lacked such potential political weight and compensated for it by a different strategy. The Social Services Director remarked on an example of his success in building upon apparent political weakness in the county:

A good example of the acceptability of my strategy is that at a recent Finance Committee meeting dealing with cuts we had been given permission to go ahead to try and put together a package of finance, which was not in any capital programme, to develop a day centre. I don't think any other committee but mine could have got that support at that particular moment of time.

The Treasurer in the same local authority assessed the social services strategy on resources with these words:

One of the reasons why Social Services have done so well is because they have deliberately kept a low profile. Their Director operates strategically and his Chairwoman has a very good relationship with the Leader which must help. I don't think Social Services have lost a major decision in the last three years. I'll give an example. The capital programme has just been chopped very much and Education has gone down from £3 million. They were not able to get a replacement project past the Finance Committee. The Social Services who complain about their lack of a large public pressure group put up a request to Finance to replace a day centre. I spoke half-heartedly against it on the grounds that Finance had a basic policy to not sanction replacement projects, and I lost, as I expected I would.

The Director of Social Services was also conscious of organizational strains in the alliance with the education department:

Recently we made strong representation to Education about proposals to cut out nursery education altogether in their cuts list. We argued that in the . . . area if this happened they would force a situation in which my department would have to make some provision for children at risk. We argued that all Education was doing was to shift expenditure. We applied some pressure and got a compromise. That pressure and some public outcry meant that Education agreed to retain nursery school provision for those children of whom we were expressing concern.

This concession by education, however, involved the social service department in a strategy inside the local authority which contradicted past strategies and created concern in the Director of Social Services:

> Recently the day before the Policy and Resources Committee, the Chairman of Education indicated he was going to make a bid for £180,000 and invited us to support that bid on the basis of the money being divided up between Education and Social Services. We were not very willing because the government's white paper had just come out, and while Education were being cut slightly more than the white paper indicated my department was being cut rather less. I felt that there was a real danger that if we pushed our luck we could provoke the Finance Committee into a backlash.

On informing the education department of their reservations, a new strategy was proposed by education, which obviously saw the importance of carrying the second largest spending department with them. The Director of Social Services continued: 'Education then told us that in that case they would ask for rather less in order to deal with nursery education. I and my Chairman then felt we had no option but to give support, but we did not feel comfortable in doing so. My strategy is not to appear to be greedy or to hassle.'

The recent retirement of the social services chairman with a close relationship to the Leader of the council meant that the Director would have to look for other mechanisms to strengthen his committee and department if the new chairman or chairwoman no longer had the same weight or authority with the Leader of the council. It can also be noted that a chief education officer has perhaps not much room to manoeuvre in his budget. The only thing he can do is to reorganize the pupil-teacher ratios. The strength of trade unions and national legislation have lessened the education department's ability to move resources about. On the other hand, the very tightness of restrictions could make it less vulnerable than a social services budget. Education is less discretionary than social services because government guidelines in white papers have been more explicit, even in the present economic climate.

The alliance in this local authority between social services and education still holds together in certain conjunctural contexts. The Chief Education Officer described the working out of such an agreement:

> As you know, before we knew what the Rate Support Grant to us would be, the Chief Officers had collectively agreed to yield up £1 million in cuts. Once we knew we had done better than expected, I, for one, was reluctant to yield up all that sum, and if I joined with Social Services our combined political strength would guarantee some clawback. At a small informal meeting between the Chief Executive, the Treasurer, Education and Social Services, it was agreed to give us back £500,000. I know the political climate was right for Social Services and Education to be let off the hook to a degree. We could not have overthrown the whole list of £x million cuts as it would have been politically impossible for the Chairman of Finance and the Leader to have gone any further in minimizing the cuts. Their party was in power at Westminster and demanded cuts.

The Treasurer in the local authority recalled the meeting:

> In spite of the agreement reached previously, I wanted to be seen to be resisting the

clawback to some extent. Not to defeat it, merely resist it. It's my job and I had just read an article in the *Financial Times* that the Environment Minister may change his financial cards and the rules yet again, so I wanted to tell the Chief Officers' Group to keep our balances just in case. I knew of course that Education and Social Services were hardest hit by the cuts.

The reputation of the social services director in being honest and trustworthy, as well as a skilful political operator who could 'deliver', was crucial to his leverage among politicians and chief officers. In a sense, this was his real political capital and he did not want to be diminished on short-term gains which could weaken him in the future. In a manner similar to the public administrators described by Heclo and Wildavsky in *The Private Government of Public Money*, the 'trust' relationship is the coin in which negotiations and deals are carried through. The Director gave an example of how fragile the 'trust' relationship can be if it is disturbed:

> Some years ago a Chairman of Committee came to see me about a complaint that we were providing an inadequate level of home help and his constituents were complaining. He went on and on. I got rather cross and told him we could only do so much with the resources given. It's no good cutting our budgets in Committee, and then complaining. The week after this he went to a Finance Committee meeting at which they were fixing the rate and there was an internal argument about at what level to fix it. He is influential and he argued for a figure of two pence more than the Leader and the Chairman of Finance wanted, provided my department was given £46,000 more to improve the home help service. All this was done outside the normal budget fixing targets. The Leader came to see me very cross as she believed I had consciously put him up to it, which I had not. She told me to stick to the normal channels of representation and not to intervene at the last minute when the rate was being fixed. Later I regained credibility but it did disturb me at the time.

This director favoured a relatively strong decision-making structure which he believed had been established. However, he noted the continued importance of subjective factors: 'The members themselves wanted to oust one of the chairmen who they thought had not been doing a particularly good job. However, when it came to a vote they felt sorry for him and they voted him back into office against the alternative candidate favoured by the Leader'. In this manoeuvre the chief officers attempted to distance themselves from all the political actors involved. While in the main they regarded most of the senior politicians as being predictable and subject to influence, they were also on guard against a complacency which would dull their political instinct. The director remarked:

> I still remember when the Chairman of Finance went behind my back to the Chairman to say, 'How much do you really want? Is it half a million?' All the objective arguments given earlier to the Finance Committee and my own Committee went by the board. In this case, without any attempt to have a rational analysis, the Chairman of Finance, a close party ally of my Chairman, said, 'We will give you half a million'. My service gained, but corporate management did not.

However, the formalism in the official ritual of decision making limits the surprises and upsets among politicians. The agenda for committees and the full council meetings is normally set by the chief officers. The county solicitor in the same county stated: 'I regard standing orders as very useful. I and only a few others probably know them sufficiently well so we are the interpreters of standing orders which gives us a certain authority over those who don't understand standing orders. It's a means of ensuring the debate is conducted according to the rules'. The director, however, was worried about the consequences of using the standing orders to limit debate among members: 'I think nothing annoys members more than using standing orders as rules for stopping them saying what they want to say. It reinforces a belief that officers are manipulating and can cause an unpleasant backlash not only against officers but also the party leaders who support them'. The consequences of publicly appearing to be manipulative and undercutting the legitimacy of politicians were greater than the consequences of officers influencing the construction of policy under the apparently neutral protection of professionalism.

A chief officer with a reputation for firmness and efficiency can draw upon support from fellow professionals as well as politicians in those policy areas which contain elements of danger. In this county the personal social services department came under public scrutiny and some criticism in a context where a man was charged with the manslaughter of a child. The criticism was that neighbours notified the social services of ill-treatment of the child in a period prior to his death. The director issued a statement to the press which stated that he had investigated and his staff had acted properly. However, continued public criticism and interest from the DHSS meant that the politicians and the director decided to establish an enquiry through the area review committee of the council. The county solicitor said:

> I was the Chairman of the Area Review Committee and I decided there should be a small panel to investigate and report to the AHA and the county council. Pressure was coming from the DHSS who were concerned that the Minister might be asked questions in parliament. The report recognized that the precipitating factor was that the magistrates in a former case concerning the child had allowed the child to go out of care back to his mother and step-father who killed him. The panel was able in its report to get the department off the hook.

It was noticeable that no politician sat on the panel which was composed only of professionals including a deputy director of social services. The symbolic importance of the report was that it strengthened the director and his political allies against a current which had reservations about the expansion of the departmental budget and also reservations about social workers generally in the county and the dominant party. The first Chairman of the Social Services Committee in the county when the director was first appointed remembered the nature of his alliance and support for the director:

> Over the years there was a change in that the department's managers acquired more power. I felt that was right, as I was against members trolling over the personal problems of individual clients. I reduced the number of meetings, which helped officers to concentrate on departmental issues and less on relationships with my back-benchers. I was still able to represent the views of members to officers.

The Chairman, a member of an old and well-established county family, also described how members would be selected for his committee:

> There was on the council an inner establishment which looked over new members. If one new member passionately wanted to get on some committee there was normally a good chance of success. If the Director knew someone was interested and could be useful he would mention it to me. I also adopted the view that if I was given a difficult member the department and I could tame him. We also went in for a certain amount of plots on who to get in as co-opted members. They could balance the odd member who might be a little bit antagonistic of Social Services and they would help civilize him.

The 'inner establishment' was, and is, of great importance in formal and informal decision making. While officially it was composed of senior councillors, it could incorporate influential chief officers.[21] The Chairman believe that even in a period of expansion there was sometimes little control over how resources were spent:

> Staff costs tend to be high, and with interest on capital compose the hard core of any service budget. The actual items in a budget which can be directly affected by members are relatively small. I remember the arguments on how much could be saved by allowing vacancies to be unfilled for three extra months and where the money could be spent. The influence and the arguments was on the margins. That gave the service a lot of protection, but upset members.

However, the margins of budget, both at the level of the authority and the department, still fuel the political system and culture which emphasizes negotiations and bargains. In the era of expansion the Chairman's tactics to gain resources were relatively simple and he used ploys related to the public 'reputation' of the county. The council had representatives of prominent and well-established county families, other than the Chairman, and they were both influential and influenced by such tactics:

> It was an effective tactic on my part to make the council uneasy that some parts of Social Services was being deprived. I kept emphasizing, in a matter-of-fact fashion, for example, that the county had a very bad record in comparison with ... county in regard to residential care for older people. Eventually enough members accepted that was bad policy and when expenditure budget plans were produced they went through the Finance Committee unchallenged. Members at council were not influenced by the quality of a particular argument at a specific meeting very much if you had not already prepared the ground over a period of time.

The reputation of the director was also important in gaining such resources, as a chief officer who had been criticized by other chief officers for inefficiency would find such roles as treasurer and chief executive not openly supportive. In an era of expansion where the national pressure on local governments was to justify an increase of social expenditure, the reputational power of the director and the political skill of the departmental allies would be of less crucial importance. The alliance between a chairman and the social services officers could also be determined by the local climate when the claims of social workers and their managers to professional status were accepted with varying degrees of coolness and reservations. The Chairman noted:

I was very keen to encourage the voluntary sector and agencies as much as possible. I had very little success in the first years after Seebohm in getting the department to be very enthusiastic. The Director was supportive but I think most social services officers were so conscious of the newness of their professional status they thought help from the voluntary sector and untrained personnel would water down their professionalism. It was one of my big failures. I had to defend the service and I found it difficult to criticize it even in private.

The Seebohm Committee had strengthened and amalgamated the various specialist services into the large personal social services departments in existence today. Before this period it was relatively usual for members and committees to monitor, intervene and to make judgements on clients. Professionalism was a response to this context which weakened the control by social workers of their work situation. One social services area manager in the county remembered this period: 'Formerly the Inspector, the Children's Officer, came here and found councillors running actual individual case-work cases. He found Area Children's Committees making day-to-day decisions on the work now entirely carried out by qualified social workers. With great skill and determination he got them out of that level of running the Children's Department.

Resistance to voluntary care and agents and resistance to members being involved in actual client care work were both responses to laymen who attempted to control their work space. Resistance involved professionals attempting to raise their status and collective group control. The same area officer assessed from his perspective the Chairman's political skill in guarding clients and professionals:

Don't forget the Chairman was an aristocrat. His timing was brilliant at committee. Several times I have seen him nudge things through by use of his social background. Don't forget most members are middle class. Once he was challenged by a member about reimbursing a women in residential care for £36 that she had stolen from her handbag. As he suggested to the committee that they make an *ex gratia* payment, one of the backwoodsmen said, 'It's all very well, Mr Chairman, but what if it had been £200?' The Chairman just looked up and said, 'We should have asked you to pay'. Most people laughed, and it went through. If it had been £200 it would have gone through. He was that good. When the backwoodsmen started to hassle social workers he safeguarded and respected them.

An ex-deputy director of social services in this authority noted the importance of the Chairman's relationships *vis-a-vis* the 'ministerial party':

Our Chairman was able to obtain a gentlemen's agreement with the Finance Committee that they would match any loan sanction we were able to get from the old Department of Health. I think we were more successful than they anticipated. We found at the end of the financial year you could often pick up a loan sanction which another authority had not been able to take advantage of.

The loyalty and commitment of this particular Chairman was primarily to the personal social services department rather than to corporate management. While he sat on other committees and expressed an interest in their work, his role on social services was of main significance to him. The ex-deputy director expressed some reservations about a vice-chairwoman of social services who also sat on the Finance Committee. He felt that to some extent her double loyalties did not work to the advantage of social services but against it. The Finance Committee had 'turned' her loyalty towards itself and in an era where virement was not automatically allowed to a spending department, she did not on the Finance Committee strongly support requests from the social services department.

The director of social services thought it still good policy not to offend the regional officers of the DHSS, but did not expect that in the 1980s they would have a major impact on their Whitehall masters. They were no longer a viable pressure group which he could use to gain control over policy and resources. Their interests as social work advisers were still linked to his, but they could not any longer influence or 'deliver' their masters. In the 1970s the regional officers, after a period of consultation, could still 'commit' their masters. He said of one project in 1977: 'We were careful to sell the project to the regional officer of the DHSS. At the London meetings they were there and the DHSS did not go back on anything previously promised'. The Director was sharply aware that various parts of the DHSS had different linkages to his department and that the DHSS itself was often in internal conflict. This could help or damage his department depending upon the particular policy issue:

> When it came to the project there seemed to be more concern between two sections of DHSS about whether we would use funds intended for the mentally handicapped section for the physically handicapped instead. They probably never contemplated in the DHSS having a project which would involve both sets of clients. So they watched each other more closely than they watched us.

In response to the cuts imposed in the 1980s the Director was very conscious that his field staff saw his role as being too compromised. The legitimacy of the cuts was strongly questioned and demands were made among field staff that he should not help the politicians. In his committee recommendations, he had suggested to the politicians that the cuts were spread so that no single part of the service should be eliminated. Some of the departmental field staff suggested that social services should adapt a strategy similar to the education department. This would have meant suggesting to the politicians and the public that an entire part of the service be totally cut and then allow county resistance among the public probably to block such cuts. The Director thought that his department did not have the same network of possible support groups as did education and such a strategy would have real dangers and would run against the grain of the political culture of the members: 'After the letters of protest about social service cuts had come into the council, I thought they were having little impact. I tried to help. I had a discussion with a local Chairman of the mentally handicapped. I suggested the parents should write to councillors. It did produce sympathy but no resources'. The lack of a strong network of pressure groups meant that instead of attempting an external strategy and being totally dependent upon a probable failure, an 'internal' strategy was followed: 'Councillors hate being hassled. I knew it and so I played it down the middle, straight. I attempted to gain sympathy and credibility. It did work as we were allowed some dispensation. We were allowed not merely to maintain the existing level of home helps service but to expand it'.

Dearlove has argued in a study of London borough councils that the ideology of councillors tended to resist those pressure groups which placed demands on them by mobilizations outside the formal mechanisms.[22] Some pressure groups were awarded legitimacy by councillors and others were ignored or marginalized. The Director was highly conscious of this councillor perception in his local government:

> If I went public and got into an open struggle with elected councillors my professional authority would be threatened. If I hassle them through open public opinion, then some influential councillors will resent that and attempt to demonstrate that their decisions on resources will not be shaken.

Even when back-bench councillors on the Social Services Committee wanted to plead almost complete exemption from the cuts at one meeting, the Director felt that this was as short-sighted a strategy as going public:

> I felt there was really no way the members on my committee had enough political influence to win exemption from cuts. If my committee had pressed the Finance Committee and Policy and Resources the plea would have been rejected. My committee then would have lost some credibility and my influence on future unpleasant decisions would have been lessened.

In this council from 1979, the volatility of 'mood' among politicians on the cuts and the percentage to be cut was extreme. Some dissent inside the regime increased the volatility. Several times leading politicians did not want to take decisions and, by so doing, narrow and close off possible options. In spite of local government's apparent openness (in comparison with central government) 'it is a closed political setting that has its own information, its own values and its own patterns of decision making'.[23] The rapid changes in central government guidelines on services and the apparent breakdown of the normal mechanisms to represent county councils at Whitehall placed strained on party cohesion. Chief officers found their normally reliable relationships with local politicians unexpectedly fragile, with a tendency to take no decisions at all just as prevalent as a tendency to take hasty decisions on ambiguous information. The weakening of normal relationships forced certain influential chief officers to plan for chaos. The budget cycle which was normally a ritual and a routine no longer seemed to be continuous with the past. In such a context, while expressing due deference to councillors, the Chief Officers' Group flowed into the planning vacuum and attempted to plan for control of the cuts. While field workers in social services doubted if their Director should manage the inflicted cuts, his own definition of professionalism and concern to limit the damage pushed him into an even closer alliance than normal with other chief officers. Conflicts still existed but they were overridden by increased dependencies. The Director noted:

> We had in the Chief Officers' Group a very useful detailed discussion of the cuts in each department which could form the basis of collective agreement among officers and which the politicians could also find acceptable. The parameters had been set by the Treasurer and Chief Executive meeting with each individual chief officer in private and identifying cuts which were both achievable and which avoided highly political issues. We built up a package of cuts to the order of £3 million as opposed to the £5 million originally suggested. We have not yet consulted the politicians but they will probably welcome our initiative, especially as we avoid issues which would generate a disproportionate amount of public response.

Attitudes to the central control departments still had traces of ambiguity and hostility as well as an acknowledgement that alienation from policies favoured by the role of chief executive and treasurer would be politically costly. At another meeting of the Chief Officers' Group, while asserting the need for greater interdependence in planning the cuts, a view was also expressed that the control departments at the centre had themselves departmental interests which were being safeguarded. Who, indeed, guards against the guardians? The Director protested:

> In my department, cuts involve loss of middle management. I am aware that the Treasurer is cutting three clerical staff and I am also aware he proposed to fill two middle management vacancies. In my department, the Principal Officer grade and its salary is only 2 per cent. In the Treasury it is 23 per cent. While I'm cutting a small valuable cadre, in practice other departments are cutting clerical and administrative grades. The main committees do not take the same critical attitude towards Treasury staffing as they do to me. Some of Social Services sit on the Finance Committee, but I cannot and will not brief these members when they sit on the Finance Committee – they are not my members when they sit on Finance.

The Director argued that one of the factors making politicians volatile on cuts is that the normally influential chief officers have declined to give further recommendations. He and other chief officers decided early in the budget year that they would provide adequate information on the implications of various options, but they desired at this stage to play 'constitutionalist' roles. An encroachment on members' roles, even if strongly desired by many members themselves, would blur the relationship with politicians. In addition, chief officers pointed out that they did not, in the main, believe in the supposed rationality behind the cuts. The Director stated: We don't want in future to risk being charged of running the authority. I said to my committee, if they want to cut by £50,000 the budget could be examined, but if they wanted £500,000 they would damage the service. They did not like that, and they don't like it spelt out like that, but you have to do it.

The Director noted that in his experience when he had agreed to prepare a list of cuts options he had become wary of writing down the options. Once a chief officer or the chief officers collectively had written down tentative cuts options, to discuss in the context of an uncertain political environment as a planning exercise only, the game was more than half lost. Once the near unthinkable had been written down as a hypothetical cuts option it was only a matter of time before it became acceptable and legitimate.

Strongly aware of this self-fulfilling prophecy as a major nuance in the psychological climate, the Director found it difficult to resist openly, and this increased in him a desire to control collectively the psychological climate of both members and professionals.

The planning decision-making system also had its limitations. It was expected to be both effective and efficient but also to strengthen the ritual of 'constitutionalism' whereby decisions were made. In practice, this was difficult to achieve as the time element tended to make vacuous and nullify a constitutionalism which would give elected members more than formal authority. The Director commented:

> Lots of difficulties appear to be created by being committed to a planning cycle which requires us to consider our target budgets far in advance of the Rate Support Grant settlement. We discussed in Chief Officers' Group why we should do it in June rather than October when we would know the RSG (Rate Support Grant). We realized that chief officers then would have little option but to allow the Finance Committee to reconcile the targets with estimates. This would mean that each individual committee would not have the opportunity within the cycle of council meetings to express its views. If the Treasurer wanted greater control and input, it would weaken all the committee structures. We all felt we would have to live with the difficulties of the present system.

The respect consciously given to the ritual constitutionalism which is the formal ideology of decision making allows chief officers to draw upon the political capital of constitutionalism when it serves their own purposes. Not allowing chief officers the automatic right to speak at council meetings, unlike committees, is tied to a custom which normally protects them from being attacked by name by members in full council. Professionalism is in part the art of giving advice to politicians and making certain they accept responsibility for political decisions. While formally chief officers are only expected to give advice and not make policy, some roles at certain times touch on grey areas. While the constitutionalism of chief officers may, on specific issues, clearly guide and formulate policy, the politicians normally turn a blind eye to it as a threat and tactically accept the half-truth that such an input is mere professionalism. The Director stated:

> I strongly suspect that the bottom parameters of the rate will be very influenced by the Chief Executive and the Treasurer though the upper limits are decided by the members. The range of rates will significantly influence the extent to which cuts will have to be made. If those two chief officers don't point out to members the implications for reductions of services they will have to face the reactions of the chief officers. They should represent us and they know it.

To that extent chief officers have common interests and common strategies. To the extent they collectively attempt to arrange trade-offs and bargains within their own group, they thus strengthen themselves before the committee system locks them into departmental conflicts. Inside the Chief Officers' Group, the Director of Social Services organized his politics around his values and role demands, and his role around his politics.

It is perhaps obvious from the examples given that each local government has its own specific culture and understandings while sharing in a national network of political and professional cultures. While C. W. Mills gently suggested that the term 'culture' is the spongiest in social science terminology, an analysis which eliminates such 'soft' data and 'subjective understandings' eliminates much else. Directors of Social Services as well as other chief officers internalize such nuances as well as constructing them through their multi-faceted activities. The majority recognize their praxis, look upon the world made for them and by them, and find it, with some reservations, good. Their worlds and multiple realities are shaped by pragmatic rules and common sense and also by sacred rituals of consent and legitimacy. Directors are, in turn, bureaucrats and 'mere servants' of the council they serve and, in part, control; the arm of the central state in the administration of services, the spokespersons and junior partners of local political elites, and, occasionally, charismatic politicians in an era and location which can reward and punish such charisma which is not institutionalized. Social workers they were once, managers perhaps they are, and politicians they are always. Their assumptive worlds matter and have consequences.

NOTES AND REFERENCES

1 Kogan, M. with W. Van Der Eyken. *County Hall and the role of the Chief Education Officer*, 1973. Bush, T. and Kogan, M. *Directors of Education*, 1982. Neve, B. Bureaucracy and politics in local government, *Public Administration*, 1977, Autumn, 291–303. Jennings, R. *Education and Politics*, 1977. For the research on managers of education services.

2 Barry, B. *Sociologists, Economists and Democracy*, 1970, 89–98.

3 Berger, P. and Luckman, T. *The Social Construction of Reality*, 1971, 158. 'With the establishment of sub-universes of meaning a variety of perspectives ... emerges, each viewing the latter from the angle of one sub-universe ... each perspective ... will be related to the concrete social interests of the group that holds it'.

4 Dunleavy, P. *Urban Political Analysis*, 1980.

5 Jones, G. W. Varieties of local politics. *Local Government Studies*, 1979, 3, 1(2).

6 Davies, B., Barton, A., McMillan. I. and Williamson, V. *Variations in Services for the Aged*, 1972.

7 Alt, J. E. Some social and political correlates of County Borough expenditures. *British Journal of Political Science*, 1971, 1(1).

8 Elcock, H. *Local Government*, 1982, 8, for CIPFA statistics.

9 Lewis, J. Variations in service provision. In Young, K. (ed.). *Essays on the Study of Urban Politics*, 1975, 66.

10 Dunleavy, P. *The Politics of Mass Housing in Britain 1945-75*, 1981.

11 Glennerster, H. *Social Services Budgets and Social Policy*, 1975, 38.

12 Webb, A. and Wistow, G. The rise which cuts. *New Society*, 23 September 1982, 502.

13 Karran, T. 'Borough politics' and 'county government' administrative styles in the old structure. *Policy and Politics*, 1982, 10(3).

14 Dunleavy, P. The limits of local government. Paper presented to the ANCAN conference, Queens University, Ontario, 1983.

15 Weber, Max. Politics as a Vocation. In Gerth, H. and Wells, C. W. (eds.). *From Max Weber*, 1948, 84. Weber also noted that generally human actors do both to a great extent.

16 Judge, K. Territorial Justice and Local Autonomy: loan sanctions in the Personal Social Services. *Policy and Politics*, 1975, 3(4).

17 Glennerster, H. Prime Cuts. *Policy and Politics*, 1980, 8(4). Also Glennerster, H. Social Service Spending in a Hostile Environment. In Hood, C. and Wright, M. (eds.). *Big Government in Hard Times*, 1980.

18 Weber, J. Secret Probe into Social Services Charges. *British Evening Post*, December 31, 1980, 1.

19 Gyford, J. *Local Politics in Britain*, 1976.

20 Booth, T. Collaboration between the Health and Social Services: Part II. *Party and Politics*, 1981, 9 (2).

21 Lee, J. M. *Social Leaders and Public Persons*, 1963, 212–4. His comments on councillors: 'if they had the necessary ability to grasp the intricacies of the administrative detail involved, constituted an informal group of 'ministers', the 'inner ring'. They in alliance with the Chief Officers constituted a ministerial party ... promotion into the inner ring depended upon making an impression upon not only one's immediate colleagues but also upon the Chief Officers and Chairmen'. Also Karran, T. Borough Politics and County Government-administrative styles in the old structure. *Policy and Politics*, 1982, 10(3). Unfortunately, studies of ministerial politics declined and vanished, with few exceptions, after 1974.

22 Dearlove, J. *The Politics of Policy in Local Government*, 1973.

23 Stewart, J. *Local Government: the conditions of local choice*, 1983, 91.

CHAPTER TEN

Professionals, the 'trust' relationship, politics and budget construction

'TRUST' RELATIONSHIPS AND PUBLIC ADMINISTRATION THEORY

Wildavsky, in his analysis of the budgeting process in British central government, argues very correctly that the bedrock of political administration is the vital importance placed on 'personal trust'.[1] The title of his chapter, rather appropriately, is 'Budgeting as trust'. He sees the culture of 'trust' as a mechanism which integrates all structures and he conceptualizes treasury/spending department relations as an expression of networks of reciprocal trust which recognize mutual dependence in the midst of conflict. This is both the culture of senior civil servants and, to a lesser extent, politicians.

To conceptualize and to recognize the trust relationship, and its importance in local government, is to locate a central absence in the study of local government structures and processes. Roles, party politics, and structures have all been given legitimacy by the researchers. The 'trust' relationship between fellow senior professionals, and between senior professionals and key public representatives, has never been analyzed. Many case studies of individual local authorities are now in existence and these have considerably advanced our understanding of local policy-making processes. They have, for example, documented the ways in which local councils make their policy decisions, and in so doing they have pointed to the growing concentration of power in a diminishing number of hands. They have indicated the increased complexity of local government administration, and the supposed privileged position which the bureaucracy occupies in relation to both the elected members and to the consumers of local authority outputs. They have focussed on the role of the political parties in local government and on how the development of the party caucus has changed traditional patterns of decision making. Yet few of these studies have managed to transcend the limitations of a view of political power which locates it entirely in the formal organs or parties.

The view generated by an empirical field-work study of budget processes in one local authority, and selective interviewing in other local authorities, is that as much important weight should be attached to the bonds which unite and unify major financial and political processes in local government, as in central government. The word 'trust' was utilized again and again by senior officers, councillors, and other personnel, as a word which captured the search for unities inside structural conditions which produce strains and conflicts. It gives contextual similarities as well as differences to the meanings of central government processes which were analyzed by Wildavsky. The 'trust relationship', so intangible to orthodox political science and organizational theory, has similarities to other cultural understandings which are located in differential institutional arrangements. Yet in local government it has a specificity of its own! It is both a form of political culture and a common occupational culture in local government. It is taken-for-granted common sense, and is thus a pivot of decision making and negotiating, to be rarely, if ever, questioned. Its importance as a crucial mechanism becomes transparent, perhaps most clearly, when it is damaged, weakened, or broken. Thus in recent years, a chief executive has been removed from office in a local authority which was studied because of the contraction and loss of trust in him as a public official, as well as for other more tangible motives. 'Trust' is a shorthand, then, for competency, straight dealing, and an ability to play by the existing rules of the game without too many other difficulties. Modifications to existing rules can be made, and are made, inside the existing rules of the game oiled by 'trust'.

'TRUST' RELATIONSHIPS AND BUDGETING THEORY

To establish and explore the hypothesis of the contextual analysis of 'trust' as both an 'oil', and as a social relationship of centrality to local government processes, it may be helpful to link it with the politics of budget construction and the main financial control system. It has been a truism that budget construction must be seen as a political process and as a by-product of a political system. Thus Wildavsky states 'If organisations are seen as political coalitions, budgets are mechanisms through which sub-units bargain over conflicting goals, make side payments, and try to motivate one another to accomplish their objectives; it may contain figures the organization hopes to receive under favourable conditions ... budget proposals often are strategies'.[2]

The ability of interest groups and pressure groups to influence and determine budget construction has now received a widespread acceptance inside the academic literature – especially in the USA. It may be the case that the recognition of the impact of such pressure groups on the budget is not the same as recognizing them as legitimate. In the UK the tendency in the academic literature is to discount the importance of the pressure groups external to the governmental machine, and to emphasize the importance of the 'trust relationship'; though in a curious manner its dynamics are taken for granted as English common sense, rather than subjects for investigation. Wright,[3] in his research on planning and controlling public expenditure in central government, concentrates on the Public Expenditure Survey Committee (PESC), whose task is to review the negotiations which have taken place between the Treasury and the departments on the levels of future expenditure. The importance of PESC as an

219

administrative device, conceived and operated by the Treasury administrators, dominates his work on state expenditure. However, Wright comments:

> The expenditure controller relies upon his knowledge of the department and of the judgement and reliability of his opposite numbers in the finance and policy divisions; knowledge acquired through the years as a result of day-to-day contact in a small community. This relationship is crucial to the effective working of the Treasury's control. It is argued that it is unnecessary for the expenditure controller to know in great detail everything the department is doing, provided that he has established a good relationship based upon mutual confidence, trust and esteem. Through the medium of that relationship he will acquire knowledge and information of the strengths and weaknesses of the department, have early warning of the initiation of new policies and . . .[4]

It is significant that after making this extremely important point it never is allowed to structure or determine the main level of explanation. The description of processes is part and parcel of a pragmatic functionalism. Functionalism is the dominant form of the analysis of politics: the unit of analysis, such as the structure of interest or pressure group, is easily located and measured in the study of institutions and governmental processes. The strength of a descriptive functionalism of this type is that it can comprehend one aspect of the total reality. Its weakness is that it finds it difficult to understand processes which are both political with a small 'p' and social. Recent approaches to the study of the politics of the budget tend more and more to assume a model of limited rationality. Thus, in the context where uncertainty over goals and outcomes prevail in resource allocation decisions, Pfeffer and Salancik[5] discuss the important role that relative power and political bargaining play in the construction of a university budget.

Bargaining and negotiating over resources is recognized in the newer literature as a form of politics. Normally, however, its conceptual use is to see such bargaining and negotiating in an individualist and instrumental perspective, unmediated by collective values. Theories of limited rationality deviate from a pure economic model of rationality by allowing for individualistic politics of bargaining. If organizations have specific collective cultures, it is difficult, if not impossible, to situate the pivots of a bargaining politics in a context which allows a weight of determination to these cultural understandings.

LOCAL GOVERNMENT BUDGETING

Strategies of bargaining over resources in local government are both horizontal and vertical. It may be useful to study the pivots of 'trust' relationships between senior professionals in local and national government. Its importance in the gaining of financial resources should form the basis for the establishment of future hypotheses. It may well be that strategically placed professionals act as the links and interpreters of the central and local government structures. Much of the expansion of local authority social services departments was built upon joint financing of projects between the relevant Whitehall department and local authorities. The politics of gauging just how far you can go in your negotiating seemed to be nine parts rational calculations by local government professionals and one part bluff. A senior social services officer from a local authority had this to say:

> For all intents and purposes we've had no capital programme for three or four years. We tended to be applying for small capital schemes because we daren't go for what we really wanted. There was a feeling in the department – 'Well, we'll never get a big capital scheme because our resource allocation is only £400,000 and our big capital scheme is £600,000'. So what we tended to go for was two intermediate cost schemes, but we would only get one of them. DHSS seem to have a principal that you would never get everything you ask for, so we would only ever get one of them. We approached the problem last year and said, 'Look we will just put the DHSS on the spot. They know that our major problem is the elderly. We've asked for a forty-five bed home, and they daren't turn us down, because if they turn us down we get nothing'. It was a gamble we took and it proved right. They were very loath to turn us down, because then it would have meant we had absolutely no capital projects, and we engineered it that way. We did not ask for three, we only asked for one, and it was a big one.

A senior colleague in the authority explained the calculation behind such a strategy:

> The DHSS sent us a form which said that the allocation will be 80 pence per head of population, so we calculated that our likely allowance would come out at £400,000, so we should have to ditch our schemes. We knew we could not do a £650,000 home for the elderly on that, so I suppose we would have to have a centre for the elderly at £250,000. That would go ahead as our bid. That's what we have done for the last two years. Then they came along last year and said, 'We're going to reduce that £400,00 even further, you are only going to get £320,000'. That drove us to desperation. We will not be driven into building things that are not our number one priority, and it was homes for the elderly that we needed ... We just had enough and we said no ... We thought we had them cornered. They'd driven the general allocation business so low that you could not do anything with it ... we knew that they would like to give everybody something ... I think we would be pushing our luck next year if we bid for another home of the elderly. They might well turn us down flat and say no, and we'd get nothing – still we need homes for the elderly.

This officer stated that the department had difficulties in gauging future bids for joint financing with the DHSS. Calculations are less easy to predict, and 'trust' in the significant other's promises tends to diminish:

> Our real dilemma is that we still need homes for the elderly, and we are uncertain as to whether we may then lose our bids altogether. The risk is greater now especially as the down-turn in allocation will continue. Do we go for another home, or do we go for something which is of lesser importance and which we may not need very much? Do we try to take it one step further and negotiate with the DHSS and say, 'Don't give us any this year and don't give us anything in 1981/2, but give us another home for the elderly in 1982/3?' The problem is that they said we were going to plan for three year periods, but to all intents and purposes that's been abandoned and I have not seen any three year plans. Forward planning nowadays tends to be a farce.

Accounting for public policy

Judge states that prior to 1975-76 the process of resource allocation was characterized,

> by an unrealistically large number of bids from local authorities, confusion amongst Directors of Social Services about the DHSS's decision-making process, and the employment of strategies with varying degrees of success, by Directors to try to maximize the number of approvals they could obtain ... it would not be a grossly misleading generalization to suggest that the majority of Directors regarded the allocation of loan sanctions as a thoroughly irrational process, and reacted accordingly ... The most popular strategy was overbidding for resources.[6]

Judge gives no examples of the ways in which senior professionals in local government social service departments attempted to impose rational 'rules of the game' on such a supposedly irrational system. Judge himself, in his work on the rationing of social service departments, adopts a technocratic, rationalist conceptualization of resource allocation, and has little sympathy for any level of politics and/or bargaining over resources.[7]

A senior officer in another local authority gave an example from the early 1970's of how a political strategy to gain resources was mounted:

> We had been careful to sell the idea of the new building projects to the regional officers of the DHSS, who in those days had more influence than they have now. This was important, because when we met in London we met at the DHSS with the Department of Employment involved. We had the regional representatives sitting in for that meeting, and they did not go back on anything that they'd promised in the meeting that they had with us in ... or on the site. Another important factor was a gentleman who was closely involved in one of the sections of the DHSS and who had not been briefed on this by his department (strangely enough he was blind). He could only be aware of the things he was told. He walked into this meeting completely green as it were, and we converted him into an ally ... Our Director knew the appropriate people in the right places at the DHSS. I think the fact that he had been a National President was a big help. He was a big believer in the telephone and undoubtedly, if he met with a blockage he would be on the telephone in no time at all to the right man. Being a figure on the national scene helped.

To this officer the 'trust' in the projects by the regional officers who were formerly professionals in the social services, the conversion of a potential enemy into an ally, and the translation of political influence and 'trust' between the national and local levels by the Director, all helped to deliver the goods.

Another senior officer in the same local authority commented:

> The authority of the regional office teams of the DHSS social work service was very much related to the strength and competency of the Principal Social Work Service Officer in the region. If you had a very strong and good one, you could gain a lot in those days. You got somewhere with them in both professional terms and organizational terms. There's a group down here who have always been a weak bunch and who have virtually no credibility in the eyes of the local service. I have had very little contact with them ... My uncharitable view of the local office is that, (a) they would not help us at all and, (b) they would not be prepared to go to Whitehall on these issues, so it's better for us to fight direct.

222

Obviously, here the 'trust' relationship has totally broken down. Reputations are made and lost on the ability of professionals to listen to a reasonable argument and, if convinced, carry along fellow professionals and political masters in the hierarchy. The former social work practitioners in the regional office lost their ability to do this and so have no reputations to be measured and traded in a 'trust' relationship. As Wildavsky dryly states, 'what is at stake goes well beyond mutual pleasantness. It is a question of building and using personal working relationships. Trust, particularly at higher levels, is created not only by talk but by action'.[8]

PROFESSIONAL RELATIONSHIPS WITH ELECTED REPRESENTATIVES

Professionals are given budgets by public representatives who themselves have a 'trust' relationship with the chief executive and the head of the Treasury. The local authority in which field work has been carried out on the local authority budgetary process has unique characteristics in terms of the psychological composition of the bulk of the key personnel, and in the context of the political and administrative history of the local authority. It has, however, broadly identical similarities to other local authorities, and thus allows tentative hypotheses to be generated.

All local authorities are faced with competing spending departments for the use of limited resources. Each year social services, for example, has to compete with other services such as education, housing and transportation in an effort to obtain sufficient resources to meet the increasing demands placed upon them by both 'objective' standards of measurement of client need and their professional perceptions. Once made, the choices of public representatives are set down in the annual revenue budget.

The process of allocating resources between departments, of course, is not totally determined locally. The local authority budget process is strongly influenced by both the percentage of funding allocated by central government and the financial regulations imposed to control spending. From 1974, local authorities have received a series of circulars exhorting them to reduce the level of their expenditure. In real terms local government has achieved a virtual standstill since 1975-6: local authorities were spending no more in 1977-8 than they were two years earlier. By 1974-5, the local authorities were spending nearly 30 per cent of public money, by 1978-9, the percentage fell to 26. This, plus the tight imposition of cash limits, has narrowed the planning mechanisms to a point where forward planning is no longer realistic, as day-to-day events swamp the local financial controllers.

In such a context, statutory regulations on service delivery standards in such areas as housing, personal social services and education have probably weakened. Senior professionals used to use statutory regulations and recommendations from central government to bargain and negotiate over resources, but weaker regulations further force politics at all levels to become more transparent and more important. The factor of local discretion has always been important and increasingly may become more so.

There are vast disparities between local authorities in the form and extent of their services which cannot be accounted for in terms of differing local 'needs'. In these services central government recommendations do not have the force of national statutory standards. The exploration of the vacant political space, other than through the determination given by party politics and their values, is perhaps one of the central conceptual weaknesses of such studies as Danziger,[9] Greenwood *et al.*,[10] and Greenwood and Stewart[11] on the determination of the local government budget.

The following is an example which may have a certain significance. A senior officer, in a spending department in a local authority in which I undertook selective interviewing, described how his social service department went against the national trend and actually gained resources. He attributed this to the importance of values held by an important member of the council's political elite:

> We were really bowled over. We had a 3 per cent cut last year and we expected to take a further cut at budget time of 1 per cent. An important council member, who was not a member of the Social Services Committee, got up and said that he regarded the work of the department as being as important as the law and order work of the police, and they were increasing manpower. It was quite unrehearsed. The Treasury adopted the stance that they were there to advise, which was a rare thing for them to do. In the end, we had a 1.6 per cent expansion, say £345,000 in the budget.

Obviously, the professionals did not gain this expansion from either a 'trust' relationship with social service politicians, or fellow professionals in the Treasury, although the latter did not attempt to block the extra money. This kind of political event is not, therefore, tied to a 'trust' relationship, but can have an importance outside of that relation. The 'trust' relationship between politicians is relatively different than the 'trust' relationship between senior professionals. Trade-offs happen through mutual exchanges in both contexts, but the estimation and calculations can be both comparable and sharply different. The 'trust' relationship between a chief officer and a committee chairman, for example, can decisively influence budget policy. Such a close relationship can be a two-edged sword, for if the latter uses the expertise of the former, it is also the case that the former can influence the latter through the information he chooses to make available, and the way he does so.

Information and expertise constitute crucial power resources in the increasingly complex world of local government. This point is not lost on the elected members themselves, and too obvious a use of such power by officers can damage the 'trust' relationship, because one of its elements is that the public must not be made antagonistic to the real, though hidden, influence of the 'servants' of the public representatives. Inside the 'trust' relationship the problem is not simply that of disparities of technical expertise. Officers are in practice called upon, not only to 'advise' on policy options, but to make a large number of routine decisions about what a policy actually 'means' once it has been decided. A chief officer, in fact, has to be an able politician and to be able to use the strength, and minimize the weaknesses, of his committee and chairperson in the negotiations over resources. The inarticulate feelings and balances amongst the

224

politicians have got to be carefully estimated and predicted. Financial resources are dependent upon a chief officer being able to master political arithmetic. Failure to do so can damage a departmental budget at the margins, but sometimes those margins can be seen as being crucially important. One chief officer argued:

> What seems to be counter-productive in this authority is a disproportionate frequency of highly articulate special pleading, and that is the factor that builds up the resistance of the silent majority. People in a rural county seem to be suspicious of people such as the Chairman of Education, who is always highly articulate. They can feel that if you have got to be that articulate then there must be something wrong with the argument, even though the logic which is being expressed is perfect. You have got to master the feel of the situation rather than the logic of the situation. And there clearly is a limit to the number of times you can make a special plea effectively. So the credibility of the various chairmen of the Committee is decided on factors other than their verbal performance at committee. Our own Chairman rarely speaks in committee and is not a particularly articulate person . . . but she is a respected person . . . So at the Finance Committee where we were dealing with cuts, we had been given permission to go ahead to try to put together a package of finance which was not in any capital programme to develop a day centre at . . . I don't think any other committee would have been able to get that decision at that particular moment in time.

Here the 'trust' between public representatives is a major factor in obtaining resources at the 'margins' in the bargaining process. An independent assessment of the use made by the chief officer of this element of a 'trust' relationship was given by a very senior officer of the Treasury when he stated:

> One of the reasons why the Social Services have done so well is that they have deliberately kept a low profile. They have not seemed to be entering the hurly-burly of competing for resources. The chief officer is a cunning operator. His chairperson has a very good relation with the Leader and gets rewarded . . . Social Services have done better than anybody I know. Joint financing has helped, but they have eaten into the percentage given to Education . . . I don't think I know of a decision that really has gone against Social Services in the last few years. To give an example, the capital programme has been chopped very much. Education has lost £2.5 million and they have not got one replacement project. They can't do it . . . The same Finance Committee, where that decision was confirmed, saw the Social Services put up a request to replace a day centre in . . . I spoke half-heartedly against it, in the sense that the basic policy is at the moment not to sanction replacement projects. I said, impartially, 'That this is going to cost £160,000, albeit a lot of money will come from outside sources'. The Finance Committee said 'Agreed'.

It may be significant that the very senior official of the Treasury spoke half-heartedly against the proposal. In another interview he stressed his great respect for the chief officer's ability to manage money, and not waste resources, and rated him above the average in competency. Part of his managerial skills was the demonstration of competency, honesty, and a style of presentation which fitted in with the cultural nuances of the public representatives. A 'trust' relationship, including a personal friendship, existed between these two, though lower down the hierarchy a very strong element of competition, as well as co-operation, was dominant in professional working relationships.

FINANCE PROFESSIONALS WITHIN SPENDING DEPARTMENTS

The links between finance professionals, mainly accountants by training, located in spending departments as well as the central control system of the Treasury, were investigated in the project. A number of significant tentative hypotheses were generated on the complexity of inter-departmental working relationships. In the building of viable working relationships of 'trust' these professionals attempt to construct viable alliances which allow for conflicts and compromises. Finance professionals in spending departments represent the interests of the spending departments in the gaining and defence of financial resources. Normally, if they are accountants, they have been trained in some office of the Treasury, and he or she must demonstrate to non-financial professionals that they can 'bring home the bacon'. This is especially important as the senior management of a spending department will accept the migrant financial professional initially for his or her financial training and ability, but may have some reservations about his or her commitment to spending department values, which may be seen as a mismatch for the values of a traditional accountant. Acceptability and 'trust' has to be earned through the success of resources gained. The finance professional, in his or her negotiations and challenges to the representatives of the Treasury, claims respect and viable work space. In the establishment of a working relationship, each actor recognizes that having one's claims accepted is not a one-shot affair.

The 'trust' relationship of professionals in negotiation is constantly in flux, as each has continuously to earn respect and status by demonstration of technical and political skills. The budget process, and the way decisions have to be very quickly reached in face-to-face interaction, means claims to competence being tested every day, and each actor is sharply aware that he or she can lose the respect of others. The temper of rapid budget construction cannot be overestimated as a major prop which compels quick decisions. Uncertainty may be felt by these professionals, but cannot be articulated too often, as it undercuts claims to competency. It can also be remarked that the boundaries of negotiations over resources, the very language in which it is discussed, and the set of phenomena to be incorporated into each negotiation, are all provided by the existence of accounting and budgetary systems in local government. Further debates about flexibility in interpretation are enhanced by possible ambiguities of accounting methods, so providing grounds for agreements and disagreements within the negotiating process. If the language of financial regulations is not seen as being totally precise, the Treasury professionals can be asked to allow multiple interpretations of financial practice.

From the perspective of a professional, the budget process can be classified into various stages. These are:

1 The process of determining the total level of resources that will be available.
2 The process of drafting initial estimates.
3 The process of determining priorities between departments.
4 The process of reducing draft estimates to meet the allocation obtained.

Each stage has a specific timetable attached to it stating when the process has to be completed.

It may be useful to start by describing some of the elements which operate when a finance officer who is not a professional accountant has to negotiate on behalf of his spending department with an accountant located in the Treasury. This accountant, for a fixed number of years, is given the post of budget liaison officer and is also given, or allowed, a certain level of power to take financial decisions. These posts are allocated to all spending departments and in some may play a crucial role in determining budget policy. In departments which themselves employ an accountant in a senior position, findings tentatively suggest that the budget liaison officer's role and influence are less important. This finance officer was in a section headed by an accountant in a senior position, and decisions had to be cleared through the head of section. He stated:

> We have to come to an agreement on things like price increases, etc ... occasionally we might get together if there's a tricky point as to whether something is to be regarded as a pay or price increase, or what they term nowadays as a volume change ... Occasionally, for the sake of requirements at every stage of budget preparation, rules have to be twisted if not broken. Flexibility is important as each budget liaison officer, and I have known six, has to learn this lesson. In our budget programme this year, we have had extra hours allocated to staff in day centres, because of the changes in the conditions of service which shortened their working week and gave them a longer holiday. So we were allowed extra hours and we have used it to put on an extra staff of one in each establishment. It's a negotiating point whether that was regarded as a pay award or a volume change. The budget officer agreed to it being a pay award in the end. This is the sort of flexible thing which you can do.

It may be remarked that this finance officer was suspected by his superior of being too deferential to the Treasury mind. Also it was privately believed that as an accountant, the budget liaison officer was in a very strong position to dominate the working relationship. It may be significant that this finance officer was unable to notice any real difference in competency between different accountants who had been budget liaison officers. Senior professionals in the spending department and the Treasury were not holders of this opinion, and they were quick to argue the differences in perspective, competency, and to measure the reputations of each former officer. It may also be useful to note that the accountant superior to the finance officer now and again had to appeal privately to the superior of the budget liaison officer, to break the agreement between the finance officer and the budget liaison officer. He rarely did this, as it disrupted his internal working relations. Occasionally, however, he would appeal to the Treasury that as professional accountants they should recognize that a non-accountant, the finance officer, had given away or had conceded too much. While this was rare, it did happen, and the mutual ties of wary respect between the deputy Treasurer and the spending department accountant, and the long-term necessity for easy and compromising relationships, would result in a new round of negotiations.

Budget liaison officers are in a central position to expand or contract their roles and the relative financial influences attached to role presentation. In a crucial sense, each budget liaison officer creates to a large extent the role played, and this creation is determined by the type of reputation lost or gained in budget politics. The amount of autonomy taken, and the respect awarded, by key professionals obviously varied considerably in the brief history of this post. One of the first budget officers was so highly regarded by the chief officer of the spending department he was attached to, that he was given a very senior post in the management structure, to represent the spending department in negotiating resources. The lower echelons of the Treasury obviously saw this as an example of a gamekeeper turned poacher. They resented him for his use of Treasury techniques and thought processes, while respecting him for both his ability to gain resources and his career mobility. Working relationships of this layer of Treasury personnel were coloured to a greater or lesser extent by this ambivalence. At a more senior level, inside the Treasury, the advantages and disadvantages of an accountant in a spending department had become part of the practical politics of the organization when dealing with this spending department. It should be noticed that only this department had a chief officer who believed that an accountant should be hired by a spending department, rather than loaned to it. The wary respect with which this officer was regarded in the Treasury is illuminated in the following comment by a very senior Treasury officer:

> Recently we had been banging the drum about the need to maintain and replace our assets. We must put the money in a proper replacement programme ... So we gave to the Education Department a certain amount of cash to replace their equipment ... The estimates turned out to be overstated, so they had something like £100,000 over when they were apparently satisfied all their requirements for replacing equipment were settled. Then they said, 'We've found a need to replace some furniture, and it seems to us ridiculous to say to a school you can have the money to replace a lathe, but your desks are collapsing and you can't have the money for that'. So we in the Treasury said it was all right and they wanted about £70,000 for replacements ... The other £30,000 they wanted to use to renew books in school libraries ... We said we are not going to use capital money, because while we were quite happy with equipment or furniture, we were not going to allow books, because we felt it was wrong in principle to use capital money on near consumable items, and they just could not accept this. They could not see what the difference was between a book that could last for five to ten years, and a lathe which would last five to ten years. They were both essential equipment items. In the end we came to a compromise where we could have allowed the money to come from revenue, but in the end the Finance Committee wouldn't do it anyway. I would think that this sort of thing would be easier to explain, or put over, in the Social Services because of ...'s training and accounting background. The Education Department just would not accept it and I think ... Social Services would have accepted and understood.

This senior Treasury officer also commented that social services, the spending department which had hired the accountant from the Treasury, also seemed to make best use of virements from a spending department's point of view. He stated:

> I think the Social Services would like to see the whole of the budget given to them and just sent over ... However, any reasonable virement suggestions we would support ... What

we will not accept, obviously, is any part of the savings which comes from the 1½ per cent staff cut, as a contribution towards extra spending somewhere else ... We would look favourably at proposals to move between budget heads staffing heads in excess of the 1½ per cent to pay for price increases. I don't think we're doing any more than making sure that they don't go off the rails ... Partly due to pressure from Social Services, we have reached a new agreement that as far as virement is concerned, they can do it if the Treasurer agrees with the service chief officer, and the chairman of the service committee and finance agree. But they must report what they've done to Finance and the Social Services. Now Social Services are the people who have made best use of the virement package probably because of ... influence ... They always come up with several virement packages; Education, on the other hand, does not.

A cautious acceptance of the organizational rewards and risks of placing an accountant in a senior position in the social services, seems to illuminate these two statements. It should be recognized that several times the most senior officials in the Treasury have expressed their distaste of future accountancy professionals moving over to spending departments on a permanent basis. The Treasury mind is most clearly demonstrated in budget negotiations. As Wildavsky argues, in the context of central government, 'the Treasurer's business is to move monies, not to spend it'.[12] In this sense, the Treasury is 'inherently reactive'. Those at the Treasury pride themselves on the ability to see through arguments misjudged by others. The slant to the 'critical scepticism' of the ideal Treasury accountant is 'hostility to hidden or built-in spending escalators'. The building of a 'trust' working relationship with accountants who not only know the mind of the Treasury, but perhaps have a more entrepreneurial interpretation of money management, is fraught with strains. Compromises, at the level of a partial softening of Treasury dogma, are the oil which activates the machinery of a 'trust' relation. However, it must be understood that professionals in the service departments are allowed to manipulate and negotiate financial regulations within certain limits. Those limits are determined in large part by the close organic link between the formal organizational structure and the centrality of accountancy professionals in the office of the Treasury.

Significantly for the bargaining relationship, the 'trust' working relationship is structurally unequal: one side can only attempt to modify the organization, while the other side is central to it. That one group of professionals outside the main financial control system view themselves as captive professionals is related to the basically alien structure of local government. The senior professionals outside the Treasury possess certain bargaining counters, such as their control over bureaucratic authority in spending departments and the alliances they build with fellow professionals in central government. The captivity of the professional can thus be significantly modified, but not transformed, by negotiations activated by powerful professionals on behalf of subordinates and themselves. The occupational weight and culture of the finance professionals in the Treasury is strikingly different. To a great extent these professionals have been given the right of control in the bureaucratic structure; so for this category the structure is not an external alien constraining organization. From their position, it has many of the characteristics of a professional organization. Finance professionals in spending departments understand this only too well. If they come from Treasury backgrounds, they understand the technology and thought processes in which they have been trained; but they have lost the organizational power base in which it is produced. One such professional remarked 'Even if I'm not as bright, tough and competent as my opposite numbers over there, I have to force myself to be competent enough to have a slight edge over them. Otherwise it can be difficult. Think of a game of football where every time you move towards the opposite side's goal you suspect the referee will blow the whistle on you'.

This finance professional was hired by a chief officer for the following reasons:

> In trying to compile the basic information about the level of resources, we naturally began to ask why certain resources were there and others were not ... Resources had been allocated for capital work and the effects of that were considerable, as the financial consequences didn't appear to be built into the revenue budget ... I think people were wary of exposing their lack of knowledge to the senior staff in the Treasurer's department who, I think, have a vested interest in keeping us ignorant of these processes.

The conscious strategy of this chief officer was to attempt to win over: to 'turn' as much as possible the budget liaison officers from the Treasury by apparently treating them as essential members of his spending department. Thus the problem of dual loyalties for such officers became intensified, though in the last resort the Treasury controlled the career structure.

The inequality of bargaining was remarked on by another finance professional in a spending department in another authority, who could pass the following comment on Treasury use of existing financial regulations:

> I always look at it as a game of monopoly. A very, very complicated game of monopoly, where the rules are changing, and where part of the fun, or part of the importance, is to be constantly abreast of the rules. Now you say to me, why then if I was to pass over there and say, well this is what I do at budget time, it's not illegal ... then I have the feeling, rightly or wrongly, that they will then amend their orders as to obstruct me from doing something.

The chief officer quoted previously could also emphasize that to enable him to claim resources for a relatively newly-formed spending department, he had to show to his sub-committee, and to the council generally, that resources were not going to be wasted. The hiring of a senior finance professional with basic loyalties to the spending department, who would negotiate in its interests, became vital. The 'trust' relationship between this chief officer and the senior staff in the Treasury, and the 'trust' relationship between the department's political allies among the councillors, became correspondingly strengthened by such a move. Ultimately, a reputation for not being able to manage forward financial planning would work against the department in the future, if the expansion in resources ever diminished. He argued that as a new department in a paradoxical position of strength and weakness in bargaining, and as a politican in negotiating resources, he had to use every available card in the pack. Trust was, and is, conditional:

> We had a very substantial level of growth, something like 16 per cent, and yet we had to tie services down, in order to contain the expansion that was taking place ... you had a lot of growth without a lot of real expansion of the level of service. That underlined the importance of coming to terms with having to plan ahead and understand the system of financial allocation, if we were going to have control over it. The need to do so became more clear as we entered into the sort of corporate debate over the allocation of resources. Other departments, over a period of years, had built up the criteria by which they were going to bid for resources. They argued that there were so many children in the schools and so many miles of road to be maintained, etc. The Social Services department initially was quite naked, in the sense that our criteria, in terms of level of service provision, were mainly internal to our professionalism. These criteria, however, were not corporately accepted in the same way that the teacher-pupil ratio was accepted, so we had to learn the rules of the game very fast. We had to develop information, knowledge and understanding of the system, in order to ensure that a fair share of the overall resources were coming in our direction ... Our need was for forward financial planning ... We looked for someone who had knowledge and experience of the financial world.

The expansion of other similar social service departments in other local authorities had a similar logic to them, whether accountants were hired or not by the chief officers.

The importance of face-to-face negotiations between finance professionals in spending departments and the Treasury cannot be merely assumed. If the budget is more or less incremental, then such negotiations affect the margins, rather than the base. It may well be that a spending department and a Treasury do not have the same perception of the importance, or lack of importance, of specific face-to-face negotiations. Working relationships may well be both related and complicated by this possible lack of a perception match between the actors.

One accountant, in a spending department in a local authority, found that to gain 'trust' in the eyes of the Treasury he was forced to attempt to control expenditure internal to the department which could be defined as wasteful expenditure by accounting values. He had himself modified his accountancy values, in order to achieve credibility in the eyes of the senior management in the spending department who were recruited from social work backgrounds, and still probably had some reservations about how far 'hard' accounting values should dominate. It may be that the monitoring by the Treasury would not pick up such 'waste', but in the context of negotiating resources he felt he had to attempt to check such expenditure. It must be added that his own commitment to the spending department and his own cluster of values motivated him in such a tactic. He remarked:

> I can give you an example where my input was nil and I thought a very strong case was totally brushed aside ... We have intermediate treatment officers who are volunteers and they do evening work, and they have never ever been paid ... What they tend to do is to take a half days holiday the next day. There was a move afoot to pay them and it was raised at the information corporate planning group. My objections were very basic. Why should we pay a lot of money for something we are already getting free? I made the

objection and I heard no more about it. It formed no part of our budget plans. Two months ago I was asked to calculate the cost of introducing a scheme to the 55 volunteers that were involved, and it came out within the region of £40,000 per annum . . . I objected most strongly, as this seemed to be a gross waste of scarce resources, because once it is paid we can never withdraw it . . . I was told to find the money. I could have scuppered it then. I could have said, 'I'm sorry I can't find the money, this was not in the budget. It's not a budgetary item, there's no allocation for it'. I did not want to appear to be obstructive. There are not many times when my advice is not taken.

The calculation here is that internally, finance personnel from non-social work backgrounds need allies in spending departments and cannot bruise or damage the vital working relationships that maintain them. Competency is judged by such social work allies in senior management as a vital element which the finance profession provides. They may, however, have strong reservations about pure accountancy values dominating internal processes. In such a context for them a 'trust' relationship has few satisfactory trade-offs.

In this authority, a budget liaison officer was allocated to the social services department who mainly interpreted this role as monitoring spending. The finance professional does not disregard the budget liaison officer, but attempts to negotiate with a deputy Treasurer or the Treasurer himself. The last type of negotiating is done through the chief officer of the spending department himself. Sometimes the 'trust' relation allows for the chief officer not to accept the finance professional's negotiation strategy, though this can shake the relationship if the chief officer's own strategy fails to work. He then loses face and is more vulnerable to the advice given next time round by the finance professional. The following example may be of some iterest:

Last year we had a very heavy underspending and that was an embarrassment. We had perfect liberty and standing orders to use virement, to transfer money from Heading A to Heading B, which we intended to do, and so we drew up a programme of about £200,000 worth of virement. Contrary to my advice the Director chose to bring it quite out in the open and tell the Treasurer in advance what we intended to do. My attitude was we were breaking no rules, we're acting in absolute accordance with standing orders; we should just go ahead and do the necessary virement. Transfer the resources bit-by-bit. But the Director chose to make it an issue with the Treasurer. As the Authority was facing a deficit, he felt as a member of a corporate team that he should be seen to be playing fair. He must have felt that while he was abiding by the letter of the law, he was contravening the spirit of it . . . I felt to hell with that. We will be grossly embarrassed by heavy underspending, and it's an excellent chance to build up our resources in the full knowledge they are going to be cut next year. If we don't spend that £200,000, it's gone for next year. We would have used that money to help us through next year's hard times. So he used his power and influence with the Chairman of the Council, who would view very dimly anybody who used virement to that extent. What happened was that the Treasurer did not have the authority to refuse us virement. So we were pressured into not using it and it collapsed. So we lost £200,000.

This finance professional argued that, with reference to resource allocations, there was very little room for manoeuvre. If his spending department, in accordance with

Government Guidelines, is awarded a 1 per cent reduction in resources or a 2 per cent growth, that figure is difficult to alter. However, bargaining over what the rate of inflation is, and in what part of the year it will either peak or fall, is seen as a legitimate element in working relationships. He stated:

> The Treasury informs us of the rate of inflation which they have used to up-date our budget. Because we are under pressure, we would select perhaps ten of the most important areas both in volume terms and percentage terms and we would check them out. Where our inflation calculation was more than theirs, we'd tell them, where it was less we would keep quiet. We can't argue about the budget figure because it's public knowledge, it's printed. We could argue about the level of spending. If they are to base the resource allocation on actual expenditure for the previous year, then there would be battles galore, but so long as they continue to do it on the budget figure, 10 per cent, on the elderly of £3.5 million, there's no argument . . . I think they expect that there will be no comeback, mainly because we have not got the available manpower to check them out very thoroughly . . . All I can do is to pick on specific items. The other day I bounced back on them and managed to get another £120,000 on agency, which is one of our big areas.

Inside this working relationship of 'trust' the finance professional, given his unequal negotiating position, thought it was a legitimate tactic to keep back information when it suited. He assesed the finance personnel in the Treasury as follows: 'I think they play the game fairly. They don't try to deprive us of resources by giving us a lower inflation rate. I've never caught them out doing that deliberately. I think they do the best they can on the information they've got. We, on the other hand, probably have more readily available information'. It was extremely important, then, for the representative of the spending department never to take information from the Treasury on trust, as this would not be acceptable even inside a 'trust' relationship. A general belief among finance personnel existed that political and technical Treasury information should always be accepted with reservations even if not openly challenged. A viable distinction between the personal honesty and competency of the Treasury personnel and the information base used sustained the 'trust' relationship. Another finance professional in a different authority argued:

> They are going to give 2 or 3 per cent on provisions when, if you asked anyone outside, they would have estimated it as more likely to be 10 or 12 per cent. I asked them how they based the figures, and it seems that they based them on the cost of providing a school meal, and they took that from the Education estimates. We objected very strongly that you could not classify a meal provided in one of our centres, or an aged person's home, with a meal provided by the Education Committee, because they produce them in tremendous bulk, whereas a lot of our establishments almost operate with corner shop purchasing. What we did was to count, using three different formulae, to show the movement of prices on provisions. We used the Retail Prices Index for one of them. We used the local evening paper that kept a shopping basket for the local housewife; and we also took an analysis of about ten or fifteen of our own homes and analyzed how costs have risen . . . All our figures were fairly similar, and they all came out at 17 to 21 per cent. We went back with this information to the Treasurer and said in no way could we accept a 3 per cent calculation of £750,000. We would lose disastrously . . . we eventually had a compromise of

about 12 per cent. They never give you what you ask for, as they never could admit that we were correct. Through such negotiating processes we gained £100,000 on that, whereas if we did not bargain we would have gained perhaps between £20,00 to £30,000.

This finance department made the following point that could generate further hypotheses about the relative importance of such financial political bargaining. The problem of relating bargaining at the margins to the ongoing base budgets could then be located:

The point of all this is that it makes allocations of resources silly, because you can get more money for your department through the mechanics of your inflation squabbling than you can through the Council saying, 'We'll agree to give the Social Services 1 per cent'. So in the past, we've maybe had £200,00 given us by the Council for growth, but we've managed to generate one way or another, maybe a total of between £600,000 to £700,000 ... We know, for example, that on provisions we gained £90,000, on Agency we got another £120,000. On income we gained another £100,000. There was, and is, a great range of different areas where we'd manage to squeeze resources of the Treasury ... We move at such a hectic pace, thank God, at budget time that nobody has any real chance to check on anybody else.

The pace of the budget cycle, as stated in this chapter earlier, should never be underestimated as a major factor in the psychology of budget politics. Timetables have to be kept and bureaucratic procedures finalized, even if professionalism is agnostic about such haste.

If the budget liaison officer has any power to make real decisions that will commit the Treasury, his or her strengths and weaknesses will be weighed up by the professionals in the spending departments. Finance professionals can make initial gains by the victories they go for in the 'trust' relationship. Too many such victories, however, entails that the Treasury representative loses his or her credibility in the eyes of the senior staff in the Treasury, and is less likely to be a useful ally when the spending department needs a Treasury insider to give them real support on a big expenditure item or policy. The politics of each system of negotiation in each local authority has certain probable similarities as well as weaknesses.

A finance professional in a social services department commented that after gaining a large amount of money on an argument on inflation items from the Treasury, 'They are becoming more expert at it now, so the chances of a big kill are less and less. It's a pity, as I always took delight in going back to the department and saying, 'Well lads, I've got you another £200,000'.

The weakness and strengths of each Treasury department's representative can only be understood if the internal politics of the major financial control system are understood. In one local authority, a Treasurer kept a very able budget liaison officer for a period of four years. In another, the post could be filled by a new accountant every year. This allows the spending departments' financial professionals to gauge their competency and to allocate the appropriate set of bargaining tactics. One finance professional argued:

For the last year the Treasury have had a very good accountant, who is very meticulous, and will have subjected figures to a fair degree of scrutiny before he lets them go, so there is not much room for manoeuvre. We are waiting for him to move, and then we will be in like hawks to pick on the new poor unsuspecting chap that comes along and is not so well versed ... I'm in a difficult position though, because there is only one of me at the moment. I have to keep remembering that if they win a minor little battle, you find that your ability to negotiate good terms is slipping from your grasp, and they will come back even harder and with more audacity later on. They may use guerilla tactics and challenge clothing next.

The finance professional also repeated a similar theme that the 'trust' working relationship is a continuous process, by which professional claims to competency are being tested in day-to-day financial encounters. Reputations are gained or diminished through the shock of such bargaining.

Lastly, this finance professional re-emphasized a point already made by other finance professionals: 'So the politicians argue and squabble about as to whether we should get £150,000 or £170,000. So often, in the last five years, it's not been very relevant, because we have already got twice that by other means. By inflation bargaining.' This professional was rather concerned that in his local authority, a book was produced last year, which has in it all the data on the budget politics of negotiating in all service departments:

So your columns should be equal, and if they are not equal it could be said that you've been fiddling. You've been redistributing resources. It picks it up very clearly. So this document could really get us now. It's tying our hands down because (I think I'll have told you in the past) ... we redirect hundreds of thousands of pounds. Now it's obvious if we have, then this accounting information works against our interests. Let's give an example. If we look at Agency under Community Homes General, the budget for 1979/80 was £303,400. With inflation on it, it's up to £351,050: but we've only budgeted £272,000. So we are making a saving there of about £80,000. Now the members would not have picked that up, because they would have compared £300,000 with £272,000 and they would not have known what the inflation negotiations had produced. They would have thought that our saving there was around £30,000 not £80,000 which it was. What this new format forces us to do, is to bring the full picture out into the open ... However, even with all that information, they didn't grasp what it was telling them. The Treasurers did not grasp it and the politicians did not grasp it. We are moving hundreds of thousands around from A to B, to B and C, and C to D, which makes their additional allocation peanuts ... So far we've escaped, though by now they may have picked this up. It's one of the funny things about local government that we spent only twenty minutes on it in the committee ... Most of the discussion was on irrelevancies and they never got round to the body of the document.

Another finance professional, who the researcher related this type of problem to, smiled. Then he condemned the competency of the financial professional in keeping informal records of transactions over bargaining. He implied that he carefully destroyed all information, as too much clarity can weaken his bargaining strength. This officer then stated: 'We work at such a pace that if you don't get caught at a particular time they won't pick you up, because we are on to something entirely different the next day.

No sooner than we had the revenue budget completed, in preparation, then we went on to the capital budget.'

A former budget liaison officer still in the Treasury, in another local authority, discussed the significance of the negotiations over the inflation rate in these terms. This officer was given a great deal of respect both by the Treasury and the spending department for his competency:

> The trouble is that neither we in the Treasury, nor the spending department, have the necessary equipment to correctly calculate the inflation rate. At best, the information base we both use is a crude guide, but negotiations on some items could be significant, as sizeable sums, in an accumulative sense, were involved; especially on that part of the budget dealing with running expenses on food, furniture, clothing, etc. The food budget was around £500,000, and if we get it wrong, the inflation rate, by say 2 to 3 per cent, that could be quite a lot of money, and the compounding effect over a short period of time would be considerable. Running expenses on food, clothing and furniture, up to 60 to 70 per cent, would have to be argued and negotiated. Only once was the food budget calculated for correctly on the inflation rate, and that was once by someone in the research unit who had a statistical training and who knew what he was doing. The trouble also is this part of the department's budget is not identical to the similar parts of other spending departments' budgets. Food, clothing, specialized furniture; all these costs are not common in spending departments. I would sometimes go along with information on other departments' budgets, as well as the rates given by retail price indexes, but of course I would not disclose the other departments' calculations to the spending department. I did not want arguments, or false agreements between spending departments, on what certain common items should be. No such information flows between departments, in my opinion, on consumption items ... It would not make the work of the Treasury easier if it did ...

This officer was rated, both by the spending department and the Treasury, as an extremely competent officer with a strong 'trust' working set of relationships in both departments. He does hint that he sees it as legitimate to withhold certain types of information, which may complicate and weaken his position of resource negotiating, as a legitimate tactic inside the 'trust' relationships. He was also very anxious that information on the tabulations provided by the Treasury he represented should not be made into a complex mystery which needed the services of a budget liasion officer and thereby reduced the role from policy-maker to an interpretative clerk. He sincerely argued that the tabulations should provide accounting information, so that budget preparation could be carried out without necessary intervention at this level from the Treasury. He stated: 'We have been very remiss on how we produce the tabulations and what is in them, as they seem to be produced in such a way that people cannot understand them without us. However, it is difficult to alter such a system.'

It is interesting to compare the lack of defensiveness over the negotiating tactic inside the 'trust' relationship, namely withholding information as a Treasury right, with the concern to spread the advantages of a simplified system of tabulations. The second was not a potential disruption of his power base of negotiating. The note of defensiveness in the voice of another finance professional (in a spending department), who saw the withholding of financial information as a legitimate tactic inside the 'trust' relationship, but still felt it was somehow wrong, can only be captured in the field-work techniques of grounded theory. As an accountant he seemed to feel, in spite of himself, that while knowledge was power it should not be used in this manner. He simply stated: 'Where our inflation calculations were more than theirs, we'd tell them. Where it was less, we'd keep mum. I don't always like it, but that's what we are forced to do.' However, on the use of hidden savings for indirect expansion, this professional took pride in his competency in negotiating with the Treasury for resources. This fear that new accounting information would come to light and weaken his bargaining position is illuminated in the following statement which also expresses his pride as a politician and as an able accountant:

> Indirect expansion through hidden savings happened every year. But this year, I had a few problems, as their information was better. It's like a card trick, wherein the first time, the first year, I actually had to show them how we do this trick, and they still did not pick it up. After that they watch your hands even closer and they may pick it up. I have the fear you can only do the same trick so many times before someone says, 'Ah! That's how you do it,' ... The information format, to compare like with like, was presented by the Chief Executive, but I see the Treasurer's hand in it ... All those hand-written pieces of paper giving results on substantive savings now collected ... The tortuous paths to raise £200,000 or £300,000, then dispersing it without it coming to light ... lest the Treasurer make a move to deprive us ... In this format, for example, it's obvious even to the weakest brain, that there's been a susbstantial change in support service's administration. £155,000 has gone up to £178,000, which looks very bad ... However, this year I got away with it. I was prepared to answer questions like that ... The first thing I did was to produce ten pages with the certain knowledge that we had been told economize on paper. The Chief Executive relented and said, 'Oh well, just put down three sides, rather than ten.' Therefore, that immediately prevented it from balancing.

CONCLUSIONS

The 'trust' relationship is not, therefore, a simple expression of trust, anymore than it was in Wildavsky's study of the mandarins at Whitehall. It allows and expresses the co-existence of conflicts and alliances. The relationship between the two elements shifts, according to the contextual politics of the issue. At the end of the day, no matter how much anger as well as professional ill-feeling is produced through such negotiations, each actor knows that they will have to meet again and again, and thus this acts as a check on a total breakdown of 'trust' as co-operation. The search for unities is an integral part of the supposedly 'non political' administrative cultures of local government at all levels, horizontal and vertical. This corresponds to the belief that gentlemen's agreements, rather than written constitutions, are best for all, as all are really given some compromise consideration which may not in fact happen under a written constitutional code of parctices. This is incorporated into a strong system of politics, with a small 'p', that both allows professionals to demonstrate competency as craftsmen, and as politicians, and to redraw existing boundaries between different parts of the organization. In the contest for available resources such skills in politics are vital.

Nevertheless, it must be emphasized that such an internal process is part of a limited consensus politics which may have worked well in the past, but whose weaknesses will become more obvious as the external environment becomes increasingly difficult to master, and central government resources lessen. The transformation to a Hobbesian politics of a ruthless war of all against all, may become the new form of collective cultural understandings in the 1980s in local government administration. Existing research is ill-prepared for such a reality.

NOTES AND REFERENCES

1 Wildavsky, A. *Budgeting: a comparative theory of the budgetary process*, 1975.
2 *Ibid.*, 4.
3 Wright, M. Planning and controlling public expenditure. In Booth, T. (ed.). *Planning for Welfare: Social Policy and the expenditure process*, 1979.
4 *Ibid.*, 35.
5 Pfeffer, J. and Salancick, G. R. *The external control of organizations: A resource dependence perspective*, 1978.
6 Judge, K. The financial relationship between central and local government. In Booth, T. (ed.). *Op. cit.*, 54–5.
7 Judge, K. *Rationing social services: a study of resource allocation and the personal social services*, 1978.
8 Wildavsky, *Op. cit.*, 71.
9 Danziger, J. *Making Budgets*, 1978.
10 Greenwood, R. *et al. Patterns of management in local government*, 1980.
11 Greenwood, R. and J. D. Stewart, *Corporate planning in English local government: an analysis with readings 1967–72*, 1974.
12 Wildavsky, *Op. cit.*, 74.

Power, reciprocity and research practices:
a semi-autobiographic appendix and note

No matter how modified, participant observation and the methods under its aegis display a tendency towards naturalism and therefore to conservatism. The ethnographic account is a supremely *ex post facto* product ... There develops, unwilled, a false unity ... The subjects stand too square in their self-referenced world. The method is also patronising and condescending – is it possible to image the ethnographic account upwards in a class society? ... The silences and enforced secrecies of the method are ultimately political silences.[1]

I have frequently been aware that social existence is disordered, ambiguous and humanly merry and many of the formal textbooks on research methods either do not fully recognize this or beyond a marginal recognition are unable to take account of this merriness. I have also been aware in the words of Nicolaus that the bulk of social research looks down rather than upwards to the social worlds of the wealthy and powerful elites. It is not just problems of access that prevent their lives being 'daily scrutinized by a thousand systematic researchers ... pried into ... analysed and cross-referenced, tabulated and published in a hundred inexpensive mass circulation journals, and written so that the fifteen year old ... could understand it and predict the actions of those who manipulate and control'.[2] Nicolaus caustically sees social research as looking down for very obvious reasons. The inability of rigid survey methods to capture the subjective realities of the minorities and the working classes of the USA allowed no predictability of behaviour. The fortunate rise of a number of qualitative methods of research, including grounded theory, while opposed by many senior social scientists as unscientific, eventually became well funded through the agencies of the managerial elite, who control sponsorship money.

In the market research practised in the UK, positivism dominated for many years. In the universities and the cultures of sociology social research was rarely dominated by positivism. In fact an anti-positivistic bias was the common theme in the teaching of research methods. Bell and Newby,[3] Abrams *et al.*,[4] and a recent collection of articles in the journal *Sociology*, all document this.[5]

In my undergraduate formative years in the late 1960's, the dominant humanism or marxism rejected the epistemologies of positivism, though empiricism was seen, apart from the followers of the early writings of L. Althusser, to be legitimate. It may well be that a weak positivist practice still existed in ways which were not openly recognized by the competing epistemologies. Hindess, a Marxist in those days, wrote a critique of both positivism and ethnomethodology which was influential,[6] and even more read Cicourel's pessimistic assault on formal methods published much earlier.[7] However, a concrete fieldwork tradition did not exist which allowed students to discuss the practice of theory in the context of the UK. The USA did, alongside a dominance of positivism, have a strong flourishing tradition of qualitative research, so we read *Street Corner Society*,[8] or the *Small Town in Mass Society*[9] if we wanted to know about the problems of operationalizing qualitative social research.

As an undergraduate, I became influenced by the cool ironical humour and critical sociology of one of the authors of *Small Town in Mass Society* who was a visiting professor. A marginal student in a marginal student cohort responded to his very American style with its conscious consciousness of power and cultural determinants. The Chicago School professionalism in later years was a weakening of this Veblen type sociology of the powerful. Bensman was, unlike the young sociologists who mainly taught me, a craftsman who respected cultural production. He saw me as a possible apprentice to his craft and fixed me up with a fellowship at Brandeis which I later turned down. His respect for C. W. Mills as a craftsman gave him a radical but resigned cutting edge. And his conscious avoidance of quantification as a form of reductionism was extremely attractive. Deeply conscious of the politics of research, he was aware, and not as a simple abstraction, that the 'public atmosphere of an organisation or community tends to be optimistic, positive and geared to the public relations image ... Any attempt in social analysis in presenting other than public relations rends the veil and must necessarily cause resentment. Moreover any organisation tends to represent a balance of divergent interests held in some kind of equilibrium by the power and status of the parties involved. A simple description of these factors, no matter how stated, will offend some of the groups in question.'[10] He was keen to argue that the research which seeks to deal with the objections raised by the powerful in an inoffensive way normally becomes banal, irrespective of its technical and methodological virtuosity. He, as a craftsman, an artist painting the canvas of American society, an ex-Trotskyist interested in power and powerlessness, committed himself to a study of the levels of power and cultural production which normally were not studied. Bensman, while conscious of the achievements of the Chicago School's West Coast followers such as Becker, Glaser and Straus, was cool about the politics dominant in their professionalization of fieldwork. To be perhaps overcrude, he knew that a positivistic method which was not able to grasp the authentic social relations of an organization, a factory, a prison, a school, and the data produced fed into elite managerial calculations, is worthless and the elites would patronize other forms of data collection, even when this is done by sociological professionals with liberal or radical private identities. The professionalization of qualitative research, while a technical advance, had an ambivalence about its political use. Like Lynd he could ask: knowledge for what ...?

While Bensman rarely discussed the epistemology of his method he was certainly closer, in his subjective opinion, than the ethnomethodologists and the interactionists to Max Weber, the classical European. He would have rejected a conception of *verstehen* which would be reducible to a phenomenological inter-subjectivity, an existentialist sociology which denies in practice historical determination. The transformation of Weber through Parsons into a subjectivist can be legitimated through a selection of neo-Kantian formulations.[11] However, it was not necessary for Bensman, who had a great admiration for G. H. Mead, to know that Weber was not Mead and that significant others have histories as well as biographical identities. As Gerth and Mills point out, when Weber came to the USA on a visit and saw 'the Greek shining the Yankees' shoes for five cents, the German acting as his waiter, the Irishman managing his politics and the Italian digging his dirty ditches',[12] his interests were not merely focussed on the persons performing such roles, but on the Yankees for whom the work is being performed. While it is accurate too that Weber and Durkheim, among others, felt it incumbent to pronounce on epistemological grounds, such statements had little or no relationship to their research. Thus, as is well know, Durkheim was a positivist when writing *The Rules of Sociological Method*, but not a positivist in *The Elementary Forms of Religious Life*. In his remarks in the beginning of *Economy and Society*, Weber was a neo-Kantian, but not in his *Religion of China*. Confronted with the advocates of grounded theory as an epistemology and Peter Winch, Weber may well decide that he is not himself a Weberian.

My postgraduate years at another English university were uneven. I had a supervisor whom I felt little empathy with and whose training at the LSE gave him little interest in qualitative data. I surprised myself by eventually completing a MSc. by thesis by relatively unstructured interviewing. In this department of sociology, a vague anthropology was resepected but no fieldwork practice to which I could relate. The culture of the academics was radically different from my last university with some exceptions. I did become friendly with a young lecturer who was later engaged in writing up his fieldwork on the labour force of the Ford Motor Company in Liverpool.[13] I became conscious of this and respected his fieldwork practice which was integrated into a socialist politics I also respected.

Beynon combined a macro Marxist political economy of the motor industry at the level of the international and national level with a brilliant qualitative fieldwork practice which located and articulated the cultures, politics and values of the shop stewards and the shop floor. There was no discussion of research methodology in this text and no attempt to discuss its sociology, but then the audience was quite consciously not a professional elite or elites but an audience of workers, especially car workers. The naturalist language was their language, taken and returned to them as the value of their labour power was not returned.

Perhaps another comparison can be made. A number of sociologists have used a qualitative, naturalist method to describe the culture of deviants and are disposed to view the entire ambience of deviance from the standpoint of the deviant persons themselves. I came across the work of these naturalists for the first time in my post-

241

graduate days, and while I felt both interest and some respect for the humanism in their project I could understand Gouldner's critique of this school of sociology very well. I responded to the argument that compared the respect given the deviant by the naturalist to a 'zoo curator who preeningly displays his rare specimens . . . he wishes to protect his collection; he does not want spectators to throw rocks at the animals behind the bars. But neither is he eager to tear down the bars and let the animals go.' Gouldner argues that coupled with an exclusion of political deviance in which men and women actively fight back on behalf of their values and interests 'the very empirical sensitivity to fine detail, characterizing this school, is both born of and limited by the connoisseur's fascination with the rare object: its empirical richness is inspired by a collector's aesthetic.'[14] Perhaps unjustly but with some correctness, Gouldner argues that the clients of this naturalist qualitative method were the liberal elites in the state who were given a critique of the unenlightened middle class bigotry. So the humanism of H. Becker and his sociological friends in the study of drug addicts, prostitutes, gamblers, night people, etc. had an audience among the very elites themselves.

I felt the justice of Gouldner's polemic on the politics of social research because it fitted in with what I felt about the ambiguous humanism of the method. The silences of the method, as Paul Willis stated, were essentially political silences.

For a number of years after coming to these conclusions I went into teaching, both in the United Kingdom and Africa, and I lost track, to some extent, of the politics of theory and research. On my return to England I applied for, and got the position of, a senior research officer on a Social Science Research Council project which was not under my theoretical control.

The project was conceptualized as a multi-disciplinary one and while it had a managerialist legitimation its possible potential seemed to be different. If I was going to be a 'hired hand', I thought it best to work in a context where qualitative research would be respected and where I, as a producer of data, might be able to influence the direction of the project as it became part of the flow of fieldwork process and practice. I found the authority structure difficult initially, as discussions on the nature of the data tended to be repetitive as the research director tended to shift his ground in reaction to his uncertainties, and the uncertainties of the two research officers became amplified because power in a *non* fieldwork context is not located in the process of research but in institutional roles. It is part of the rhythm of the total research cycle that the sponsor recedes as an important reference group after the grant has been received, and is only again reasserted as a significant other when findings are to be discovered, written up and reported. If a grant holder who has formal institutional power is not located in the research process itself, he or she is conscious, no matter what happens between the time the money is given and the research cycle is perhaps artificially completed, that the sponsor is still thinking in the original terms of the project, in spite of the passage of time and the new experiences gained from carrying out the research. As a result, the director is obliged to come up with findings that in some way relate to the original research hypothesis as worked out with and for the sponsor. If, as Vidich and Bensman argue, from 'the perspective of the individual researcher all group and bureaucratic research is a form of torture',[15] then the lack of control and non location in data of a research director may be equally tortuous. I must confess that while the two research officers knew the predicament of the project director and sometimes even joked about it, our problems seemed to be greater.[16] Only as the production of data emerged would the two researchers relex their professional defences against the initial attempt to assert a bureaucratic rhythm over them. Power, in the research team, began to lose its abstract monolithic quality, as human relationships began to build up and, equally importantly, the research officers began to accumulate and write from their data. In such a new context, while the director had the formal power to fire the researchers and to write their references, as well as having authority relationships through the supervision of their PhDs, the negative power of the researchers in control of field data and as interpreters of field data came to be felt and led to further negotiations and modifications of the research. The grantholder's decision, at a relatively early stage, to adopt a method of 'loose delegation' based upon the notion that 'good people' have been hired and they will perform best if left to 'get on with it', conflicted with his consciousness as the sponsor of the research. However, the ability to use tight control with unstructured research processes can only be maintained if the grantholder is able to spend a significant amount of time in the fieldwork itself and insist on very frequent feedback, especially when hypotheses and procedures have to be modified. The grantholder's 'conversion' to an anti-positivistic model of fieldwork research also undercut tight control over the research process and allowed space to be created for the internal discourses of the research team. By the end of the project, the real influence of the researchers was not congruent with their relatively lowly formal status. The substance of the grantholder's advice to the researchers, whose loyalties were to their conception of the project rather than to their nominal chain of command, was almost a paraphrasing of the anthropologist Evans-Pritchard's norms of fieldwork. These could be summed up as 'don't upset the natives, behave like gentlemen (preferably English gentlemen), keep off the women, take quinine daily' and, most importantly, 'play it by ear'. While we, the researchers, became different people as we both experienced, with some amusement, the research process itself, the grantholder has yet to make a statement on the impact of the researchers themselves on his multiplicity of roles. He could share at the University the excitement, though not the boredom, of the revaluation of data but the mediations on him were different in quality and texture.

Both fieldwork researchers had a strong interest in power though they may have had fundamental differences on how it can be measured. I found my interests in the study of the relatively powerful met by the concentration on the formal 'servants' of the local government political system, the elite professionals, who in practice had often an important input into public policies. This reconciled me to the project as it integrated my private political identity, which was interested in the low accountability in a formally democratic political system, with my sociological interests (and fascination) with the study of elite power on, and over, decision making. It allowed my outside interests to mesh with my job as a hired hand. Few managerialist projects allow or would allow such a reconciliation.

I found my professional identity as a middle-class researcher potentially useful in a utilitarian sense in that the elite professionals with whom I built up relationships, while not sharing my psychological and cultural patterns, found sometimes something of value in chatting to me. My role as an outsider perhaps was of use here. Reciprocity is always difficult to measure. M. Dalton, author of the well-known work, *Men Who Manage*, described in vivid detail, his attempt to acquire salary sales and other confidential information from the firms on which he was doing research. He was successful in using secretaries to get him information to which he would not normally have been privy. Dalton openly acknowledges that an exchange of favours won their co-operation. I was troubled (and I am not a feminist) by his statement that when 'women secretaries are treated as intellectual menials they are disposed to be communicative with those who show awareness of their insights and knowledge of affairs'. Manipulation can be easy as well as self deceptive.[17]

I felt a genuine sympathy and even respect for the elite professionals in their struggle to control their work situation and their public services in the structural clash between central and local governments which especially became the pattern from 1979. In the early stages of the project when I feared the veto power of these professionals over my research identity, my respect was less strong than when I gained acceptance as a fellow professional. In one sense I was sharply aware that, for temporary periods, in my relief at gaining limited access I has 'surrendered' to the object of study and I had to escape my captivity. Like an obsession in a dawning love affair, such captivity undercuts the dialectic of involvement and detachment, but at times it can overwhelm.[18] At other times my political identity came to my rescue and my captivity and integration was lessened by the belief that local government was normally the property of local elites, sometimes benevolent and sometimes not. Nevertheless, I favoured the autonomy of local government and to that extent I became its advocate. This may not have had a relationship to the increased openness of access I had as a researcher. It may be remarked with some pride (after all, a professional can take pride in his identity), that I am the only researcher in the United Kingdom to gain access to confidential meetings of the top strata of corporate managers in local government. I also found myself becoming the advocate of a particular spending department in interviews with certain influential local politicians, something no participant observer classically can take pride in. I resented the attack on the managerial craftsmenship and values of the managers of certain public services I believed in. All this took place inside a structural legitimation crisis for local government where the personnel of local government utilized what public support they could find (including the presence of a lowly researcher) in the populist attacks in folk lore, mass media and central government circles, on the inefficiency and expensiveness of local government. Only in a crisis do organizations normally show their hidden as well as constitutionalist processes of power and decision making, another lesson C. W. Mills taught.[19]

NOTES AND REFERENCES

1 Willis, P. *Learning to Labour*, 1977, 194.

2 Nicolaus, M. The ASA Convention. *Catalyst*, 1969, 103–6.

3 Bell, C. and Newby, H. (eds.). *Doing Sociological Research*, 1977.

4 Abrams, P. *et al.* (eds.). *Practice and Progress: British Sociology 1950–1980*, 1981.

5 Special issue: 'The teaching of research methodology', *Sociology*, 1981, 15(4).

6 Hindess, B. *The Use of Official Statistics in Sociology*, 1973.

7 Cicourel, A. V. *Method and Measurement in Sociology*, 1964.

8 Cohen, A. *Street Corner Society*, 1956.

9 Vidich, A. and Bensman. J. *Small Town in Mass Society*, 1968.

10 Vidich, A. and Benman, J. *Op. Cit.* 407–8.

12 Horowitz, I. L. Max Weber and the Spirit of American Sociology, *Sociological Quarterly*, 1964, 5 (4).

12 Gerth, H. and C. W. Mills (eds.). *From Max Weber*, 1948, 15.

13 Beynon, H. *Working for Ford*, 1973.

14 Gouldner, A. *For Sociology*, 1973, 38–9.

15 Vidich, A. J. and Bensman, J. The Springdale Case. In Vidich, A. J. *et al.* (eds.). *Reflections on Community Studies*, 1971, 323.

16 Tomkins, C. *et al.* The Social Process of Research. *Accounting, Organisations and Society, 1980, 5(2), 247–262.*

17 Dalton, M. Preconditions and Methods in *Men Who Manage* in Hammond, P. E. (ed.). *Sociologists at Work*, 1964.

18 Wolff, K. H. Surrender and Community Study in Vidich, A. J. *et al.*, *Op. Cit.*, 233–268.

19 It is a pity that the only valuable study of UK universities by Moudie, G. and Eustice, R. (*Power and Authority in British Universities*, 1974) was written in an epoch when financial resources though tight, were not dramatically and arbitrarily cut. The constitutional model of formal academic power in university government may be significantly modified if such a study was replicated in the years 1981 and 1982.

DAVID ROSENBERG BIBLIOGRAPHY

Review of 'Campus Power Struggle by Howard S. Becker, Aldine, 1970', *The Sociological Review*, 19(1), 1971, 115-16.

The sociology of the police and institutional liberalism (draft polemic), *Unpublished paper*, 1971.

To advise, assist and befriend – English probation work as a form of social work, MSc Thesis, University of Bristol, 1972.

Extended review of 'For Sociology: renewal and critique in sociology today' by Alvin W. Gouldner, Allen Lane, 1973', *The Sociological Review*, 23(4), 1975, 967-71.

Extended review of 'Working for Ford by Huw Beynon, Allen Lane and Penguin, 1973', *The Sociological Review*, 22(4), 1974, 630-6.

Review article of 'Modern revolutions' by John Dunn, CUP, 1972', *The African Review* 4(3), 1974, 481-90.

Extended review of 'Fascism and Dictatorship by N. Poulantzas, New Left Books, 1974', *The Sociological Review*, 24(3), 1976, 658-75.

Review article of 'C. van Onselen, Chibaro: African mine labour in Southern Rhodesia 1900-1933, Pluto, 1976', *The African Review*, 7(2), 1977, 106-18.

The origins and functions of sociological and historical theories of underdevelopment, *Unpublished paper*, 1977.

The development of the marxist theory of imperialism, *Unpublished paper*, 1977.

Extended review of 'Classes in contemporary capitalism' by Nicos Poulantzas. New Left Books, 1975', *The Sociological Review*, 1978, 26(3), 679-94.

'Some myths on the African working class: the construction of social science theory and its political function', Institute of Development Studies, University of Nairobi, 1978 (Working Paper, 294).

With Tomkins, C. and I. Colville. 'The social process of research: some reflections on developing a multi-disciplinary accounting project'. *Accounting, Organisations and Society*, 1980, 5(2), 247-62.

With Tomkins, C. and I. Colville. *The social process of research: some reflections on developing a multi-disciplinary accounting project*, Centre for the Study of Organizational Change and Development, University of Bath, 1980 (Working Paper, 80/02).

With Tomkins, C. and P. Day. 'A work role perspective of accountants in local government service departments'. *Accounting, Organizations and Society*, 1982, 7(2), 123-37.

Review of 'The Police, Autonomy and Consent by M. Brogden. Academic Press, 1982', *The Sociological Review*, 1983, 31(4), 800-802.

With Tomkins, C. 'The politics of mass housing in Britain, 1945-1975: A Study of corporate power and professional influence in the welfare state by Patrick Dunleavy. Clarendon Press, 1981', *The Sociological Review*, 31(1), 1983, 116-29.

Review of 'State, Class and Recession by S. Clegg, G. Down and P. Boreham (eds.), Croom Helm, 1983, *The Sociological Review*, 32(1), 1984, 152-3.

'The Politics of Role in Local Government: perspectives on the role set of Treasurers in their relationships to Chief Executives', *Local Government Studies*, 10(1), 1984, 47-62.

'Budgets and Human Agency: Do the men have to be dragged back in?' *Sociological Review*, 33(2), 1985, 193-220.

'The Languages of Role: Treasurers in UK Local Governments', *Policy and Politics*, 13(2), 1985, 155-774.

'The Assumptive Worlds of Managers of Personal and Social Services in UK Local Government', *Local Government Studies*, 11(4), 1985.

'Professionals, the "Trust" Relationship, Politics and Budget Construction: a Case Study of Local Government', *Accounting, Organisations and Society*, 1985.

POEMS

Overnight or Coffee, Manoeuvres, Serious Relations, *Ambit*, 1980, 83, 39-40.

REFERENCES

Abrams, P., *Historical Sociology*, Open Books, 1982.

Abrams, P., Deem, R., Finch, J. and Rock, P. (eds.). *Practice and Progress: British Sociology, 1950-1980*, Allen and Unwin, 1981.

Adorno, T. W., *Against Epistemology: A Metacritique: Studies in Husserl and the Phenomenological Antinomies*. Blackwell, 1982.

Aiken, M. and Bacharach, S. The urban system, politics and bureaucratic structure: a comparative analysis of 44 local governments in Belgium, in Karpik, L. (ed.), *Organization and Environment: Theory, Issues and Reality*, Sage, 1978, 199-251.

Albrow, M., *Bureaucracy*, Macmillan, 1970.

Albrow, M., The Study of organisations – objectivity or bias? In Gould, J., (ed.), *Penguin Social Sciences Survey, 1968*, Penguin, 1968, 146-167; see also Salaman, G. and K. Thompson, (eds.), *People and Organisations*, Longman, 1973, 396-413.

Alexander, A., *Local Government in Britain since Reorganisation*, Allen and Unwin, 1982a.

Alexander, A., *The Politics of Local Government in the United Kingdom*, Longman, 1982b.

Alexander, A., The rate-capping missile which could miss the target. *Municipal Journal*, 1983, 2nd September, 1302-1303.

Alt, J. E., Some social and political correlates of county borough expenditures. *British Journal of Political Science*, 1971, 1(1) 49-62.

Althusser, L., *Lenin and Philosophy, and Other Essays*, New Left Books, 1971.

Arnold, J. and Hope, A. *Accounting for Management Decisions*, Prentice-Hall, 1983.

Ashford, D. E., Resources, spending and party politics in British Local Government. *Administration and Society*, 1975, 7(3), 286-311.

Ashford, D. E., A Victorian drama: the fiscal subordination of British Local Government. In Ashford, D. E. (ed.), *Financing Urban Government in the Welfare State,*. Croom Helm, 1980, 71-96.

Bachrach, P. and Baratz, M. S. Decisions and non-decisions: an analytical framework. *American Political Science Review*, 1963, 57, 632-642.

Badie, B. and Birnbaum, P. *The Sociology of the State*, University of Chicago Press, 1983.

Barry, B., *Sociologists, Economists and Democracy*, Collier-Macmillan, 1970.

Bealey, F., Blondel, J. and McCann, W. P. *Constituency Politics: a study of Newcastle-under-Lyme*. Faber, 1965.

Beattie, J. H. M., On understanding ritual. In Wilson, B. R. (ed.), *Rationality*, Harper and Row, 1971, 240-268.

Bebbington, A. and Ferlie, E. *Budgeting and Planning in the Social Services Departments in the face of cutbacks*. Personal Social Services Research Unit, University of Kent, 1980 (PSSRU Discussion Paper, 172).

248

Becquart-Leclercq, J., Relational power and systemic articulation in French local polity. In Karpik, L., (ed.), *Organization and Environment: Theory, Issues and Reality*, Sage, 1978, 253-292.

Beetham, D., *Max Weber and the Theory of Modern Politics*, Allen and Unwin, 1974.

Bell, C. and Newby, H. (eds.), *Doing Sociological Research*, Allen and Unwin, 1977.

Benington, J., *Local Government becomes Big Business*, CDP Publication and Intelligence Unit, 1976.

Benton, T., Objective interests and the sociology of power, *Sociology*, 1981, 15(2), 161-184.

Benton, T., Realism, power and objective interests. In Graham, K. (ed.), *Contemporary political philosophy: radical studies*, CUP, 1982, 7-33.

Berger, P. L. and Pullberg, S. Reification and the sociological critique of consciousness, *New Left Review*, 1976, 35, 56-71.

Berger, P. L. and Luckman, T. *The Social Construction of Reality: A Treatise in the Sociology of Knowledge*, Penguin, 1971.

Berreman, G. D., *Behind Many Masks: Ethnography and Impression Management in a Himalayan Village*. Society for Applied Anthropology, 1962, (Monograph; no. 4). Also Bobbs-Merrill Reprint Series; A-393.

Beynon, H., *Working for Ford*, Allen Lane, 1973.

Bhaskar, R., *The Possibility of Naturalism: A Philosophical Critique of the Contemporary Human Sciences*, Harvester Press, 1979.

Blowers, A., Checks and balances: the politics of minority government. *Public Administration*, 1977, 55, 305-316.

Blowers, A., *The Limits of Power: The Politics of Local Planning Policy*, Pergamon Press, 1980.

Blunkett, D., A truly public transport. *New Statesman*, 1982, 19th February, 8-9.

Boaden, N., *Urban Policy Making: Influence on County Boroughs in England and Wales*, CUP, 1971.

Bocock, R., *Ritual in Industrial Society: A Sociological Analysis of Ritualism in Modern England*, Allen and Unwin, 1974.

Booth, T. A., Collaboration between the health and social services, part 2: a case study of joint finance, *Policy and Politics*, 1981, 9(2), 205-226.

Branson, N., *Poplarism, 1919-1925: George Lansbury and the Councillors' Revolt*, Lawrence and Wishart, 1979.

Briggs, A., *Victorian cities*, New edn Penguin, 1968.

Brogden, M., Policy authority: the denial of conflict. *Sociological Review*, 1977, 25(2), 325-349. See also McGrew, A. G. and M. J. Wilson (eds.), *Decision Making: Approaches and Analysis: A Reader*, Manchester University Press, 1982, 327-340.

Brogden, M., *The Police: Autonomy and Consent*, Academic Press, 1982.

Bucher, R and Stelling, J. Characteristics of professional organisations. *Journal of Health and Social Behaviour*, 1969, 10(1), 3-15.

Bulmer, M., (ed.), *Sociological Research Methods: An Introduction*, Macmillan, 1977.

Bulpitt, J. G., *Party Politics in English Local Government*, Longman, 1967.

Burchell, S., Clubb, C., Hopwood, A., Hughes, J. and Nahapiet, J. The roles of accounting in organizations and society. *Accounting, Organizations and Society*, 1980, 5(1), 5-27.

Burgess, T. and Travers, T. *Ten Billion Pounds: Whitehall's Takeover of the Town Halls*, Grant McIntyre, 1980.

Burrell, G. and Morgan, G. *Sociological Paradigms and Organization Analysis: Elements of the Sociology of Corporate Life*, Heinemann Educational, 1979.

Bush, T. and Kogan, M. *Directors of Education*, Allen and Unwin, 1982.

Caiden, N. and Wildavsky, A. *Planning and Budgeting in Poor Countries*, Wiley, 1974.

Caulcott, T., How treasurers are holding services to ransom over costs. *Local Government Chronicle*, 1983, 4th November, 1208-1209.

Chartered Institute of Public Finance and Accounting, *General and Rating Statistics, 1980-81*, The Institute, 1982.

References

Child, J., Organisational structure, environment and performance: the role of strategic choice. *Sociology*, 1972, 6, 1-22. See also Salaman, G. and K. Thompson, *People and Organizations*, Longman, 1973, 91-107.

Cicourel, A. V., *Method and Measurement in Sociology*, Free Press, 1964.

Clapham, D., Corporate planning and the cuts. *Local Government Policy Making*, 1983, July, 28-33.

Clapham, D., Rational planning and politics: the example of local authority corporate planning. *Policy and Politics*, 1984, 12(1), 31-52.

Clegg, S., Organization and control. *Administrative Science Quarterly*, 1981, 26, 545-562.

Clegg, S., and Dunkerley, D. *Organisation, Class and Control*, Routledge and Kegan Paul, 1980.

Clegg, S., *Power, Rule and Domination: A Critical and Empirical Understanding of Power in Sociological Theory and Organizational Life*, Routledge and Kegan Paul, 1975.

Clements, R. V., *Local notables and the city council*, Macmillan, 1969.

Cockburn, C., *The local state: management of cities and people*, Pluto Press, 1977.

Cohen, A., *Two-dimensional man: an essay on the anthropology of power and symbolism in complex society*, Routledge and Kegan Paul, 1974.

Cohen, G., Issue networks in the analysis of inter-governmental relations: the role of inspectors at central and local government levels in furthering equal opportunity in education for ethnic minorities. *Policy and Politics*, 1982, 10(2), 217-237.

Collins, C. A., Hinings, C. R. and Walsh, K. The Officer and the councillor in local government. *Public Administration Bulletin*, 1978, 28, 34-50.

Connolly, W., *Legitimacy and the State*, Blackwell, 1984.

Cooke, P., Class interests, regional restructuring and state formation in Wales. *International Journal of Urban and Regional Research*, 1982, 6(2), 187-204.

Cooper, D. J., Hayes, D. and Wolf, F. Accounting in organized anarchies: understanding and designing accounting systems in ambiguous situations. *Accounting, Organizations and Society*, 1981, 6(3), 175-191.

Cooper, N. and Stewart, J. Local government, budgets closer to targets. *Public Finance and Accountancy*, 1982, 9th June, 17-21.

Coser, L., *The functions of social conflict*, Routledge and Kegan Paul, 1956.

Covaleski, M. A. and Dirsmith, M. W. Budgeting as a means for control and loose coupling. *Accounting Organizations and Society*, 1983, 8(4), 323-340.

Crouch, C. (ed.), *State and economy in contemporary capitalism*, Croom Helm, 1979.

Crozier, M., *The bureaucratic phenomenon*, Tavistock, 1964.

Crozier, M. and Thoenig, J. C. The regulation of complex organised systems. *Administrative Science Quarterly*, 1976, 21, 547-570.

Cyert, R. M. and March, J. G. *A behavioural theory of the firm*, Prentice-Hall, 1963.

Dalton, M., *Men who manage: fusions of feeling and theory in administration*, Wiley, 1959.

Dalton, M., Preconceptions and methods in *Men who manage*. In Hammond, P. E. (ed.), *Sociologists at work: essays on the craft of social research*, Basic Books, 1964, 50-95.

Danziger, J. N., A comment on 'The politics of the budgetary process in English local government'. *Political Studies*, 1978a 26(1), 109-115.

Danziger, J. N., *Making budgets: public resource allocation*, Sage, 1978.

Davies, B., Barton, A., McMillan, I. S. and Williamson, V. *Varieties in services for the aged*, Bell, 1972.

Davies, J. G., *The evangelistic bureaucrat: a study of a planning exercise in Newcastle upon Tyne*, Tavistock, 1972.

Day, R. and Day, J. V. A review of the current state of negotiated order theory: an appreciation and a critique. *Sociological Quarterly*, 1977, 18(1), 126-142.

Dearlove, J., *The politics of policy in local government: the making and maintenance of public policy in the Royal Borough of Kensington and Chelsea*, Cambridge University Press, 1973.

Dearlove, J., *The re-organization of British local government: old orthodoxes and a political perspective*, Cambridge University Press, 1979.

Dempster, M. A. H. and Wildavsky, A. On change: or, there is no magic size for an increment. *Political Studies*, 1979, 27(3), 371-389.

Dennis, N., *Public participation and planners' blight*, Faber, 1972.

Denzin, N. K., *The research act in sociology: a theoretical introduction to sociological methods*, Butterworths, 1970.

Deutscher, I., Words and deeds: social science and social policy. *Social Problems*, 1966, 13(3), 235-254.

Di Maggio, P. J. and Powel, W. W. The iron cage revisited: institutional isomorphism and collective rationality in organizational fields. *American Sociological Review*, 1983, 48, 147-160.

Ditton, J., (ed.), *The view from Goffman*, Macmillan, 1980.

Doig, A., *Corruption and misconduct in contemporary British politics*, Penguin, 1984.

Douglas, D. J., Managing fronts in observing deviance. In Douglas, J. D. (ed.), *Research on deviance*, Random House, 1972, 93-115.

Douglas, M., *Natural symbols: explorations in cosmology*, Penguin, 1973.

Douglas, M., *Purity and danger: an analysis of the concepts of pollution and taboo*, Routledge and Kegan Paul, 1966.

Duke, V. and Edgell, S. *Local authority spending cuts and local political control*, Mimeo, 1983.

Duke, V. and Edgell, S. *Public expenditure cuts in Britain and local authority mediation*, Mimeo, 1982.

Duncan, S. S. and Goodwin, M. The local state: functionalism, autonomy and class relations in Cockburn and Saunders.*Political Geography Quarterly*, 1982, 1(1), 77-96.

Dunleavy, P. and Rhodes, R. A. W. Beyond Whitehall. In Drucker, H. (ed.), *Developments in British politics*, Revised edition, Macmillan, 1984, 106-133.

Dunleavy, P., *The limits of local government*, Mimeo, 1983 (Paper presented to ANCAN Conference, Queens University, Kingston, Ontario, March 1983).

Dunleavy, P., *The politics of mass housing in Britain, 1945-1975: a study of corporate power and professional influence in the welfare state*, Clarendon Press, 1981a.

Dunleavy, P., Professions and policy change: notes towards a model of ideological corporatism. *Public Administration Bulletin*, 1981b, 36, 3-16.

Dunleavy, P., Protest and quiescence in urban politics: a critique of some pluralist and structuralist myths. *International Journal of Urban and Regional Research*, 1977, 1, 193-218.

Dunleavy, P., *Theories of the State and society and the study of central-local relations*, Mimeo, 1978 (paper commissioned by the SSRC Panel on Central/Local Government Research).

Dunleavy, P., *Urban political analysis: the politics of collective consumption*, Macmillan, 1980.

Edelman, J. M., *The symbolic uses of politics*, University of Illinois Press, 1964.

Elcock, H., *Local government: politicians, professionals and the public in local authorities*, Methuen, 1982.

Elcock, H., Tradition and change in Labour Party politics: the decline and fall of the city boss. *Political Studies*, 1981, 29(1), 439-447.

Eley, G. and Nield, K. Why does social history ignore politics? *Social History*, 1980, 5th May, 249-271.

Elliott, B. and McCrone, D. *The city: patterns of domination and conflict*, Macmillan, 1982.

Ferlie, E. and Judge, K. Retrenchment and rationality in the personal social services. *Policy and Politics*, 1981 9(3), 311-330.

Fielding, A. G. and D. Portwood, Professions and the state: towards a typology of bureaucratic professions. *Sociological Review*, 1980, 29(1), 23-53.

Flynn, R., Urban managers in local government planning. *Sociological Review*, 1979, 27(4), 743-753.

Foster, C. D., Jackman, R. A. and Perlman, M. *Local government finance in a unitary state*, Allen and Unwin, 1980.

Foucault, M., *The archaeology of knowledge*, Tavistock, 1972.

251

References

Fraser, D., *Urban politics in Victorian England: the structure of politics in Victorian cities*, Leicester University Press, 1976.

Friedland, R. O., *Power and crisis in the city: corporations, unions and urban policy*, Macmillan, 1982.

Garrard, J. A., The history of local political power: some suggestions for analysis. *Political Studies*, 1977, 25(2), 252-269.

Garrard, J. A., Social history, political history and political science: the study of power. *Journal of Social History*, 1983a, 16(3), 105-121.

Garrard, J. A., *Leadership and power in Victorian industrial towns, 1830-1880*, Manchester University Press, 1983b.

Gaventa, J., *Power and powerlessness: quiescence and rebellion in an Appalachian valley*, Clarendon Press, 1980.

Geertz, C., *Interpretations of Culture*, Basic Books, New York, 1973.

Gerth, H. and Mills, C. W. (eds.), *From Max Weber: essays in sociology*. Routledge and Kegan Paul, 1948.

Giddens, A. and Held, D. (eds.), *Classes, power and conflict: classical and contemporary debates*. Macmillan, 1982.

Ginsburg, N., *Class, Capital and social policy*, Macmillan, 1979.

Glaser, B. G. and Strauss, A. L. Discovery of substantive theory: a basic strategy underlying qualitative research. *American Behavioural Scientist*, 1965, 8(6), 5-12.

Glennerster, H., Korman, N. and F. Marslen-Wilson, Plans and practice: the participants' views. *Public Administration*, 1983, 61, 253-264.

Glennerster, H., Prime cuts: public expenditure and social services planning in a hostile environment. *Policy and Politics*, 1980a, 8(4), 367-382.

Glennerster, H., *Social service budgets and social policy*, Allen and Unwin, 1975.

Glennerster, H., Social service spending in a hostile environment. In Hood C. and M. Wright (eds.), *Big government in hard times*, Martin Robertson, 1980b, 174-196.

Gluckman, M., *Custom and conflict in Africa*, Blackwell, 1973.

Goffman, E., *Behaviour in public places: notes on the social organization of gatherings*, Free Press, 1963.

Goffman, E., *Interaction ritual: essays on face-to-face behaviour*, Penguin, 1972a.

Goffman, E., *The presentation of self in everyday life*, Penguin, 1971.

Goffman, E., *Relations in public: miscrostudies of the public order*, Penguin 1972b.

Goffman, E., Role distance. In Goffman, E., *Encounters: two studies in the sociology of iteraction*, Bobbs-Merrill, 1961, 83-152.

Goldie, N., The division of labour among mental hospital professionals – a negotiated or an imposed order? In Stacey, M., M. Reid, C. Heath and R. Dingwall, (eds.), *Health and the division of labour*, Croom Helm, 1977, 141-161.

Gough, I., *The political economy of the welfare state*, Macmillan, 1979.

Gouldner, A. W., The sociologist as partisan: sociology and the welfare state. In Gouldner, A. W. *For sociology: renewal and critique in sociology today*, Allen Lane, 1973, 27-68.

Grant, W. P., Local councils, conflict and 'rules of the game'. *British Journal of Political Science*, 1971, 1(2), 253-256.

Grant, W. P., Non-partisanship in British local politics. *Policy and Politics*, 1973, 1(3), 241-254.

Green, D. G., Inside local government: a study of a ruling Labour group. *Local Government Studies*, 1980, 6(1), 33-49.

Green, D. G., *Power and party in an English city: an account of single-party rule*, Allen and Unwin, 1981.

Greenwood, R., Changing patterns of budgeting in English local government. *Public Administration*, 1983, 61, 149-168.

Greenwood, R. and Stewart, J. D. (eds.), *Corporate planning in English local government: an analysis with readings, 1967-72*, Knight, 1974.

Greenwood, R., Fiscal pressure and local government in England and Wales. In Hood, C. and M.

Wright, (eds.), *Big government in hard times*, Martin Robertson, 1981, 77-99.

Greenwood, R., (*et al.*), *In pursuit of corporate rationality: organisation developments in the post-reorganization period*, Inlogov, 1976.

Greenwood, R., Hinings, C. R., Ranson, S. and Walsh, K. Incremental budgeting and the assumption of growth: the experience of local government. In Wright, M. (ed.), *Public spending decisions: growth and restraint in the 1970's*, Allen and Unwin, 1980a, 25-48.

Greenwood, R., *Incremental budgeting: antecedents of change*, Mimeo, 1984.

Greenwood, R., The local authority budgetary processes, In Booth, T. A. (ed.), *Planning for welfare: social policy and the expenditure process*. Blackwell, 1979, 78-96.

Greenwood, R., (*et al.*), *The organisation of local authorities in England and Wales, 1967-75*, Inlogov, 1975.

Greenwood, R., (*et al.*), *Patterns of management in local government*, Martin Robertson, 1980b.

Greenwood, R., Hinings, C. R. and Ranson, S. The politics of the budgetary process in English local government. *Political Studies*, 1977, 25(1), 25-47.

Greenwood, R., Pressure from Whitehall. In Rose, R. and E. Page, (eds.), *Fiscal stress in cities*, Cambridge University Press, 1982, 44-76.

Greenwood, R., Hinings, C. R. and Ranson, S. A rejoinder to Danziger's comment. *Political Studies*, 1978, 26(1), 116-118.

Gunther, R., *Public policy in a no-party state: Spanish planning and budgeting in the twilight of the Franquist era*, University of California Press, 1980.

Gyford, J., *Local politics in Britain*, Croom Helm, 1976.

Habermas, J., *Towards a rational society*, Heinemann, 1971.

Hampton, W., *Democracy and community: a study of politics in Sheffield*, Oxford University Press, 1970.

Harloe, M., *Swindon: a town in transition: a study in urban development and overspill policy*, Heinemann, 1975.

Harre, R. and Secord, P. F. *The explanation of social behaviour*, Blackwell, 1972.

Harrington, T., Explaining state policy-making: a critique of some recent 'dualist' models. *International Journal of Urban and Regional Research*, 1983, 7(2), 202-281.

Haynes, R. J., *Organisation theory and local government*, Allen and Unwin, 1980.

Haywood, S., Decision-making in local government: the case of an 'independent' council. *Local Government Studies*, 1977, October, 41-55.

Heclo, H. H., The councillor's job. *Public Administration*, 1969, 47, 185-202.

Heclo, H. H. and Wildavsky, A. *The private government of public money: community and policy inside British politics*, Macmillan, 1974.

Held, D., *Introduction to critical theory*, Hutchinson, 1980.

Held, D., *et al.* (eds.), *States and societies*, Martin Robertson, 1983.

Hennock, E. P., Finance and politics in urban local government, 1835-1900. *Historical Journal*, 1963, 6(2), 212-225.

Hennock, E. P., *Fit and proper persons: ideal and reality in 19th century urban government*, Edward Arnold, 1973.

Hepworth, N. P., Local authority expenditure. *Three Banks Review*, 1980, 127, 3-24.

Hill, D. M., *Democratic theory and local government*, Allen and Unwin, 1974.

Hill, M. J., *The sociology of public administration*, Weidenfeld and Nicolson, 1972.

Hindess, B., The 'phenomenological' sociology of Alfred Schutz. *Economy and Society*, 1972, 1(1), 1-27.

Hindess, B., Power, interests and the outcomes of struggles. *Sociology*, 1982, 16(4), 498-511.

Hindess, B., *The use of official statistics in sociology: a critique of positivism and ethnomethodology*, Macmillan, 1973.

Hinings, B., *et al. Management systems in local government*, Inlogov, 1979.

Hinings, C. R., Greenwood, R. and Ranson, S. Contingency theory and the organization of local authorities: Part 2: Contingencies and structure. *Public Administration*, 1975, 53, 168-190.

References

Hinings, C. R., Greenwood, R., Ranson, S. and Walsh, K. The organizational consequences of financial restraint in local government. In Wright, M. (ed.). *Public spending decisions: growth and restraint in the 1970's*, Allen and Unwin, 1980, 49-67.

Hinings, C. R. and R. Greenwood, Research into local government reorganisation. *Public Administration Bulletin*, 1973, 15, 21-38.

Hirst, P. and Woolley, P. *Social relations and human attributes*, Tavistock, 1982.

Hollis, M., *Models of man: philosophical thoughts on social action*, Cambridge University Press, 1977.

Homans, G. C., Bringing men back in. *American Sociological Review*, 1964, 29(6), 809-818.

Hood, C. and M. Wright, (eds.), *Big government in hard times*, Martin Robertson, 1981.

Horowitz, I. L., Max Weber and the spirit of American sociology. *Sociological Quarterly*, 1964, 5 (4), 344-354.

Houlihan, B., The professionalisation of housing policy making: the impact of housing investment programmes and professionals. *Public Administration Bulletin*, 1983, 41, 14-31.

Howton, F. W. and Rosenberg, B. The salesman: ideology and self-imagery in a prototype occupation. *Social Research*, 1965, 32(3), 277-298.

Hughes, E. C., The humble and the proud: the comparative study of occupations. *Sociological Quarterly*, 1970, 11(2), 147-156.

Hughes, E. C., *The sociological eye: selected papers on institutions and race*, Aldene, Atherton, 1971.

Hughes, E. C., *The sociological eye: selected papers on work, self and the study of society*, Aldene, Atherton 1971.

Isaac, J., On Benton's 'Objective interests and the sociology of power': a critique. *Sociology*, 1982, 16(3), 440-444.

Jackson, R. M., *The machinery of local government*, 2nd edition, Macmillan, 1965.

James, F., *The prison-house of language; a critical account of structuralism and Russian formalism*, Princeton University Press, 1972.

Jennings, R., *Education and politics: policy-making in local education authorities*, Batsford, 1977.

Jessop, B., Capitalism and democracy: the best possible political shell? In Littlejohn, G., B. Smart, J. Wakeford and N. Yuval Davies, (eds.), *Power and the state*, Croom Helm, 1978, 10-51.

Johnson, C., Dandeker, C. and Ashworth, C. *The structure of social theory*, Macmillan, 1984.

Johnston, R. J., *Geography and the state: an essay in political geography*, Macmillan, 1982.

Jones, A., The politics of educational planning in County Durham, 1979, Mimeo.

Jones, G. W., How to save local government. In Institute of Economic Affairs. *Town hall power or Whitehall pawn?* The Institute, 1980, 129-141 (Readings in Political Economy; 25).

Jones, G. W., Varieties of local politics. *Local Government Studies*, 1979, 1(2), 17-32.

Jones, G. W., Stewart, J. and Travers, T. *The way ahead for local government finance: the response to the Green Paper, Alternatives to Domestic Rates (Cmnd 8449)*, Inlogov, 1982.

Jonsson, S., Budgeting behaviour in local government: a case study over 3 years. *Accounting, Organizations and Society*, 1982a, 7(3), 287-304.

Jonsson, S., *A city administration facing stagnation: political organization and action in Gothenburg*, Swedish Council for Building Research, 1982b.

Judge, D., The financial relationship between central and local government in the personal social services. In Booth, T. A. (ed.), *Planning for welfare: social policy and the expenditure process*, Blackwell, 1979, 23-50.

Judge, K., *Rationing social services: a study of resource allocation and the personal social services*, Heinemann, 1978.

Judge, K., Territorial justice and local autonomy: loan sanctions in the personal social services. *Policy and Politics*, 1975, 3(4), 43-69.

Kantor, P. and David, S. The political economy of change in urban budgetary politics: a framework for analysis and a case study. *British Journal of Political Science*, 1983, 13(3), 251-274.

Karpik, L., (ed.), *Organization and environment: theory issues and reality*, Sage, 1978.

Karran, T., 'Borough politics' and 'county government' administrative styles in the old structure. *Policy and Politics*, 1982, 10(3), 317-342.

Keat, R. and Urry, J. *Social theory as science*, Routledge and Kegan Paul, 1975.

Keith-Lucas, B. and Richards, P. G. *A history of local government in the 20th century*, Allen and Unwin, 1978.

Keith-Lucas, B., *The unreformed local government system*, Croom Helm, 1980.

Kellner, P. and Lord Crowther-Hunt., *The civil servants: an inquiry into Britain's ruling class*. Macdonald, 1980.

Kemp, T., *Theories of imperialism*, Dobson, 1967.

Kesselman, M., *The ambiguous consensus: a study of local government in France*, Knopf, 1967.

Kogan, M. with W. Van Der Eyken, *County hall and the role of the chief education officer*, Penguin Education, 1973.

Laffin, M., Professionalism in central-local relations. In Jones, G. W., (ed.), *New approaches to the study of central-local government relationships*, Gower, 1980, 18-27.

Lambert, R. J., A Victorian national health service: state vaccination 1855–71. *Historical Journal*, 1962, 5(1), 1-18.

Larson, M. S., *The rise of professionalism: a sociological analysis*, University of California Press, 1977.

Lawrence, P. R. and Lorsch, J. W. *Organisation and environment*, Harvard University Press, 1967.

Lee, J. M., Wood, B., Soloman, B. W. and Walters, P. *The scope of local initiative: a study of Cheshire County Council, 1961-1974*, Martin Robertson, 1974.

Lee, J. M., *Social leaders and public persons: a study of county government in Cheshire since 1888*, Clarendon Press, 1963.

Levine, C. H. and I. S. Rubin, (eds.), *Fiscal stress and public policy*, Sage, 1980.

Levine, C. H., More on cutback management: hard questions for hard times. *Public Administration Review*, 1979, March/April, 179-183.

Levine, C. H., Organizational decline and cutback management. *Public Administration Review*, 1978, July/August, 316-325.

Levine, C. H., Rubin, I. S. and Wolohojian, G. G. *The politics of retrenchment: how local governments manage fiscal stress*, Sage, 1981a.

Levine, C. H., Rubin, I. S. and Wolohojian, G. G. Resource scarcity and the reform model: the management of retrenchment in Cincinnati and Oakland. *Public Administration Review*, 1981b, November/December, 619-628.

Levitin, T. E., Role performance and role distance in a low status occupation: the puller. *Sociological Quarterly*, 1964, 5(3), 251-260.

Lewis, J., Variations in service provision: politics at the lay-professional interface. In Young, K., (ed.), *Essays on the study of urban politics*, Macmillan, 1975, 52-77.

Leys, C., *Politics in Britain: an introduction*, Heinemann Educational, 1983.

Lindbloom, C. E., The science of 'muddling through'. *Pubic Administration Review*, 1959, 19(2), 79-88.

Lomer, M., The chief executive in local government, 1974-76. *Local Government Studies*, 1977, 3(4), 17.40.

Lukes, S., *Power: a radical view*, Macmillan, 1974.

Lukes, S., *Essays in social theory*, Macmillan, 1977.

Lukes, S., Power and structure. In Lukes, S., *Essays in social theory*, Macmillan, 1977, 3-29.

McCall, G. J. and Simmons, J. L. (eds.), *Issues in participant observation: a text and reader*, Addison-Wesley, 1969.

Macdonald, K. M., Professional formation: the case of Scottish accountants. *British Journal of Sociology*, 1984, 35(2), 174-189.

McGrew, A. G. and Wilson, M. J. (eds.), *Decision making: approaches and analysis: a reader*,

References

Manchester University Press, 1982.

McLennan, G., Held, D. and Hall, S. (eds.), *State and society in contemporary Britain: a critical introduction*, Polity Press, 1984.

Malpass, P., Professionalism and the role of architects in local authority housing. *RIBA Journal*, 1975, 82(6), 6-29.

Mangham, I., *Interactions and Interventions in Organizations*, John Wiley, 1978.

Manis, J. G. and Meltzer, B. N. (eds.), *Symbolic Interaction: a reader in social psychology*, 2nd edition, Allyn and Bacon, 1972.

March, J. G. and Simon, H. A. *Organizations*, Wiley, 1958.

Marshall, A. H., *Financial administration in local government*, Allen and Unwin, 1960.

Marshall, J., (ed.), *The history of Lancashire County Council*, Martin Robertson, 1977.

Martlew, C., The state and local government finance. *Public Administration*, 1983, 61, 127-147.

Maslen, A. T. J., The politics of administrative reform: the special review of Lambeth Borough Council. *Local Government Studies*, 1983, May/June, 45-65.

Maud, *Sir*, J., and Finer, S. E. *Local government in England and Wales*, Oxford University Press, 1953.

Melling, J., (ed.), *Housing, social policy and the state*, Croom Helm, 1980.

Merton, R. K., Bureaucratic structure and personality. In Merton, R. K. *Social theory and social structure*. Enlarged edition, Free Press, 1968a, 249-260.

Merton, R. K., *Social theory and social structure*. Enlarged edition, Free Press, 1968.

Metcalfe, J. L. Organizational strategies and inter-organizational networks. *Human Relations*, 1976, 29(4), 327-343.

Meyer, J. W. and Rowan, B. Institutionalized organizations: formal structure as myth and ceremony. *American Journal of Sociology*, 1977, 83(2), 340-363. See also Zey-Ferrel, M. and M. Aiken, (eds.), *Complex organizations: critical perspectives*, Scott, Foresman, 1981, 303-322.

Midwinter, A., *Budgetary reform in local government: a political analysis*, 1984 Mimeo. (Paper prepared for the Governmental Budget Under Stress Conference, University of Manchester, 18-19 May 1984).

Midwinter, A. and Page, E. (eds.), Cutting local spending: the Scottish experience, 1976-1980. In Hood, C. and M. Wright, (eds.), *Big government in hard times*, Martin Robertson, 1981, 56-76.

Midwinter, A., Keating, M. and Taylor, P. 'Excessive and unreasonable': the politics of the Scottish hit list. *Political Studies*, 1983, 31, 394-417.

Miliband, R., *Capitalist democracy in Britain*, Oxford University Press, 1982.

Mills, C. W., Situated actions and vocabularies of motive. In Horowitz, I. L. (ed.), *Power, politics and people: the collected essays of C. Wright Mills*, Oxford University Press, 1967, 439-452.

Minns, R., The significance of Clay Cross: another look at district audit. *Policy and Politics*, 1974, 2(4), 309-329.

Moodie, G. C. and Eustace, R. *Power and authority in British universities*, Allen and Unwin, 1974.

Mommsen, W. J. *The age of bureaucracy: perspectives on the political sociology of Max Weber*, Blackwell, 1974.

Mouzelis, N. P., *Organisation and bureaucracy: an analysis of modern theories*, Routledge and Kegan Paul, 1967.

Neve, B., Bureaucracy and politics in local government: the role of local authority education officers. *Public Administration*, 1977, Autumn, 291-303.

Newby, H., Bell, C., Rose, D. and Saunders, P. *Property, paternalism and power: class and control in rural England*, Hutchinson, 1978.

Newman, O., *The challenge of corporatism*, Macmillan, 1981.

Newton, K. and Sharpe, L. J. Local outputs research: some reflections and proposals. *Policy and Politics*, 1977, 5, 61-82.

Newton, K., Role orientation and their sources among elected representatives in English local politics. *Journal of Politics*, 1974, 36, 615-636.

Newton, K., *Second city politics: democratic processes and decision-making in Birmingham*, Clarendon Press, 1976.

Nicolaus, M., The A.S.A. convention. *Catalyst*, 1969, Spring, 103-106.

O'Connor, J. R., *The fiscal crisis of the state*, St Martin's Press, 1973.

Olesen, V. L. and Whittaker, W. E. Role-making in participant observation: processes in the researcher-actor relationship. *Human Organization*, 1967, 26(4), 278-281.

Olsen, J. P., Local budgeting: decision-making or a ritual act. *Scandinavian Political Studies*, 1970, 5, 85-115.

Olson, O., *An accounting system in an organizational gap: something about the system, more about its misfits.* Centre for Applied Research, Norwegian School of Economics and Business Administration, 1983.

Ostrom, E., A public service industry approach to the study of local government structure and performance. *Policy and Politics*, 1983, 11(3), 313-341.

Paddison, R., *The fragmented state: the political geography of power*, Blackwell, 1983.

Page, E., Grant consolidation and the development of intergovernmental relations in the USA and the UK. *Politics*, 1981, 1.

Pahl, R. E., Socio-political factors in resource allocation. In Herbert, D. T. and D. M. Smith (eds.), *Social problems and the city: geographical perspectives*, Oxford University Press, 1979, 33-46.

Panitch, L., Trade unions and the state: the limits of corporatism. *New Left Review*, 1981, 125, 21-43.

Parry, G. and Morris, P. When is a decision not a decision? In Lrenk, I., (ed.), *British Political Sociology Yearbook, Vol. 1: Elites in Western Democracy*, Croom Helm, 1974, Ch.11, 317-336.

Perkins, H., *The origins of modern English society, 1780-1880*, Routledge and Kegan Paul, 1969,

Pettigrew, A. M. Information control as a power resource. *Sociology*, 1972, 6(2), 187-204.

Pettigrew, A. M., On studying organizational cultures. *Administrative Science Quarterly*, 1979, 24, 570-581.

Pfeffer, J. and Salancik, G. R. Organisational decision making as a political process: the case of a university budget. *Administrative Science Quarterly*, 1974, June, 135-150.

Pfeffer, J. and Salancik, G. R. *The external control of organisations: a resource dependence perspective.* Harper and Row, 1978.

Pfeffer, J., *Power in organisations*, Pitman, 1981.

Pfeffer, J., Power in university budgeting: a replication and extension. *Administrative Science Quarterly*, 1980, 637-653.

Phillips, D. L., *Knowledge from what? Theories and methods in social research*, Rand McNally, 1971.

Platt, J., *Realities of social research: an empirical study of British sociologists*, Sussex University Press, 1976.

Porter, R., *English society in the 18th century*, Penguin, 1982.

Pugh, D. S. (ed.), *Organisation theory: selected readings*, Penguin, 1971.

Pugh, D. S. and Hickson, D. J. *Organisational structure in its context: the Aston Programme 1*, Saxon House, 1976.

Ranson, S., Hinings, B., Leach, S. and Skelcher, C. *Domination and distribution in policy planning networks*, Inlogov, 1980. (Paper presented at SSRC Conference on Central-Local Relations, March 14-16, 1980).

Ranson, S., Hinings, B., Greenwood, R. and Walsh, K. Values preferences and tensions in the organisation of local government. In Dunkerley, D. and Salaman, G. (eds.), *International Yearbook of Organization Studies 1980*. Routledge and Kegan Paul, 1980a, Ch. 11, 197-221.

Ranson, S., Hinings, C. R. and Greenwood, R. The structuring of organisational structures. *Administrative Science Quarterly*, 1980b, 25, 1-17.

Ravetz, A., *Remaking cities: contradictions of the recent urban environment*, Croom Helm, 1980.

Regan, D. E., *A headless state: the unaccountable executive in British local government*, University of

References

Nottingham, 1980 (Inaugural lecture).

Regan, D. E., *Local government and eduction*, Allen and Unwin, 1977.

Rhodes, R. A. W., Analysing intergovernmental relations. *European Journal of Political Research*. 1980, 8, 289-322.

Rhodes, R. A. W., Hardy, B. and Pudney, K. *Constraints on the national community of local government: members, 'other governments' and policy communities*, Department of Government, University of Essex, 1983a. (Discussion paper; no.6).

Rhodes, R. A. W., Continuity and change in British central-local relations: 'the Conservative threat', 1979-83. *British Journal of Political Science*. 1984, 14, 261-283.

Rhodes, R. A. W., *Control and power in central-local government relations*, Gower, 1981.

Rhodes, R. A. W., *'Corporate bias' in central-local relations: a case study of the Consultative Council on Local Government Finance*, Department of Government, University of Essex, 1982. (Discussion paper; no.1).

Rhodes, R. A. W., The lost world of British local politics? *Local Government Studies*, 1975, 1(3), 39-60.

Rhodes, R. A. W., Hardy, B. and Pudney, K. *'Power-dependence' theories of central-local relations: a critical assessment*, Department of Government, University of Essex, 1983b. (Discussion Paper; No.7).

Richards, P. G. *The reformed local government system*, Allen and Unwin, 1973.

Richardson, J. J. and Jordan, A. G. *Governing under pressure: the policy process in a post-parliamentary democracy*, Martin Robertson, 1979.

Rose, R. and Page, E. Chronic instability in fiscal systems. In Rose, R. and E. Page, (eds.), *Fiscal stress in cities*, Cambridge University Press, 1982, 198-245. See also Centre for the Study of Public Policy, University of Strathclyde, 1982 (Studies in Public Policy; 104).

Rosenberg, D., Tomkins, C. and Day, P. A work role perspective of accountants in local government service departments. *Accounting, Organizations and Society*, 1982, 7(2), 123-137.

Rubin, I. S., Preventing or eliminating planned deficits: restructuring political incentives. *Public Administration Review*, 1980a, November/December.

Rubin, I. S. Retrenchment and flexibility in public organizations. In Levine, C. H. and I. S. Rubin, (eds.), *Fiscal stress and public policy*, Sage, 1980b, 159-178.

Rubin, I. S., Retrenchment, loose structure and adaptability in the University. *Sociology of Education*, 1979, 52, October, 211-222.

Rubin, I. S., Universities in stress: decision making under conditions of reduced resources. *Social Science Quarterly*. 1977, 58(2), 242-254.

Rubinstein, W. D., The end of 'old corruption' in Britain, 1780-1860. *Past and Present*, 1983, 101, 55-86.

Said, E. W., *Orientalism*, Routledge and Kegan Paul, 1978.

Salaman, G. and Thompson, K. (eds.), *People and organisations*, Longman, 1973.

Salaman, G., Towards a sociology of organisational structure. *Sociological Review*, 1978, 26 (3), 519-554. See also Zey-Ferrell, M. and M. Aiken, (eds.), *Complex organizations: critical perspectives*. Scott, Foresman, 1981, 22-45.

Salaman, G., *Work organizations: resistance and control*, Longman, 1979.

Saunders, P., *Social theory and the urban question*, Hutchinson, 1981.

Saunders, P., They make the rules. *Policy and Politics*, 1975, 4, 31-58.

Saunders, P., *Urban politics: a sociological interpretation*, Penguin, 1980.

Saunders, P., Why study central-local relations? *Local Government Studies*, 1982, March/April, 55-65.

Sbragia, A. M., *Capital markets and central-local politics in Britain: the double game*. Centre for Study of Public Policy, University of Stratchclyde, 1983. (Studies in Public Policy, 109), *and* reprinted by Division of Research, Graduate School of Business Administration, Harvard

University.

Sbragia, A., Cities, capital and banks: the politics of debt in the United States, United Kingdom and France. In Newton, K., (ed.), *Urban Political Economy*, St Martin's Press, 1981, 200-220.

Scott, M. B. and Lyman, S. M. Accounts. *American Sociological Review*, 1968, 33(1), 46-62.

Self, P., *Administrative theories and politics*, Allen and Unwin, 1972.

Sharkansky, I., Budgeting amidst triple-digit inflation: the case of Israel. *British Journal of Political Science*, 1984, 14, 73-88.

Sharpe, L. J., *Incremental theory and budgeting: a modest test*, 1984, Mimeo. (Paper presented at Conference on Governmental Budgets under Stress, University of Manchester, 18th May 1984).

Skinner, D. and Langdon, J. *The story of Clay Cross*, Spokesman Books, 1974.

Smart, B., Foucault, sociology and the problem of human agency. *Theory and Society*, 1982, 11(2), 121-141.

Smith, B. C., *Policy making in British government*, Martin Robertson, 1976. *Sociology*, 1981 15(4). Special issue: the teaching of research methodology.

Stacey, M., Batstone, E., Bell, C. and Murcott, A. *Power, persistence and change: a second study of Banbury*, Routledge and Kegan Paul, 1975.

Stacey, M., *Tradition and change: a study of Banbury*, Oxford University Press, 1960.

Stanworth, P. and A. Giddens, (eds.), *Elites and power in British Society*, Cambridge University Press, 1974.

Stanyer, J., *Understanding local government*, Martin Robertson, 1976.

Stebbins, R. A., The unstructured research interview as incipient interpersonal relationship. *Sociology and Social Research*, 1972, 56(2), 164-179.

Stewart, J., From growth to standstill. In Wright, M., (ed.), *Public spending decisions*, Allen and Unwin, 1980, 9-24.

Stewart, J., Jones, G., Greenwood, R. and Raine, J. *In defence of local government*, Inlogov, 1981.

Stewart, J., *Local government: the conditions of local choice*, Allen and Unwin, 1983.

Strauss, A. L., *Mirrors and masks: the search for identity*, Martin Robertson, 1977.

Study Group on Local Authority Management Structures, *The New Local Authorities: Management and Structures* (Bains Report), 1972.

Taylor, J. A., The Consultative Council on Local Government Finance: a critical analysis of its origins and development. *Local Government Studies*, 1979, May/June, 7-35.

Therborn, G., *The ideology of power and the power of ideology*, Verso, 1980.

Thoenig, J. C., State bureaucracies and local government in France. In Hanf, K. and F. W. Scharpf, (eds.), *Interorganisational policy making*, Sage, 1978, 167-197.

Thrasher, M. and Dunkerley, D. *Analysing urban policy implementation: a social exchange perspective*, European Meeting of Urban Researchers, 1981.

Thrasher, M., The concept of central-local government partnership: issues obsured by ideas. *Policy and Politics*, 1981, 9(4), 455-470.

Thrasher, M. and Dunkerley, D. *Inter-governmental exchange relations*. 1981, Mimeo.

Thrasher, M. and Dunkerley, D. A social exchange approach to implementation analysis. *Social Science Information*, 1981, 21(3), 349-382.

Tomkins, C., Rosenberg, D. and Colville, I. The social process of research: some reflections on developing a multi-disciplinary accounting project. *Accounting, Organisations and Society*, 1980, 5(2), 247-262.

Urry, J. and Wakeford, J. (eds.), *Power in Britain: sociological readings*, Heinemann Educational, 1973.

Urry, J., Role analysis and the sociological enterprise. *Sociological Review*, 1970, 18, 351-363.

Vidich, A. J. and Bensman, J. *Small town in mass society: class, power and religion in a rural community*. Revised edition, Princeton University Press, 1968.

References

Vidich, A. J. and Bensman, J. The Springdale case: academic bureaucrats and sensitive townspeople. In Vidich, A. J., J. Bensman and M. R. Stein, *Reflections on community studies*, Harper and Row, 1971, 313-349.

Waller, P. J. *Town, city and nation: England, 1850-1914*, Oxford University Press, 1983.

Webb, A. and Wistow, G. Public expenditure and policy implementation: the case of community care. *Public Administration*, 1983, 61, 21-44.

Webb, A. and Wistow, G. The rise which cuts. *New Society*, 1982, 23 September, 501-502.

Weber, J., Secret probe into social services charges. *Bristol Evening Post*, 1980, 31st December (front page story).

Weber, M., Politics as a vocation. In Gerth, H. H. and C. W. Mills, (eds.), *Max Weber: essays in sociology*, Routledge and Kegan Paul, 1948, 77-128.

Weber, M., *The theory of social and economic organization*, Free Press, 1964.

Weick, K. E., Stress in accounting systems. *Accounting Review*, 1983, 58(2), 350-367.

Wildavsky, A., *Budgeting: a comparative theory of budgetary processes*, Little, Brown, 1975.

Wildavsky, A., *The politics of the budgetary process*, Little, Brown, 1964.

Wildavsky, A., Rationality in writing: linear and curvilinear. *Journal of Public Policy*, 1981, 1(1), 125-140.

Wilding, P., *Professional power and social welfare*, Routledge and Kegan Paul, 1982.

Williams, G. A., The concept of 'Egemonia' in the thought of Antonio Gramci: some notes on interpretation. *Journal of History and Ideas*, 1960, 21(4), 586-599.

Willis, P. E., *Learning to labour: how working class kids get working class jobs*, Saxon House, 1977.

Wilson, B. R. (ed.), *Rationality*, Harper and Row, 1971.

Winkler, J. T., Corporatism. *European Journal of Sociology*, 1976, 17(1), 100-136.

Wolff, K. H., Surrender and community study: the study of Loma. In Vidich, A. J., J. Bensman, and M. R. Stein, *Reflections on community studies*, Wiley, 1964, 233-263.

Wolfinger, R. E., Non-decisions and the study of local politics. *American Political Science Review*, 1971, 65(4), 1063-1080.

Wolin, S. S., *Politics and vision: continuity and innovations in Western political thought*, Allen and Unwin, 1961.

Wright, M., Planning and controlling public expenditure. In Booth, T. (ed.), *Planning for Welfare: social policy and the expenditure process*, Blackwell, 1979.

Wrong, D. H., The oversocialised conception of man in modern sociology. In Wrong D. H., *Skeptical sociology*, Heinemann, 1977, Chapter 2, 31-54.

Yearly, C. K., The 'Provincial Party' and the megalopolises: London, Paris and New York, 1850–1910. *Comparative Society and History*, 1973, 15(1), 51–88.

Young, K., *Local politics and the rise of party: the London Municipal Society and the Conservative intervention in local elections, 1894-1963*, Leicester University Press, 1975.

Young, K., and Kramer, J. *Strategy and conflict in metropolitan housing: suburbia versus the Greater London Council, 1965-75*, Heinemann, 1978.

Young, K., Values in the policy process. *Policy and Politics*, 1977, 5(3), 1-22.

Zey-Ferrell, M. and Aiken, M. (eds.), *Complex organizations: critical perspectives*, Scott, Foresman, 1981.

Zimmerman, D. H., Record-keeping and the intake process in a public welfare agency. In Wheeler, S. (ed.), *On record: files and dossiers in American life*, Russell Sage Foundation, 1969, 319-354.

INDEX

261

Index